The Blackwell Guide to

Business Ethics

—— Blackwell Philosophy Guides ——

Series Editor: Steven M. Cahn, City University of New York Graduate School

Written by an international assembly of distinguished philosophers, the *Blackwell Philosophy Guides* create a groundbreaking student resource – a complete critical survey of the central themes and issues of philosophy today. Focusing and advancing key arguments throughout, each essay incorporates essential background material serving to clarify the history and logic of the relevant topic. Accordingly, these volumes will be a valuable resource for a broad range of students and readers, including professional philosophers.

The Blackwell Guide to
Business Ethics

Edited by

Norman E. Bowie

Copyright © Blackwell Publishers 2002

First published 2002

2 4 6 8 10 9 7 5 3 1

Blackwell Publishers Inc.
350 Main Street
Malden, Massachusetts 02148
USA

Blackwell Publishers Ltd
108 Cowley Road
Oxford OX4 1JF
UK

Library of Congress Cataloging-in-Publication Data has been applied for.

ISBN 0-631-22122-0 (hardback); 0-631-22123-9 (paperback)

British Library Cataloguing in Publication Data
A CIP catalogue record for this book is available from the British Library.

Typeset in 10/13pt Galliard
by Graphicraft Limited, Hong Kong
Printed in Great Britain by MPG Books Ltd, Bodmin, Cornwall
This book is printed on acid-free paper.

Contents

Contents

Notes on Contributors

Mary Beth Armstrong is a Certified Public Accountant and Professor of Accounting at Polytechnic State University, San Luis Obispo, California. She has written two books and numerous articles on ethics in public accounting and she provides continuing education courses on ethics in accounting for California CPAs. Professor Armstrong serves on, and has chaired, the American Accounting Association's Professionalism and Ethics Committee and the Committee on Professional Conduct of the California Society of Certified Public Accountants.

John R. Boatright is the Raymond C. Baumhart, S.J. Professor of Business Ethics in the Graduate School of Business at Loyola University of Chicago. He has published widely in professional journals on topics of business ethics. His most recent books are *Ethics and the Conduct of Business* and *Ethics in Finance*. He currently serves as the Executive Director of the Society for Business Ethics and is past president of the society.

Norman E. Bowie is the Elmer L. Andersen Chair in Corporate Responsibility at the University of Minnesota. His most recent publication is *Business Ethics: A Kantian Perspective* (Blackwell 1999). His textbook with Tom Beauchamp has just been published in its sixth edition. Professor Bowie has been Dixons Professor of Business Ethics and Corporate Responsibility at the London Business School and a fellow in Harvard's Center for Ethics and the Professions.

Thomas L. Carson is Professor of Philosophy at Loyola University of Chicago. He is the author of four books, the most recent of which is *Moral Relativism*. He is currently working on a book entitled *Lying and Deception: Theory and Practice*.

Joanne B. Ciulla is Professor and Coston Family Chair in Leadership and Ethics at the Jepson School of Leadership Studies, the University of Richmond. She publishes in the areas of business ethics, leadership studies, and the philosophy of work. Her most recent book is *The Ethics of Leadership*. Professor Ciulla has also held a UNESCO Chair in Leadership Studies at the United Nations University's leadership academy.

James J. Clarke is Associate Professor of Finance at Villanova University. He has written in the area of interest rate risk, investments, and bank strategic planning. Professor Clarke is also on the faculty of the America's Community Bankers' National School of Banking and has served on the faculty of the American Bankers Association's Stonier Graduate School of Banking.

Carl Cranor is Professor of Philosophy at the University of California, Riverside. He has published numerous books and articles on theoretical issues in risk assessment and the philosophy of science in the regulatory and tort law. His most recent book is *Are Genes Us? The Social Consequences of the New Genetics*. Professor Cranor has served on the State of California's Proposition 65 Science Advisory Panel, California's Science Advisory Panel on Electric and Magnetic Fields, and the National Academy of Sciences Panel to Czechoslovakian Academy of Sciences.

Richard T. DeGeorge is University Distinguished Professor of Philosophy and Business Administration and Director of the International Center for Ethics in Business at the University of Kansas. He is the author of over 160 articles and author or editor of 19 books. Professor DeGeorge is completing a book on ethical issues in information technology. He has been the President of the American Philosophical Association and is currently President of the International Society of Business, Economics and Ethics.

Joseph R. DesJardins is Professor of Philosophy at the College of St. Benedict, St. Joseph, Minnesota. He has written numerous articles in business ethics and environmental ethics. His two most recent texts are *Contemporary Issues in Business Ethics* and *Environmental Ethics*. Professor DesJardins is the current editor of the Society for Business Ethics Newsletter.

Thomas J. Donaldson is the Mark O. Winkelman Professor at the Wharton School of the University of Pennsylvania and the Director of the Wharton Ethics Program. He has written broadly in the area of business values and professional ethics. He is the author of several books the most recent of which is *Ties That Bind: A Social Contracts Approach to Business Ethics*. His book *Ethics in International Business*, was the winner of the 1998 SIM Academy of Management Best Book Award.

Thomas W. Dunfee is the Kolodny Professor of Social Responsibility and Director of the Carol and Lawrence Zicklin Center for Business Ethics Research at the Wharton School of the University of Pennsylvania. He is the author of numerous articles on business ethics and business law as well as the author of several books, the latest of which is *Ties That Bind: A Social Contracts Approach to Business Ethics*. He recently accepted the appointment of Vice-Dean of the Undergraduate Division at Wharton.

Ronald F. Duska holds the Charles Lamont Post Chair of Ethics and the Professions at the American College. He is the author of numerous articles in business ethics with a special emphasis on the insurance industry. His most recent book is *Education, Leadership and Business Ethics: A Symposium in Honor of Clarence Walton*. He served for ten years as the Executive Director of the Society for Business Ethics.

R. Edward Freeman is the Elis and Signe Olsson Professor of Business Administration and Director of the Olsson Center for Ethics at the Darden School, University of Virginia. Professor Freeman's books include *Strategic Management: A Stakeholder Approach, Corporate Strategy and the Search for Ethics*, and *Environmentalism and the New Logic of Business: How Firms Can Be Profitable and Leave Our Children a Living Planet*. He is also the editor of the Ruffin Series in Business Ethics (Oxford University Press). He has received many teaching awards and has been a consultant and speaker for companies around the world.

Kenneth E. Goodpaster is the David and Barbara Koch Chair in Business Ethics at the University of St. Thomas, St. Paul, Minnesota. He has published widely on topics in business ethics in professional journals; his case book *Policies and Persons: A Casebook in Business Ethics* has recently been published in its third edition. He has also co-produced an Internet-based textbook and a fully online graduate course in business ethics.

Thomas M. Jones is Professor of Management and Organization in the Graduate Business School at the University of Washington. He has published widely in professional journals on stakeholder theory, ethical decision-making models, corporate social performance, corporate governance and simulation models. He has been Connelly Visiting Scholar at Georgetown University.

Daryl Koehn is the Cullen Chair of Business Ethics at the University of St. Thomas, Houston, Texas. She has written extensively in the field of ethics; several of her articles have been translated into Chinese, Spanish, and Bahasi. Among her books is *Trust in Business: Barriers and Bridges*. She previously held the Wicklander Chair of Professional Ethics at DePaul University. She founded one of the first electronic journals – the *Online Journal of Ethics*. Professor Koehn is chair of the Houston 2012 Olympics Ethics Committee.

Patrick E. Murphy is Professor of Marketing and Chair of the Marketing Department at the University of Notre Dame. He is the author of numerous articles and books on marketing ethics. His most recent book is *Eighty Exemplary Ethics*

Statements. He was listed as one of "the top researchers in marketing" and has been a Fulbright Scholar to the University College Cork, Ireland.

Lisa H. Newton is Professor of Philosophy, Director of the Program in Applied Ethics and Director of the Program in Environmental Studies at Fairfield University. She has published a large number of articles on ethics in politics, law, medicine, and business. Her text *Taking Sides: Controversial Issues in Business Ethics and Society* has just been published in its sixth edition. Professor Newton is on the editorial board of a number of professional journals and frequently consults with hospitals, nursing homes, and home health care services.

Manuel Velasquez is Charles J. Dirksen Professor of Business Ethics at Santa Clara University. He is the author of numerous articles in business ethics. He is the author of a major case book in business ethics and his text *Philosophy: A Text with Readings* is now in its sixth edition. Professor Velasquez is past President of the Society for Business Ethics.

Patricia H. Werhane is the Peter and Adeline Ruffin Professor of Business Ethics and Senior Fellow at the Olsson Center for Applied Ethics in the Darden School at the University of Virginia. She is the author of numerous articles and books on business ethics. Her latest book is *Moral Imagination and Managerial Decision-Making.* She is the past president of the Society for Value Inquiry, the Society for Business Ethics, and the former editor-in-chief of *Business Ethics Quarterly.*

Andrew C. Wicks is Associate Professor of business ethics in the Graduate Business School at the University of Washington. He has published numerous articles in professional journals on such topics as stakeholder theory, trust, managed care, the new economy, and total quality management. Professor Wicks received his PhD in Religious Ethics at the University of Virginia.

Introduction

Norman E. Bowie

Business Ethics received the attention of philosophers in the mid-1970s – although the subject certainly existed before that time – especially in many Catholic institutions. It also received the attention of some management professors in the Social Issues in Management Division of the Academy of Management. These management professors were almost all social scientists and brought a different approach to the subject. One of the recent trends in business ethics has been closer cooperation between philosophers and social scientists in business ethics research.

Business Ethics was one of the applied philosophy areas that seemed to thrive once normative ethics and political philosophy became more respectable, that is not long after Rawls published his classic, *A Theory of Justice*. The growth of the field has been phenomenal. In thirty years, three journals have been created along with a separate society, The Society for Business Ethics (SBE). Membership has grown to approximately 600. Business ethics courses are offered both in philosophy departments and in schools of business; benefactors have created a number of endowed chairs in the area, and Jobs for Philosophers always advertises a number of openings in the area. If business ethics is a fad, it is a fad that has lasted for over thirty years and one that continues to have resilience. However, some philosophers in the field of business ethics are somewhat more pessimistic about the role that philosophy will play in the future of the discipline, for example, see Bowie (2000).

This *Blackwell Guide to Business Ethics* is designed to acquaint the reader with three distinct areas in business ethics. The first section of the book focuses on issues of theory and pedagogy. The second section features articles that focus on ethical issues in several of the functional areas of business and on some specific business practices. The third and final section provides an overview to some of the areas that the editor believes will be important in the future.

Part I

From a theoretical standpoint, most business ethicists criticized the leading theory of the function of business adopted by economists and finance professors. That was a more audacious undertaking than one might realize, since US legal institutions backed the conventional theory, which could be rigorously formulated, and had as its spokesperson a highly articulate Nobel Prize winner in Economics, Milton Friedman. Friedman argued that the social responsibility of business (the ethical obligation of business managers) is to seek profits for the stockholders. Under the leadership of Ed Freeman, an alternative stakeholder theory of the firm was presented. On the stakeholder theory the obligation of business (business manager) is to consider, weigh, and balance the needs of the firm's stakeholders. Stakeholder theory is still developing. Debates continue as to who are the stakeholders, how should their interests be balanced – that is are the obligations of business to some stakeholders more important than its obligations to other stakeholders – and how the weighing of stakeholder interests is to be done. Freeman has recently even argued that there is not one stakeholder theory but many.

With that challenge in mind, it seems logical to begin this *Guide to Business Ethics* with an article on stakeholder theory. That article, written with the cooperation of philosophers and management theorists traces the history of the stakeholder approach, explains where it is at present and where it might be and ought to be going in the future. It is worth pointing out that although debate over the nature of stakeholder theory continues, stakeholder terminology has been widely adopted in the business community. This represents a rare instance where philosophical terminology becomes part of the popular lexicon. In addition many corporations have adopted codes of ethics or mission statements that articulate normative stakeholder theory and principles. And recently international agreements such as the Caux Roundtable Principles for Business have been drafted, organized, and adopted around stakeholder principles.

Despite the widespread acceptance of stakeholder language, many theoretical issues remain to be resolved. A dominant paradigm is to distinguish instrumental stakeholder theory from normative stakeholder theory. Freeman criticizes that way of looking at stakeholder theory because it reinforces the notion that there is a sharp distinction in management between the non-moral and moral use of stakeholder theory. Several scholars have argued for convergent stakeholder theory where the normative prescriptions are both sound ethically and instrumentally (i.e., those prescriptions contribute to corporate profit.) The Jones, Wicks and Freeman article explores this issue and suggests future research topics in stakeholder theory – both theoretical and empirical. Their article concludes by considering four basic challenges that stakeholder theory faces and ways these challenges might be met.

Although most business ethicists remain partial to the stakeholder approach, philosophical explanations and defenses of the stockholder theory have been proposed. In this volume John Boatright provides an explanation and defense of one version of stockholder theory. Boatright casts his explanation and defense in terms of the broad issue of corporate governance. He starts with Michael Jensen's account of the corporation as a nexus of contracts among the various corporate stakeholders. All stakeholders – with one important exception – he explains, are able to write contracts that essentially protect their interests. The group that cannot write such a contract is the stockholders. Thus stockholders bear a number of important risks and the inducement for stockholders to take the risk is that they receive the profits. And to protect their interests from the self-interested behavior of managers (what finance theorists call agency problems), stockholders are legitimately entitled to govern the firm. The existence of agency problems, the assumption of risk on the part of the stockholders, and the inability of stockholders to enter into contracts that fully protect their interests give stockholders a legitimate right to the profits of the firm and the right to govern it. That is why stockholders are special and that is why, Boatright would contend, the interests of stockholders should not be treated on a par with the interests of the other stakeholders, even if the law permitted it.

One of the more vexing issues in philosophy is the issue of relativism. Relativism is an issue in business ethics because international corporations want to know if they should do in Rome as the Romans do. Some answers given to that question are not especially philosophical. Many companies argue that they will not compromise their basic values and that when doing business abroad or setting up subsidiaries, they will insist on a set of values that are to be adhered to universally. Where core values are not at issue, international corporations will do in Rome as the Romans do. Of course, some companies do not see the importance of a set of core values and they will do in Rome as the Romans do as well. For those companies that do have core values and impose them internationally, the philosopher wants to know whether those core values are sufficiently congruent with ordinary morality. Too often, the critics argue, the core value of short-term profitability has trumped ordinary morality. Thus international companies have been criticized for using sweatshop manufacturers as suppliers, for closing plants in industrialized countries in order to take advantage of "obscenely" low wage scales in third world countries, and for moving plants abroad to take advantage of weak environmental laws. International companies have been strongly criticized by non governmental agencies (NGOs) and as a result a number of international agreements have been or are being forged to govern the conduct of international corporations. One of the most inclusive and broadest agreements is The UN Global Compact. A number of companies including British Petroleum, Unilever, Deutsche Bank, Ericsson, Novartis, and Nike have endorsed the nine principles. However, most international corporations are not signatories to these agreements and the agreements that are endorsed still need critical scrutiny.

In the past Richard DeGeorge has argued that in considering the obligations of international firms from industrialized countries like the USA, companies from these countries should be held to a higher standard. More specifically, in discussing the situation in Russia in the 1990s he argued that Russian firms operating in Russia were permitted to do some things that firms from industrialized countries were not permitted to do (DeGeorge, 1993). For example, Russians would be permitted to "bribe" in certain circumstances, but American firms would not be allowed to bribe at all. The most comprehensive theory of how companies should behave when operating across national boundaries is that of Thomas Donaldson and Thomas Dunfee. An overview of their work constitutes chapter 3. Donaldson and Dunfee have a place both for universal moral norms and for ethical relativism. There are universal norms of conduct that they call hypernorms that result from a convergence of the great philosophical and religious traditions as well as from international agreements. Business conduct, such as bribery, that is in violation of those hypernorms is not morally permitted. However, practices not in violation of the hypernorms are permitted and may vary from society to society. Thus there is considerable moral free space for legitimate divergent behavior. Certainly one of the major tasks of international business ethics is to discover whether there really are hypernorms and to identify them. Alternatively international corporations might negotiate such norms through international agreements.

One of the earlier debates in business ethics centered on whether self-regulation was better than government regulation as a means to ensure ethical corporate conduct. The passage in 1991 of the Federal Sentencing Guidelines has given major emphasis to a legal compliance based model. Nonetheless, most business people would prefer self-regulation to government regulation on the grounds that they are closer to the problem and want the flexibility to put their own house in order. But is this practical when what is manufactured are toxic substances? Can business be trusted in cases like this? In his essay Carl Cranor argues that recent developments in regulatory law-particularly in the regulation of toxic substances- have tilted the balance in favor of business. The reason for this tilt is found in the severe demands that courts make regarding scientific evidence concerning the certainty of harm. Cranor argues that the 1970s administrative law in this area arose out of the failure of tort law to solve the problems. Regulatory laws try to protect us from harm in advance by specifying what should be done. However, the federal legislation in this area has different standards of risk acceptance; there is no uniform standard on what counts as acceptable risk. Cranor discusses the advantages and disadvantages of both tort and regulatory law and concludes that the protection of the public requires both.

Cranor then turns his attention to a number of legal developments that he believes weaken the effectiveness of both regulatory and tort law. First, regulatory law may preempt tort law and thus in some cases prevent victims from achieving compensation. More important are legal decisions that specify what is to count as valid scientific evidence in regulatory and tort law. Before 1993, the parties had considerable discretion with respect to what counted as adequate scientific evidence. But that changed with the Daubert decision in 1993. That decision allowed judges to call upon their own court appointed scientific experts to determine what scientific evidence should be allowed into court and what should not be so allowed. Less stringent requirements regarding regulatory law resulted from the Benzene case fifteen years earlier. Well philosophically speaking, how stringent should the requirements be? Cranor contends that there is a lot of uncertainty and ignorance concerning the effects of toxic substances and that as a result decisions will tend to go against those with the burden of proof. Scientific means for resolving uncertainty and ignorance take time – up to six years for animal studies and even more if human studies are required. And it takes even longer for scientific interpretation and acceptance of test results. It took sixty years to prove that benzene caused leukemia. Cranor also argues that scientists are more predisposed to ruling out false positives (things that are thought to be toxic when they are not) while regulatory agencies are more interested in ruling out false negatives (things thought not to be toxic when they really are). If the standard of the scientists is to prevail, public risk is increased. Cranor then discusses three court decisions that allow what he considers to be unreasonable risk to be inflicted on the public.

Business ethicists are invariably challenged by assertions that ethics cannot be taught – that if you have not learned to be ethical by age five you will not learn how to be ethical in a business ethics class. Since this assertion is an empirical claim, it is easy to be taken aback. However, the assertion is false. Two essays in this volume speak to that issue. Manuel Velasquez's contribution considers the issue of how we ought to reason when we do work in applied ethics. Velasquez begins with an explanation and criticism of what he defines as the standard account of moral reasoning. Under the standard account, moral reasoning proceeds by subsuming particular cases under general rules. In this model, moral reasoning is hierarchical with specific moral judgments at the bottom of the hierarchy and general abstract moral principles such as Kant's categorical imperative, Mill's principle of utility or Rawls's difference principle at the top of the hierarchy. What distinguishes many moral theorists is how many and which principle or principles are at the top of the hierarchy. As Velasquez points out, the reasoning that one uses to defend the moral principle at the top of the hierarchy must be different from the reasoning that goes on at the other levels of the hierarchy. Velasquez describes and criticizes a number of proposals for defending these most general moral principles. In the second half of his paper, Velasquez considers alternatives to the standard approach of moral reasoning. One alternative is virtue theory. Virtue theorists argue that moral reasoning moves from character to action. A courageous person ought to act courageously. In reasoning this way, a virtue theorist does not use general rules in the same way as the standard model. Virtue theorists do not reason by subsuming particular cases under general rules. Rather they reason from a particular virtue to what acting in accordance with that virtue would require in practice (in particular situations.) Another group of theorists, particularists, focus on the uniqueness of each moral situation. Given the "fact" that situations in the moral life are so different, moral reasoning cannot proceed by general rules. Rules are at most heuristic. The form of moral reasoning most amenable to the particularists, is casuistry. Interestingly casuistry is closed tied to the case method that is heavily used in business education.

In his essay on the case method in business ethics, Kenneth Goodpaster shows how the case method provides a means for teaching ethics – even to adults. The case method Goodpaster asserts is a tool for moral insight. Looked at in this way, business ethics is less about providing content to be learned than critical inquiry that leads to the habits that provide moral insight. And moral insight does not come from the application of one of the standard ethical theories to an ethics issue in business. Rather, all the traditional theories have their role to play. Goodpaster identifies this as the pluralistic approach to using ethical theories in case studies. Goodpaster argues that pluralism does not degenerate into relativism and he insists that his view is not relativistic. Finally, we teach ethics through both theory and practice. In this way ethics education is a life-long process and is hardly learned at your mother's knee.

But how does an instructor accomplish that and what features of the case are important? Goodpaster then presents a diagram that illustrates a case analysis technique (a CAT scan) that any instructor might use as he or she teaches by the case method. Goodpaster concludes his essay by explaining how ethics can most effectively be integrated into the business curriculum.

Part II

Business ethics research and teaching tend to be organized in one of two ways. First, it can be organized around the functional areas in management education, accounting, finance, marketing, human relations, operations management, and strategic management. This volume includes essays on ethical issues in human resources, accounting, and marketing. Research and teaching are also organized around the various issues that affect the primary corporate stakeholders, employees, shareholders, and customers. As a practical matter, the two ways of organizing tend to overlap. Thus most of the ethical issues in finance are concerned with management's obligations to stockholders, ethical issues in human resources tend to focus on management's obligations to employees, and ethical issues in marketing tend to focus on management's obligations to customers. One of the gaps in both these approaches is the issue of management's obligations to the environment. Some theorists have tried to maintain the stakeholder organization by classifying the environment as the silent stakeholder. Whatever the merit of that approach, the obligations of management to the environment are a important topic in business ethics; they are also an important topic in the allied discipline of environmental studies. In this volume, Joseph DesJardins provides an overview of the ethical issues facing business with respect to the environment and attempts to provide his own perspective on how best to approach those issues.

The first two articles in this section look at some of the ethical issues that are specific to the functional disciplines of accounting and marketing. Accounting is a functional area in business where ethical concerns are traditionally prominent, although the technical issues in the field have sometimes discouraged philosophers from making a major contribution. Accountants, unlike most others in business, are considered professionals and as a result there is a specialized body of professional accounting ethics. In chapter 7, accounting professor and certified public accountant (CPA) Mary Beth Armstrong provides an overview of many of the prominent ethical issues in accounting. As philosophers review the issues she discusses, they should find ample opportunities for ethical analysis. Professor Armstrong begins by distinguishing managerial accountants from public accountants. Since these accountants perform very different functions, their moral obligations differ. Managerial accountants work for corporations and thus their situation is analogous to professional engineers who work for business firms. There is often a conflict between the demands of the business and their professional obligations. Armstrong documents a number of these conflicts within budgeting, internal auditing and internal reporting. Many of these issues present conflicts of loyalty. The managerial auditor is to act as a check on management, yet he or she is part of the management team. To whom is ultimate loyalty owed – the management team or the accounting profession? Many managerial accountants belong to the Institute of Managerial Accountants, which has a code of conduct that seems to give priority to loyalty to the profession over loyalty to the firm.

Most accountants in public accounting firms are CPAs. Traditionally the chief task of public accounting firms was to audit public corporations. On the face of it there is an issue of independence since the primary obligation of CPAs is to the investing public, but the corporations being audited do the hiring and firing of public accounting firms. This perception that public accountants may not be truly independent is only enhanced by the growth of consulting within public accounting firms. These firms may provide consulting in the computer area that provides very profitable contracts. Would the auditors from that public accounting firm be more cautious in their audit statement when the consulting arm of the firm has a large contract with the client being audited? Armstrong specifies many of the suggestions that have been made to deal with this conflict of interest. One change that is being implemented is to have the audit committee of the Board of Directors be the client rather than the top management team. Whether this change in perspective is sufficient to provide "true" independence is hotly debated. Another ethical issue in accounting includes the "expectations gap." This gap exists because the investing public seems to expect the accounting profession to provide more information about a firm than the profession believes it can or should provide. Thus there is a gap.

Armstrong maintains that accounting is a practice in MacIntyre's sense and that there are a number of resulting virtues that accountants should have – specifically independence, integrity, objectivity, due care, confidentiality, and concern for the public interest. Armstrong points out that there is much discussion of the virtue of independence and as we have seen above, achieving that virtue can be extremely difficult.

Armstrong also discusses the regulatory environment and the relationships that exist among the public accounting firms, the professional accounting self-regulatory bodies and the SEC. She points out that these relationships have not been harmonious of late and that greater coordination and respect is required. Armstrong concludes her essay by pointing out how much the accounting industry and profession have changed. She argues that in spite of these changes, there are certain core values that should be retained. Most of the ethical issues in accounting have a long history and present an opportunity for philosophers and accountants to work together cooperatively to try and resolve them.

One of the most active areas in business ethics has been in the area of marketing ethics. Interestingly, this is one of the areas where the number of business academics exceeds the number of philosophers who are doing writing and research in the area. Professors of marketing have had an interest in ethical issues in their field since at least the 1960s. Patrick E. Murphy provides an overview of that forty-year-old history. Murphy distinguishes the normative issues from the descriptive issues in marketing ethics. Interestingly some of the normative positions have been empirically tested. For example, deontological reasons rather than consequentialist reasons are behind the decisions to discipline unethical marketers. Philosophers of social science and science may find Murphy's critique of some of the research methodologies in marketing to be of special interest. Another interesting finding is that company codes of ethics do not have much to say on the issue of marketing despite the pervasiveness of those issues.

Among the more prominent issues in marketing ethics is target marketing to the physically, cognitively, socially, and motivationally vulnerable. This issue has been of particular concern to George Brenkert. Other normative issues that are discussed in some depth are bribery, counterfeiting, the gathering of competitive information, and organizational leadership. One of the great examples of ethical business is from marketing ethics – the decision of Johnson and Johnson to stop making capsules after the Tylenol poisonings. Some of the issues including privacy in e-commerce, social responsibility, and leadership relate to other comprehensive discussion of these issues in other chapters. Marketing provides some ethical issues that are unique to it – cause marketing, target marketing, and the practice of slotting. Murphy concludes his article by suggesting ways that marketing teaching and research could be improved. One item that needs immediate action is greater integration between marketing ethics and business ethics research. Finally, Murphy's call for updated and expanded cases in marketing ethics fits well with Goodpaster's analysis (chapter 6) concerning the importance of cases in the teaching of business ethics.

The stakeholder most prominent in marketing ethics is the customer. One issue in marketing ethics – deceptive advertising and sales practices – is so prominent in the business ethics literature that it is the subject of an article in its own right. The main point of interaction here is when a customer decides to buy a product. Corporations spend huge amounts of money advertising products and services on television and radio, in newspapers and magazines and on billboards along

America's highways. Some believe that American culture is saturated with commercial advertising. Advertising clearly influences purchases or it would not be done. Another point of contact in the purchasing decision is the salesperson. The chief ethical problems regarding advertising and sales revolve around issues of information disclosure and deception. Those issues are the focal point of the article by Thomas Carson. Carson begins his piece by showing that lying and deception and deception and information nondisclosure are distinct concepts. He then contends that deception is wrong and that an important issue is to decide what counts as a deception. To answer that question, he reviews current law governing deceptive advertising. Carson believes with other critics of Federal Trade Commission policy, that the law is too lenient with respect to puffery – claims that product x is the very best of that type. He agrees that such claims do deceive and that companies making such claims should be held to stronger legal and moral account.

Why should that matter? What is wrong with deceptive advertising? Deceptive advertising causes one to have false beliefs and acting on those beliefs can cause harm – harm to consumers who get the wrong product or pay more for a product and harm to competitors who are deprived of the sale. That's why competitors bring many false advertising suits. Deceptive advertising also violates Kant's categorical imperative and Carson's version of the golden rule.

Carson then turns to the ethics of sales. Here, the central issue is information disclosure. How much information is the salesperson morally obligated to provide to a buyer? Carson points out that law now severely limits the doctrine of caveat emptor (let the buyer beware) Sales transactions are governed by an implied warranty of merchantability and are protected by the Uniform Commercial Code. Carson, like many business ethicists, thinks that ethics requires more disclosure of information than is required by law. A golden rule principle will then provide an answer to the question: What should the seller disclose to the buyer? Carson adopts his own version of the golden rule and articulates and defends six principles that an ethical salesperson should follow in dealing with a customer. In following those principles, salespeople will avoid lying and deception and provide the ethically appropriate amount of disclosure. In the course of his discussion, Carson provides a rich and subtle analysis of a number of sales examples.

Financial services are a product where there is a huge information asymmetry between the seller and the buyer. Wherever there is severe information asymmetry, there is a temptation to take advantage of the vulnerability of the consumer. Ronald Duska and James Clarke provide an extensive review of the ethical issues that arise in financial markets. Since the workings of financial markets are opaque even to the well educated, Duska and Clarke provide a clear definition of the various kinds of financial markets and the laws that govern them. They argue that financial markets provide a valuable service to society and that the popular portrayal of them as unethical is one-sided and unfair. As Duska and Clarke argue financial markets are the fundamental element of a free market system and are instrumentally beneficial in bringing about the highest overall standard of living in history. Duska and Clarke provide an analysis of why financial markets are efficient, but they also argue that if certain fundamental moral principles were not adhered to, financial markets would collapse. At the center of these ethical principles is the basic moral principle, "Your word is your bond." Although some practices within the financial services industry can be (are) obviously unethical, e.g., fraud, many other practices have been challenged as ethically questionable but there is no firm determination as to whether those practices are morally permissible or morally unacceptable. Some of the examples from Duska and Clarke include determining how much disclosure is necessary in the sale of financial instruments and whether accountants should do consulting for the firms they audit. Duska and Clarke then show how the use of two moral principles,

1   avoid deception and fraud, and
2   honor your commitments

can help to resolve the issue as to whether certain practices are ethically accept-able or not. They cast light on how some of the ethical issues in financial services can be addressed. The article concludes with an examination of some of the organizational and institutional barriers that stand in the way of ethical behavior, especially behavior that puts the interests of the client first.

Perhaps the stakeholder group that has received the most attention from business ethicists is the employee. I suspect that one reason for this attention is the existence of a principle in labor law known as employment at will. That doctrine which is accepted as law in most states accepts the employment rela-tionship as one that, in the absence of contract or violation of law, can be ended by either party at any time for good reason or bad, or even for no reason or reason immoral. By and large, business ethicists have been united in their objec-tion to the employment at will doctrine. The reigning consensus seems to be that the employment relationship should be governed by the fact that employees have certain rights including a right to work, a right to privacy, and even a right to meaningful work. Business ethicists often ground these rights in Kantian moral theory.

Against this consensus that Kant's principle of respect for persons requires that people have a right to work, or even a right to meaningful work, stands Daryl Koehn. Professor Koehn has a two-fold argument. First, Kant's respect for persons principle does not entail a right to work, and secondly, there is no right to work. In support of the former, Professor Koehn points out that work frequently does not enhance a person's self-respect. Now one might accept these arguments and then turn them around to show that the respect for persons principle entails more than a right to work; it entails a right to meaningful work. However, such a move would run afoul of Professor Koehn's second objection, that the con-textually bound historical nature of rights would show that there cannot be a right to work, and thus there is no right to meaningful work. In the course of her argument, Koehn has many insightful comments on the nature of work itself.

Business ethicists have been criticized with justification that they have focused on the obligations of employers to employees but have said little about the duties that employees owe to employers. One reason for this emphasis may be the belief on the part of business ethicists that there is an imbalance of power in the employer/employee relationship and that the more powerful employers have abused their power and treated employees unjustly. However, as Koehn points out, if a right to meaningful work were to be accepted, then it is only fair that corporations be granted the right to accountable performance from their employees.

The next right to be analyzed and questioned is the employee's right to privacy. Koehn points out that the right to privacy is historically bounded and that, currently, technology poses grave challenges to any right to privacy. The right to privacy is also under challenge from the law. If the law holds an employer accountable for the sexual harassment of employees, then an employee cannot expect that his or her e-mails can be completely private.

Professor Koehn's final discussion centers on the notion of comparable worth. Her basic argument is that there is no way to operationalize that concept within management. There are too many competing ingredients and too much disagreement. Even if one could agree on what constituted comparable worth, the redistributive effects would be contentious and undermine the efficiency of labor markets. Comparable worth cannot be substituted for the traditional labor market.

Nearly every text in business ethics contains a section on ethics and the environment. Given the importance of the issue of business's responsibility to the environment, an essay on that topic is included in this volume. In doing so, however, it should be pointed out that the environmental ethics has developed as a field of its own; there are many issues in environmental ethics that are outside the normal parameters of business ethics. Professor Joseph DesJardins, who is recognized both as an environmental ethicist and a business ethicist provides the discussion for the responsibility of business to the environment. In the early part of his essay, DesJardins introduces a set of concepts and distinctions that challenge the way traditional ethicists such as utilitarians and Kantians would look at the environment. What are the implications of these new ways of looking at an ethical issue for management's responsibilities to the environment? DesJardins distinguishes different attitudes that a manager might take to the environment. From a neoclassical perspective, the manager has no obligation to the environment *per se*. The duties of the manager are limited to following the law and basic ethical customs. DesJardins is willing to grant that morality does not require that business shoulder the sole responsibility for environmental protection. However, DesJardins argues that obligations are created when we can preserve or produce things of value. Arguing from the perspective that entities other than human beings have intrinsic value, DesJardins argues that certain policy decisions are reasonable as a means to preserve and produce environmental value. First, pollution should be minimized. Second, renewable resources should be favored over non-renewable resources. Third, when

non renewable resources must be used, they should be used in a way that provides equal opportunity to all and benefits the least well off. Using them to
support a consumerist lifestyle is immoral. Fourth, environmentally sensitive natural
areas should be preserved. That includes wetlands and species needed to preserve
biodiversity. DesJardins argues persons holding different ethical theories and
justifications for preservation would endorse these policy recommendations.

Once we admit that the environment, or at least some nonhuman elements
of it, has intrinsic value, then a market based neoclassical approach is inadequate.
First, the high growth orientation of business overlooks the fact that such growth
is hardly environmentally benign. Or more accurately the view that the regulated
market will provide corrective mechanisms to overcome externalities fails to consider a number of important facts. First, you do not regulate until a significant
amount of damage is done. A huge depletion of fish is required before fishing is
regulated. Endangered species and wilderness areas are irreplaceable public goods.
In those cases the damage cannot be undone. Second, business does not simply
respond to consumer demand; business helps creates that demand. Thus it is naïve
to think that business need only wait and then respond when consumers turn a
darker shade of green. Business has the wherewithal through marketing techniques to make consumers a darker shade of green. But that is not the end of the
critique. DesJardins reviews some of the new economic thinking that will require
that all of us, including business, rethink some of our assumptions about growth.
We need to realize that natural resources are not like other factors of production.
Sustainable growth must become a part of business policy. There are biophysical
limits to growth. With that in mind DesJardins describes how business would
need to be restructured to provide sustainable growth. In doing so DesJardins calls
on the work of Hawken, A. Lovins and H. Lovins as articulated in their book,
Natural Capitalism. Such thinking is not utopian. DesJardins provides a number
of examples where such thinking is already transforming business practice.

Part III

The final section of this volume anticipates some new areas in business ethics that
will provide areas for teaching and research in the twenty-first century. The four
areas I have chosen are ethical issues in computer technology and e-commerce,
ethical issues in biotechnology, ethical issues in health care, and ethical issues in
leadership.

Richard DeGeorge has taken business ethicists to task for not directing more
of their attention to ethical issues in information technology. DeGeorge reminds
us that computers are machines that are designed, maintained, and used by human
beings. We cannot ignore an ethical issue with the phrase "computer error."
DeGeorge then discusses some of the major ethical issues in information technology that deserve the attention of philosophers. The first is privacy. DeGeorge

explains how the collection of personal information has been enhanced by the use of computers and other advances in information technology. If privacy is to be protected, consumers need to give informed consent to the collection and distribution of personal information and they need to be sure that, if consent is given, that the information will be kept appropriately confidential. Moreover, if the information contains errors, consumers also need to be assured that these errors will be corrected. One of the more controversial issues in this area is what should count as informed consent. Another concerns the electronic surveillance of employees. What kinds of surveillance are legitimate and what kinds are illegitimate?

When one focuses on the Internet, one sees how privacy might need to be compromised for the greater good. Internet users often like anonymity especially when participating in "chat rooms." However, anonymity makes it easier to avoid responsibility and to engage in illegal or unethical solicitations or acts. The problem is particularly difficult when romance or sexual activity is involved. Another test for complete privacy is presented by encryption. Encryption protects privacy, but it protects the privacy of the criminal and potential terrorist as well as the privacy of the ordinary citizen. How to balance the right to privacy in the use of the Internet with the demands of the public good remains a difficult ethical question.

Most of us have experienced "bugs" in software. However, consumers seem to accept these "bugs" in computers and computer software but would never accept such defects in other products. To make matters worse, DeGeorge points out that some software companies produce beta versions that most likely contain "bugs" that will be discovered by the users. Often this is done to beat a competitor to the market. But surely, at the very least, the consumer should be informed. And why shouldn't we expect the same level of quality control from software companies that we expect from other manufacturers of consumer products? Besides sometimes a flaw in software will crash the computer and damage other files. But, unlike other products, software companies are not held responsible for the damages they cause.

Not all ethical malfeasance is on the software manufacturers. In the area of intellectual property rights, customers commit some malfeasance. Copyright protection and patentability present extremely complex legal and ethical issues. DeGeorge walks us through current law on these matters and indicates where substantial ethical issues remain.

The rise of the computer has given rise to a new way of doing business – e-commerce. In the late 1990s, investors were so enamored with e-commerce that they bid the stock price of e-commerce businesses to unbelievable heights. This changed when the bubble burst just after the turn of the century. But e-commerce and the ethical issues related to it are here to stay. Should the products of e-commerce be taxed? Should those employed in e-commerce but working at home be eligible to be covered by workman compensation laws? How can consumers be protected from fraud or even from having their identity stolen?

The last set of ethical issues DeGeorge considers focuses on the impact of technology on human values and the way we conceive of ourselves as human beings. Will computers and robots with computer chips inside them be our servants or our masters? As we interact through computers, what impact will that have on our social nature? Will the technological revolution increase the gap between the haves and the have nots? Since the answer to that question is likely to be in the affirmative, what should be done to correct that disparity? Will the widespread use of the Internet enhance democratic institutions or subvert them? These are some of the questions that will engage future business ethicists.

One of the more radical changes in America in the 1990s was the growth of health maintenance organizations (HMOs). Their growth is in large part attributable to the skyrocketing cost of health care caused in part by the prevalence of third party payment schemes. The HMO was designed to make health care more efficient and thus to slow the escalating costs of health care. But as health care became more like a business, a set of unique ethical problems arose. A dramatic picture of these problems is presented in the case of John Worthy that opens Patricia Werhane's essay on ethical issues in health care. This case illustrates a number of the major points that Werhane wants to make. First, one needs to evaluate ethical issues in health care in terms of systems thinking. Second, one must understand health care as involving a myriad of relationships, and thus the ethics of health care organizations is bound to be complex. Werhane first shows that Milton Friedman's injunction that a firm maximize its profits ought not be applied without qualification to the healthcare management industry. Rephrasing Friedman, Werhane argues that the social responsibility of any healthcare organization is to improve the health of the patient population so long as it stays with the rules of the game. But what are the rules of the game and how is this objective to be accomplished? Given the myriad relationships, Werhane adopts the stakeholder model for attacking the problem. One of the tasks of management, perhaps the major task, is to set priorities when the interests of the stakeholders conflict. For Werhane, the priority in health care organizations goes to the patient. The second most important stakeholder according to Werhane is the healthcare professional and her first obligation should be to the patient. But if the healthcare professional were to take that as her mandate, she would be in conflict with the financial goals of the organization. And, in such conflicts, financial goals are in third place behind the welfare of the patient and the judgment of the healthcare professional.

Anomalies in the healthcare industry create further problems. Patients have many disanalogies with ordinary customers; they are vulnerable, often poorly informed, and frequently not responsible for paying for the services they receive. Thus we have another reason for not applying traditional business models and the business ethics that underlie them to healthcare organizations.

Werhane points out that we hold healthcare organizations morally accountable as well as individual healthcare individuals. But given the complex relationships that exist among multiple parties, it is often difficult if not impossible to ascribe responsibility. (Werhane does point out that in her view a systems approach does not lead to the abrogation of personal responsibility.) Thus, when mistakes are made, a systems approach is often the best way to go. What would a systems approach require? It would require that a problem within the system be looked at from a number of perspectives. This will broaden the approach to the problem. It enables us to understand another's point of view. It enables us to outline the boundaries and thus to be clear what is not included in the system. Finally, it enables us to exercise our moral imagination. Werhane concludes her piece by applying a systems approach to patient consent and the privacy of medical records and thereby enriches the discussion of those concepts.

Lisa Newton addresses some of the unique issues that arise in the biotechnology industry. She begins by noting that there are objections, usually based in theology, to obtaining this kind of knowledge at all and she recognizes that some environmentalists will object to biotechnology on the grounds that it endangers biodiversity. Rather than focus on these issues she addresses three dilemmas presented by the business of biotechnology. First, she focuses on the safety of genetically modified foods. Newton considers all the arguments that have been raised against the safety of genetically modified foods and finds them wanting. It seems that genetically modified foods are safe to eat. It also seems to her that crops that are bioengineered to protect against insects and herbicides are generally safe to use in the environment and that, on balance, bioengineered crops may help the environment more that hurt it. But Newton is hardly a partisan of that view as she recognizes that all the data are not in. Second, she reflects on whether discovered genes, proteins, and other basic elements of life should be considered private property. In this case as well. Newton considers the arguments made in favor of allowing the genes, proteins, and other basic elements to be patented, or at least the processes that lead to their manipulation. The arguments are not conclusive and Newton ends up as a skeptic with respect to their being patented as private property. Although she also recognizes that patents help drive technological discovery. Third, Newton considers whether knowledge about a person's genes and their defects should be kept private and out of the hands of health insurance companies. Newton sees a genuine dilemma here. We already allow insurance companies to discriminate on the basis of characteristics that increase their risk; young drivers, smokers, etc. Allowing them to discriminate on the basis of knowledge about our genes is arguably just one more step. On the other hand, knowledge of our genetic structure gets at the very essence of who we are. Shouldn't the right to privacy cover that information? Newton concludes that there is no easy solution to that dilemma. Issues in the biotechnology industry have created severe challenges to ethical theory and ethical decision-making. Business ethicists should find this both exhilarating and anxiety producing.

Leadership studies is a field within business that has received increasing attention of late. What are the characteristics of a leader and how can ordinary managers become leaders? Some issues within leadership studies are grist for the mill of business ethicists. Joanne Ciulla, a contributor to both business ethics and leadership studies, has provided an overview of how classic writers and social scientists have conceived leadership. She then moves on to her interesting ethical analysis – the importance of trust in leadership. Ciulla argues that the right question to ask about leadership is "What is good leadership?" We want leaders to be both effective and good. Ciulla further argues that effective and moral leadership is in large part situation dependent. We have moved away from the most rigid forms of auto-cratic management to a period where employees are demanding more of a say in the workplace. Leaders and followers share the goals of the organization; the goals are not simply imposed top to bottom. A number of factors account for this change – among them a better educated work force, expert power in the hands of employees, and even a more vigilant media that will report on workplace abuse. These changes require that we look at the relation a leader has with her followers. What is the key ingredient that would make that relationship an ethical one? Ciulla argues that the key ingredient is trust; it is the trust of the followers that determines the success of today's leaders. Ciulla concludes with some speculation about the future. She argues that the growth of international business and the diversity of followers will require bridge leaders – leaders who can build connec-tions among diverse followers.

This volume is certainly not the last word as a guide to business ethics. Tech-nology and globalization are changing the nature of business. The power of business seems to be growing and many of our non business institutions are evolving into businesses. As these forces continue to spread and expand, so will the number of ethical questions in business that deserve the attention of moral philosophers.

References

Bowie, N. E. 2000: Business Ethics, Philosophy and the Next 25 Years, *Business Ethics Quarterly*, 18, 7–20.

DeGeorge, R., 1993: International Business Ethics, Russia and Eastern Europe, *Social Responsibility; Business, Journalism, Law and Medicine*, 19, 5–23.

Part I

Theoretical and Pedagogical Issues

Chapter 1

Stakeholder Theory: The State of the Art

Thomas M. Jones, Andrew C. Wicks, and R. Edward Freeman

Introduction

The purpose of this chapter is to examine an approach to both business and business ethics that has come to be called "stakeholder theory." While there is disagreement among stakeholder theorists about the scope and precise meaning of both "stakeholder" and "theory," we shall take "stakeholder theory" to denote the body of research which has emerged in the last 15 years by scholars in management, business and society, and business ethics, in which the idea of "stakeholders" plays a crucial role.

For those unfamiliar with the stakeholder literature, the term "stakeholder" came into wide-scale usage to describe those groups who can affect, or who are affected by, the activities of the firm (Freeman, 1984). "Stakeholder theory" began as an alternative way to understand the firm, in sharp contrast to traditional models which either:

a) depicted the world of managers in more simplistic terms (e.g. dealing with employees, suppliers and customers only), or
b) which claimed the firm existed to make profits and serve the interests of one group (i.e. shareholders) only.

In the former case, Freeman argued that the world of managers had become much more complex, and that the traditional models of managerial activity tended to divert the attention and efforts of managers away from groups who were vital to the success (or failure) of firm initiatives. It was only by embracing this broader, "stakeholder" picture of the world that managers could adequately understand this more complex reality and undertake actions that enable the firm to be successful. In terms of case (b), stakeholder theorists claim that traditional models of the firm put too much emphasis on shareholders to the exclusion of other stakeholders who deserve consideration and to whom managers have obligations. While stakeholder theorists reject neither the notion that firms need to make money, nor that managers have moral duties to shareholders, they claim that managers also have duties to these other groups. In summary, stakeholder theorists have argued for two basic premises: that to perform well, managers need to pay attention to a wide array of stakeholders (e.g. environmental lobbyists, the local community, competitors), and that managers have obligations to stakeholders which include, but extend beyond, shareholders. Regardless of which of these two perspectives individual stakeholder theorists emphasize in any given paper, almost all of them regard the "hub and spoke" model depicted in Figure 1.1 as adequately descriptive of firm-stakeholder relationships.

In terms of what follows, our analysis will be divided into four sections. We shall briefly examine the history of the idea of stakeholders and discuss the origins of some contemporary theoretical issues. Then we shall analyze the current state of the art of stakeholder theory. We go on to suggest some future directions for scholars interested in pursuing these ideas, and finally, we suggest some challenges that have emerged within stakeholder theory.

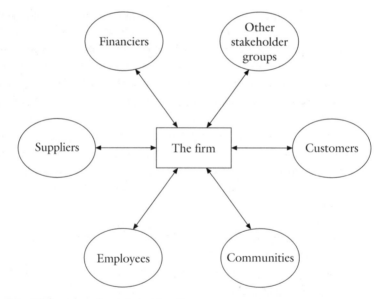

Figure 1.1   Hub and spoke stakeholder diagram

The Origins of the Stakeholder Concept

For many contemporary scholars, organized thinking about the stakeholder concept began with Freeman's seminal book, *Strategic Management: A Stake-holder Approach* (1984). But, as Freeman himself acknowledges, the general idea antedated his book by at least several years, perhaps by centuries. To gain a full understanding of the history of the concept, one first needs to explore the related notion of corporate social responsibility and some of its antecedent ideas and then review related themes from the literatures of corporate planning, systems theory, and organization theory.

Corporate social responsibility

Corporate social responsibility, defined by Jones as "the notion that corporations have an obligation to constituent groups in society other than stockholders and beyond that prescribed by law or union contract" (1980, pp. 59–60), clearly has "stakeholders" at its core. The origins of corporate social responsibility also show concern for stakeholders, even if this specific term wasn't used. Eberstadt (1973) argues that concepts analogous to social responsibility have been with us for centuries, even millennia. For example, in classical Greece, business was expected to be of service to the larger community. In the Medieval period, roughly 1000–1500 AD, a good businessman was honest "in motive and actions" and used his profits in a socially responsible manner (Eberstadt, 1973). For centuries, the idea of "noblesse oblige" – roughly defined as "the responsibility of rulers to the ruled" – represented an analogous concept among members of the European aristocracy. If one assigns similar responsibilities to members of an economic aristocracy in America, a country without a hereditary aristocracy, the analogy is not farfetched. This conclusion is particularly compelling since the power wielded by corporate managers (and owners, during the "robber baron" era) may in many cases rival that of their European aristocracy counterparts.

Furthermore, although they didn't use the term corporate social responsibility, Berle and Means, in their classic work on the separation of ownership and control, *The Modern Corporation and Private Property*, invoked the general concept. They did not bemoan this separation of ownership and control as many economists did, but rather noted that it liberated managers to serve the larger interests of society. In their words:

> The control groups have, rather, cleared the way for the claims of a group far wider than either the owners or the control. They have placed the community in a position to demand that the modern corporation serve not alone the owners or the control but all society (1932, p. 312).

This conclusion must have seemed somewhat odd to followers of a debate between Berle and E. Merrick Dodd in the pages of the *Harvard Law Review* (1932) and the *University of Chicago Law Review* (1935) from 1931 to 1935. Although Dodd persuasively advocated a broader set of corporate responsibilities, Berle didn't concede the point until 1954 in *The Twentieth Century Capitalist Revolution*.

Berle and Means were not alone among scholars who advocated broader responsibilities for business executives in the 1930s. The noted author Chester I. Barnard stressed the fundamentally instrumental role of the corporation in *The Functions of the Executive* (1938). The purpose of the firm, he argued, was to serve society; corporations were means to larger ends, rather than ends in themselves.

Many businesspeople also took steps to publicly embrace the idea of social responsibility. In a post-depression (and post-WWII) fit of defensiveness about the virtues of capitalism and a propaganda blitz intended to "sell" capitalism to the American public, they began to adopt postures of broad responsibility to corporate constituents (Cheit, 1956). Included in these pronouncements, common in the 1950s, were depictions of executives as corporate "statesmen" who balance the manifold interests of society in their decisions. In some sense, corporate social responsibility, as an ideal at least, was imposed on business by business itself. It wasn't until outsiders began to question the results of this statesmanship that corporate social responsibility began to acquire a larger external group of advocates. It was also during this period that Howard Bowen published his path-breaking book, *Social Responsibilities of the Businessman* (1953). Bowen wrote of the gathering intellectual force of the doctrine that business leaders are "servants of society" and that "management merely in the interests (narrowly defined) of stockholders is not the sole end of their duties" (1953, p. 44).

Each of the historical and intellectual predecessors discussed thus far focus on what Donaldson and Preston (1995) call the normative aspects of stakeholder theory. Although no one used the term "stakeholder" at the time, these perspectives held that corporations *should* behave in ways that were quite different than those prescribed by the conventional goal of the firm. According to this alternative perspective, firms should be operated in order to serve the interests of customers, employees, lenders, suppliers, and neighboring communities as well as stockholders.

Corporate planning

Another set of antecedent ideas approached the stakeholder question from a quite different angle, however. As Freeman and Reed (1983) and Freeman (1984) carefully document, a strain of stakeholder thinking was also developing in the corporate planning literature and related work. The term "stakeholder" was first used at the Stanford Research Institute in 1963 and was employed to connote groups "without whose support the organization would cease to exist" (Freeman, 1984).[1] To SRI researchers, corporate planning could not proceed effectively without some understanding of the interests of stakeholder groups. In this view and in many views derived from it, attention to stakeholder concerns was clearly subsidiary to some other, dominant interest – stockholder returns or firm survival, for example. Ansoff's *Corporate Strategy* (1965) dealt with the stakeholder notion by arguing for the existence of two types of corporate objectives – economic and social – with social objectives being secondary to economic objectives. Although these secondary objectives might constrain or modify the pursuit of the primary (economic) objectives, they were in no way to be regarded as "responsibilities."

In the contemporary vocabulary of Donaldson and Preston (1995), managers should be concerned about stakeholders only for *instrumental* reasons – as a means to improve the financial performance of the firm. One of the extensions of this instrumental use of stakeholder thinking was environmental scanning, a process by which planners attempted to forecast changes in the social environments of firms. With better assessments of these environments, better economic forecasts and, ultimately, better corporate strategic plans could be made.

Systems theory

Freeman (1984) also points to the systems theory literature in his historical account of the development of the stakeholder concept. The works of Churchman (1968) and Ackoff (1970) figure prominently in this history. According to the systems view, many social phenomena cannot be fully understood in isolation. Rather, they must be viewed as parts of larger systems within which they interact with other elements of the system. In this context, the concept of "stakeholders in a system" has meaning quite different from that employed by authors in the strategy literature (Freeman, 1984). According to Ackoff (1974), stakeholders must play a participatory role in the solution of systemic problems. In this framework, the optimization of the goals of individual components of the system (sub-system goals) is to be pursued only to an extent compatible with the pursuit of overall system goals. The intrinsic value of subsystem interests is clearly subordinate to overall system interests.

Organization theory

According to Freeman (1984), organization theorists were also important forerunners of the formal development of the stakeholder concept. In particular, he considers Rhenman (1968), who offers a formulation of stakeholder-based ideas very similar to that of the corporate planners. A leading edge thinker of his era. Rhenman[2] designates "the individuals and groups which depend on the company for the realization of their personal [and, presumably, group] goals and on whom the company is dependant" as stakeholders (Freeman, 1984, p. 41). Other "pre-stakeholder" ideas from organization theorists include the notion of "organization-sets" (Evan, 1966), an "open-systems" approach (Katz and Kahn, 1966; Yuchtman and Seashore, 1967), organizational "clientele" (Thompson, 1967), as well as contributions by Emery and Trist (1965) and Dill (1958), among others. The work of Pfeffer and Salancik (1978) is probably the organization theory most directly analogous to a stakeholder approach. Their concept of "resource dependence" captures the reliance of organizations on providers of key resources and support in a formal way. The reliance of other groups on "resources" from the firm is not emphasized in resource dependence theory, although many of the relationships in question are clearly reciprocal in nature.

However, some organization theorists (Pennings and Goodman, 1977) were concerned with the full range of "outputs" of organizations, rather than just efficiency or, in the case of corporations, profit. These scholars often stressed the difference between efficiency and effectiveness, the latter being defined in terms of the appropriateness of an organization's output. Nord (1983) made explicit the normative nature of any measurement of organizational output. In the process, he (perhaps inadvertently) linked the organizational effectiveness literature to the explicitly normative literature of corporate responsibility. A more detailed account of developments in organizational effectiveness can be found in Ehreth, who argues that "organizational effectiveness is not an objective state but is a relational construct that fits the needs and interests of constituencies" (1987, p. 9).

Although this brief summary cannot do justice to the intellectual antecedents of stakeholder theory, it does suggest that those who have done academic work on stakeholder theory have not done so without guidance from scholars in related fields. Those contributions are hereby gratefully, if not fully, acknowledged. And, it is noted that some of the ongoing arguments within the stakeholder theory literature – many of which cut to the core of its purpose and design – are indebted to its multidisciplinary origin. Each discipline brings a slightly different set of assumptions, implicit norms, and methods to the development of stakeholder theory.

The Current State of the Art of Stakeholder Theory

The past 15 years have seen the development of the idea of stakeholders into an "idea in good currency." Talk of stakeholders is increasingly common within business and academic circles. There are scores of essays focusing on stakeholders within management as ethics and social issues become more salient, and as our attention expands beyond the strict focus on shareholders. Even restricting our attention to academic writings still leaves a myriad of different work (spanning empirical and normative research), the exact relationships among which are often difficult to identify. The question is, what kind of shared underlying themes and ideas make up stakeholder theory? That is, if we examine the current state of the art within this field, what sort of theory do we find?

Donaldson and Preston (1995) provided one influential method for synthesizing the array of work that had been done to date. They advanced four key ideas that they claimed were central to stakeholder theory which make it a distinctive theory rather than a set of disparate ideas about "stakeholders." According to Donaldson and Preston (1995), stakeholder theory is *descriptive, instrumental, normative* and *managerial*. It is *descriptive* in the sense that researchers advancing stakeholder theory attempt to talk about, or describe, what the corporation is (i.e. how people at the corporation behave). They then compare that to some larger schematic to evaluate their performance (e.g. do they act as though the stakeholder or shareholder model is driving their behavior?). Stakeholder theory is *instrumental* in that researchers advance "if . . . then" types of propositions, specifically, that acting according to stakeholder management principles will be associated with positive outcomes for the corporation. Donaldson and Preston (1995) then claim that the central strand of stakeholder theory, and the "glue" which holds the theory together, is its *normative* content – claims that focus on what managers ought to do. Stakeholder management principles set out the legitimate interests of various stakeholders (including but going beyond shareholders) in the corporation and use these as a basis for determining how managers should behave. Indeed, it is this distinctive normative core which helps give shape and substance to the first two strands. This normative strand provides a descriptive story or script (i.e. respect the legitimate interests of stakeholders) one could use to compare to real managerial behavior to see if they are similar or different. These normative commitments provide a set of behaviors one might test to see the performance implications (i.e. the "if . . . then" statements characteristic of instrumental theory). Finally, Donaldson and Preston (1995) claim that stakeholder theory is *managerial,* in that it aims to shape and direct the behaviors of managers at the corporate in a specific and systematic way.

The core appeal of the Donaldson and Preston (1995) article is that it provided order and coherence where many saw chaos and confusion. Stakeholder researchers in business ethics, business and society, strategy, human resources, and other disciplines intuitively sensed that there was a connection to the writings of their peers, but there were few theoretically developed ideas linking their work together beyond the recognition that groups beyond shareholders had legitimacy at the corporation. Though it didn't resolve a number of key looming problems,[3] the Donaldson and Preston (1995) typology appeared to provide part of this missing link. It offered an umbrella to cover existing research in stakeholder theory, organize it into distinct strands (i.e. descriptive, instrumental, normative), and direct future work (i.e. to make sure it is coherent and follows the typology set out in their article). It also helped to combat the perception that stakeholder theory was an amorphous and ill-defined construct, born of good intentions, but doomed to fail for its breadth, its emphasis on people rather than profits, and its inability to direct the day-to-day behavior of managers.

However, there emerged voices of dissent to this grand reconciliation. Freeman (1994, 1999, 2000) took direct aim at the Donaldson and Preston (1995) typology for two main reasons. First, Freeman saw their work as reinforcing, rather than overcoming, the separation thesis. Second, he thought the sharp conceptual separation among normative, descriptive and instrumental was untenable.

In terms of the first criticism, Freeman has long been concerned with the importance of language and metaphor and how this shapes existing practice. The separation thesis posits that people, for the most part, tend to see the language and concepts of ethics and business as separate and that they occupy distinct realms (e.g. ethics deals with altruism and concern for others; business deals with selfishness and profits). The difficulty is trying to find a way to get these two realms back together, or at least to overlap enough so that you can convince managers that being good at their job doesn't mean they have to be a-, or im-moral. Freeman points out that the problem with the two realms is not that some people are happy to keep them separate while others want to bring them closer together, but that this metaphor for thinking about business and ethics is fundamentally misguided. Business ethics should instead be about how we understand the nature of business, as a morally compelling and interesting domain of human activity that could never be devoid of morality (i.e. so the divide never occurs in a wholesale or systematic way). For Freeman, the Donaldson and Preston (1995) article makes the mistake of setting up stakeholder theory as the foil to shareholder theory, thereby reinforcing the idea that ethics (i.e. stakeholder theory) is fundamentally different from business (i.e. shareholder theory) and managers have to choose between them. For this reason, Freeman (1994, 1999, 2000) didn't want to make stakeholder a specific and singular theory that could be compared to shareholder theory. Rather, he sought to make stakeholder theory a genre of research in which any account of the firm that posits a purpose for the firm and a set of responsibilities of managers is a "stakeholder theory." Under this view, the shareholder theory is itself a "stakeholder theory." The purpose of this move is to underscore the normative underpinnings of any theory of the firm and to help make us all better critics of corporations by forcing us to evaluate whether a given corporation has a compelling answer to questions regarding the purpose of the firm and the obligations of managers to stakeholders.

Freeman also objected to Donaldson and Preston's (1995) work because he claimed it sharply divided conceptual categories that are not fundamentally different. Following Quine, Davidson, Rorty, and other modern pragmatists, Freeman argued that a sharp separation of these modes of inquiry is neither conceptually plausible nor pragmatically desirable. Indeed, sharply separating facts and values, normative and empirical inquiry, risks reinforcing the separation thesis all over again (Wicks and Freeman, 1998). Freeman claims that these modes of inquiry are interrelated and together make up a coherent answer to the stakeholder question: what is the purpose of the corporation and in whose interests should it be run? Any adequate answer to that question, he claims, is a normative core or narrative. It will have aspects of what Donaldson and Preston (1995) call descriptive, instrumental and normative discourse and all play a key role in providing a compelling theory or narrative. No one element can be sharply separated and no one strand does the primary "work" of creating a compelling and justified theory.

A recent article by Jones and Wicks (1999) attempted to reconcile these viewpoints on stakeholder theory. They identified two distinct strands within the literature: the "single-theory" view expressed by Donaldson and Preston (1995) and the genre of normative cores view laid out by Freeman (1994). The authors (Jones and Wicks) claim that there is room to see significant convergence among these competing perspectives, even as the underlying methods, paradigms, and assumptions may differ significantly. They argue that stakeholder theorists are committed to developing normative cores (i.e. accounts of the purpose of the firm and obligations of managers) that can lay some persuasive claim to instrumental soundness (i.e. that firms running on these principles can survive and thrive in a competitive economy). To make the case that these views are convergent, the authors appeal to the normative interests of core stakeholders. Jones and Wicks (1999) argue that whatever else these groups want, they also wish to see the firm be profitable, and thus, they have a normative interest in the instrumental outcomes associated with the firm's normative core. The authors use this argument as the basis for positing that core stakeholder principles should not just be morally sound, but capable of keeping the firm economically viable.

This view does not take sides on the merits of the normative, instrumental, and descriptive typology, nor does it embrace the single theory or genre of theories view. It does, however, directly challenge a central claim of the Donaldson and Preston (1995) account, that normative and instrumental are clearly distinct and that the normative is the only arena where one can find justification for stakeholder theory. Jones and Wicks (1999) give the theory a more pragmatic orientation by claiming that both normative and instrumental theory provide critical resources in creating a justified stakeholder theory.

The remaining question from this discussion is what makes stakeholder theory unique? What stands out that is not common to other theories within management? Clearly, other theories talk about stakeholders, at some level. As simple descriptive terminology, the term "stakeholders" has thoroughly infected our language, particularly because of the growing need to attend to groups beyond shareholders to operate the firm as a going concern. Given this conceptual innovation, it makes little sense to talk about theories where managers don't manage stakeholders (i.e. all management theories do, at some level), or where firms lack stakeholders (i.e. all firms do have stakeholders). Thus, the terminology of stakeholder, by itself, is not what distinguishes stakeholder theory. Rather, as Donaldson and Preston (1995), Freeman (1994, 1999, 2000), and Jones and Wicks (1999), seem to agree, the distinctive element to stakeholder theory is its normative focus. Though the questions posed by each are different, all three papers center on the importance of answering the question: what is the purpose of the firm and to whom are managers obligated? In itself, posing this question is a considerable shift from existing theories of management that seek almost exclusively to address descriptive and/or instrumental claims. Stakeholder theory provides an effort to make theories of management explicitly accountable for their normative content and to highlight the moral underpinnings of "business" as we know it.

Perspectives on the Future of Stakeholder Theory

Although stakeholder theory has made substantial advances over the past decade, much work remains to be done. To begin with, the vast majority of stakeholder-based research papers that have been published to date are either theoretical or conceptual in nature. Given that theory building in a stakeholder framework can take on several forms, three of which – normative, instrumental, and descriptive – were described by Donaldson and Preston (1995), it is no surprise that theoretical perspectives dominate the literature.

This dominance notwithstanding, more theoretical work is needed. For example, narrative interpretation, advocated by Freeman (1994), and described by Jones and Wicks as ". . . the creation of narrative accounts of moral behavior in a stakeholder context" (1999, p. 209), has not been exhausted as a genre of research. In particular, we are aware of no narrative stakeholder theories based on theories of distributive justice. Although unconventional even in the already unconventional world of narrative stakeholder theories, such distributive justice-based accounts – for example, a Rawlsian "difference principle" based theory or an "entitlements" based theory derived from the work of Nozick (1975) are not beyond imagination. An account based on "effortocracy" could also be formulated in a narrative format.

According to Donaldson and Preston, instrumental stakeholder theory "is used to identify the connections, or lack of connections, between stakeholder management and the achievement of traditional corporate objectives (e.g., profitability, growth) (1995, p. 71). To date, only one formally presented instrumental stakeholder theory has been advanced. Jones (1995) argues that firms whose managers are able to create and sustain mutually trusting and cooperative relationships with their stakeholders will achieve competitive advantage over firms whose managers cannot. Other instrumental stakeholder theories are certainly possible and the instrumental realm might constitute a fertile ground for new stakeholder theory development.

According to Jones and Wicks (1999), the real challenge to stakeholder theorists is the creation of "convergent" stakeholder theory. Convergent stakeholder theory is theory that is simultaneously morally sound in its behavioral prescriptions and instrumentally viable in its economic outcomes. According to these authors, narrative accounts (or, for that matter, any normative stakeholder theory) without some evidence (broadly defined) as to their practicability, are of little value. Similarly, instrumental stakeholder theory that calls for adherence to behavioral standards that are not morally sound should also have little appeal to scholars with a stakeholder orientation. Recall that the most basic normative tenet of stakeholder theory is the view that the claims of all legitimate stakeholders have intrinsic value. It follows that stakeholder theory with serious moral deficiencies should not be acceptable to stakeholder theory advocates. Although Jones and Wicks (1999) do not fully develop Jones's (1995) "mutual trust and cooperation" instrumental theory into a formal convergent theory, they do suggest the general outlines of an extension of that type. Extending the idea of possible development of additional normative theories presented above, convergent theory based on these normative premises – the difference principle, entitlements, and effortocracy – is also possible. Finally, Donaldson and Dunfee's (1994) Integrative Social Contracts Theory (ISCT) would seem to be a good candidate for development into a convergent stakeholder theory.

The world of business practice also provides some potentially rich sources for doing stakeholder theory research. Works like Collins and Porras' *Built to Last* (1994) and Paine's "Managing for Organizational Integrity" (1994) both focus on companies that provide the more complex and morally interesting approaches to running a firm that are at the heart of stakeholder theory. Indeed, much of what drives the work of the authors of these works is a sense of the limitations and shallowness of describing the corporation as solely about making profits and enriching shareholders. One could describe the "corporate ideology" of the firms profiled by Collins and Porras (1994) and the "integrity strategy" of the firms described by Paine, as (at least partial) normative cores. These works, and others like it from the practitioner realm, hold special promise to address the managerial and practical challenges of stakeholder theory. That is, such work draws clear connection between values and purpose on the one hand and managerial activity on the other (i.e. it is managerial), and these resources provide credible conceptual and anecdotal evidence as to how a given firm's normative core may enable it to be highly competitive within the marketplace (i.e. it is practical/workable).

Another avenue of theoretical development in stakeholder theory involves descriptive theory – theory that purports to explain and (perhaps) predict how managers will actually behave in the context of stakeholder relations. It must be acknowledged that neoclassical microeconomic theory, based on the assumption of rational self-interested behavior on the part of economic actors, represents a legitimate and highly developed version of this type of theory. The fact that many stakeholder theory advocates dispute the moral foundations of both the processes and outcomes of the theory notwithstanding, neoclassical theory is authentic descriptive stakeholder theory. Although Jones and Wicks (1999) express doubt that a theory with the breadth and depth of neoclassical economic theory will emerge from the stakeholder theory framework, several other approaches are possible. Papers currently working their way through the review process at various journals show considerable promise. For example, one manuscript merges prospect theory, resource dependence theory, and organizational life cycle theory in an attempt to explain which stakeholder groups will be attended to at various points in a firm's development. Another paper, an empirical effort, examines the relative preference (of student groups) for "across-decision" attention to stakeholder interests as opposed to "within-decision" methods. Within-decision methods attempt to strike a balance among the interests of stakeholder groups within individual decisions; across-decision methods merely attempt to balance those interests over time, in essence, relying on an implicit set of IOUs to produce long-term equity among stakeholder groups. A descriptive stakeholder theory based on Donaldson and Dunfee's (1994) Integrative Social Contracts Theory is conceivable as well.

The emphasis to date on theoretical work should not understate the importance of empirical efforts in the interest of advancing stakeholder theory. As noted by Jones and Wicks (1999), instrumental theory is empirical theory. It matters a great deal whether or not the establishment and maintenance of mutually trusting and cooperative relationships do, in fact, lead to competitive advantage as predicted by Jones (1995). In addition, empirical evidence is one means of addressing the "practicability" facet of convergent stakeholder theory (Jones and Wicks, 1999). Economically disastrous outcomes resulting from normative prescriptions do not meet the test of good convergent theory. Similarly, descriptive theory, as it begins to emerge, will need to be tested. As noted above, one form of descriptive theory – within-decision versus between-decision methods – has already been subjected to empirical testing. The Academy of Management Journal published a recent collection of such papers.

"Large N" statistical studies are not the only way of producing empirical evidence, however. Case studies can also shed useful light on empirical questions. Case studies have the added advantage of the potential development of "grounded" theory, wherein theoretical possibilities are developed from the study of actual business practices and actual managerial behavior. Participant-observer studies of actual firms, particularly exemplary ones, may well be a productive extension of the case study method. Kochan and Rubenstein's (2000) participant observation study of Saturn is an example of a recent powerful contribution.

Another means of enhancing understanding of stakeholder relationships is through computer simulations. By nature, stakeholder relationships are multilateral and multifaceted, making them fertile ground for computer modeling, albeit modeling of a fairly sophisticated type. Despite the difficulties of programming such relationships, computer simulations hold out the promise of the rapid examination of very complex phenomena, and hence for a net increase in our knowledge of the value of stakeholder theory.

Challenges for Stakeholder Theory

There are four main theoretical challenges for stakeholder theory that will ultimately affect the usefulness of stakeholder theory for academics, business people, or both:

1 The problem of definitions
2 The background theory problem
3 The problem of pluralism
4 The problem of value creation and trade, and ethical theory

We shall explain each in turn, but we caution that these issues are interrelated, and that within each are complex theoretical and practical problems.

The problem of definition

Much has been written about the original definitions of "stakeholder" as "any group or individual who can affect or is affected by the achievement of an organization's objectives" (Freeman, 1984). Such a definition is implicitly appealing to strategic management scholars and executives. These are precisely the groups that can affect the firm, hence, precisely the groups whose relationships with the firm need to be shaped and influenced. However, some have argued that such a wide definition implies that "terrorists" are stakeholders, thus making "stakeholder" lose its implicit legitimacy. Others have argued that the term should be restricted to those groups who are definitional of the firm. For instance, in most businesses, customers, suppliers, communities, financiers, and employees all have a clear stake in the firm.

Recently, Phillips (2001) has suggested that such stakeholders be called "intrinsic" or "definitional" while other groups are stakeholders instrumentally, in so far as they affect the definitional stakeholders. He argues that firms have common moral obligations to both definitional and instrumental stakeholders, but have special obligations only to definitional stakeholders. Thus, the interesting question, on this analysis, becomes what does the firm owe to a customer, (and the reciprocal question of what a customer owes to a firm by virtue of being a customer).

Alternatively, if the narrow definition defines who has a stake, then it is incumbent to give an account of who and what counts as a "community." In a recent paper, Dunham et al. (2001) have suggested that if "community" is interpreted widely enough, then the narrow definition of stakeholders expands into the wide definition, once community is understood to consist of a collection of those interests that share some commons, or a political entity defined by competing interest groups.

This argument raises the next challenge; namely, it is imperative to pay more attention to the background theories that are at work. The upshot of these differing views of definition is that it is difficult to say what kinds of moral obligations are at work, when the very nature of who has the obligation is obscure. More practically, if who is a stakeholder is imprecise, it is difficult to formulate priority rules about whose interests count and when they come into play. However, since definitions are embedded in the background normative theory shaping such inquiry, perhaps an analysis of the background theory problem will provide some useful resources for addressing these issues as well.

The background theory problem

Given its multidisciplinary origins, much of the disagreement about stakeholder theory is diagnosable as differing sets of background theories at work. For instance, in the strategy literature there has traditionally been little concern with ethics and values, so the more subtle problems of definition are difficult to appreciate. (One solution to this problem is to define strategy theorists out of the stakeholder theory realm and note their much closer affinity to resource dependence theory.) Mitchell et al. (1997) have suggested a typology of features that determine which stakeholders are most important from three different points of view. However, this very typology assumes that managers are the best judges of stakeholder interests and/or behavior, and implicitly assumes that managers' or firms' judgments are the ones that should be used to determine stakeholder salience.

There are some scholars who have suggested that stakeholder analysis of the corporation must proceed from within a framework that acknowledges that the corporation is a legal entity – a legal fiction. Thus, corporate law and its itinerant compatriots, the law of torts, contracts, and agency, must serve a central role in any stakeholder theory that is to have practical significance. At this point, those who advocate this position have the burden of demonstrating that the legal view aids understanding of stakeholder phenomena. It is useful, however to note with Orts (1997) that "the law" in the form of dozens of "stakeholder statutes" no longer clings to a model that holds shareholder hegemony as a central value.

Philosophers and economists, such as Donaldson and Preston, have suggested that both philosophy and economics are the critical foundational fields, and Donaldson and Dunfee discuss cultural norms that can be shared and justified across particular cultures, making the social sciences, writ large, appropriate background disciplines. Scholars concerned with environmental issues have suggested that the environment be seen as a stakeholder. Such claims, and the background assumptions behind them, are based in environmental sciences (writ large) and bring it into play as a background theory.

With such an impressive array of potential background theories, perhaps it is foolhardy to wish for one, univalent *stakeholder theory*. Indeed, some stakeholder theorists (Freeman, 1994, 1999, 2000; Jones and Wicks, 1999) have already abandoned the quest. In an overlooked part of Donaldson and Preston's (1995) seminal paper, they suggest that ultimately stakeholder theory must be managerial. They write:

> The stakeholder theory is **managerial** in the broad sense of that term. It does not simply describe existing situations or predict cause-effect relationships; it also recommends attitudes, structures, and practices that, taken together, constitute stakeholder management. Stakeholder management requires, as its key attribute, simultaneous attention to the legitimate interests of all appropriate stakeholders, both in the establishment of organizational structures and general policies and in case-by-case decision making. This requirement holds for anyone managing or affecting corporate policies, including not only professional managers, but shareowners, the government, and others. Stakeholder theory does not necessarily presume that managers are the only rightful locus of corporate control and governance. Nor does the requirement of simultaneous attention to stakeholder interests resolve the longstanding problem of identifying stakeholders and evaluating their legitimate "stakes" in the corporation. The theory does not imply that all stakeholders (however they may be identified) should be equally involved in all processes and decisions (p. 67).

If stakeholder theory is managerial in this sense, a point readily conceded by many stakeholder scholars, we have to open the possibility that it is possible to have more than one theory that is useful. In fact, we might propose that any particular stakeholder theory is a function of a set of background conditions and a particular normative core, as articulated in so-called "convergent stakeholder theory" (Jones and Wicks, 1999). What would be necessary is a typology of stakeholder theories, each of which would contain a set of propositions that spell out the connections between the particular way that a set of firms can do business from within a particular normative core. Such an approach would naturally lead us to the third challenge to stakeholder theory.

The problem of pluralism

Suppose that there can be multiple stakeholder theories, each based on a normative core and a set of background disciplines. Each theory would describe how firms might actually realize that normative core, and the propositions that connect the normative core to other facets of the enterprise. In addition each particular stakeholder theory might have a set of instrumental propositions, such as "if you want to create shareholder value, you should manage the firm in a sustainable manner" or "if you want to manage the firm in a sustainable manner, you must pay a great deal of attention to environmentalists-critics of the corporation." The very language used to frame these propositions might differ depending on the framing assumptions that make up the particular theory. Each particular theory might well produce a different set of tradeoffs or priorities among stakeholder groups.

In this thicket of pluralism, what would be the role of an overarching "stakeholder theory"? Perhaps it would simply be, as we argued above, the role of genre: pointing out what a set of related theories have in common, and then coming to see them as related along particular dimensions.

Suppose however, that we assume that a particular stakeholder theory in its well-worked out form, might give an executive or a stakeholder a reason for acting in a certain manner. Surely, there is room for conflict among fully specified stakeholder theories. Indeed, any stakeholder theory based on normative theory from moral philosophy will almost certainly be in conflict with other such theories, given that the conflicts among normative theories are well documented. The existence of such "a reasonable pluralism" may well induce the search for a "minimalist" stakeholder theory, or a set of basic conditions that all normative cores must meet to be legitimate. This would both constrain and direct the creative, pluralistic drive to find an array, perhaps a wide array, of normative cores within stakeholder theory (Freeman, 1994, 1999, 2000; Wicks and Freeman, 1998). Akin to the public-private distinction on which political philosophers such as Rawls (1993) have relied, we could evaluate actions across (and perhaps independent of) various stakeholder genres according to such criteria. Some candidates for such a minimalist or public set of reasons would include those principles articulated by Freeman (2000) as giving rise to stakeholder capitalism, or the suggestions by Jones and Wicks (1999) for convergent stakeholder theory.

The problem of value creation and trade, and ethical theory

Traditionally, theories of business have begun and ended with economic logic. Business has been seen, wrongly as we argued above, as a way of creating "economic" value, with ethics perhaps serving as a side constraint. And, business ethics in general, and stakeholder theory in particular, have been developed within a framework of existing ethical theory that assumes that business is primarily concerned with its economic (narrowly defined) logic. Not surprisingly, ethical theory has little to say about business, or the way that value is created and traded. Yet, human beings have been value-creators and traders long before they were political philosophers. The practice of business has a long history, yet the existing body of ethical theory on which most business ethicists and stakeholder theorists rely pays almost no attention to the cultural and moral norms of value creation and trade. Werhane (1991) has suggested that Adam Smith saw the centrality of ethics to business, but even Adam Smith did not see the centrality of business to ethics. If the institution (i.e. business) in which most people spend the majority of their lives working, finding meaning (intrinsic and instrumental) and forging relationships with others is not central to the development of principles about how human beings interact and should interact, then the resulting ethics is likely to be sterile at best, and extremely difficult to apply at worst.

It seems to us that once we admit that business has to be responsible in some sense to stakeholders, and that stakeholders are moral agents as well as members of groups such as "customers," "communities," "shareholders," etc., then the door is opened for a complete rethinking of ethics and ethical theory. Certainly anyone reading this essay will conclude that this rethinking is well under way. Such a project is large in scope, and probably generalizable across the "disciplines" of applied ethics. We need to understand from an historical perspective just how value creation and trade have come about. We need to understand its different forms, how it has emerged across nation states, and why it appears to be a remarkably resilient institution. Connecting stakeholder theory to the very foundations of value creation of trade, to the foundations of entrepreneurship, is an important future project, one begun by Venkataraman (2001). Much work, however, remains to be done.

Conclusion

Though it is relatively new, we have shown that stakeholder theory has a rich heritage and a promising future. We traced the intellectual and historical roots of stakeholder theory in order to give the reader a deeper appreciation of what stakeholder theory is and what it may become. It seeks to do what no other theory within business and organization studies has tried: to openly address the critical questions about what firms ought to do, and to make such questions central to any account of the firm. We have ended with an array of possibilities for where scholars may take future research, knowing that we have only scratched the surface. While the diversity of backgrounds, methodologies, and perspectives of stakeholder theorists creates numerous difficulties, it also opens up tremendous opportunities for interesting and innovative work. It is with the challenge of taking on these creative endeavors that we leave the reader, and where we see the greatest promise for both stakeholder theory and organization studies.

Notes

1   Recently, Mr. Giles Slinger has revisited the early history of the idea of stakeholders. Through more extensive interviews, and the examination of a number of historical documents, Slinger rewrites the history as told in Freeman (1984). The essential difference is that the early use of the stakeholder idea was not particularly oriented towards the survival of the firm. Slinger's argument can be found in his doctoral dissertation, Essays on *Stakeholders and Takeovers*, (Slinger, 2001). An abridged version is in "Spanning the Gap: The Theoretical Principles Connecting Stakeholder Policies to Business Performance" (Slinger, 1998).
2   For a history of the development of the stakeholder concept in Scandinavia, and Rhenman's role in that development, see Nasi (1995).
3   Their typology claims that groups other than shareholders have legitimate interests, but it doesn't specify who these groups are, how we determine what their legitimate interests are, or how we resolve conflicts among stakeholder interests. It also didn't provide a specific answer to the definitional problem that threatened to make stakeholder theory vacuous: who is a stakeholder and why does the firm have a special obligation to them? Finally, though it claims to be managerial, it is not immediately clear how the central claims of this article would translate into any managerially specific behaviors.

References

Ackoff, R. 1970: *A Concept of Corporate Planning*. New York: John Wiley.

Ackoff, R. 1974: *Redesigning the Future*. New York: John Wiley.

Ansoff, I. 1965: *Corporate Planning*. New York: McGraw Hill.

Barnard, C. I. 1938: *The Function of the Executive*. Cambridge: Harvard University Press.

Berle, A. 1954: *The Twentieth Century Capitalist Revolution*. New York: Harcourt-Brace.

Berle, A. and Means, G. 1932: *Private Property and the Modern Corporation*. New York: Commerce Clearing House.

Bowen, H. 1953: *Social Responsibilities of the Businessman*. New York: Harper.

Cheit, E. 1956: *The Business Establishment*. New York: John Wiley.

Churchman, W. 1968: *The Systems Approach*. New York: Dell Books.

Collins, J. and Porras, J. 1994: *Built to Last*. New York: Harper.

Dill, W. 1958: Environment as an influence on managerial autonomy. *Administrative Science Quarterly*, 2 (4), 409–43.

Dodd, E. M., Jr. 1932: For whom are corporate managers trustees? *Harvard Law Review*, 45,1145.

Dodd, E. M., Jr. 1935: Is the effective enforcement of the fiduciary duties of corporate managers practicable? *University of Chicago Law Review*, 2, 194.

Donaldson, T. and Dunfee, T. 1994: Integrative social contracts: A communitarian conception of economic ethics. *Economics and Philosophy*, 11 (1), 85–112.

Donaldson, T. and Preston, L. 1995: The stakeholder theory of the corporation: concepts, evidence, and implications. *Academy of Management Review*, 20 (1), 65–91.

Dunham, L., Liedtka, J. and Freeman, E. 2001: Community: The soft underbelly of stakeholder theory. *Darden School Working Papers*. Charlottesville, Va.

Eberstadt, N. 1973: What history tells us about corporate responsibility. *Business and Society Review*, 7, 76–81.

Ehreth, J. 1987: Development of a competitive constituency model of organizational effectiveness and its application to a Health Services Organization. *Doctoral Dissertation*. University of Washington Graduate Business School.

Emery, F. and Trist, E. 1965: The causal texture of organizational environments. *Human Relations*, 18, 21–31.

Evan, W. 1966: The organization set: Toward a theory of inter-organizational design. In J. Thompson (ed.) *Approaches to Organizational Design*. Pittsburgh: University of Pittsburgh Press, 175–90.

Freeman, E. 1984: *Strategic Management: A Stakeholder Approach*. Boston: Pitman.

Freeman, E. 1994: The politics of stakeholder theory: Some future directions. *Business Ethics Quarterly*, 4 (4), 409–22.

Freeman, E. 1999: Divergent stakeholder theory. *Academy of Management Review*, 24 (2), 233–6.

Freeman, E. 2000: Business ethics at the millennium. *Business Ethics Quarterly*, 10 (1), 169–80.

Freeman, E. and Reed, D. 1983: Stockholders and stakeholders: A new perspective on corporate governance. *California Management Review*, 25 (3), 88–106.

Jones, T. 1980: Corporate social responsibility revisited, redefined. *California Management Review*, 22 (3), 59–67.

Jones, T. 1995: Instrumental stakeholder theory: A synthesis of ethics and economics. *Academy of Management Review*. 20, 92–117.

Jones, T. and Wicks, A. 1999: Convergent stakeholder theory. *Academy of Management Review*, 24, 206–21.

Katz, D. and Kahn, R. 1966: *The Social Psychology of Organizations*. New York: John Wiley.

Kochan, T. and Rubenstein, S. 2000: Towards a stakeholder theory of the firm: The Saturn Partnership. *Organizational Science*, 11 (4), 367–86.

Mitchell, R., Agle, B. and Wood, D. 1997: Toward a theory of stakeholder identification and salience: Defining the principle of who and what really counts. *Academy of Management Review*, 22, 853–86.

Nasi, J. 1995: A Scandinavian approach to stakeholder thinking: An analysis of its theoretical and practical uses, 1964–1980. In J. Nasi (ed.) *Understanding Stakeholder Thinking*. Helsinki: LSR-Julkaisut Oy, 97–115.

Nord, W. 1983: A political-economic perspective on organizational effectiveness. In K. S. Cameron and D. A. Whetten (eds), *Organizational Effectiveness: A Comparison of Multiple Models*. New York: Academic Press, 95–133.

Nozick, R. 1975: *Anarchy, State and Utopia*. New York: Basic Books.

Orts, E. 1997: A North American legal perspective on stakeholder management theory. In F. Patfield (ed.) *Perspectives on Company Law*, 2, 165–79.

Paine, L. S. (1994): Managing for organizational integrity. *Harvard Business Review*, 2, 106–17.

Pennings, H. and Goodman, P. 1977: *New Perspectives on Organizational Effectiveness*. San Francisco: Jossey Bass.

Pfeffer, J. and Salancik, G. 1978: *The External Control of Organizations*. New York: Harper.

Phillips, R. 2001: Stakeholder legitimacy: A preliminary investigation. *Georgetown University Business School Working Paper*. Washington, D.C.

Rawls, J. 1993: *Political Liberalism*. New York: Columbia University Press.

Rhenman, E. 1968: *Industrial Democracy and Industrial Management*. London: Tavistock.

Slinger, G. 1998: Spanning the gap: The theoretical principles connecting stakeholder policies to business performance. *Centre for Business Research, Department of Applied Economics Working Paper*. University of Cambridge.

Slinger, G. 2001: *Essays on Stakeholders and Takeovers*. Cambridge University Ph.D. Thesis, Department of Applied Economics, in press.

Thompson, J. 1967: *Organizations in Action*. New York: McGraw Hill.

Venkataraman, S. 2001. Stakeholder value equilibration and the entrepreneurial process. *Business Ethics Quarterly*. Ruffin Series No. 3, in press.

Werhane, P. 1991: *Adam Smith and his Legacy for Modern Capitalism*. Oxford: Oxford University Press.

Wicks, A. and Freeman, E. 1998: Organization studies and the new pragmatism: Anti-positivism, and the search for ethics. *Organization Science*, 9 (2), 123–40.

Yuchtman, E. and Seashore, S. 1967: A system resource approach to organizational effectiveness. *American Sociological Review*, 32, 891–903.

Further Reading

Harrison, J. and Freeman, E. 1999: Stakeholders, social responsibility, and performance: Empirical evidence and theoretical perspectives. *Academy of Management Journal*, 42 (5), 479–87.

Chapter 2

Ethics and Corporate Governance: Justifying the Role of Shareholder

John R. Boatright

Corporate governance is concerned broadly with who has the right to control the activities of a firm and how this right ought to be exercised. The answers to these questions constitute the main body of corporate law. In the USA, the law assigns a central role to shareholders. Specifically, the shareholders of a corporation have the ultimate right of control as well as a claim on all profits. In addition, corporate law imposes a fiduciary duty on managers to serve the shareholders' interests. Although corporate governance varies from one country to another, the American model is widely admired and emulated. However, many thoughtful people consider the shareholder-centered corporation to be morally unacceptable. In particular, critics charge that corporate governance, as practiced in the USA, unjustifiably neglects the rights and interests of other constituencies, such as employees, customers, suppliers, and communities.

This chapter examines the standard argument for the role of shareholders in corporate governance. Many different justifications for American corporate law have been offered over the years but, in the past three decades, a new economic approach has come to dominate the study of corporate law. In brief, this approach views the corporation as a nexus of contracts among its various constituencies and regards governance structures as attempts by these groups to reduce the costs of contracting. The argument examined here results from the application of this economic approach to the shareholders' role. Although the argument is not universally accepted, even critics acknowledge its power and influence. More-over, critics of the argument have not succeeded in developing an alternative theoretical approach that could ground a different system of corporate gover-nance. This lack of a rival theory does not mean that the economic approach to corporate law is sound, but only that, at the present time, this approach frames the discussion.

The position taken in this chapter is that the central role of shareholders in American corporate governance is fully justified. Not only does the standard argument provide adequate support for the particular bundle of rights that corporate law assigns to shareholders, but it does so in a way that permits adequate consideration of the rights and interests of other constituencies or stakeholders. However, the defense of this position turns on many complex and controversial issues that are difficult to resolve. To the debate, each side brings different factual assumptions about the effectiveness of alternative economic arrangements as well as different value judgments about how economic activity ought to be conducted and what it should achieve. Agreement about such matters is unlikely, and so the best that can be achieved in this chapter is a clarification of the issues that advances the debate.

The Contractual Theory

The standard argument for the role of shareholders in corporate governance is founded on an economic approach that is commonly called the new institutional economics or the new economics of organizations. Until recently, neoclassical economic analysis offered only a rudimentary theory of the firm (Hart, 1989), but in the 1970s, economists, building on the pioneering work of Ronald Coase (1937), developed a powerful theory utilizing agency cost and transaction cost economics (Alchian and Demsetz, 1972; Williamson, 1975, 1985; Klein et al., 1978; Jensen and Meckling, 1976; Fama and Jensen, 1983a, 1983b). These economists followed Coase in modeling the firm as a nexus of contracts, in which each corporate constituency, including employees, customers, suppliers, and investors, supplies some asset in return for some gain. These contracts include not only explicit legal contracts, such as employment and sales contracts, in which the terms are clearly specified, but also long term relationships built on implicit contracts or shared understandings. In addition, the law plays a critical role in contracting. First, legislative statutes provide "standard form" or "off the shelf" contracts that save the parties the need to write contracts for each transaction and also serve when the parties are unable to contract face to face. Second, judicial interpretations often "fill in" the gaps in written contracts that do not cover every situation (Easterbrook and Fischel, 1991).

Contracting is the principal means by which we conduct our economic affairs and structure economic relations. The contracts that constitute a corporation are distinguished by the fact that they are all made with a legal fiction that we call the firm. The firm is a common signatory of these contracts and the entity that connects them to form a nexus (Hansmann, 1996). Many of these contracts, such as consumer purchases, are simple market exchanges, but others are more complex arrangements. Employment contracts, for example, include a pledge by an individual to accept orders and act in the best interest of the employer. Such open-ended obligations are necessary because the contracts of employees and many other constituencies cannot anticipate and address every contingency.

Perhaps the most complex arrangement of all is that between a firm and its shareholders.

In Coase's account (1937), a firm is a *hierarchy* – that is, a structured system of authority relations. Through voluntary contracting, individuals create firms because they can generally achieve with others more than they can alone in the marketplace. By becoming an employee, in a hierarchical firm, for example, an individual submits to the authority of a superior, but in return that person is able to earn more than is possible as an independent contractor in a market. Thus, for Coase, markets and hierarchies constitute two fundamentally different means for economic coordination. The former coordinates by exchange, the latter by direct control. However, Alchian and Demsetz observe that corporations do not exercise hierarchical authority like a state. The firm, they assert, "has no power of fiat, no authority, no disciplinary action any different in the slightest degree from ordinary market contracting between any two people" (Alchian and Demsetz, 1972, p. 777). The extent to which firms are hierarchies that rely on authority relations is an important issue to be examined later, but these writers agree that, in the last analysis, firms are built on voluntary market exchanges.

In all market exchanges, rational economic actors are assumed to seek the greatest benefit for the least cost in order to maximize their own welfare. The costs to be considered in an exchange include not only the costs of the benefit obtained but also the costs of making the exchange itself. That is, contracting has costs, and when individuals join with others in productive activity, these contracting costs can be substantial. In general, then, rational economic agents would seek to organize production in ways that lower the costs of contracting. Indeed, Coase explains the existence of firms in this way. Why, he asks, do firms exist at all? Why does all economic activity not take place in an open market? The answer is that the transaction costs of working out in a market all of the contracts that would be required are very high and that these costs could be greatly reduced by organizing production in hierarchies. Thus, in Coase's account, firms result from efforts by individuals to contract in ways that lower transaction costs.

Firms provide many benefits because, in general, people's economic assets, especially their knowledge and skills, bring a greater return when they are utilized with the assets of others in joint production. However, joint production also introduces many problems, and the costs of contracting arise mainly from efforts to solve these problems and from any loss due to the failure to find a solution. One important kind of cost is that incurred in monitoring the performance of others. When several people work together, it may be possible for one or more to contribute less and yet collect the same as everyone else. Alchian and Demsetz (1972) argue that workers in this situation would hire a monitor whose task is to ensure that everyone contributes equally. To the question "Who monitors the monitors?" they respond that such monitoring would be unnecessary if the monitor were offered the residual revenues or the profit of the enterprise. In short, workers would voluntarily agree to assign profits to a third party who could solve the monitoring problem.

Monitoring is part of a more general problem arising from conflicting goals. Organizations bring together people with their various goals, most of which are aimed at advancing their own interests. An economic organization of any size must develop mechanisms for enabling people with different goals to cooperate productively. This is accomplished, in part, by structuring many business relations as agency relations, in which one person, an *agent,* agrees to act on behalf of another, the *principal* (Jensen and Meckling, 1976). Agency relations are critical to the organization of a firm, but they also involve costs, both in monitoring agents' performance and in suffering any loss from nonperformance. The task of monitoring agents is especially acute when there is *asymmetric information* (as when one person has information that others lack) and *incomplete information* (as when certain information is not and perhaps cannot be known). These features are most pronounced in the case of the managers of an enterprise, who are generally better informed about important matters and must be trusted in their judgment about the future (which, of course, cannot be known with assurance). The agency costs of controlling managers are enormous and constitute a major portion of the total cost of contracting in a firm.

Other contracting costs arise from risks that are created by entering into contractual relations. One kind of risk results from providing firm-specific assets that cannot easily be removed from production. For examples, employees who develop skills that are of use only to their current employer or a supplier who invests in machinery to make parts with only one buyer become "locked into" their position. Not only may the other parties take advantage of this lock-in. but the benefit of a long-term relation may be upset by unforeseen developments. For example, a supplier's sole customer may discontinue a product or find another source. In addition, a relation such as that between a firm and its employees or suppliers may be very complex, with the result that the parties may be unable to anticipate and plan for every situation. This is especially true when people have "bounded rationality" due to a limited ability to acquire and process information (Simon, 1955, 1957, 1979, 1997). So people take risks when they enter into a long-term relation from which they cannot easily withdraw (lock-in), whose dimensions cannot be fully grasped (complexity), and whose future they cannot predict (uncertainty). The cost of protecting oneself against these risks or incurring a loss because of them are also part of the costs of contracting.

The fundamental proposition of the economic approach to the study of the corporation is that all economic organizations can be understood as a nexus of contracts that results from bargaining among all the relevant constituencies or contracting parties, each of which is seeking to gain the maximum benefit from engaging in a joint productive enterprise. The challenge for each group is to contract with a firm so as to obtain the greatest benefit at the lowest cost, which is primarily a matter of reducing the costs of contracting. More specifically, this means developing long-term relations in a cooperative endeavor with protection against the risks of lock-in, complexity, and uncertainty. The managers of a firm, who have the task of making these contracts on behalf of the firm, face the same challenge of organizing joint production in a way that reduces contracting costs to the maximum feasible extent. Managers thus serve as an intermediary between the various constituencies, contracting with each one in a way that coordinates the contracts made with the others.

The Shareholder's Contract

A business enterprise requires many inputs. Economists classify these as land, labor, and capital. In addition, a firm needs managerial expertise to coordinate these inputs. Neoclassical economics assumes that each provider of an input owns that input and that a manager or entrepreneur is the owner of the firm, who buys inputs, sells the output, and pockets the difference. That is, profit is the compensation received by the manager-owner for his or her contribution of managerial talent. However, this is not the only possibility. We could imagine a group of workers who hire managers to coordinate their productive activity and who keep the profits for themselves. Alternatively, the sellers of an input, such as grain farmers, or the buyers of an output, such farmers who buy seeds and fertilizer, could hire managers to organize the sale of their grain or the purchase of seeds and fertilizer, respectively. These are examples of worker-owned, supplier-owned, and customer-owned firms, and these forms of enterprise, usually called cooperatives, are quite common (Hansmann, 1996). In most large, publicly-held corporations, the providers of capital are the shareholders, but the role of shareholder or owner can be held by any group.

Although shareholders are commonly called the owners of a corporation, the concept of ownership as applied to the modern corporation is different from its ordinary use (Schrader, 1996). No group "owns" General Motors, for example, in the same way that a person owns an automobile or a home. Rather, shareholders have a certain bundle of rights, which include the right of control and the right to receive the residual revenues or profits (Hansmann, 1996). (Residual revenues are the net earnings of a firm, which is to say the revenue that remains after all fixed obligations are met.) The right of control and the right to the residual are logically separate, which is to say that they could be held by different groups. Indeed, in a not-for-profit corporation, trustees exercise control but are legally barred from any personal benefit. (However, a nonprofit corporation, strictly speaking, has no owners; it is an asset held in trust for some beneficiaries.) In practice, the right of control and the right to residual earnings go together because the right to the residual would be insecure without control. No group without a right to residual earnings would have an incentive to operate a for-profit corporation so as to maximize these earnings. (Trustees, who have a legal duty to run a nonprofit corporation in the interest of the beneficiaries, are assumed to be altruistic.) The right of ownership to a thing could also be shared by two or more groups. For example, employees and investors could jointly exercise control of a firm and split the profits. However, shared ownership encounters practical problems that explain its relative infrequency.

That shareholders have the rights to exercise control and to receive the residual revenues is a matter of definition: the shareholders or owners are whatever group or groups have these rights. Although employee-owned corporations and various kinds of cooperatives exist, the most common form of organization for large firms is ownership by the suppliers of equity capital. The key question, then, is why, in most instances, equity capital suppliers are the shareholders. That is, why is investor ownership the form of economic organization taken by most corporations and the standard form in corporate law? This question seeks an *explanation* for the dominance of the investor-owned corporation, but our concern here is ultimately with *justification*. So we also need to ask why this form of organization is justified. However, the contractual theory of the firm provides both an explanation and justification.

The contractual theory itself is not logically tied to any assignment of rights to any constituency. It does not specify which group has the right of control or the right to the residual. All groups are free to bargain for these rights. Moreover, the specific content and extent of shareholder rights, as well as the rights of other constituencies, are also matters for bargaining. For example, shareholders do not have an absolute right of control but rather a narrow set of legal rights that confer *de jure* power on such matters as the election of directors, proxy proposals, charter revisions, and mergers and acquisitions. On many important matters, shareholders have the ultimate say, but they have little voice in day-to-day operations. The business judgment rule shields many management actions from shareholders suits, thereby giving managers considerable legal authority. In some instances, bond covenants and loan agreements give other investors besides shareholders rights to intervene in certain matters. In practice, the shareholder legal right of control is limited in scope and shared with other groups, and the details are matters to be determined by contracting.

Furthermore, *de facto* control is exercised by many corporate constituencies. Without the benefit of any legal right of control, employees, customers, and other groups can influence corporate decisions by setting the conditions for their cooperation. In particular, public interest groups can exert powerful pressure on corporations by mobilizing public opinion and influencing government. Even if shareholders claim the residual, many groups make claims on a company's total revenues. An environmental group that forces a corporation to spend more money on pollution control, for example, has determined the use of some revenues. Corporate philanthropy also involves a diversion of revenue to nonshareholder groups. The right to residual revenues is merely claim on the portion of a corporation's total revenues that remain after other groups have already exacted their share, and many groups might prefer to bargain for a greater share of the revenues that are not counted as part of the residual.

In addition to the kinds of contracting costs introduced so far, there are other costs that attach specifically to the assumption of the right of control and the right to residual earnings. Although these rights are usually regarded as benefits, their exercise involves costs that must be considered by any group that seeks to be the shareholders or owners of a firm. Henry Hansmann (1996) identifies these "costs of ownership" as the costs of controlling managers, the costs of collective decision making, and the costs of risk bearing. The first two costs are involved in the right of control and the latter in the right to the residual.

First, controlling managers incurs costs whenever there is a separation of the legal right of control and *de facto* day-to-day control of a corporation, which Berle and Means (1932) called the separation of ownership and control. In firms that are still run by the owners, there is no divergence of interests inasmuch as the managers and the shareholders are the same persons. However, Berle and Means observed that as corporations have grown in size and outlive the founders, their operations are increasingly controlled by professional managers whose interests differ from those of the shareholders. The assumption is that managers, if not restrained, would seek to enrich themselves by lavish pay and extravagant per-quisites. Other possibilities include self-dealing (for example, owning a supplier), competition with the firm (as in taking an investment opportunity for oneself instead of the firm), and excessive retention of earnings (also known as "empire building"), which inflates the size of the firm and hence the managers' importance. These costs are a form of agency costs and include both the costs of monitoring managers and the losses that result from a failure to prevent them from pursuing their interests to the detriment of the firm.

Second, decision making is a costly process even when only one person has control because of the need to gather and process information. When two or more people make decisions collectively, further costs are incurred in resolving the inevitable disagreements. Even people with the same interest may differ in their judgment of the most effective course of action, but differences of interest create more profound conflicts. For this reason, the costs of ownership are reduced when only one constituency has control. However, the members of any given constituency may have conflicting interests, which result in some decision-making costs. For example, investors may have different risk preferences or time horizons that lead them to favor or oppose certain decisions. Moreover, the costs of decision making include not only the cost of this investment but also any losses caused by less than the best decisions. Good decision making in an organization requires a substantial investment, but no amount of money can guarantee that the best decisions will be made, so some losses of this kind are inevitable.

Third, business is an inherently risk activity, and this risk can be shared by everyone or borne by a single group. Any corporate constituency that provides an asset to the firm in return for a claim on residual revenues assumes a large portion of the risk of the enterprise and in so doing provides a service to everyone else. Every contractor with a firm assumes some risk, but all legal obligations to those with fixed contracts must be met before residual claimants receive any of a firm's revenues. Residual claimants are not guaranteed any specific return, and their payment is the only obligation that a firm can fail to make without becoming insolvent. Thus, bondholders who are not paid can force a company into bankruptcy, while shareholders can only count their losses. The right to the residual is a benefit that is often thought to make shareholders especially privileged, but it comes at a price, namely the cost of bearing the residual risk.

We are now in a position to understand terms why certain investors would contract with a firm to be the owners or the shareholders, and why other constituencies would contract differently and be willing to allow these investors to assume this role. The contractual theory explanation, in brief, is that the system of corporate governance that prevails in most large, publicly held corporations is that which enables all constituencies to gain the greatest benefit from joint production at the lowest contracting cost. Many business organizations adopt other governance structures, such as those of sole proprietorships, partnerships, cooperatives, mutual companies, and the like, but the theory explains these as well by noting how the costs and benefits are altered by different conditions. There is no one ideal form of corporate governance that is appropriate in all circumstances, and rational contractors will experiment to find the most suitable forms.

This brief explanation omits many critical details, and so we need to understand more specifically how systems of corporate governance result from contracting by all of the relevant constituencies. That is, how do we get from contract to corporate governance?

From Contract to Corporate Governance

People with capital are as necessary for production as workers and the suppliers of raw materials, but they are not owners of an enterprise merely in virtue of providing capital. Indeed, lenders and bondholders, who provide capital do not have the right of control or a right to residual revenues. The investors who provide equity capital generally hold these rights. Equity capital, by definition, is capital that is provided without the obligation to repay over time the principal with interest that defines loans and bonds. It is capital that is provided for the life of the firm with whatever guarantees the investors can obtain. From the investors' point of view, there must be some advantage in providing equity capital rather than debt capital. From a company's point of view, there must be some advantage in obtaining equity rather than debt capital. In theory, a firm could obtain all the capital it needs by borrowing – that is, by taking on debt – but there are many disadvantages to operating in this manner. The creation of the investor-owned firm could be explained from either point of view, but it is perhaps better explained by asking why firms would seek equity capital and what they need to do to attract it.

Capital, like any other input, is obtained in a market. Managers of firms seek capital at the lowest cost, while the owners of capital seek the highest return. There is a limit to the amount of capital that a firm can raise through borrowing from banks and issuing bonds because of the increasing risk. As a firm's debt obligations consume a greater portion of its revenues, the ability of the firm to make its debt payments becomes less certain. If the risk is shared with all constituencies, then they will each demand higher returns for their inputs, or else go to other firms where the risk is lower. Not only the costs of capital but also the costs of labor and raw materials rise with the risk. The solution is to persuade one class of investors to provide capital in return for a firm's residual revenues, so that those investors assume a preponderance of the risk. Sole proprietorships and partnerships function without shareholders, but the individuals involved assume great risk. Such firms typically require little capital or else have great difficulty raising sufficient capital, and they occasionally "go public" to share risk and obtain needed capital. Less frequently, public firms will "go private" through a management buyout or a takeover in which the new owners assume greater risk and provide their own capital.

Managers of firms can obtain capital at a lower cost if they reduce the risk to investors. For example, the interest rate on bonds is lower for firms that obtain a higher rating from investor services companies such as Moody's and Standard & Poor's. The risk for residual risk bearers can be reduced by the adoption of forms of corporate governance that address the major contracting costs, especially the costs of ownership. Corporations have wide latitude in choosing governance structures. First, in the USA, corporate law is the province of the states, and so states can compete for charters by varying the terms they offer. Although some writers complain of a "race to the bottom," in which states compete to offer terms that favor management over shareholders (Cary, 1974), others argue that competition among the states produces corporate law that strikes an ideal balance (Winter, 1977; Romano, 1993). Second, much corporate law is "default" legislation that can be "contracted around" by parties that so choose. That is, corporate law provides a basic model that corporations may alter to suit their needs. So the reduction of contracting costs is a major consideration in the adoption of specific forms of corporate governance by a firm. By choosing one governance structure over another, firms compete with each other in attracting equity capital, and firms that make a mistake in their choice pay a price in the market for capital.

If choosing a system of corporate governance is a matter of determining which constituency can assume the role of owner at the lowest cost, the task might seem to be daunting because of the information required. However, if this choice is left to the market, then the best forms of corporate governance will emerge through contracting among all the relevant constituencies. That is, employees, customers, suppliers, investors, and other groups, will calculate for themselves the costs and benefits of ownership, as well as the costs and benefits of other arrangements, and express these calculations in the marketplace. Governance structures that are not efficient will disappear, along with the firms that adopted them, in a Darwinian struggle for the "survival of the fittest." Thus, corporations need not be designed in one fell swoop by some knowing mind but can emerge from the myriad choices of individuals over time. However, a theoretical explanation of the cost-reducing advantages of the dominant system of investor ownership can be offered by considering the three costs of ownership, namely the costs of controlling managers, the costs of collective decision making, and the costs of risk bearing.

First, no constituency would assume the costs of controlling managers unless the expected returns exceed the costs. Generally, residual risk bearers, who reap the full benefit of improvements in management performance, gain the greatest return from incurring these costs. In the standard argument, residual risk bearers ought to have control because they have the greatest incentive to monitor management performance and to expend time and effort in overseeing a firm's operation. Insofar as any constituency fills this role effectively at the lowest cost, other constituencies are benefited automatically by improved firm performance. Moreover, no constituency without a claim on the residual would have an incentive to spur management to improved performance if their returns do not increase as a result, which is usually the case. For example, workers' pay is determined mainly by the market for labor, and so employees ordinarily do not receive higher wages if a company is more profitable. (At the same time, their wages usually do not suffer if the firm falters.) Similarly, customers do not receive goods more cheaply and suppliers cannot command a higher price merely because a company is successful because, as with wages, the price of goods is determined by the market.

In practice, the shareholders of American corporations have little incentive to control managers. Given the pattern of fragmented holdings among diversified investors, shareholders in the United States ought to be "rationally disinterested" in the performance of any given firm. Mark Roe (1991) points out that the most efficient form of corporate governance is probably a small group of investors with concentrated holdings because they would have the greatest incentive to closely monitor managers. Such a pattern prevails in Germany, for example, but concentrated holdings have been prevented in the USA by laws that reflect a distrust of powerful financial institutions. Thus, Roe argues, politics as well as markets have shaped corporate law. Hansmann (1996) concedes that American shareholders are not very effective monitors, but argues that investor ownership is still better than the alternatives because it assures everyone that somebody else's interests will not be primary. In addition, Hansmann observes, there is extensive regulation in the USA, such as accounting standards and securities law, as well as an active press, all of which leads managers to act in the shareholders' interest.

Second, investors with a claim on the residual, which is to say equity capital providers, are commonly regarded as the group that can make decisions at the lowest cost. Decision making costs arise primarily from efforts to resolve conflicts among those with control. For this reason, any governance structure in which control is shared – between investors and employees, for example – would be fraught with conflicts because of differing objectives, and considerable time and effort would be required to make sound decisions. Not all members of any one constituency, such as employees or customers, have the same objectives, but equity capital providers are typically the least conflicted group. In the standard argument, equity capital provides have the advantage of a single, clear objective that is capable of directing decisions, namely increasing residual revenues or profits. This objective is one that potentially benefits all constituencies because a successful firm creates more wealth that is available for distribution to all.

Third, equity capital providers are usually the constituency best able to bear risk. This ability is due primarily to the opportunity of shareholders to diversify their holdings. The value of an investor's portfolio of shares in a large number of companies will generally not be affected by the fortune of a single company but will fluctuate with the broader market. Employees, by contrast, are not able to diversify the risk of unemployment. In addition, wealthy investors are typically less risk averse than other groups and hence more willing to accept greater risk for the prospect of a higher return. Again, less affluent employees generally prefer the safety of a known paycheck to the uncertainty of receiving a portion of the residual.

For these reasons, equity capital providers can generally incur the costs of ownership at lower cost than other constituencies with the result that the total contracting costs of all constituencies is reduced. Under some circumstances, however, there are benefits to some other constituency that make it advantageous for that group to obtain control. For example, employee ownership typically occurs in troubled companies in which employees are asked to accept lower pay to enable the firm to survive or else assume greater risk, including the nonpayment of promised wages or even unemployment. The potential loss to employees who are locked into such a firm may offset the costs of ownership and lead them to seek control. In addition, customers who are forced by a single seller to pay high prices may reduce their overall costs by forming a cooperative in which they control the supplier. Similarly, suppliers, such as milk producers or cranberry growers, who have only one customer can avoid loss from the market power of the buyer by obtaining control. Land O' Lakes and Ocean Spray are examples of producer cooperatives for the marketing of dairy products and cranberry juice respectively.

Whether a corporation is owned by investors, employees, customers, suppliers, or some other constituency is determined by the costs and benefits of ownership as reflected in the market choices made by each group. The standard argument holds that whatever the assignment of ownership, the resulting system of corporate governance is optimal not only for the constituency with control and a claim on the residual but also for all other constituencies. However, the idea that all groups can benefit from ownership by one group requires further explanation.

Protecting Other Constituencies

In the contractual theory, every constituency enters into a relationship with a firm. Although contracts are used by each group to build its relationship, the type of contracts and the terms of these contracts are different because each group has unique contracting problems that require tailor-made solutions. We have previously observed that the problems of contracting are due primarily to the need to protect firm specific assets under conditions of complexity and uncertainty. In practice, there are a great many ways for all constituencies to protect themselves and to plan long-term, beneficial relationships with a firm, and the means chosen by one group need not be, and probably will not be, the same as those adopted by another. The important question is whether each group is adequately protected. That is, are they all well served by the multiplicity of relationships that constitute the nexus-of-contracts firm?

The standard argument holds that, in general, the interests of nonshareholder constituencies are best protected by a variety of safeguards that are unrelated to the right of control. In contrast, shareholder interests are very difficult to protect by the same kind of safeguards, and so control rights are the means that best protect the uniquely vulnerable interests of shareholders. This part of the argument involves several points.

First, it should be noted that contracting is not the only source of protection for corporate constituencies. In particular, each group can seek to avoid lock-in, and doing so is advantageous to the extent that the gains exceed any loss. For example, a supplier has greater protection when it sells to many buyers. A supplier might make more profit by selling only to one firm, but the resulting lock-in creates greater risks that must be weighed against the benefits. Generally, consumers who make one-time purchases and have a wide selection can avoid being locked in, as can employees with highly marketable skills in a tight labor market. In short, the marketplace itself provides a form of noncontractual protection.

Second, each constituency can seek to write contracts that cover every aspect of a relationship and anticipate every contingency. Many sales contracts have detailed provisions concerning the rights and obligations of each party, and union contracts provide a similar level of protection for employees. Such explicit contracting involves considerable direct transaction costs, as well as other indirect costs from a lack of flexibility. (For example, union employees might be more productive without certain work rules in their contracts, but if they cannot trust employers to share the productivity gains with them, then they are better off with the productivity hindering rules.) An alternative to relatively complete, explicit contracts is relational contracting (Macaulay, 1963; Macneil, 1978; Goetz and Scott, 1981). Relational contracts generally commit the parties to some common goal rather than a specific course of action, and compliance with the contract is judged not by whether some action is performed but whether each party has made a "best effort" attempt to achieve the goal (Goetz and Scott, 1981). The most prominent use of relational contracting is the creation of agency relations, whereby a principal seeks to overcome the contracting problems caused by complexity and uncertainty, as well as information asymmetry, by engaging another person as an agent.

Third, the legal system provides many protections. In addition to offering standard form contracts and gap-filling judicial interpretations, the law also creates many rights and obligations. For example, customers benefit from consumer protection legislation that sets safety standards, as well as from tort law that enables them to sue for injury from defective products. In addition, many terms of sale, including warranties, are set by law. On the whole, consumers in the United States are very well protected by a combination of explicit contracts and legal safeguards. Similarly, employees are well protected by the vast body of employment law and by worker protection legislation; and investors, such as bondholders, are protected by the body of securities law and by the Bankruptcy Code (which specifies the rights of debt holders in the event of insolvency).

Turning now to the position of shareholder/owners, which is any constituency that has the right of control and a right to residual revenues, the right of control itself is the chief means for protecting the right to the residual. Control by itself confers no benefit and would not usually be sought as an end for its own sake. The value of control lies rather in what it enables one to achieve. Ordinarily, control is of value to residual risk bearers because this is a relatively effective means and, more importantly, virtually the only means for them to safeguard their promised return. By contrast, groups that have no claim on the residual are usually better protected by other safeguards.

Residual risk bearers are uniquely vulnerable because of their inability to write detailed, complete contracts with a firm. The gain for residual risk bearers comes only when a firm is well run, but because of the complexity and uncertainty involved in management, the steps to be taken cannot be specified in advance. This raises no problem for owners who exercise day-to-day control, but with the separation of ownership and control (Berle and Means, 1932), shareholders need some means for ensuring that managers run the firm so as to maximize residual returns. The power of shareholders to elect directors – who in turn hire managers, evaluate their performance, and set their compensation – provides some protection. In addition, the market for managerial talent and especially the market for corporate control disciplines managers, and the law further serves to protect shareholders by such means as disclosure requirements, a prohibition on insider trading, and provisions for shareholder suits. An especially important legal safeguard is the fiduciary duty of managers to operate a firm in the shareholders' interest.

That the fiduciary duties of managers are owed primarily to the shareholders is a source of great controversy. Many critics of corporate governance focus on fiduciary duty as the key feature of the shareholder-centered corporation (Marens and Wicks, 1999) and call for an expansion of this duty to all stakeholder groups (Evan and Freeman, 1993). Arguably, fiduciary duties play a less important role in corporate governance than critics assume. They serve primarily to prevent directors and top managers from abusing their position to enrich themselves and others (Clark, 1985), and in this role fiduciary duties benefit all constituencies. Although suit can be brought for breaches of fiduciary duties, their enforcement depends less on legal sanctions than on moral force. In general, a party to an explicit contract has a stronger legal claim that the beneficiary of a fiduciary duty.

The main value of fiduciary duties is to create an open-ended obligation to act in the interest of another in situations where precisely stated obligations are not possible. Two parties who could write complete explicit contracts would have no need for fiduciary duties. To a great extent this describes the situation of nonshareholder constituencies. However, fiduciary duties are particularly well suited to the contracting problems faced by shareholders, whose contract with the firm cannot be fully specified.

Jonathan R. Macey describes fiduciary duties as "a method of gap-filling in incomplete contracts" (Macey, 1991, p. 25). He writes, "Fiduciary duties are a corporate governance device uniquely crafted to fill in the massive gap in this open-ended bargain between shareholder and corporate officers and directors" (Macey, 1991, p. 41). All contracts are incomplete to some extent, and so would not other constituencies benefit from this kind of gap filling? Macey's reply is that judicial decisions fill in gaps of the contracts involving employees, customers, suppliers, and other nonshareholder groups. In short, fiduciary duties are only one means of gap filling (judicial decision making is the other), and other con-stituencies have an effective alternative to fiduciary duties (namely, relying on the courts to interpret their contracts with a firm). Moreover, the effectiveness of fiduciary duties is decreased when they are shared (Macey and Miller, 1993). If management owed fiduciary duties were owed to every corporate constituency, then they would be of benefit to none.

It is worth noting that fiduciary duties are not owed solely to shareholders. Many states have modified the fiduciary duty principle in the event of a takeover bid to permit the consideration of other constituencies (Orts, 1992). The Employ-ment Retirement Income Security Act (ERISA) imposes a fiduciary duty on management in the handling of employees' retirement funds (Little and Thraikill, 1977). These developments reflect a judgment by legislatures and courts that the contracting problems of nonshareholder constituencies in these situations are best addressed by means of fiduciary duties.

The argument for assigning fiduciary duties primarily to shareholders, then, is that this arrangement solves a critical contracting problem for this group; that this solution would be less effective if fiduciary duties were owed to other groups as well; and that, in any event, other groups have more effective means for solving their contracting problems.

The Justification of Corporate Law

The contractual theory of the firm, as presented so far, holds that American cor-porate law represents what people would have negotiated had they been able to do so (Easterbrook and Fischel, 1991). This claim assumes that much corporate law ratifies the economic choices individuals have in fact made and also reflects the attempts of legislators and judges to anticipate the choices that the parties might have made. In both instances, there is a search for governance forms that reduce the costs of contracting, which is to say a search for the most efficient ownership structures. Insofar as corporations result from private contracting, they can be justified in the same way as any outcome from free market exchange. However, just because people would contract so as to create a given form of corporate governance, it does not follow that this form is justified. Put differently, efficient structures are not for that reason just. Efficiency is a moral good, but it may not be the only morally relevant consideration in corporate governance.

A guiding ethical principle of the contractual theory is that whenever possible people should be free to choose the terms of their economic relations with others. This principle can be grounded either in libertarianism, which makes individual freedom of choice a fundamental value, or in utilitarianism, which justifies free market choices for the reason that they produce higher levels of welfare. Both libertarianism and utilitarianism require many background conditions for the justification of the outcome of people's free choices. Economists commonly stress the need for perfect competition, perfect information, and the absence of force and fraud, and they also recognize instances of market failure that may require government regulation. Moreover, an organizational form can be morally justified as an outcome of contracting only if the conditions for fair contracting are satisfied. That is, any ethical theory that grounds the principle of free choice must enable us to determine when a contract is genuinely fair and not the result of coercion, fraud, or unfair advantage taking.

Although the standard contractual argument for the prevailing system of corporate governance might be criticized on the grounds that the conditions for fair contracting are not satisfied, the critics generally mount a broader challenge to the idea that corporate law should be formed merely by considering how individuals do or would contract. Specifically, critics charge that a contractual approach:

1 reinforces existing imbalances of power among various constituencies and even creates a bias in favor of shareholders;
2 fails to address adequately the social costs or externalities of corporate activities; and
3 overlooks the public nature of corporations and their role in society.

Let us examine each of these charges briefly.

Safeguards and power

Objection The contractual theory assumes that each constituency is able to protect itself by selecting the safeguards that are best suited to its situation. These safeguards take many forms, and, according to the theory, the fact that shareholders protect themselves with the rights of ownership does not necessarily give them any advantage over employees or customers who rationally choose other means of protection. However, if safeguards must be bargained for, then the inequality of power that exists in every society will be reflected in the law of corporate governance. A largely disempowered workforce, for example, might be unable to secure adequate safeguards in a process of bargaining, while ultrapowerful investors gain more than their rightful share. More importantly, all individuals have some rights that they should not have to bargain for in a market. Everyone should be treated fairly and have his or her interests taken into account. In short, moral treatment is not a good to be distributed in a market but a precondition for all economic activity.

Reply   First, inequality of power, which is a serious moral concern, exists primarily between individuals in a society rather than between corporate constituencies. All of us are consumers and members of communities; most people are employees, and an increasing number are investors, especially through pension funds. As a result, a substantial equality of power among these groups may coexist with great inequality among individuals. The contractual argument is open to criticism for a lack of equality only if one or more groups, such as employees or consumers, have unequal power *as a group*. Moreover, our concern in these various roles should be the greatest overall benefit. That is, employees (who are also consumers) should be willing to accept less in wages if, by doing so, they gain even more as consumers through lower prices. An instructive example is provided by Japan, where the relatively privileged position of employees is offset by very high consumer prices and very low returns on savings. Arguably, individual Japanese might be better off on balance if they were less well off as employees.

However, this reply does not address the serious inequality that remains. Many workers in the USA, for example, have a much weaker bargaining position than their counterparts in Europe, and this inequality is not wholly offset by the benefits they receive as consumers or investors. When companies reduce their workforce in order to increase profits, it appears that employee interests are being sacrificed to those of shareholders. Some critics argue that the current law of corporate governance unduly favors shareholders and that the law ought to be changed to redress this imbalance of power. Their proposals include extending the fiduciary to shareholders to include other stakeholders, giving stakeholder groups representation on boards of directors, and reducing limited liability for shareholders (Millon, 1995). Each of these proposals needs to be carefully evaluated, but contractual theorists are skeptical about the efficacy of using legal rules to change the outcome of bargaining in a market. Merely changing the rules of corporate governance is unlikely to compensate for any underlying inequality of power since more powerful groups could respond by extracting concessions on other matters (Maitland, 2001). In short, legal rules are weak instruments to correct imbalances of power. However, the rules of corporate governance profoundly affect the efficiency of firms, and so any change designed to reduce inequality must be weighed against the loss of efficiency.

The point that rights should not have to be bargained for involves two misconceptions. First, contracting itself presupposes a right to contract and certain minimal conditions, such as the absence of force and fraud, and certain kinds of treatment of others is wrong, notwithstanding any contractual agreements. For example, exposing employees to unreasonably dangerous working conditions is morally impermissible, even with their consent. However, above a moral minimum, the rights and obligations of parties may justifiably be open to negotiation. Thus, employers and employees may justifiably bargain over the level of safety, recognizing that the choice may involve a tradeoff with other goods, such as wages. The contractual theory holds that most of the rights involved in corporate governance are not part of a moral minimum but are rightfully subject to bargaining. We have already noted that no group has a prior claim on corporate control and that any group can assume this role. The crucial question, therefore, is not whether some rights exist antecedently – some definitely do – but which rights exist antecedently and which result from contracting.

Second, the moral requirement that everyone's interests ought to be taken into account does not preclude a fiduciary duty to run a corporation in the interests of shareholders (Marens and Wicks, 1999). In the contractual theory, the interests of employees, customers, and other constituencies are best served, generally, if managers make major corporate decisions with a view only to the interests of shareholders. (Such decisions can also be described as those that utilize resources most efficiency and create the greatest wealth for society.) If this claim is true, then nonshareholder constituencies would consent to a system of governance in which their interests are not explicitly considered by management, assuming, of course, that their interests are already adequately protected by other means. This does not mean that their interests are not taken into account. Rather, they are taken into account *in the contracting process*, out of which the nexus-of-contracts corporation is formed. Similarly, we should not expect a creditor to consider our interests in collecting a debt. Our interests are taken into account when we borrow money, but when a loan comes due, there is nothing to be done but to observe the agreement. Overall, a system of lending is in our interest, and insisting that a creditor consider our interest in deciding whether to collect a loan would undermine this system.

The problem of social cost

Objection Business activity benefits society, but it also imposes social costs. A fiduciary duty to serve the interest of shareholders alone permits, indeed seems to require, that managers disregard these costs to society in the pursuit of shareholder benefits. Social costs are commonly viewed as *externalities*, which are costs of production that are not borne by the producer. A company that pollutes, for example, is able to utilize a resource for which others pay the cost. Not only do managers have a duty to ignore externalities, which are costs to society, but they should seek to avoid internalizing such costs, by investing in pollution control, for example. Such a disregard of social costs cannot be justified by the contractual theory when contracts between two parties affect third parties. Not only should contractors be aware of third-party effects as a matter of morality, but no contract can be justified if it wrongfully harms others. Thus, any contract between a firm and its shareholders must be made with a concern for the interests of other constituencies, and no contract can justify actions that are morally wrong.

Reply The problem of social cost is twofold. First, all costs of production should be weighed against the benefits, which is to say that production should be maximally efficient. Regardless of who bears the cost, society as a whole should gain the greatest possible benefit in return. Second, the costs (as well as the benefits) should be distributed in an equitable manner. In theory, bargaining in a nexus-of-contracts firm revolves around both the costs and the benefits of joint productive activity. That is, workers bargain not only for wages (a benefit) but also for safe and healthy working conditions (because injury and illness are costs). Thus, the distribution of social costs is, to some extent, built into structure of a firm. Furthermore, it should matter little, from a theoretical point of view, whether costs are externalized or internalized. If internalized costs are passed along to consumers in higher prices, for example, then consumers still bear the costs. The problem with externalization is that it leads to an inefficient utilization of resources. The objection, then, is not that firms create externalities but that they impose social costs that reduce efficiency and are distributed unfairly.

There are many ways to address both of these problems of social costs. That managers should have a duty to consider the effects on other constituencies akin to their fiduciary duty toward shareholders is one solution but not necessarily the most effective. For example, workers could arguably obtain more protection from workplace hazards by bargaining for better working conditions or by lobbying for government regulation. Similarly, consumer protection legislation, environment protection laws, and a host of other regulatory regimes provide far more protection to various constituencies than a reliance on managerial good will. The legal system prevents the imposition of social costs by means other than regulation. For example, tort law enables people who are wrongfully harmed to sue for damages and thereby limits the ability of managers to inflict certain kinds of harm on people. Thus, the law does not permit two contracting parties to harm third parties in violation of their rights.

In addition, markets can serve to internalize costs and thereby secure both efficiency and fairness. Ronald Coase (1960) argued that externalities would not result in an inefficient allocation of resources if there were a clear assignment of property rights for all resources and means for enforcing these rights at no cost. Under such conditions, the cost of all resources would be fully factored into economic choices. This insight (called Coase's theorem) underlies an approach to pollution, for example, that assigns rights to pollute and requires firms exceeding pollution limits to purchase the rights from less polluting firms. A well-designed market-based pollution control system may be not only efficient but also fair, by distributing costs in accord with market choices.

Contractual theorists no less than their critics are concerned with the problem of social costs. They disagree principally over the use of corporate governance as a solution. Contractual theorists agree with the assessment of Easterbrook and Fischel (1991) that we should seek to distribute both the costs and the benefits of productive activity in the way that all parties would agree to were they able to bargain. The form of corporate governance reflects the choices that these parties would make about governance structures, but these choices have little bearing on decisions about the utilization of resources. How we make these decision is very important, but, as Easterbrook and Fischel (1991, p. 39) conclude, "To view pollution . . . or other difficult moral or social questions as *governance* matters is to miss the point."

The public/private distinction

Objection In the contractual view, business organizations are private associations of individuals who contract with each other to achieve their own (private) ends. However, corporations are not merely private associations; they are also public institutions, created by society and endowed with certain privileges, in order to serve important public goals. Although individuals have a right to contract with others in the course of engaging in business, the right to incorporate, with its attendant privileges, is granted by society to serve some socially beneficial purpose. Moreover, conceiving the corporation as an essentially private association deprives employees and other groups from active participation in decision-making. On the contractual view, a corporation is a hierarchy, not a democracy. Thus, employees, for example, are expected to work as directed by their superiors. However, Christopher McMahon (1994) argues that the use of authority in business organizations is morally permissible only if it is democratically exercised. That is, all affected groups should have a significant voice in major corporate decisions.

Reply The contractual approach starts with the assumption that individuals create organizations not only to serve their own ends but also to achieve common goals in cooperation with others. The earliest large US corporations were formed to build railroads, produce steel, and engage in other activities that require the marshalling of vast resources. The reasons for incorporating must be stated in a corporation's charter. Thus, corporations *do* serve some larger purposes. These may vary according to the aims of their founders, but they invariably involve the provision of economic goods and services. The founders may also choose whether to incorporate as a for-profit or not-for-profit organization. This choice does not affect the purposes of the corporation but determines how it is governed. For example, for-profit and not-for-profit hospitals have the same end – to provide healthcare – but the former is controlled by trustees on behalf of society, the latter by directors, who represent the shareholders. The not-for-profit form is appropriate if donors contribute the assets of the hospital; the latter, if the assets are obtained from investors. Ultimately, the governance structure for a hospital will reflect how it is financed.

Although corporations may be said to exist with the permission of society in some sense, we grant the privileges that enable individuals to do business in the corporate form because of the need for large-scale economic organization in the production of most economic goods. We also gain maximum benefit from corporations when they operate efficiently. The contractual theory assumes that finding the most efficient organizational forms or governance structures is a difficult task and that, for the most part, this task is best left to the marketplace. The problems are sufficiently complex that a market approach – which leaves individuals free to experiment and allows experience to show us the best solutions – is more likely to succeed than an approach that views these problems as matters of public policy. Of course, we need to make sure that important public concerns are adequately addressed. The main issue here between contractual theorists and their critics is whether the public interest should be served directly by making corporations public institutions or served indirectly by leaving corporations in private hands, subject to public controls.

For example, a public or not-for-profit hospital, no less than a for-profit facility, should operate efficiently, making the best use of its resources to provide high quality medical care. However, a public good, such as caring for indigent patients, may be more easily served by a not-for-profit hospital due to its comparative freedom to balance efficiency with other goals. The resulting inefficiency has a price, but it is a price that society is willing to pay to ensure that those unable to pay do not go without treatment. By contrast, a for-profit hospital would seek to avoid the care of indigent patients in order to maximize the return to shareholders. However, the public good of caring for indigent patients could be achieved within a system of for-profit hospitals by such means as government regulation that requires treatment or government payment for such services. Both sides agree that we want to obtain the best medical care for the allocated resources consistent with achieving other socially desirable goods, such as equal access to medical care. In short, we need to make some trade-off between equity and efficiency. As long as the members of a society agree on *what* trade-off to make, *how* the trade-off is made should be immaterial. The same trade-off could be made with a system of for-profit or not-for-profit hospitals, and so the crucial question is which system works best overall. This is an empirical matter to be decided by experience and not a normative judgment about the public or private nature of the corporation.

Similarly, whether corporations should be more democratic instead of being hierarchical is also a question of what works best in practice for all those involved. Workers who want a voice in decision-making are free to organize themselves as employee-owned firms. However, we have already observed that monitoring and decision-making costs might lead them to submit to the control of managers and to assign them the right to all profits. Williamson (1985) observes that workers might also seek to sell an employee-owned firm to investors in order to obtain capital on more favorable terms. Thus, workers might agree to join a hierarchical firm and forgo a democratic workplace in order to gain more than they could otherwise. If they make this decision, then they are exercising their freedom to choose, and depriving people of the freedom to make this decision would be coercive. Furthermore, one joins a hierarchical firm by becoming an agent, and agency relationships are a ubiquitous feature of business. Attorneys, accountants, bankers, and a host of others agree to become agents and serve others – in return for ample compensation, of course – and so there is no reason why the situation of employees or any other group serving as agents should be regarded as morally undesirable.

Conclusion

The argument presented in this chapter relies on an economic approach in which corporate governance is, first and foremost, a search for the most efficient forms of economic organization. This approach assumes that the justification for any resulting system of corporate governance is not that it embodies some ethical ideal but that it reflects individual economic choices expressed through contracting in a market. However, the market in this case is primarily a means for creating forms of economic organization, and in contracting we consider not only efficiency but also ideals. Our economic choices reflect our preferences, and these include the kinds of organizations and ultimately the kind of a society that we want. In short, our moral desires are embodied in markets (Dunfee, 1999). Our current system of corporate governance has evolved through trial and error, with careful evaluation at each step, and the freedom to experiment with different organizational forms enables us to choose those we consider best.

It follows from this economic approach that there is no one ideal form of corporate governance. Not only will many organizational forms exist within any given society, but different forms will be suited for different historical periods. Moreover, corporate governance will vary greatly around the world, as people solve the problems of economic organization in accord with their cultural, historical, political, and legal traditions. Global competition will punish countries with inefficient governance structures, but many different efficient forms of organization are still possible. Consequently, corporate governance in the United States, Europe, and Asia may converge to some extent while still retaining certain distinctive features. Corporate governance is also constantly evolving in response to changing conditions, and so it is difficult to predict the governance structures that might be adopted in the twenty-first century.

References

Alchian, A. A. and Demsetz, H. 1972: Production, information costs, and economic organization. *American Economic Review*. 62, 777–95.

Berle, Jr., A. A. and Means, G. C. 1932: *The Modern Corporation and Private Property*. New York: Harcourt, Brace & World.

Cary, W. L. 1974: Federalism and corporate law: Reflections upon Delaware. *Yale Law Journal*. 83, 663–705.

Clark, R. C. 1985: Agency costs versus fiduciary duties. In J. W. Pratt & R. J. Zeckhauser eds *Principle and Agents: The Structure of Business*. Boston: Harvard Business School Press, 55–79.

Coase, R. H. 1937: The nature of the firm. *Economica*. N.S., 4, 386–405.

Coase, R. H. 1960: The problem of social cost. *Journal of Law and Economics*. 3, 1–44.

Dunfee, T. W. 1999: Corporate governance in a market with morality. *Law and Contemporary Problems*. 62, 129–57.

Easterbrook, F. H. and Fischel, D. R. 1991: *The Economic Structure of Corporate Law*. Cambridge: Harvard University Press.

Evan, W. and Freeman, R. E. 1993: A stakeholder theory of the modern corporation: Kantian capitalism. In T. L. Beauchamp and N. E. Bowie (eds). *Ethical Theory and Business*. 4th edn, Englewood Cliffs, NJ: Prentice Hall, 75–84.

Fama, E. F. and Jensen, M. C. 1983a: Separation of ownership and control. *Journal of Law and Economics*. 26, 301–25.

Fama, E. F. and Jensen, M. C. 1983b: Agency problems and residual claims. *Journal of Law and Economics*. 26, 327–49.

Goetz, C. J. and Scott, R. E. 1981: Principles of relational contracts. *Virginia Law Review*. 67, 1089–150.

Hansmann, H. 1996: *The Ownership of Enterprise*. Cambridge: Harvard University Press.

Hart, O. 1989: An economist's perspective on the theory of the firm. *Columbia Law Review*. 89, 1757–73.

Jensen, M. C. and Meckling, W. H. 1976: Theory of the firm: Managerial behavior, agency costs, and ownership structure. *Journal of Financial Economics*. 3, 305–60.

Klein, B., Crawford, R. G. and Alchian, A. A. 1978: Vertical integration, appropriable rents, and the competitive contracting process. *Journal of Law and Economics*. 21, 297–326.

Little, Jr., H. S. and Thraikill, L. T. 1977: Fiduciaries under ERISA: A narrow path to tread. *Vanderbilt Law Review*. 30, 1–38.

Macey, J. R. 1991: An economic analysis of the various rationales for making shareholder the exclusive beneficiaries of corporate fiduciary duties. *Stetson Law Review*, 21, 23–44.

Macey, J. R. and Miller, G. P. 1993: Corporate stakeholders: A contractual perspective. *University of Toronto Law Journal*. 43, 401–24.

Macneil, I. F. 1978: Contracts: Adjustment of long-term economic relations under classical, neoclassical, and relational contract law. *Northwestern University Law Review*. 72, 854–905.

Maitland, I. 2001: Distributive justice in firms: Do the rules of corporate governance matter? *Business Ethics Quarterly*. 11, 129–43.

Marens, R. and Wicks, A. 1999: Getting real: Stakeholder theory, management practice, and the general irrelevance fiduciary duties owed to shareholders. *Business Ethics Quarterly*. 9, 273–93.

Macaulay, S. 1963: Non-contractual relations in business: A preliminary study. *American Sociological Review.* 28, 55–67.

McMahon, C. 1994: *Authority and Democracy: A General Theory of Government and Management.* Princeton, NJ: Princeton University Press.

Millon, D. 1995: Communitarianism in corporate law: Foundations and law reform strategies. In L. E. Mitchell (ed.) *Progressive Corporate Law.* Boulder, CO: Westview, 31–3.

Orts, E. W. 1992: Beyond shareholders: Interpreting corporate constituency statutes. *George Washington Law Review.* 61, 14–135.

Roe, M. 1991: A political theory of American corporate finance. *Columbia Law Review.* 91, 10–67.

Romano, R. 1993: *The Genius of American Corporate Law.* Washington, DC: The AEI Press.

Schrader, D. E. 1996: The oddness of corporate ownership. *Journal of Social Philosophy.* 27, 104–27.

Simon, H. A. 1955: A behavior model of rational choice. *Quarterly Journal of Economics.* 69, 99–118.

Simon, H. A. 1957: *Models of Man.* New York: Wiley.

Simon, H. A. 1979: Rational decision-making in business organizations. *American Economic Review.* 69, 493–513.

Simon, H. A. 1997: *Administrative Behavior.* New York: Free Press. Original publication: 1947.

Williamson, O. E. 1975: *Markets and Hierarchies: Analysis and Antitrust Implications.* New York: Free Press.

Williamson, O. E. 1985: *The Economic Institutions of Capitalism.* New York: The Free Press.

Winter, Jr., R. K. 1977: State law, shareholder protection, and the theory of the corporation. *The Journal of Legal Studies.* 6, 251–92.

Further Reading

Maitland, I. 1994: The morality of the corporation: An empirical or normative disagreement? *Business Ethics Quarterly,* 4, 445–58.

Chapter 3

Untangling the Corruption Knot: Global Bribery Viewed through the Lens of Integrative Social Contract Theory

*Thomas W. Dunfee and
Thomas J. Donaldson*

Global managers often must navigate the perplexing gray zone that arises when two cultures – and two sets of ethics – meet. Consider these two scenarios:

- Competing for a bid in a foreign country, you are introduced to a "consultant" who offers to help you in your client contacts. A brief conversation makes it clear that this person is well connected in local government and business circles and knows your customer extremely well. The consultant will help you to prepare and submit your bid and negotiate with the customer . . . for a substantial fee. Your peers tell you that such arrangements are normal in this country – and that a large part of the consulting fee will go directly to staff people working for your customer. Those who have rejected such help in the past have seen contracts go to their less-fussy competitors.
- A developing country in Africa solicits bids for a dam on a major river. Your firm submits a bid based on your substantial experience in building similar structures. The contract is awarded to an Indonesian firm having little experience in building the type of dam required. You suspect that a bribe has been paid to the government official in charge of awarding the contract. You later hear that the winning proposal involves substandard materials and design. You genuinely believe that the dam is likely to collapse in the future and cause great loss of life.

What should you do in such cases? "Bribery is just like tipping," some people say. "Whether you tip for service at dinner; or, bribe for the benefit of getting goods through customs – you pay for a service rendered." But while many of us balk at a conclusion that puts bribery on a par with tipping or that suggests we should violate our personal values when in another culture, we cannot say why. In the case of the African dam, one appears to confront a choice among evils. If one does nothing, the contract will go to a less qualified bidder, and even worse, the lives of people living near the dam may be endangered. But if one complains, it not only seems like sour grapes, but by exposing the corruption, one risks endangering the representatives of one's firm. Ultimately *can* there be any solution to such problems?

This chapter describes a systematic way to think through the problems of bribery and its possible responses. In order to untangle the corruption knot, we will show how to apply two key concepts from the "social contracts" approach we develop at length in our book, *Ties That Bind* (Donaldson and Dunfee, 1999). We focus on bribery as part of the international issue of corruption because of its enormous importance in today's global business environment. Further, we believe that public attitudes about bribery are changing, making matters even more challenging for beleaguered managers facing the temptation of bribery. Academics, public policy makers, officials of public international organizations, and corporate managers all must consider the full implications of widespread global bribery. But we also focus on bribery for the practical reason that our space in this book is limited, and we believe that treating one global ethics topic well is preferable to treating many badly.[1]

Integrative Social Contracts Theory

We wrote the book, *Ties that Bind*, out of our conviction that answering today's questions require a new approach to business ethics, one that exposes the implicit understandings or "contracts" that bind industries, companies, and economic systems into moral communities. It is in these economic communities, and in the often unspoken understandings that provide their ethical glue, that we believe many of the answers to business ethics quandaries lie. Further, we think that answering such questions requires the use of a yet deeper, and universal "contract" superseding even individual ones. The theory that combines both these deeper and thinner kinds of contracts we label "Integrative Social Contracts Theory," or "ISCT" for short.

ISCT does not overturn popular wisdom. While it asserts that the social contracts that arise from specific cultural and geographic contexts have legitimacy, it acknowledges a *limit* to that legitimacy. It recognizes the moral authority of key transcultural truths, for example, the idea that human beings everywhere are deserving of respect. The social contract approach we detail holds that any social contract terms existing outside these boundaries must be deemed illegitimate, no matter how completely subscribed to within a given economic community. In this sense, all particular or "micro" social contracts, whether they exist at the national, industry, or corporate level, must conform to a hypothetical "macro" social contract that lays down moral boundaries for any social contracting. ISCT thus lies midway on the spectrum of moral belief, separating relativism from absolutism. It allows substantial "moral free space" for nations and other economic communities to shape their distinctive concepts of economic fairness, but it draws the line at flagrant neglect of core human values.

ISCT is derived from a thought experiment in which rational contractors are assumed to rely upon a limited set of core assumptions in framing their search for a common economic ethics, where "economic ethics" refers to the principles establishing the boundaries of proper behavior in the context of the production and exchange of goods and services.

These are as follows:

- All humans are constrained by bounded moral rationality. This means that even rational persons knowledgeable about ethical theory cannot always divine good answers to moral problems without being acquainted with community-specific norms.
- The nature of ethical behavior in economic systems and communities helps determine the quality and efficiency of economic interactions. Higher quality and more efficient economic interactions are preferable to lower quality and less efficient economic interactions.
- All other things being equal, economic activity that is consistent with the cultural, philosophical, or religious attitudes of economic actors is preferable to economic activity that is not.

In virtue of these three propositions, we argue further that individual contractors would desire the option to join and to exit economic communities as a means of leveraging their ability to achieve the benefits of either greater efficiency or greater compatibility with preferred religious, philosophical, or community norms.

The hypothetical members of the global economic community would be capable of considering which norms would be best to guide all business activity in a way that achieves fairness. In this hypothetical state of nature, we argue that such rational global contractors would agree to the following *de minimis* macro-social contract setting the terms for economic ethics:

1 Local economic communities have moral free space in which they may generate ethical norms for their members through microsocial contracts.
2 Norm-generating microsocial contracts must be grounded in consent, buttressed by the rights of individual members to voice and exit.
3 To become obligatory (legitimate), a microsocial contract norm must be compatible with hypernorms.

4   In cases of conflicts among norms satisfying macrosocial contract terms 1–3, priority principles must be established through the application of rules consistent with the spirit and letter of the macrosocial contract.

Here are the ISCT priority principles, or "rules of thumb":

1   Local community norms have priority unless adopting them harms members of another community.
2   Local community norms designed to resolve norm conflicts have priority unless adopting them harms members of another community
3   The more global the source of the norm, the greater the norm's priority.
4   Norms essential to the maintenance of the economic environment in which the transaction occurs have priority over norms potentially damaging to that environment.
5   Patterns of consistency among alternative norms add weight for priority.
6   Priority is given to well-defined norms over less well-defined ones.

Thus, under the approach delineated in ISCT, it is important to make use of hypernorms, or, in other words, universal principles applicable to all cultures and actions. Second, many problems dissolve when existing microsocial contracts found within relevant communities are carefully identified and proper priority is established among them.

Resolving Problems in Global Business Ethics: Is there Evidence for Microsocial Contracts and Moral Free Space?

No one doubts that cultural differences abound in global business activities (Donaldson and Dunfee, 1999, pp. 213–33). The deeper question is whether these differences imply different microsocial contracts for different cultures where members truly affirm authentic, legitimate norms that nonetheless conflict with those operating in other cultures. Might it be the case that in every instance of cultural difference, one side is invariably more "right" than the other? If so, the task of an international manager is simply to discover what the "right" norms are, and act accordingly. *TIES*s notion of the "microsocial contract" provides a tool for interpreting the significance of ethical differences, and it is a tool that we will use frequently in the remainder of this chapter.

Kluckhorn (1955), Hofstede (1980), Turner and Trompenaars (1993) and many other management theorists have shown the importance of cultural differences to business – but the further issue of the ethical implications of many of these differences remains unexplored. For example, researchers have documented the importance of understanding the time sensitivity of the Swiss in contrast to the time laxity of South Americans, or the group orientation of the Japanese in contrast to the individualism of the Americans. To fail to understand such differences, modern managers realize, triggers missteps and financial losses. But the importance of understanding *ethical* differences among cultures is much less well understood – a puzzling oversight, since ethical differences often have ringing consequences.

On a positive note, the clearer picture of the significance of cultural differences slowly emerging during the last decade has shed light on ethical differences. In one study, for example, thousands of international managers around the world were asked this question:

> While you are talking and sharing a bottle of beer with a friend who was officially on duty as a safety inspector in the company you both work for, an accident occurs, injuring a shift worker. The national safety commission launches an investigation and you are asked for your evidence. There are other witnesses. What right has your friend to expect you to protect him?

Three choices were offered as answers:

1 A definite right?
2 Some right?
3 No right?

Here the explicit ethical notion of a "right" and the implicit notion of the duties of friendship are in play. The results of the questionnaire were striking, with cultural patterns perspicuous. To cite only one set of comparisons, approximately 94 percent of US managers and 91 percent of Austrian managers answered "3," i.e., "no right," whereas only 53 percent of French and 59 percent of Singaporean managers did (Turner and Trompenaars, 1993).

Surveys of international managers also show striking differences between cultural attitudes towards profit. When asked whether they affirmed the view that "The only real goal of a company is making profit," 40 percent of US managers, 33 percent of British managers, and 35 percent of Austrian managers affirmed the proposition, in contrast to only 11 percent of Singaporean managers, and only 8 percent of Japanese managers selected (Turner and Trompenaars, 1993).

Or, consider studies undertaken of the striking differences about everyday business problems. One study of Hong Kong managers revealed that Hong Kong managers rank taking credit for another's work at the top of a list of unethical activities, and, in contrast to their Western counterparts, rank it more unethical than bribery or gaining of competitor information. The same study showed that among Hong Kong respondents, 82 percent indicated that additional government regulation would improve ethical conduct in business, whereas only 27 percent of American respondents did (MacDonald, 1988).

Resolving Problems in Global Business Ethics:
Is there Evidence for Universal Principles or "Hypernorms?"

Short of a relativism in which anything goes, making sense of bribery means separating better from the worse in global business practices. If blatant bribery is wrong everywhere, then some conceptual scheme appears necessary to declare it wrong. But is any moral scheme universally valid? Are there any hypernorms, i.e., universal moral principles, that can be used to separate better from worse? "Hypernorms" we define as "principles so fundamental to human existence that . . . we would expect them to be reflected in a convergence of religious, philosophical, and cultural beliefs" (Donaldson and Dunfee, 1994, p. 265). As expressed by Walzer, such universal principles would be a thin "set of standards to which all societies can be held – negative injunctions, most likely, rules against murder, deceit, torture, oppression, and tyranny"(Walzer, 1994, p. 10).

An obvious question, then, is how best to ascertain the existence and content of hypernorms. In *TIES* we describe the efforts of anthropologists, political scientists and philosophers, among others, who are searching for a convergence of beliefs and values at the global level. Scholars from many cultures and academic disciplines are asking similar questions about what humans commonly believe. A promising starting point, thus, would be an attempt to identify the extent of convergence among the convergence scholars themselves.

Frederick (1991) studied six intergovernmental compacts (including the Organization for Economic Cooperation and Development's (OECD) Guidelines for Multinational Enterprises, the Helsinki Final Act and the International Labour Organization's (ILO) Tripartite Declaration of Principles Concerning Multinational Enterprises) to identify principles common to the set. Similarly, one could look to the statements of global organizations as potential sources of hypernorms. The Caux Principles developed by the Caux Round Table, a group of senior executives from Asia, Europe and North America who meet annually in Caux, Switzerland, are a prime example; so too is the document *Towards a Global Ethic*, produced by the Council for a Parliament of the World's Religions. From these and elsewhere, some promising samples of hypernorms can be drawn. Here are three candidates:

- Firms should adopt adequate health and safety standards for employees and grant employees the right to know about job-related health hazards (Frederick, 1991, p. 166).
- You should not lie; speak and act truthfully (*Toward a global ethic* 1993: Chicago, IL: Council for a Parliament of World Religions, p. 11).
- Businesses (should be expected to) honour their obligations in a spirit of honesty and fairness (*Caux Round Table Principles for Business* 1994: Washington, DC: Caux Round Table Secretariat, s. 2, Principle One).

Finally, there are shortcuts that managers can use to identify hypernorms for the purpose of making ethical decisions. As a first step a manager could look to the type of general references cited above. The explicit purpose of the "Caux Principles," for example, is to provide guidance for practical business situations. Second, the manager could try to imagine the likely public response if the action being contemplated were to appear as the lead story on the international edition of CNN, or on the front page of the *Financial Times.* This global version of the traditional local newspaper test may serve to encourage one to think in terms of whether actions might violate widespread understandings of right and wrong. A similar approach would be for a manager to ask herself whether or not the proposed action might be seen as violating an important tenet of one of the major world religions. Finally, a manager could ask a diverse set of peers whether a proposed course of action violates a global ethical principle.

Hypernorms thus bound the moral free space of communities, and in this sense the approach of ISCT marries the familiar role of social norms within distinct communities with a conception of manifest universal principles.

Let us next examine the perplexing problem of bribery and corruption in international business through the lens of ISCT.

Key International Issue: Corruption[2]

Corruption is widely condemned, but also widely practiced (Donaldson and Dunfee, 1999, pp. 213–33). Some firms establish procedures to ensure that others do not bribe their employees, even as those same firms use bribes to obtain business. Surprisingly firms from countries where domestic corruption is minimal often play a major role as bribe-payers into corrupt environments. Many explanations arise for these seemingly inconsistent acts. Companies' participation in some forms of corruption may stem from competitive necessity and the belief that by bribing they are respecting local cultural norms. Or, they may feel that they are being extorted by locals, who are the real culprits. Finally, they may throw up their hands, proclaiming their inability to control rogue employees. Despite such excuses, consensus is growing in many professional sectors, as well as in the general public, that something must be done about bribery. Hence, a confluence of factors has produced a changing environment in which corruption is now viewed as a key global problem.

Consider three typical instances of sensitive payments. The first involves low-level bribery of public officials in some developing nations. In these nations it may be difficult for any company, foreign or national, to move goods through customs without paying low-level officials a few dollars. The payments are relatively small, uniformly assessed, and accepted as standard practice. Indeed, the salaries of such officials are sufficiently low that the officials require the additional income. One suspects the salary levels are set with the prevalence of bribery in mind.

Or consider a second kind of bribery where a company competes for a bid in a foreign country, and where, to win the competition, a payment must be made, not as it happens to a government official, but to the employee of a private company. Nonetheless, in this instance, it is clear that the employee of the private company, instead of passing on the money to the company, will pocket the money. In a modified version of this scenario, the bribe may even happen one level deeper. For example, a company competing for a bid may be introduced to a "consultant" who offers to help in client contacts (see the example that begins this chapter). There are many variations of this kind of bribery, including one where the payment is made to a senior manager for the approval of large, phantom, cost overruns incurred by the bribe-paying supplier.

Third, and most significant, is bribery involving large sums of money paid to public sector officials for the granting of public works projects, or permissions to buy land or do business within the bribe receivers' country.

It is not obvious at first blush what ISCT has to say about such scenarios, or where even to place the practices on an ISCT conceptual map. Do practices involving such payments reflect principles that count as ISCT "authentic norms?" Or, do the payments invariably turn out to be direct violations of hypernorms, and hence may be placed in the "illegitimate" arena of ISCT norms? Or, instead, does the making of bribes in places where they are common qualify as expressions of "moral free space?"

Again, ethical views about business vary around the globe. Bribery is no exception. Not only does the incidence of bribery vary, but so too its perception as unethical. In one study, for example, modern Greeks perceived the actions in some bribery scenarios as being less unethical than Americans (Tsalikis and LaTour, 1995). In another, Hong Kong managers were shown to be somewhat less critical of bribery than their American counterparts (MacDonald, 1988). And Tsalikis and Wachukwu (1991) showed that ethical reactions to bribery vary, noting in particular that Nigerians perceive some bribery scenarios as more ethical than Americans.

From the vantage point of ISCT, then, are there ethical problems with bribery? The answer is "yes," as the following sections clarify:

Violating a microsocial norm

From the standpoint of the bribe recipient, the acceptance of a bribe usually violates a microsocial norm specifying the duties of the agent, i.e., the bribe recipient, to the principal, i.e., the employing body, such as the government, private company, etc.

Perhaps the most obvious problem with bribery is that it typically involves the violation of a duty by the person accepting the bribe to the principal for whom that person serves as an agent. Note that in the cases described above, the bribe recipient performs an action at odds with the policies established by his employer.

The customs official accepts money for a service that he was supposed to provide anyway. In the case where a company competes for a bid or seeks approval of a cost overrun, the approving manager pockets the money in violation of company policy and the company is shortchanged. In other words, if the money belongs to anyone, it belongs to the customer's company, not to the individual employee. In the typical case of high-level public sector bribery, the public official violates the public trust and his obligation to society in virtue of his role.

Such policies may or may not be written down. Often they are explicit, but even where they are not, they usually reflect well-understood, implicit agreements binding the employee or official as agent to the interests of his employer or nation (the principal.) In short, even when not formally specified, such duties flow from well-understood micro-social contracts existing within the relevant economic community.

But while this rationale shows one ethical problem with bribery, it is inconclusive. To begin with, it shows the ethical problem with *accepting* a bribe, but says nothing about *offering* a bribe. Has the person making the payment also committed an ethical error? Second, while violating a duty to an employer is one reason for considering an act unethical, why could this reason not be overridden by other reasons? Perhaps other microsocial contracts in the culture firmly endorse the ethical correctness of bribe giving and bribe taking. Perhaps these microsocial contracts, along with an employee's legitimate interest in supporting his family, etc., override the prima facie obligation of the employee to follow the policies of his employee. It makes sense to explore the further implications of ISCT.

Violating an authentic norm

Bribery is typically not an authentic norm. The mythology is that bribery is accepted where it flourishes. This image is badly distorted. Despite the data mentioned earlier that shows variance in how unethical various people regard bribery, that is to say, how it compares with *other* unethical activity, there is a surprising amount of agreement that bribery *is* unethical.

All countries have laws against the practice. This is a striking fact often overlooked by individuals that have something to gain by the practice. "There is not a country in the world," writes Fritz Heimann, "where bribery is either legally or morally acceptable." That bribes have to be paid secretly everywhere, and that officials have to resign in disgrace if the bribe is disclosed, makes it clear that bribery violates the moral standards of the South and the East, just as it does in the West" (Heimann, 1994).

Some countries, even ones where the practice has flourished, not only outlaw it, but prescribe draconian penalties. "In Malaysia, which is significantly influenced by the Moslem prescriptions against bribery, execution of executives for the offense of bribery is legal" (Carroll and Gannon, 1997). In China in 1994, the President of the Great Wall Machinery and Electronics High-Technology Industrial

Group Corp., Mr. Shen Haifu, was executed by a bullet to the back of his neck for bribery and embezzlement offenses. In 2000, several prominent Chinese officials were sentenced to death for bribery including the former vice-chair of the national legislature. Chinese academics and managers often speak of the great social cost incurred due to the current level of bribery. Under ISCT, this has the implication that even among a community of bribe payers, bribery cannot necessarily be established as an authentic norm. And, even when a norm can be found to exist among a set of bribe-soliciting public officials and bribe-paying global managers, it is never sufficient to consider just those communities. Instead, the norms of all communities affected by the bribes must be considered. The citizens who get overpriced, poor quality public services as a result of the bribes can be expected to hold an anti-bribery norm. Similarly, the owners of the organization victimized by the betrayal of its managers would oppose the practice or bribery. Under the priority rules set forth in ISCT, these anti-bribery community norms would be expected to have priority and to override the norms of the pro-bribery communities.

In short, in many if not most instances, the necessary condition imposed by ISCT that the norm be authentic, i.e., that it is both acted on *and* believed to be ethically correct by a substantial majority of the members of a community, simply appears false. Further, whenever a bribery norm does satisfy the requirements for recognition as an authentic norm, it will be subject to being overridden by the anti-bribery norms of affected communities. To the extent that these expectations are true, most instances of bribery would fail the ISCT moral free space test.

Hypernorm violation

Even this last consideration, however, leaves a nagging doubt behind. In particular, is bribery only wrong because most people dislike it? Is there nothing more fundamentally *wrong* with bribery? Suppose, hypothetically, that the world came to change its mind over the next thirty years about bribery. Suppose that in some future state, a majority of people finds bribery to be morally acceptable? If so, would bribery be ethically correct? In such a world would reformers who spoke out against bribery be speaking illogical nonsense?

The answer to this question turns on the further question of whether a hypernorm disallowing bribery exists. For if such a hypernorm existed, then no legitimate microsocial norm could support bribery, and, in turn, it would deserve moral condemnation even in a world whose majority opinion endorsed it.

One can argue that high-level public sector bribery, in and of itself, violates a hypernorm (Donaldson and Dunfee, 1999). Philip Nichols (1997) cites specific references from each of the world's major religions condemning bribery. "Corruption is condemned and proscribed," he writes, "by each of the major religious and moral schools of thought. Buddhism, Christianity, Confucianism, Hinduism, Islam, Judaism, Sikhism, and Taoism each proscribe corruption. Adam

Smith and David Ricardo condemned corruption, as did Karl Marx and Mao Tse Tung" (Nichols, 1997, pp. 321–2). Bribes have resulted in collapsing bridges and buildings, in the deaths of children from tainted drugs, and in the diversion of food intended for starving peoples. Many bribes have a direct negative effect on human well-being. In fact, a multicultural set of authors exploring the implications of ISCT explicitly identified a hypernorm condemning bribery (Fritzsche et al., 1995). However, the condemnation of coarse public sector bribery still leaves unresolved the status of many other forms of bribery, including private sector bribery and the many other permutations of public sector bribery. To deal with those, we now consider whether other hypernorms can be identified that condemn bribery.

At least two hypernorms may be invoked in seeking a more fundamental condemnation of bribery. The first is obvious. To the extent that one places a positive, transnational value, on a *right to political participation*, large bribes of publicly elected officials damage that value. For example, when Prime Minister Tanaka of Japan in the 1970s bought planes from the American aircraft manufacturer Lockheed, after accepting tens of millions of dollars in bribes, people questioned whether he was discharging his duties as a public official correctly. In addition to the fact that his actions violated the law, the Japanese citizenry was justified in wondering whether their interests, or Tanaka's personal political interest, drove the decision. Implicit in much of the political philosophy written in the Western world in the last three hundred years, in the writings of Rousseau, Mill, Locke, Jefferson, Kant, and Rawls, is the notion that some transcultural norm supports a public claim for the citizenry of a nation state to participate in some way in the direction of political affairs. Many – see, for example, Shue (1980), Donaldson (1989) and the *Universal Declaration of Human Rights* – have discussed and articulated the implications of this right in current contexts. If such a right exists, then it entails obligations on the part of politicians and prospective bribe givers to not violate it. In turn, large-scale bribery of highly elected public officials – the sort that the Lockheed Corporation engaged in the 1970s – would be enjoined through the application of a hypernorm. It would, hence, be wrong regardless of whether a majority of the members of an economic community, or even the majority of the world's citizens, endorsed it.

Notice, however, that the political participation hypernorm misses one kind of case. Suppose it is true that large-scale pay-offs to public officials in democratic or quasi-democratic countries are proscribed by considerations of people's right to political participation. In such countries, bribery may defeat meaningful political rights. But many countries in which bribery is prevalent are not democratic. Bribery in countries such as Zaire, Nigeria and China may nonetheless not have a direct effect on political participation by ordinary citizens that is directly repressed by authoritarian governments.

Other troubling questions may be raised. How about much smaller pay-offs to public officials? And how about bribes *not* to public officials, but to employees of corporations? It seems difficult to argue that small, uniformly structured bribes to customs officials, or bribes to purchasing agents of companies in host countries, seriously undermine the people's right to political participation. These questions prompt the search for yet another hypernorm relevant to the issue of bribery.

A second hypernorm does appear relevant to the present context. It is what we have called the economic hypernorm of "necessary social efficiency." That hypernorm requires that economic agents utilize resources efficiently concerning goods in which their society has a stake (Donaldson and Dunfee, 1999, pp. 139–73). The hypernorm arises because all societies have an interest in husbanding public resources, developing strategies to promote aggregate economic welfare and, in turn, of developing efficiency parameters to do so. These we have called in *TIES* "N-Strategy Efficiency Parameters." Like mathematical parameters, they help determine the specific form of the N-Strategy function but not its general nature. Efficiency parameters resemble N-Strategies in sometimes being formal, and at other times informal.

Formal and informal proscriptions on bribery may be viewed as informal efficiency parameters. Indeed, nations and NGOs who oppose bribery most commonly cast their opposition in terms of the damage that bribery does to the economic efficiency of the nation state.

This raises an obvious question: *Is* bribery inefficient? Certainly *if* it is inefficient, the economic consequences must be significant in light of the sheer amount of money involved. While it is impossible to determine the current, precise level of corrupt bribery, one estimate by the World Bank placed the total amount of bribery involved in international trade at $80 billion per year (Walsh, 1998). What is more, a recent World Bank survey of 3600 firms in 69 countries found that 40 percent of businesses pay bribes (Omestad et al., 1997). In industrial countries 15 percent of businesses were found to pay bribes, but in the former Soviet Union this figure jumps to over 60 percent (Omestad et al., 1997).

Corruption *is* inefficient for identifiable reasons. First, it limits the ability of governments to perform vital functions and may even threaten overall governmental effectiveness. The *Financial Times* reported that "deep corruption [in China] is corroding the exercise of state power" (Kynge, 1997). Falsified accounts to cover up corruption have had the effect of rendering China's official statistics "virtually meaningless"(ibid). In Ecuador, it is estimated the government could pay off its foreign debt in five years if corruption was brought under control. It is estimated that corruption costs the country $2 billion every year (Transparency International). And in Argentina, corruption in the customs department defrauded the government out of $3 billion in revenues: Officials estimated that 30 percent of all imports were being under-billed and approximately $2.5 billion of goods were brought into the country under the guise of being labeled "in transit" to another country, thus illegally avoiding import taxes altogether (Argentines Give Import to Fraud Crackdown, *Financial Time* London, 3 December 1997, p. 5.). Corruption also influences government spending, moving it out of vital functions such as education and public health, and into projects where public officials can more easily extract bribes (Mauro, 1998).

The personal financial gains secured by corrupt public officials explain why these problems persist. In Mexico, suspicions surround the ability of Raul Salinas, the brother of former President Carlos Salinas, to amass a fortune of over $120 million while a public official (Walsh, 1998). Two former presidents of South Korea were convicted of developing a fund of over $900 million while they were in office in the 1980s and 1990s (Guggenheim, 1996). At the local level, in Grenoble, France, the city mayor was convicted for personally receiving $1.8 million in 1989 while selling the city water system.

Corruption imposes tremendous costs on business. While American companies complain of lost contracts due to the FCPA, other countries complain of the bribes their firms must pay to obtain those contracts. For example, German companies are estimated to pay an aggregate of over $3 billion in bribes to obtain business contracts abroad (Guggenheim, 1996). In certain countries, the costs of doing business due to bribes significantly impair the ability to make a profit. In Indonesia, it is estimated that 20 percent of business costs are bribes to bureaucrats (Honest trade: 'A global war against bribery', *Economist*, 16 January 1999, p. 22.) In Albania, approximately one-third of potential profits are lost to bribe payments (ibid).

As the economist Kenneth Arrow noted years ago, "a great deal of economic life depends for its viability on a certain limited degree of ethical commitment" (Arrow, 1973, p. 313). To the extent that market participants bribe, they interfere with the market mechanism's rational allocation of resources, and their actions impose significant social costs. When people buy or sell on the basis of price and quality, with reasonable knowledge about all relevant factors, the market allocates resources efficiently. The best products relative to price, and, in turn, the best production mechanisms, are encouraged to develop. But when agents accept defective goods or pay more than they have to in order to divert money into personal pockets, the entire market mechanism is distorted. By misallocating resources, bribery damages economic efficiency (Sen, 1997). As economists Bliss and Di Tella (1997) note, "Corrupt agents exact money from firms." Corruption affects, they observe, the number of firms in a free entry equilibrium, and in turn increases costs relative to profits. In contrast, "the degree of deep competition in the economy increases with lower overhead costs relative to profits; and with a tendency toward similar cost structures." Corruption can even be shown to exact a cost on additional social efforts to improve economic welfare, including industrial policy initiatives (Ades and Di Tella, 1997), and on predictability in economic arrangements.

Bribery, then, is objectionable on both moral and economic grounds. Nonetheless, it is worth noting that practical solutions to problems of bribery are notoriously difficult to implement, and usually involve a shift of focus to deeper levels of society. At the precise level at which most managers confront bribery, bribery eludes a fully satisfactory solution. This is because from the standpoint of an individual manager working in some global regions, refusing to bribe can mean losing business. Sales and profits are typically lost to the more unscrupulous companies, and the unethical company benefits at the expense of the more ethical company. Indeed, both the ethical *company* and the ethical *individual* are victims. (Of course, companies mitigate the damage to employees caught in this bribery trap when they communicate clear policies, and when they support employees who follow those policies.) A fully satisfactory answer, hence, lies not at the level where individuals face bribery, but at deeper levels, i.e., at the level of the firm, the competitive environment, and ultimately, the host country's background institutions. Many theorists argue that such deeper, institutional reform entails a narrowing of the dramatic gap that now exists between civil servant and private sector pay, a new mindset or "social contract" among government officials and corporate managers, and a toughening of the sanctions designed to ensure legal compliance in host countries. In short, the practical solution to bribery demands changes in social and economic structures so as to facilitate a more level playing field that aligns incentives *away from* rather than *toward* long-standing practices of bribery.

Conclusion

In this chapter, we have identified the three tools that ISCT provides for analyzing the complex phenomenon of bribery. First, ISCT's concept of a microsocial contract has application directly to the act of accepting a bribe. When applied, it becomes obvious that most acts of bribery violate one of the legitimate microsocial norms that specify the duties of the agent, i.e., duties of the bribe recipient to the principal, that is, to the employing body such as the government or a private company. Second, ISCT's distinction between authentic v. inauthentic norms in microsocial contracts reveals that most microsocial norms allowing bribery are *not* authentic norms. Finally, ISCT's concept of a "hypernorm" shows that bribery usually violates at least one of two distinct hypernorms, namely, the universal right to political participation, and the economic hypernorm of "necessary social efficiency."

Notes

1 Much of this section is derived from Thomas Donaldson and Thomas W. Dunfee, 2001, Précis for: Ties that bind. *Business and Society Review*, 105 (4), 436–43.
2 Much of this section is derived from David Hess and Thomas Dunfee, 2001, Fighting corruption: A principled approach: The C2 principles (combating corruption). *Cornell International Law Journal*, 33 (3), 593–626.

References

Ades, A. and Di Tella, R. 1997: *National champions and corruption: some unpleasant interventionist arithmetic.* Paper presented at the University of Pennsylvania, Philadelphia.

Arrow, K. J. 1973: Social responsibility and economic efficiency. *Public Policy,* 3 (21), 300–17.

Bliss, C. and Di Tella, R. 1997: *Does competition kill corruption?* Paper presented at the University of Pennsylvania, Philadelphia.

Carroll, S. J. and Gannon, M. J. 1997: *Ethical Dimensions of International Management.* Thousand Oaks, CA: Sage.

Donaldson, T. 1989: *The Ethics of International Business.* New York: Oxford University Press.

Donaldson, T. and Dunfee, T. 1994: Towards a unified conception of business ethics: Integrative social contracts theory. *Academy of Management Review,* 19 (2), 252–84.

Donaldson, T. and Dunfee, T. 1999: *Ties that Bind: A Social Contract Approach to Business Ethics.* Harvard University Business School Press.

Frederick, W. C. 1991: The moral authority of transnational corporate codes. *Journal of Business Ethics,* 10 (3), 165–77.

Fritzsche, D. J., Hou, P. Y., Sugai, S. and Dun-Hou, S. 1995: Exploring the ethical behavior of managers: A comparative study of four countries. *Asia Pacific Journal of Management,* 12 (2), 37–61.

Guggenheim, K. 1996: Corruption, not revolutions or coups, topples governments these days, *L.A. Times,* October 6, sec. A, p. 4.

Heimann, F. F. 1994: Should foreign bribery be a crime? *Transparency International,* 2.

Hofstede, G. 1980: *Culture's Consequences.* Beverly Hills, CA: Sage.

Kluckhorn, C. 1955: Ethical relativity: Sic et non. *Journal of Philosophy,* 52, 663–77.

Kynge, J. 1997: "China uncovers falsified accounts in state groups," *Financial Times* (London), Wednesday, December 24, p. 7.

MacDonald, G. M. 1988: Ethical perceptions of Hong Kong/Chinese business managers. *Journal of Business Ethics,* 7, 835–45.

Mauro, P. 1998: Corruption: Causes, consequences, and agenda for further research. *Finance & Development,* 35 (1), 11–14.

Nichols, P. M. 1997: Outlawing transnational bribery through the World Trade Organization. *Law and Policy in International Business.* 28 (2), 305–86.

Omestad, T., Hurtey, M., Lovgren, S., Palmer, C. C. B. and Cunningham, V. 1997: Bye-bye to bribes: The industrial world takes aim at official corruption. *US News & World Report,* December 22, 22.

Sen, A. 1997: Economics, business principles, and moral sentiments. *Business Ethics Quarterly,* 7 (3), 5–15.

Shue, H. 1980: *Basic Rights: Subsistence, Affluence, and U.S. Foreign Policy.* Princeton, NJ: Princeton University Press.

Tsalikis, J. and LaTour, M. S. 1995: Bribery and extortion in international business: Ethical perceptions of Greeks compared to Americans. *Journal of Business Ethics,* 4, 249–65.

Tsalikis, J. and Wachukwu, O. 1991: A comparison of Nigerian to American views of bribery and extortion in international commerce. *Journal of Business Ethics,* 10 (2), 85–98.

Turner, C. H. and Trompenaars, A. 1993: *The Seven Cultures of Capitalism.* New York: Doubleday.

Universal Declaration of Human Rights 1948: Reprinted in T. Donaldson and P. Werhane (eds) (1979). *Ethical Issues in Business*: 252–5. Englewood Cliffs, NJ: Prentice Hall.

Walsh, J. 1998: A world war on bribery. TIME, June 22, 16.

Walzer, M. 1994: *Thick and Thin: Moral Argument at Home and Abroad.* Notre Dame, IN: University of Notre Dame Press.

Further Reading

Simons, Marlise, 1996: U.S. enlists rich nations in move to end business bribes, *N.Y. Times*, 12 April, see. A, p. 10.

Transparency International. *Corruption Reports.* <http://www.transparency.de>

Chapter 4

The Regulatory Context for Environmental and Workplace Health Protections: Recent Developments

Carl Cranor

"[I]t is the mark of an educated man to look for precision in each class of thing just so far as the nature of the subject admits. . . ."

Aristotle, *Nichomachean Ethics* 1094^{b}24–8

The legal environment for protecting employees and the general public from exposures to toxic substances has undergone substantial changes since 1980. The regulatory environment appears to be much more hospitable to businesses than it was before this date. In the present circumstances, firms can defend their cases before regulatory agencies or tort law courts to a large extent on the claim that there is not definitive evidence that possible toxicants have been shown to cause harm. This is the result of the paucity of scientific evidence that can be provided, the difficulty establishing such claims, the post-market burdens and standards of proof that must be met in the regulatory law and in torts, and the legal changes that have occurred during the last twenty years. As a consequence, employees in industries using toxic substances and the general public appear to be less well protected by the law than they once were and than they could be.

This situation is not beyond redress, however. Courts have constrained agencies and district court judges both, demanding much greater scientific evidence in support of legal change. They could issue decisions that would recognize, in the spirit of Aristotle, that courts and agencies should only demand the degree of evidence and precision of support that is appropriate for the institution in question. Appellate courts could signal lower courts and agencies that they need not demand the most certain and best supported scientific evidence, if that would distort the aims of the legal institution in question. Were they to do this, courts by their decisions would provide greater workplace and public health protections consistent with reliable scientific judgments on which businesses could rely. Whether they will remains to be seen.

In arguing for the above claims, I first review some of the legal institutions for regulating toxic substances, focusing on the tort law and then the administrative law. After introducing a framework for assessing these different areas of the law, I then consider how recent court decisions concerning the use of scientific evidence have modified these legal contexts.

Legal Framework for Regulating Toxic Substances

The focus of this discussion is limited to the institutional protections for human health that might arise from exposure to toxic substances in the general environment – environmental health protections – and in the workplace – workplace health protections. Although citizens also seek protections from the degradation of the air, water, land, and groundwater, as well as protections for wilderness areas and endangered species, I restrict this discussion to keep it manageable. As a further constraint, I focus on health harms or risks to human health arising from exposures to toxic substances, with carcinogens providing the main, but not the only example. This is hardly the whole of environmental health protections, but it provides enough of the main features of the regulatory environment in which businesses must work and some of the social and philosophical issues that arise therein to outline some of the main issues.

The tort law

The tort law aims to secure the rightful borders of our possessions and ourselves by *making us whole* should we suffer damage from others by their "crossing the borders" of our rights or our possessions. (Nozick, 1974) Typically, to bring a legal action and seek compensation for the injuries suffered, one must have suffered a legally compensable injury as a result of the violation of the law by another. Thus, one must show that another's conduct violated the law and that the violation caused the injuries in question. The aim is to restore the victim to the status quo ante before the injury occurred, to make the victim whole again. Although a plaintiff (the complaining party) typically must have been injured before having a right to legal redress, like the criminal law there are also less direct deterrence effects, such as discouraging similar conduct by others, as well as modifying the particular defendant's behavior.

Both environmental and workplace health protections began mainly in the tort, or personal injury, law. The tort law of the late nineteenth and early twentieth century failed to provide much protection from workplace harms, however, because employers could defend themselves fairly easily against such claims. Progressive legislation of the 1920s and 1930s sought to replace the poorly functioning tort law with workers' compensation laws, but these, in turn, have not lived up to the promise they might have had at the outset. (McGarity and Shapiro, 1993). By the late 1960s and early 1970s, there was considerable political motivation for providing better workplace protections by means of different legal institutions.

Just as early workplace health protections began with the tort law, so too did environmental health protections. While much current environmental legislation owes some of its structure and substance to tort law doctrines, here too, the tort law suffers from a number of shortcomings that undermine some of its effectiveness for "regulating" toxic substances that threaten human health (discussed below) (Rodgers, 1977).

Suffice it to say at this point that the spate of federal and state environmental laws passed in the early 1970s addressing both workplace and general environmental protection were responses to the inadequacy of existing legal institutions at the time. Since the main institutions were the tort law, workers' compensation law and a few nascent regulatory laws, it was the failure of these – and perhaps largely the failure of torts – that led to a new era in environmental protection.

Administrative law

Responding to the shortcomings of existing institutions, Congress (and state legislatures) ushered in a new era in the early 1970s by passing a wide range of administrative (or regulatory) laws. These aimed at remedying shortcomings of existing institutions and dealing better and more comprehensively with environmental problems.

Administrative or regulatory laws are creations of a legislature, either state or federal. Legislatures pass such laws to cope with problems that are too particular and require too much detailed attention for a legislature itself to address. For example, a legislature might decide in broad outline that workplaces should not pose greater risks to health than those that exist for the wider non-working populations or that the populace should not be exposed to toxic substances through consumer products or environmental pollutants. However, a legislature is not well prepared to formulate and implement detailed exposure guidelines and regulations to address particular toxic substances. Thus, administrative agencies serve to carry out the general law and policies of a legislature under the guidance of the executive branch of government or under the guidance of an agency independent of the executive (so called "independent" agencies).

Regulatory laws are explicitly preventive. They seek to protect our rights by preventing harms from materializing in the first place (typically to large numbers of people) by specifying in advance how certain activities must be done. They aim to provide prospective guidance compared with retrospective punishments or compensation for injuries victims suffer that are typical of the criminal or tort law, respectively.

Congress first passes enabling legislation, authorizing the creation of an administrative agency or extending the authority of an existing agency to address the social problems of concern. In the early 1970s, the US Congress passed a number of laws aimed at protecting the people's health, either from environmental or workplace toxicants. These laws included, *inter alia*, Occupational Safety and Health Act [OSHA] (1970), the Clean Air Act (1970), the Clean Water Act (1972), the Consumer Product Safety Act (1972), the Safe Drinking Water Act (1976) and the Toxic Substances Control Act (1976), as well as significant amendments to the Federal Insecticide, Fungicide and Rodenticide Act (1972) and the Food, Drug, and Cosmetic Act (1968).

Some laws ("premarket" laws) aim to intercept toxic substances before they enter commerce and endanger persons (TSCA, FIFRA, and the FDCA). The vast majority authorizes agencies to detect existing risks to the public from substances in the market or to employees in the workplace and to remove or reduce the risks before they materialize into harm ("postmarket laws") (US Congress OTA, 1987).

In creating administrative laws, Congress typically authorizes an agency to address a group of problems and conduct appropriate scientific inquiries to identify and remedy them, e.g., whether the problem is exposure to vinyl chloride, asbestos, or cotton dust in the workplace or exposure to contaminants in plastic bottles, in drinking water, or in rivers and streams. Once a problem and appropriate methods for addressing it have been identified, the agency has the authority to *issue a proposed regulation* addressing it, e.g., reducing concentrations of asbestos or benzene in the workplace. Legislation normally provides for a comment period during which an agency is obliged to hear and take comments from interested parties.

Following this, it typically then issues a *final regulation* that has the force of law and can be enforced by the agency unless there is a legal challenge. Issuing a regulation by an agency is an act of creating law quite specific to the problem at issue. If the regulation is issued in accordance with procedures specified in the legislation (or in procedural statutes) and the regulation is not challenged by an affected party in an appellate court, it has the force of law. If the law is appealed either on grounds that it was created by means of invalid procedures or it is substantively flawed, then typically the legal appeals would have to be exhausted before it has the force of law. If the regulation, or a portion of it, is invalidated, then the invalid sections lose their legal force. The agency would then have to revisit the problem and reissue a regulation.

The substantive legal provisions specifying the extent of risk permitted under the law implicitly establish a Congressionally enacted philosophy about the distribution of benefits and burdens from toxic substances and the costs of controlling them under the statute. In short, who bears the risks of uncertainty and what considerations, if any, outweigh potential risks from toxic substances are at least implicitly specified by the statute. Some have "no risk" provisions, e.g., portions of the Food Drug and Cosmetic Act governed by the Delaney Clause. According to that, if a food additive causes cancer in humans or in appropriate animal tests, it is deemed "unsafe" and is not allowed as a food additive. Other statutes express different views. The Clean Air Act authorizes the EPA to regulate risks from toxic air contaminants by issuing regulations that provide for an "ample margin of safety." This may permit the EPA to issue "health-related standards" based upon ambiguous or incomplete data. Other statutes authorize risk-risk balancing – weighing the risk to human health from exposure to a regulated substance against the risk to human health from not having the substance in commerce – e.g. provisions for food additives under the Food, Drug and Cosmetic Act prior to 1958. Still others authorize risk-benefit balancing in the issuance of regulations, e.g., some provisions of the Toxic Substances Control Act. Finally, some statutes authorize agencies to use the "best practicable" or the "best available" technology to reduce exposures to potentially toxic substances, rather than aiming to clean up pollutants in the ambient air or water to a certain concentration level. In recent years some statutes have combined best available technology provisions with provisions aimed at cleaning up the ambient environment to some appropriate "safe" or "low risk" level (recent amendments to the Clean Air Act) (US Congress, OTA, 1987).

These distributive views may be modified somewhat as the laws are implemented – as regulations are written, carried out, enforced, and adjudicated – although agencies cannot stray too far from the language of the statutes. As I discuss below, this distribution can also be affected by procedural requirements that are imposed on the amount of scientific evidence needed before regulation can occur under the statutes.

The relationship between the tort and administrative law

Even though regulatory laws were enacted aiming to remedy shortcomings in the tort (and other) laws at the time, both regulatory and tort law have a role in "regulating and controlling" toxic substances. What the proper relationship between torts and the regulatory law should be is a complex one, raising political and moral philosophic issues, as well as issues of comparative institutional strengths and weaknesses. Of course, the actual relationship between the two areas of law is currently negotiated or settled by how the institutions in fact interact. These are products of court decisions, as well as political decisions that emanate from legislatures and regulatory agencies. And, there will be some flux in this as the law changes. Yet there are substantial philosophic issues in these debates, some of which I consider.

Philosophic issues One major philosophic debate concerns the appropriateness and extent of governmental intervention in the lives of citizens and in the business marketplace. The tort law (along with the criminal law) tends to be favored over the use of regulatory law to protect people from toxic substances by those who emphasize the importance of liberty and freedom from governmental interference. This includes philosophic libertarians and perhaps some philosophic liberals.

Philosophic libertarians elevate "the claim of individual freedom of action, and [ask] why state power should be permitted even the interference represented by progressive taxation and public provision of health care, education and a minimum standard of living" (Nagel, 1975). Furthermore, libertarians tend to have a negative view of governmental institutions.

Libertarians tend to argue for use of the tort law rather than regulatory law. Regulatory law places constraints on people's lives and how they run their businesses in order to prevent harms and risks of harm to employees' or the general public's health, whereas the tort law permits interference with persons only if they actually invade the interests of and harm others.

The tort law not only would be endorsed by libertarians, but it also fits well with a kind of atomistic view of society and

> the "invisible hand conception of the law." This metaphor conveys the idea that individuals in society can take care of themselves acting in accordance with their own rights and conceptions of what they need; with protections for their rights they can fulfill these needs through the goods and services provided by the economic market. And they can take care of themselves through the tort law when they are injured by seeking [redress] from the wrongdoer. . . . [T]here is no need to address and no legal problem for the law to redress, unless and until someone has brought a complaint [of wrongful injury] before a court (Cranor, 1993).

Libertarians represent one extreme on a spectrum from no or little government regulation of private activity aimed at preventing harm to others up to greater governmental regulation. They tend to adopt an almost non-rebuttable presumption against governmental intervention except to compensate or punish others for harm inflicted. Libertarianism, however, is only as plausible as the normative foundations of it, which others have critiqued, but I cannot pursue (Nagel, 1975, p. 137).

While libertarians emphasize the freedom from interference from others (including the government) as well as freedom to innovate and to develop new ideas, opponents of this extreme view call attention to the importance of other morally salient considerations that bear on the choice of institutions.

Philosophic liberals advocate a rebuttable presumption for using the least governmentally intrusive means to protect citizens from harm (Schuck, 2000, p. 51). Moreover, since liberal theorists

> put high value on other goals, such as justice, or happiness, or culture, or security, or varying degrees of equality, they were prepared to curtail freedom in the interests of other values and, indeed, of freedom itself. For, without this, it was impossible to create the kind of association that they thought desirable. Consequently it is assumed . . . that the area of men's free action must be limited by law . . . [However], there

ought to exist a certain minimum area of personal freedom which must on no account be violated; for if it is overstepped, the individual will find himself in an area too narrow for even that minimum development of his natural faculties which alone makes it possible to pursue, and even to conceive, the various ends which men hold good or right or sacred. It follows that a frontier must be drawn between the area of private life and that of public authority. Where it is to be drawn is a matter of argument, indeed of haggling (Berlin, 1997 [1969, p. 118]).

This is, of course, a statement of classical liberalism in the tradition of J. S. Mill, but it does not take one very far. The issue that divides one liberal from another is the "haggling" over the proper scope of freedom, the tradeoffs of freedom versus other normative goals, and the appropriate role of public authority. In discussions concerning the proper role of the tort compared with regulatory law, this is often expressed in terms of a comparative institutional analysis with a normative basis provided by considerations of liberty, pursuit of happiness (expressed in some form of utilitarianism), protection from harm, some form of equality, or other normative considerations. Consider just one philosophic position that provides a rationale for more stringent health protections than would be provided by the tort law. This is the social contract view that owes its contemporary articulation to John Rawls. According to this political philosophy the principles of justice for guiding the fundamental institutions of a society are those that appropriately informed persons would agree to under fair conditions. Rawls and others have argued that in such conditions one of the principles to which such decision-makers would agree is a principle of *fair equality of opportunity*. Individuals have fair equality of opportunity if "those who are at the same level of talent and ability, and have the same willingness to use them . . . have the same prospects of success regardless of their initial place in the social system. . . ." (Rawls, 1971, p. 75). Since serious diseases and death undermine one's opportunities, this principle would authorize protections for people's health by means of several different institutions as a means to securing their equal opportunity to pursue the good things of life.

A background presupposition is that health protections have "normal functioning as a human being" as its goal. Thus, health protections, much like education, have great strategic importance in securing social opportunities. If persons contract diseases that lead to death, long-term illnesses, or especially debilitating conditions, such as cancer, reproductive diseases, birth defects, adverse neurological conditions, this will impair or undermine altogether their equality of opportunity in the community. Thus, it is not only inadequate to compensate people after the fact of disease to restore them to their previous normal functioning; on this account it is *unjust* not to take steps to prevent them from contracting easily preventable diseases in the first place. It is part of providing them fair opportunities equal to others in the community (Daniels, 1985).

To secure persons fair equality of opportunity, one needs institutions that provide, *inter alia*, for public health, environmental cleanliness, preventive medical services, occupational health and safety, and food and drug protections (Daniels, 1985; Cranor, 1993, p. 170). Such institutions would seek to prevent the risks of disease from environmental and workplace exposures to toxic substances from materializing into harm. It is the resulting serious *harm* and debilitating or life-threatening diseases that undermine a person's fair opportunity in a community (although it is conceivable that concern about risks also poses problems). However, to prevent the harm from materializing, a community must take steps to reduce the risks of such harms to some low and appropriately fair level. And, this must be done in a more comprehensive and consistent way than the adventitious deterrence the tort law provides. That is, if one knows that exposure to asbestos or benzene will likely cause debilitating or life threatening diseases for persons, or that exposure to lead will lower the IQ in and lessen the brain function of children, these are cases for preventive intervention.

Articulating the fair equality of opportunity principle helps to place in relief fundamentally different rationales for the tort and the regulatory law. The tort law is largely concerned with correcting wrongs done to others – making them whole again – justified mainly by a principle of corrective justice. The rationale for utilizing administrative laws is to prevent in a more comprehensive way the risks of disease from toxic substances from materializing into harms that undermine one's fair chances at the good things of life. Protecting health goes a long way toward preventing and correcting some of the inequities that may result from the bad luck of disease that may be induced by alterable social institutions or practices. This is especially true for *humanly caused* and preventable diseases that might result from firms or individuals not taking sufficient care in how they handle and control toxic substances or in not doing sufficient research into the harmful properties of substances.

The above sketch of some moral and political rationales of different institutions are only part of a more extensive analysis of approaches to preventing workplace and environmental health harms from toxic substances. They can be augmented and deepened by comparing different institutional approaches to the problems.

Comparative institutional analysis On its face the tort law appears to be a woefully inadequate institution for addressing and "regulating" toxic substances, because ordinarily it requires that someone actually be harmed by exposure to a toxicant before there are legal grounds for legal intervention. Because it is retrospective, there are limited and uncertain prospective protections provided by the deterrent threat of a tort suit or by an actual finding of accountability.

Nonetheless, there is some deterrent effect from torts, but how much is not entirely clear. A Rand Corporation study indicates that in product liability cases the tort law is far more protective than other areas of the law, including regulatory law (Eads and Reuter, 1983). For one thing, the small, poorly funded, Consumer Product Safety Commission, designed to provide some consumer protection, is relatively ineffective compared with larger environmental protection agencies, e.g., EPA, FDA, and OSHA. For another, there are special features of the consumer market that may enhance the effect of torts. Deterrence is substantially aided by the power of publicity and public opinion when a consumer product is identified as one likely to cause harms to others. For areas of our lives more hidden from public view, the tort law may not have such significant effects.

Deterrence by the tort law results from the uncertainty posed by the possibility of sanctions in any given case. And the extent of deterrence may vary across the variety of state and federal jurisdictions, so there may not be uniform treatment from jurisdiction to jurisdiction. This complicates business planning and undermines uniform protections for citizens in different jurisdictions. Moreover, there are, in general, several reasons specific to torts for thinking that this institution will not function very well to protect the public from exposures to toxic substances.

Establishing a factual basis for a typical tort action is more difficult than establishing a factual basis for a regulatory action, which further complicates the deterrent effect. Most tort actions are not based upon the risk of injury, but upon concrete injuries or invasions of interests defendants caused particular plaintiffs. Moreover, a generalized showing that the substance in question causes the kind of harm from which the plaintiff suffered is not sufficient. The plaintiff must show that a particular defendant's action was the proximate cause of the plaintiff's particular harm. Thus, when tort actions involve toxic substances, evidence of injuries, which requires the use of scientific evidence, makes proof of injury more difficult. (This is developed further in the section on science and the law.)

In addition, even if plaintiffs are successful in winning a suit and authorized to collect compensation for injuries suffered, the defendants may be judgment proof – unable to pay the compensation awarded. Thus, winning a suit does not ensure that the victim is made whole following an injury. It would be better for the community for firms to internalize the costs of prevention imposed by a regulatory agency than to risk the chance that firms would be judgment proof and victims would go uncompensated.

Moreover, the tort law is atomistic; it addresses the harm that occurred and aims to restore the victims to the status quo ante. Ordinarily, it does not address in a comprehensive way the circumstances that led to the harm. Rectification of those circumstances is left to the wisdom and self-interest of defendants. Further, it does not necessarily address all of those who might be in harms' way from the similar activities of other individuals, firms or whole industries.

Many toxic substances result in diseases that have substantial latency periods before they materialize into harm – a significant time-delay between exposure to a substance and manifestation of disease in a way that can be clinically detected. This may be because the diseases progress via a biological mechanism that produces a disease slowly, such as cancer, or because their effects are multigenerational. Long latency periods complicate identification of cause and effect relationships.

Additionally, risks from toxic substances tend to have low probabilities of materializing into harm, but when they do, many will have catastrophic consequences for individual victims, such as cancer or reproductive effects, or for the larger society (in the case of a nuclear meltdown or radioactive releases).

Thus, toxic substances tend to present low probability, high consequence risks that materialize into harm for some.

Some issues concerning torts can be deepened by utilizing a substantial review of the tort and administrative law by two legal scholars, Clayton Gillette and James Krier in 1990. They analyzed the functional ability of torts and regulatory law to reduce what they called "public risks" to an optimal level. Public risks are "manmade 'threats to human health or safety that are centrally or mass-produced, broadly distributed, and largely outside the individual risk bearer's direct understanding and control'" (Gillette and Krier, 1990, p. 1028). Such risks tend to result in harms that materialize and are diffusely "spread over many victims, so the costs to any one victim might be small even though the aggregate cost to the total victim population is very large." Examples include harm from chemical additives, mass-produced vaccines, nuclear power plants, leakage and contamination in the disposal of nuclear wastes, the production of synthetic chemicals, which may be toxic, carcinogenic, mutagenic, or teratogenic (Gillette and Krier, 1990, p. 1029). (Of course, some harms can also be substantial to individual victims.)

There are "*structural* features" of public risks that pose access barriers to plaintiffs successfully bringing a suit in the first place. Such risks reduce the chances that injured parties will identify the source of harm and decrease the odds that victims will identify a commonalty of interests between themselves and others injured by a particular exposure. Moreover, this can even be a problem for occupationally caused harms where people work at the same facility.

As a result, some individual victims may be tempted to free ride on the collective good of a lawsuit brought by others. That is,

> [t]he characteristic diffuseness of public risks. . . . can mean small costs per victim notwithstanding large losses in the aggregate. From the individual litigant's perspective, a relatively small injury usually will not warrant the substantial costs associated with proving a case and recovering a judgment. The situation is aggravated by process concerns, legal doctrines that complicate the plaintiff's job. . . . for example, the requirement of identifying a particular defendant who more probably than not caused the plaintiff's injury (Gillette and Krier, 1990, p. 1047).

Thus, "public risk [tort] litigation is structurally biased against victim *access*. Victims who might wish to seek redress in the courts confront significant obstacles that diminish the incentive to sue." As a consequence "public risk litigation is probably marked by too few claims and too little vigorous prosecution, with the likely consequence that too much public risk escapes the deterrent effects of liability." "The producers of public risks will be inclined to overindulge, absent signals that align their self-interest with the larger social interest. . . . Because the signal emanating from the courts is thus weakened, there is likely to be too much public risk." Consequently, "access bias, *viewed in isolation*, may make the expected value of the signal generated by court judgments too low . . . because the social costs they represent are not brought to bear on producer decision making" (Gillette and Krier, 1990, pp. 1054–6).

However, access bias against plaintiffs is counterbalanced by process bias favoring plaintiffs. That is, if plaintiffs could overcome access biases and make it into court, then the procedural and substantive rules of the tort law as well as juries tended to favor plaintiffs. The end result, they argue is that there was probably not too much and not too little public risk that was within the proper scope of the tort law.

Nonetheless, there remain the problems noted above with torts to help control exposures to toxic substances. With such limitations, it was not surprising that there was a political movement in the early 1970s to enact a number of laws that created or strengthened administrative agencies to address problems posed by toxic substances. Agencies administering *premarket* regulatory statutes hold out the promise of intercepting substances before any damage is done as the argument from the equality of opportunity principle suggests. Even agencies administering *postmarket* regulatory statutes have advantages over the tort law in terms of comprehensively addressing problems of toxic substances and providing reasonable protections for those affected. By relying on animal studies, not waiting for human deaths, agencies can accumulate information about which substances pose substantial risks of harm to humans and take preventive action before those risks materialize.

However, not all is well with regulatory agencies despite appearances that they have advantages over the tort law.

Administrative agencies require a permanent bureaucracy to investigate risks of harm, devise approaches to addressing them, write the regulations and enforce them. This is a social cost to which there may be philosophical or economic objections.

Administrative approaches are subject to great political pressures in the legislative, rulemaking and rule applying processes. For example, since administrative law is a product of legislation, its creation is subject to all the political pressures that can be brought to bear by interest groups. And, the political pressure does not end with legislation. Interpreting the statute, creating an agency, if that is needed, and then issuing regulations all are subject to similar pressures. And, as time passes there is a substantial risk of a regulatory agency being "captured" by the industries that it aims to regulate, which further reduces its effectiveness.

In addition, recent presidential administrations and anti-regulatory Congresses have found other ways of frustrating the health protective intent of legislation. Presidential administrations have reduced agency budgets or subjected public health regulations to stringent review by the Office of Management and Budget in order to ensure that the regulations pass a "cost–benefit" analysis. Recent Congresses hostile to environmental health legislation have reduced funding for many of the agencies or tried to pass legislation to slow their activities by demanding more cost-benefit analysis of or "good science" in support of regulations. In political discussions the demand for "better science" in support of regulation has almost become a code word for slowing regulation.

Moreover, when we return to Gillette's and Krier's analysis, they conclude that regulatory agencies have probably permitted too much public risk from toxic substances within their ambit. The public faces substantial access bias in the agencies because of the same free rider problems that plague torts, but without the personal motivation that exists in torts to bring problems of toxic substances to the attention of regulators. Regulated industries, by contrast, have substantial advantages in bringing their concerns to the agencies, since they are highly organized and have concentrated economic interests at stake.

Finally, even if public risks did not have the structural features that create an imbalance of access to agencies, agency experts tend to view risks or acceptable risks much more like regulated industry than like the general public. As a consequence agency experts would regulate risks much more the way industry would than the general public would want. As Gillette and Krier correctly point out, there are simply *different conceptions of [acceptable] risk* at stake in these debates (Gillette and Krier, 1990; Cranor, 1995). Agencies and regulated industries tend to share one view, the broader, non-technically trained public another. Thus, even if all else were equal, from the public's point of view there would be too much risk from toxic substances.

This failure, however, they argued in 1990 was to some extent countered by appellate court review of agency actions. Judges tended to review agency actions in a way that counterbalanced agency tendencies to allow too much risk from toxic substances. Thus, while agencies probably permitted too many risks from toxic substances, courts tended to require agencies to curtail them. On balance then, there was not an inappropriate amount of risk from toxic substances resulting from the interaction of agencies and the judiciary. Whether this balance remains, we consider below.

The need for both torts and the regulatory law

Even if agencies did not suffer from any of the political problems indicated above, there may be occasions when the regulations are simply not adequate to protect all those exposed, especially those who are particularly sensitive or vulnerable to the substance in question. That is, agencies might not succeed in making regulations sufficiently protective, as occurred in several attempts to regulate asbestos, benzene, vinyl chloride, and arsenic (US Congress, OTA, 1987). Simply put, it can be difficult to craft regulations to protect all. Or sufficiently protective regulations may be simply too costly to implement compared with the importance of an industry to the economy.

To the extent that administrative agencies fail to provide sufficient protection from toxicants and people are harmed as a result, there remains a need for the tort law to provide compensation to injured parties. Historically, the tort law served as an important backup to regulatory law in providing incentives for asbestos manufacturers and installers to provide better protections for those exposed to asbestos-bearing products. Anecdotal evidence in the mid-1980s suggested that tort law sanctions resulting from suits against pesticide manufacturers led to improved regulatory legislation from Congress to address protections from pesticide exposures. Moreover, even though there have been reasonably good regulatory protections from benzene, people continue to allege harm from it and seek tort law compensation (*Chambers v. Exxon Corp.*, 81 F. Supp. 2d 66b 2000). The compensatory function of torts has helped to alert consumers and firms to some of the potential problems concerning low level exposures to potentially toxic substances, thus performing warning and deterrence functions.

There are, thus, good reasons for having both a well-functioning tort system and a well-functioning regulatory system to provide protections from toxic substances.

There have been, however, some legal developments that jeopardize both. In some areas of the law, where an agency has legal authority to address a substance and has done so, state or federal tort law courts may be precluded from hearing the cases of plaintiffs injured by the substance. In short, federal regulatory law may *pre-empt* the tort law (*Cipollone v. Liggett Group, Inc.*, 505 US 504, 1992). This has become more prevalent in recent years. When preemption occurs, if regulatory agencies have not done their jobs in protecting the public and there is no redress available through the tort law, any victims of exposure to toxic substances may simply be out of luck.

The Interaction of Science and Law in Regulating Toxic Substances

The above issues existed and shaped the interaction between torts and regulatory law before some comparatively recent legal developments concerning the use of scientific evidence in the law. These decisions have had a substantial impact on the efficacy of these legal institutions and their interactions.

In addressing public health issues that arise from toxic substances, scientific information is critical.

> [E]nvironmentally-caused harms pose . . . complex problems, because the causal agents typically are invisible, operate by obscure mechanisms, are difficult to trace and result in diseases or other injuries which [may] have long latency periods before they are manifested. Thus, the causal mechanisms tend to be obscure, unlike those we associate with the grosser forms of harm about which we are usually concerned [in the tort law]. Moreover, an environmentally-caused harm typically is a disease, impairment of health or incapacitation that is indistinguishable from diseases or incapacities with quite different etiologies. That is, except in rare cases the environmental cause does not leave a "signature." . . . Finally, . . . [many] scientific fields that might permit us to discover and accurately assess the risks from toxic substances are in their infancy (Cranor, 1997, p. 137).

As a result, detecting, identifying and substantiating the harms in question involves subtle, time-consuming scientific detective work and, often, molecular investigations. These facts about the need for scientific evidence and the difficulties of providing it overlay the preceding discussion concerning the features of different legal institutions to regulate toxic substances. The use of scientific evidence in both areas of law was substantially influenced, and, I would argue, complicated by US Supreme Court decisions in the last two decades. Moreover, political uses of science have complicated the debates about comparative institutional advantages.

Before 1980, regulatory agencies were given a great deal of discretion by appellate courts in deciding how to regulate and how much scientific support had to be provided for regulations. Before 1993, parties to tort disputes had considerable discretion in presenting expert witnesses. And, federal judges had considerable latitude in admitting or excluding evidence in toxic tort cases that came before them. (Of course, there were some limitations on how much they could control the presentation of evidence in cases at the bar, but much of this changed in1993.)

In 1980, a US Supreme Court decision – the Benzene case *Industrial Union, AFL-CIO v. American Petroleum Inst.*, 448 US 6007 1980 – ruled invalid a regulation issued by the OSHA (that reduced exposure to benzene in the workplace) largely because there was insufficient empirical scientific substantiation of the regulation.

In *Daubert v. Merrill-Dow Pharmaceutical* (509 US 579 1993), the Supreme Court issued a ruling concerning the role of federal trial court judges in admitting scientific evidence and scientific expert testimony in toxic tort cases. In each instance, the courts had choices in how they approached the issues and in each case there are, I believe, problems with the decisions.

The background of the two different decisions by the Supreme Court 13 years apart was quite different. In the *Benzene* case a *plurality* insisted that the OSHA must find on the basis of *empirical evidence* that there is a "significant risk" to employees at current exposure levels and that it is more likely than not that the risk will be substantially reduced at proposed exposure levels in its regulation. It must rely more on documented empirical findings and less on policy judgments or scientific assumptions in reaching conclusions about permissible exposure levels to toxic substances. Moreover, the Court and the agency had legitimate disagreements in interpreting the legislation authorizing OSHA's regulations. The court's view is final. This was a controversial decision; nearly half the court believed that OSHA had sufficient legislative and constitutional discretion to continue to regulate as it had without the added burden of considerably more scientific documentation for its regulations.

In *Daubert*, the Court's *unanimous* decision came against a different background. Individual litigants in a toxic tort suit must provide their own scientific experts to testify to the plausibility of the scientific support for their position. The quality of such experts and the quality of scientific evidence in support of their testimony can vary considerably. The plaintiffs' bar has been particularly criticized for such practices, but a poor scientific foundation for one's claims is not restricted to plaintiffs. In some cases – and there is only anecdotal evidence – litigants' experts' foundation for their testimony was probably not well supported by defensible scientific evidence. In *Daubert* itself, while early scientific studies suggested that the anti-morning sickness drug Bendectin caused shortened limb birth defects, subsequent studies, generated by the litigation, failed to find sufficient support for that claim to pass judicial scrutiny of the scientific evidence. Ultimately few plaintiffs' cases were successful.

A second example concerns silicon breast implants that were alleged to cause systemic autoimmune disorder. Marcia Angell, editor of the *New England Journal of Medicine*, claimed that the experts in those cases did not have a sound scientific basis for their testimony

> Scientific testimony in the courtroom is often at most only marginally related to scientific evidence. . . . [T]oo often [experts] are merely adding a veneer to a foregone, self-interested conclusion. Sometimes they spin theories that they say are supported by their expertise or experience. Or they may refer vaguely to research. Very often, however, the "research" is their own and it is unpublished and unavailable. The point is that they are not required to produce their evidence, and they usually do not. The result is a growing gap between scientific reality and what passes for it in the courtroom. The *Daubert* decision was a brave step toward remedying the situation, but it was not enough (Angell, 1996).

That some individual litigants were using experts whose testimony was not well grounded in science is quite different from the activities of federal agencies whose peer-reviewed science and policy decisions (made in light of the purposes of the statute) guided regulations. Agencies were utilizing respectable science of the time together with policy considerations that are legitimate under the legislation to support regulations.

However, it is arguable that the appellate courts in both the tort and regulatory cases perceived that when legal decisions are based on scientific claims, they should be founded on better evidence. Certainly, some commentators have advocated such a view for a number of years. The *Daubert* court explicitly argued that expert testimony must be reliable and based upon the scientific method. The *Benzene* court argued that OSHA must base its decisions more on scientific *findings* and less on scientific assumptions, safety factors and policy decisions (although agencies may continue to utilize such considerations).

A more implicit message may have been that both regulatory agencies and toxic tort litigants were intruding too much into the business of American business. Some on the *Benzene* court explicitly articulated this view, arguing that OSHA was out of control, imposing too great a burden on American businesses by its regulations. Thus, some justices sought to exert greater control over OSHA (and perhaps implicitly on other agencies) by utilizing a strong misreading of the legislation and by imposing some evidentiary and scientific constraints on OSHA's basis for legislation. The *Daubert* Court did not explicitly make such a point, although the Court in a subsequent decision came quite close to making this point. (*General Electric v. Joiner*, 522 US 136, 1997)

The effect of the Benzene *decision on the requirements for scientific evidence in regulatory law*

Typically, when an agency regulation is issued it will be upheld by appellate courts unless the agency acted "arbitrarily or capriciously" in issuing it. (A few agencies are reviewed under a different standard.) Agencies have this scope of discretion on the theory that there are a variety of approaches to the problem, that agency personnel better understand the issues and thus are better able than an appellate court to evaluate plausible approaches. Moreover, a presidential administration should be able to have the flexibility to pursue its political objectives in implementing laws passed by Congress.

The *Benzene* case ushered in a requirement for more detailed scientific support for regulation in the form of empirically based risk assessment, and perhaps was an early warning of a concern about the costs of regulations. On its face, this does not seem unreasonable. After all, should not government decisions rest on scientifically sound findings? It is arguable, however, given agency reactions to the *Benzene* case and agency interpretations of it, that it had a substantial chilling effect on regulatory activity by OSHA and other federal agencies, greatly slowing their activities and perhaps discouraging them from issuing more health-protective regulations (discussed below).

The *Benzene* case could have been decided differently. Minimal changes in this highly visible and influential decision could easily have made quite a difference in the regulatory context and led agencies to issue, and reviewing courts to permit, much more health-protective regulations than has subsequently tended to be the case. The Court could have permitted the regulation to stand. OSHA had reasonably good evidence that benzene was a carcinogen and took preventive steps within its authority to protect employees' health, given the scientific evidence that was available in 1978. (It now appears that the proposed 1978 exposure standard of 1 ppm benzene over an eight-hour period might have been too high by a factor of five or ten. (Infante, 1992)) Another possibility is that the Court could have selected different aspects of the statute to emphasize in its ruling, such as the fact that OSHA is required to protect workers from "material impairment of health or functional capacity" even if they are exposed to a toxic substance for a "working lifetime" and that Congress recognized that OSHA must work at the "frontiers of scientific knowledge." Either of these would have argued for a more health-protective and discretion-recognizing interpretation of the statute. The *Benzene* decision greatly increased the legal pressure on agencies to perform detailed, science-intensive risk assessments in support of regulations. This arguably has resulted in many fewer substances being considered for regulation by OSHA or by other agencies. OSHA has also almost been legally barred from considering analogs of expedited regulations in order to address the hundreds of toxic substances in US workplaces.

There are, of course, winner and losers in such decisions. While the *Benzene* case made regulation more difficult and left employees at risk, it also eased some of the legal burdens on industries manufacturing and using toxic substances and left them freer to conduct business as they see fit. Whether such results are on balance desirable is a complicated issue, but I believe it has not been.

One major issue this case raises is what is a reasonable standard of scientific evidence needed to take regulatory action under a post-market statute to prevent risks of harm from materializing into harm and what are some of the consequences of different decisions?

The effect of the Daubert *decision on the need for scientific evidence in toxic tort cases*

In the tort law, the *Daubert* decision did two things: it explicitly required district court judges to serve as gatekeepers for admitting scientific evidence and experts, and it provided some presumptive considerations to guide whether experts had an appropriate scientific foundation for their testimony.

Much of this decision is salutary in requiring appropriate scientific methodology to support the testimony of an expert. An important philosophic and social issue in the decision is how certain the scientific foundation must be for expert testimony when evidence is so sparse and uncertain in most toxic tort cases. In this case also, the court had choices in its decision and opted for more rather than less restrictive rules for admitting scientific evidence. It remains to be seen what the effect of this decision will be as courts grapple with these issues. Although it is still early in the debate, some decisions suggest that many courts will require, and even more commentators are recommending, that the scientific foundation for expert testimony must satisfy fairly stringent standards of proof. A more recent decision suggests that it will be even more difficult for plaintiffs to introduce scientific evidence into toxic tort cases. As a result of these decisions, toxic tort law not only risks being even less protective than previously, but also, despite plaintiffs having a preponderance of evidence standard of proof to carry, will depart even further from the aims of the tort law. With these decisions, the Court is approaching a requirement that plaintiffs must establish their conclusions with considerable scientific certainty before they can recover damages in the tort law and before it can have its deterrent effect on defendant's actions in exposing the public to toxic substances. While the law in this area is far from settled, preliminary indications are not reassuring.

Philosophic issues concerning the use of scientific evidence in tort and regulatory law

How stringent the evidentiary requirements are for both the tort and regulatory law makes considerable difference in the overall functioning of these institutions. This becomes quite apparent from the context in which the issues are framed.

First, in post-market contexts the status quo continues until a legal case is made for change. If there is harm or risk of harm in the status quo, this continues. If there is no harm or no risk of harm, this also continues. Moreover, such contexts invite the idea, explicitly endorsed by the law, that the status quo is acceptable, permissible, or proper, until there is justification for changing it. For this reason the law erects barriers in the form of burdens of proof (designating which party has to make a legal case for changing the status quo) and standards of proof (the degree and kind of certainty with which the case must be made). The more stringent these are before legal action is authorized, the more difficult it is to change the status quo.

Second, any *uncertainty* about the factual foundations for regulatory or tort law change in legal relationships adds to the legal barriers and makes the legal task more difficult, depending upon how much ignorance and uncertainty must be removed in carrying burdens of proof and in meeting the required standards of proof.

Third, there is spotty, but persuasive data suggesting that ignorance and uncertainty about the toxic properties of substances is pervasive, even massive. To the extent this is true, the need to remove uncertainty creates extremely high factual barriers for agencies issuing postmarket regulataions or for tort law plaintiffs to satisfy before legal action can be taken. If there is considerable ignorance about such substances, legal decisions will always go against the party with the burden of proof (Cranor and Eastmond, 2001).

Fourth, it is difficult scientifically to remove the lack of information and uncertainty. The typical tests for discerning the toxic properties of substances are slow and do not provide quick answers to common questions about their safety. Just obtaining the basic toxicity data from laboratory and animal tests by the most expeditious schedule requires at least six years. If human data are insisted upon, this extends the period even further. Human studies involve the use of tests that are comparatively insensitive, tests that risk missing or underestimating a toxic effect. These problems are exacerbated when substances have toxicity properties with substantial latency periods, such as carcinogens, some reproductive toxins and some neurotoxins.

Consider benzene, an important industrial product and by now a well-known human carcinogen. Benzene was implicated in the 1890s of causing various blood diseases. In the 1920s, it was reported to cause leukemia. However, documentation and wide scientific acceptance of benzene's leukemogenic properties did not come for another sixty years. In 1974, the World Health Organization's

International Agency for Research on Cancer noted that it could only indicate that a relationship between benzene exposure and the development of leukemia was "suggested" by case reports and one case-control study. By 1987, the same organization found that benzene "*is* carcinogenic to man" (IARC, 1987). At present, scientists and public health organizations are better prepared to act upon evidence of harm, but for scientists to be alerted to a problem and then to conduct the needed tests to substantiate it takes considerable time and resources. There have been similar delays in documenting the harms from other substances.

The concerns just expressed apply only to the typical *scientific tests*. When this is conjoined with how *scientists'* assess such tests, this probably extends the period of ignorance and uncertainty. Scientists' approaches to data interpretation are likely to exacerbate delays associated with conducting the basic battery of tests. Just because tests have been completed does not mean that there is scientific *acceptance* of them, which may take considerably longer. And, if there is an insistence for legal purposes on a scientific *consensus* about what the tests show this will take longer yet. Scientists typically approach new data and theories with considerable skepticism. Thus, there must be a period after test data have been published for the scientific community to assimilate and accept the results as correct (or sufficiently correct for the purposes needed).

Moreover, at least some scientists are likely to have extremely stringent conceptions of the degree of scientific certainty needed before data and theory results are accepted as well as a demanding conception of the factual mistakes that must be avoided. Both views, if present, are likely to increase factual barriers to a scientific basis for legal action.

Fifth, there are more subtle but related points about institutional norms and issues about how much and which kinds of ignorance and uncertainty must be removed to address regulatory and tort law issues.

Consider first institutional norms. Scientific practice implicitly adopts a certain normative approach toward preventing factual mistakes that might result from scientific inquiry. The tort law and regulatory law implicitly have somewhat different approaches from each other and from scientific practice toward similar mistakes.

In scientific practice, scientists seek strongly to prevent false positive mistakes from occurring, from identifying substances as toxic when they are not. Scientists appear to protect much less strongly against false negatives, that is, substances being identified as non-toxic when they are toxic. Regulatory law seems to differ quite sharply from this; the presuppositions here appear to protect more against false negatives than against false positives, although this varies with the law in question. (Recall the different statutory approaches to risks.) The tort law is intermediate between the two. As judged by the ultimate burden of persuasion that must be satisfied in tort suits, it appears indifferent between legal mistakes that favor defendants (legal false negatives) and mistakes that favor plaintiffs (legal false positives) (with factual errors contributing to legal errors) (Cranor, 1993).

The subtle tension between these institutions creates the following problems. If the scientific distribution of errors of factual mistakes is insensitively adopted in legal contexts, this will tend to dominate the approach to the distribution of mistakes in the legal institutions. Thus, insensitive prevention of factual false positives in the needed scientific studies may skew the legal outcome in regulatory or tort law contexts, where prevention of such mistakes is of somewhat lesser concern. Moreover, in statistical studies the foundations of much scientific research, the aim to prevent false positives mathematically increases the chances of false negatives. Scientific insistence on preventing false positives consequently increase false negatives, the prevention of which is of greater legal concern. And, various scientific practices can have a similar effect, e.g., demanding more and better evidence, demanding the removal of considerable uncertainty, subjecting scientific claims to considerable scrutiny and skepticism (Cranor, 1993). In short, if the scientific requirements for the law are not designed sensitively for the legal context in question, the demand for a good scientific foundation can distort the law.

There is a further point: which kinds of ignorance and uncertainty must be removed for legal purposes? Considerable detail could be provided here, but consider one example. Some federal judges in toxic tort cases have required that a litigant alleging that a substance causes harm must show not only a relation between exposure to a substance and harm to humans, but also the biological mechanism of action. While understanding biological mechanisms is important for basic toxicological research, it is rarely needed for identifying a substance as harmful (but it can help). A scientific requirement for the purpose of understanding toxicity may not be needed to identify toxicological harms. More significantly, biological mechanisms of action are understood for very few substances; to require such understanding for every toxicant is tantamount to requiring the impossible in many cases. Other courts have required multiple kinds of evidence that are not needed for tort law purposes.

Sixth, the combined effects of post-market burdens and standards of proof, pervasive ignorance and uncertainty about toxicants, scientific practices, and tensions between the goals of science and legal institutions indicated above tend to have a substantial impact on regulation, parties to litigation and on corporate behavior.

In post-market settings, there is a strong temptation to insist on the most demanding conceptions of scientific evidence and to require that they be established with the highest degree of certainty, since no regulation occurs until the requisite legal burdens have been satisfied. There are examples of both temptations from regulatory and tort law. If courts are not discriminating in their review of such cases this can distort the legal setting. Moreover, firms can usually find skeptical scientists to emphasize uncertainty and what is not known or understood about the toxicity of substances, which in turn may contribute to stringent conceptions of science or to conclusions that the scientific record is inadequate for the legal conclusion in question.

When the government in a regulatory case or a plaintiff in a tort law suit has the burden of establishing a harm or risk of harm, there are incentives for firms to take advantage of the uncertainty and ignorance surrounding the toxicity of a substance. It is relatively easy to argue, as the tobacco industry did for many years, that a harm or risk of harm is "not proven scientifically." This also comports well with scientific approaches to uncertainty. Since in absence of evidence to the contrary, scientists would urge that they simply do not know what a substance's properties are.

What is the effect of these judicially imposed scientific requirements on regulatory law? In 1990, Gillette and Krier argued that in regulatory law the public was disadvantaged by both access and process bias, but this tended to be counterbalanced by judicial intervention. How are things two decades later after some major court rulings on scientific evidence in the law?

The short answer appears to be that citizens are less well protected against public risk because courts are constraining agency attempts to reduce exposures to toxic substances. Moreover, legislative and executive branch institutions have further burdened the agencies in their efforts to regulate health hazards. Prior to the late 1980s, Gillette and Krier argued that courts were making agencies do more to regulate toxic substances; now the courts and other institutions tend to control the agencies and make them regulate such risks *less*, even less than the agencies have sought to do. Consider three examples:

In 1989, OSHA issued a regulation to update its exposure standards to toxic substances in the workplace by incorporating permissible exposure levels for 428 toxic substances recommended by the American Conference of Governmental Industrial Hygienists, a private organization that tends to be dominated by industry experts. This regulation was initially opposed by labor but supported by some industry trade groups and opposed by others. The Eleventh Circuit Court of Appeals struck down the agency action. It held that OSHA "failed to establish that existing exposure limits in the workplace present a significant risk of material health impairment or that new standards eliminated or substantially lessened the risk; and . . . OSHA did not meet its burden of establishing that its 428 new permissible exposure limits (PEL) were either economically or technologically feasible" (*American Federation of Labor and Congress of Indus. Organizations v. Occupational Safety and Health Admin., US Dept. of Labor*, 1992). This decision, echoing some of the language of the *Benzene* case, and illustrating the scientific and procedural burdens that OSHA must satisfy, makes it extremely difficult for the agency to take expedited action on the hundreds of toxic substances in the workplace.

In 1989, the EPA issued a rule under section 6 of the Toxic Substances Control Act (TSCA) "to prohibit the future manufacture, importation, processing and distribution of asbestos in almost all products." Asbestos is a known carcinogen that has caused lung cancer, mesothelioma, and other diseases in thousands of people, often at rather low exposures levels. This rule was reviewed by the Fifth Circuit Court of Appeals, invalidated and remanded to the agency for further consideration. More generally, the court ruled that any TSCA rulemaking must be designed to prevent "unreasonable" risks, which is similar to a test from tort law that balances the risks and benefits of an action. Thus, the agency not only must find a reasonable relationship between the severity of injuries prevented and the costs of preventing them, but it must also engage in a *comparative risk analysis* of injuries prevented by the ban compared with injuries resulting from substitute products. The agency is not required to seek out and test all possible substitutes, but "when an interested party comes forward with credible evidence that the planned substitutes present a significant, or even greater toxic risk than the substance in question, the agency must make a formal finding on the record that its proposed action still is both reasonable and warranted under TSCA" (*Corrosion Proof Fittings v. EPA*, 947 F.2d 1201, 5th Cir. 1991, p. 1230). Thus, the court appears to mandate a qualified comparative risk judgment, such that the agency must not only consider the risks and benefits of reducing them under the regulation, but also the risks that might be incurred from substitute products, e.g., greater deaths from brakes not made from asbestos (provided that this is raised by an interested party) (p. 1207).

Nearly a decade after these two decisions, the Court of Appeals for the District of Columbia invalidated a rule issued by the EPA to reduce particulate air contaminants, among other contaminants. That court held, *inter alia*, that EPA's construction of Act on which EPA relied in revising [particular matter] and ozone [standards] effected [an] unconstitutional delegation of legislative power ... [and that its] "decision to regulate coarse particulate matter indirectly was arbitrary and capricious (*American Trucking Association v. US EPA*, 175 F.3d 1207 DC Cir. 1999).

Aspects of each of these decisions criticize the agency in question for failing to provide sufficient scientific support for its regulation, the seeds of which were planted in the *Benzene* case. And, the courts often introduce other considerations that further burden an agency's action. What effect does this have on the regulatory environment?

These cases of the past decade appear to exacerbate the problems to which Gillette and Krier called attention in 1990. Access for the public has not changed. Regulated industries continue to have lobbying advantages compared with the public. Court decisions have tended to further burden agency actions aimed at reducing risks from toxic substances. The combined effect is to keep current risks in existence, thus over time not decreasing and perhaps increasing risks to which workers and the public are exposed.

Most significantly, the courts now appear to be additionally constraining the agencies from addressing those risks beyond what the agencies are willing to do. Beginning with the *Benzene* case through *AFL-CIO v. OSHA* and *Corrosion Proof Pipe Fittings* to *American Trucking* an increased emphasis on scientific and technical support for regulations has increased the barriers which agencies must overcome to address risks of concern to the American public. In short, if agencies were permitting too much public risk in 1990, the court decisions in the last decade have exacerbated the problem.

In 1990, Gillette and Krier were optimistic that federal judges were spurring agency action to produce greater protections – requiring them to curtail public risks to a greater extent than the agencies were inclined – and permitting toxic tort cases to have a significant deterrent effect on companies through the tort law.

Their hope of 1990 has been dashed, I believe. Appellate courts no longer appear to spur agencies to provide greater protection from toxic substances, and *Daubert* and its progeny at the appellate and district court levels have placed greater procedural barriers in front of plaintiffs that reduce the deterrence signals sent from successful toxic tort suits.

It is difficult to provide definitive arguments about torts because decisions on the admissibility of scientific evidence are so decentralized across federal district and appellate courts. However, a growing body of scholars is concerned about the impact of *Daubert* and its progeny on the tort law (Cranor and Eastmond, 2001). The Supreme Court increased judicial gatekeeping responsibilities on the admission of evidence and made such decisions difficult to overturn on appeal (*General Electric v. Joiner*, 522 US 136, 1997). Moreover, there appear to be inconsistencies within and between circuits on how scientific evidence is treated. It appears that courts within the different circuits are tending to review evidence much more stringently than they were before the *Daubert* decision. Some circuits appear to make it quite difficult to get evidence and scientific experts admitted, while others appear to be doing quite a good job in reviewing and admitting evidence. Some trial and appellate courts appear to violate scientific standards of evidence evaluation in their decisions.

It now appears more difficult for plaintiffs to have scientific experts admitted in toxic tort cases, simply because federal judges must scrutinize experts in a way that they did not need to prior to *Daubert*. How will this affect the law?

In 1990, Gillette and Krier argued that the public was disadvantaged in torts by access bias, but benefited from process bias. However, the *Daubert* decision has diminished process bias and actually increased some access bias to toxic tort plaintiffs. Judicial scrutiny of scientific experts is part of the legal process once plaintiffs are in court and this has made it more difficult for plaintiffs to go beyond preliminary hearings. Some plaintiffs will never be able to present their claims to juries because judges will exclude their technical experts with good, but not the best evidence, thus effectively ending their cases. Judicial scrutiny could also be considered as part of plaintiff access, since a litigant's case can be precluded at such an early stage of the trial process and the *Daubert* hurdles will result in lawyers willing to take fewer toxic tort cases. Thus, it appears that the balance of access and process bias has been upset compared to the circumstances existing prior to *Daubert*.

Conclusion

The legal environment for protecting employees and the general public from exposures to toxicants has changed, perhaps quite significantly, subsequent to the *Benzene, Daubert* and other decisions. The postmarket regulatory environment is likely much more hospitable to businesses because they can rest their cases before agencies or tort courts on claims of scientific uncertainty and on the claim that there is not definitive evidence that possible toxicants have been shown to cause harm. This is the result of the paucity of scientific evidence, the difficulty establishing such claims and the postmarket burdens and standards of proof that must be met in the regulatory law and in torts. Employees in industries using toxic substances and the general public appear to be less well protected by the law than they once were and than they could be.

This situation is not beyond redress however. Courts have constrained agencies and district court judges both. They could issue decisions that would recognize in the spirit of Aristotle that they should only demand the degree of evidence and precision that is appropriate for the institution in question. Appellate courts could signal lower courts and agencies that they need not demand the most certain and the best supported scientific evidence, if that would distort the aims of the legal institution in question. Were they to do this, courts by their decisions would permit and encourage greater workplace and public health protections consistent with reliable scientific judgments on which businesses could rely. Whether they will or not remains to be seen.

References

Angell, M. 1996: *Science on Trial: The Clash of Medical Evidence and the Law in the Breast Implant Case*. London and New York: W. W. Norton & Company.

Berlin, I. 1997: Two concepts of liberty. *The Proper Study of Mankind*. New York: Farrar, Strauss and Giroux, 191–242. Originally written in 1969.

Cranor, C. F. 1993: *Regulating Toxic Substances: A Philosophy of Science and the Law*. New York: Oxford University Press.

Cranor, C. F. 1995: The use of comparative risk judgments in risk management. In A. M. Fan and L. W. Chang (eds) *Toxicology and Risk Assessment*, Marcel Dekker, Inc., 817–33.

Cranor, C. F. 1997: A philosophy of risk assessment and the law: a case study of the role of philosophy in public policy, *Philosophical Studies*, 85, 135–62.

Cranor, C. F. and Eastmond, D. A. 2001: Scientific ignorance and reliable patterns of evidence in toxic tort causastion: Is there a need for liability reform? *Law and Contemporary Problems*, 64(4), Autumn, 5–48.

Daniels, N. 1985: *Just Health Care*. New York: Cambridge University Press.

Eads, C. and Reuter, P. 1983: *Designing Safer Products: Corporate Responses to Product Liability Law and Regulation*. Santa Monica, CA: Rand Corporation.

Gillette, C. P. and Krier, J. E. 1990: Risk, courts and agencies. *University of Pennsylvania Law Review*, 38, 1077–109.

IARC (International Agency for Research on Cancer) 1987: *Monographs, Vol. 107*. Lyon, France: WHO.

Infante, P. 1992: Benzene and leukemia: the 0.1 ppm ACGIH proposed threshold limit value for benzene. *Applied Occupational Environmental Hygiene*, 7, 253–62.

McGarity, T. O. and Shapiro, S. A. 1993: *Workers at Risk: The Failed Promise of the Occupational Safety and Health Administration.* Westport Connecticut: Praeger.

Nagel, T. 1975: Libertarianism without foundations. *Yale Law Journal* 85: 136–49.

Nozick, R. 1974: *Anarchy, State and Utopia.* New York: Oxford University Press.

Rawls, J. 1971: *A Theory of Justice.* Cambridge: Harvard University Press.

Rodgers, W. H. Jr., 1977: *Handbook on Environmental Law.* St. Paul Minn.: West Publishing Co.

Schuck, P. 2000: The Limits of Law. *Yale Law Report.*

US Congress, OTA (Office of Technology Assessment) 1987: *Identifying and Regulating Carcinogens.* Washington, DC: US Government Printing Office.

Further Reading

Amdur, M. O., Doull, J., and Klaassen, C. D. (eds) (1991) *Casarett and Doull's toxicology.* New York: Pergamon Press.

Berger, M. A. 1997: Eliminating general causation: Notes towards a new theory of justice and toxic torts. *97 Columbia Law Review.* 2117–52.

Berger, M. A. 2000: The Supreme Court's triology on the admissiblity of expert testimony. *Reference manual on scientific evidence.* 2nd edn. Washington, DC: Federal Judicial Center. 9–38.

Cranor, C. F., Fischer, J. A., Eastmond, D. A. 1996: Judicial boundary-drawing and the need for context-sensitive science in toxic torts after Daubert v. Merrell-Dow Pharmaceutical. *The Virginia Environmental Law Journal,* 16, 1–77.

Keeton, W. P., Dobbs, D. B., Keeton, R. E. and Owen, D. G. 1984: *Prosser and Keeton on Torts,* 5th edn. St. Paul, Minn: West Publishing Co.

Chapter 5

Moral Reasoning

Manuel Velasquez

Moral reasoning is the process of thinking by which a person arrives at judgments about the particular or general requirements of morality. Such reasoning may lead to judgments about the morality of particular behaviors, persons, institutions, or states of affairs, or of general types of behaviors, persons, institutions, or states of affairs. It may also lead to judgments about the more general requirements of morality such as the requirements embodied in abstract moral rules or principles used to evaluate the morality of acts, persons, institutions, and states of affairs. Examples of the former kinds of judgments include the judgment that it was morally wrong for General Electric managers to fix prices during the 1960s, as well as the judgment that price-fixing agreements in a market economy generally are morally wrong. Examples of the latter include John Stuart Mill's utilitarian principle that "actions are right in proportion as they tend to produce happiness, wrong as they tend to produce the reverse of happiness" (Mill, 1957 [1861]), Immanuel Kant's categorical imperative that one ought to "act only on that maxim that can be willed to become a universal law" (Kant, 1964 [1785]) and John Rawls' "difference principle" which holds that social and economic inequalities are just only if they are "to the greatest benefit of the least advantaged" and "open to all under conditions of equality of opportunity" (Rawls, 1971). The aim of moral reasoning is to arrive at judgments about morality that are reasonable, i.e., that can be justified by an appeal to reasons, evidence, proofs, or other rationales for one's judgments and so can help us live moral lives in a reasonable manner.

We will examine, first, a widely accepted conception of moral reasoning, and discuss several problems and issues debated by those who accept this standard conception. We will next examine some alternative conceptions of moral reasoning that challenge the standard one, and discuss also some of the issues and problems raised by these alternatives. It is important to notice that a particular theory of moral reasoning can be understood to be either a descriptive theory of how people in fact reason about the requirements of morality, or a normative theory of how people, ideally, ought to reason about the requirements of morality. The theories discussed here are all normative theories of moral reasoning, i.e., theories of how moral reasoning should proceed if one is to arrive at reasonable or justified judgments about morality.

The Standard Conception of Moral Reasoning

For many ethicists, moral reasoning about the morality of particular persons, acts, institutions, and states of affairs, (or types of acts, persons, institutions, and states of affairs) is primarily a matter of subsuming particular cases (or types of cases) under more general principles or rules. On this conception of moral reasoning, one reasons about the morality of an action to be performed in a certain set of circumstances by ascertaining the features of that action in those circumstances, and then determining whether those features would qualify the action as moral or immoral according to the criteria set out in certain more general moral rules that express the requirements of morality. On this view, then, moral reasoning about the morality of particular actions, persons, institutions, or states of affairs would have a three-part structure:

1   The reasoning involved in grasping the highly abstract moral rules or moral principles that embody the general requirements of morality
2   The reasoning involved in ascertaining the features that an action (or person, or institution, or state of affairs) performed in a certain set of circumstances possesses (a process that may require empirical or factual information about the action and its circumstances)
3   The moral judgment reached by determining whether the features of the action, in light of the general requirements of morality, qualifies the action as moral or immoral.

If one accepted Mill's utilitarian principle, for example, then to reason to an adequate judgment about whether price-fixing in a market economy is morally wrong would involve determining whether price-fixing tended to produce more happiness or unhappiness, a determination that would presumably involve gathering the facts related to the empirical effects of price-fixing. If one accepted Kant's categorical imperative, one would have to determine, instead, whether price-fixing could be willed as a universal practice in a market economy, which would require an inquiry into whether a market economy could be sustained if price-fixing were a general practice in that economy. And if one accepted Rawls' difference principle, one would reason about whether price-fixing produces inequalities that maximally benefit the least advantaged members of society and how it affects equality of opportunity, both of which would require ascertaining the facts about price-fixing.

This conception of moral reasoning (i.e., the view that moral reasoning proceeds by subsuming particular cases under general rules) suggests that it is possible to arrange all or at least many of our moral judgments in hierarchical arrays of increasing generality. At the bottom would be judgments about the morality of concrete actual or planned actions; higher up would be judgments about the morality of general types of actions; higher up still might be judgments about the morality of a range of types of actions, all of which possess some general feature or features; at the very top would be the supreme and so most general or abstract moral principles – such as the utilitarian principle or the categorical imperative – indicating which general features all wrong or right actions – or all wrong or right actions of a certain class – have in common. The judgments at any given level in these hierarchical arrays would subsume the less general judgments in the level below them. Moral reasoning, then, can be conceived as the process of drawing out the logical relations among these hierarchies of judgments, so that the morality of a judgment at a lower level would be determined by seeing whether and how it is related to judgments at a next higher level.

It should not be thought that those who hold the standard conception of moral reasoning leave no room for moral discernment or judgment. The kinds of general moral principles that ethicists have suggested – the utilitarian principle, for example, and the categorical imperative – are highly abstract and general, forcing those who use the principles in their reasoning to engage in considerable interpretation and judgment about what exactly these abstract moral principles mean and exactly what, in detail, they require. The utilitarian principle, for example, leaves considerable room for the exercise of judgment about what counts as happiness, as well as about the scope of the principle of utility. Judgment is also required to determine whether particular features of actions, persons, institutions, or states of affairs are the kinds of features that are relevant to the abstract moral principles.

A key controversy among those who accept the standard conception of moral reasoning, of course, is the question of what general principles should be used to determine the morality of particular acts, persons, institutions or states of affairs. Each of the major ethical theories proposes distinct general principles, and these general principles in turn require that moral reasoning take into account a range of considerations that are not taken into account in moral reasoning governed by other general principles. Each theory, consequently, implies a distinct view of how moral reasoning proceeds. Mill's utilitarian theory, for example, implies that moral reasoning about behaviors is essentially reasoning about the consequences that behaviors will have on the happiness (or unhappiness) of sentient beings. Kant's theory implies that moral reasoning about action is essentially a matter of reasoning about what is possible or willable as a universal practice, regardless of the consequences on human happiness. And Rawls' theory holds that moral reasoning about social arrangements is a matter of reasoning about the impact these arrangements have on the fortunes of the least advantaged and on equality of opportunity. Consequentialist or teleological theories conceptualize

moral reasoning about the morality of actions as reasoning about their consequences: the good or bad results that actions will produce. Non-consequentialist
or deontological theories view moral reasoning as reasoning about something
other than, or in addition to, consequences. While teleological theories hold that
claims about what is good are basic, and judgments about what actions are right
are derivative from these, deontological theories hold that at least some claims
about what actions are right are basic insofar as moral reasoning does not determine their rightness by ascertaining whether those actions will promote some
antecedently identified goods. Mill's theory is a teleological theory while Kant's
theory is a deontological one.

Not only are ethicists at odds about which principles should play the role of
the supreme moral principles, they also disagree about how many such topmost
principles there are. Many of the classical ethicists have been ethical monists,
arguing that there is a single moral principle that serves as, or should serve as,
the supreme principle in all moral reasoning. But others have advocated ethical
pluralism, an approach that claims that moral reasoning requires a plurality of
general principles which cannot be reduced to any single principle. Kant (1964
[1785]), for example, was a monist and claimed that "all imperatives of [moral]
duty can be derived from this one [categorical] imperative as their principle."
Several contemporary philosophers (Hare, 1975; Gewirth, 1987; Gensler, 1996)
have proposed as the supreme principle adaptations of the so-called Golden Rule
("Do unto others as you would have them do unto you," Matthew 7:12) versions
of which are prominent in virtually all religious traditions (Wattles, 1996). On
the other hand, Ross (1930), Nagel (1979), Stoker (1990), as well as several
natural law ethicists such as Finnis (1983), have claimed that morality requires an
irreducible plurality of general principles. Those who favor ethical monism argue
that a plurality of principles inevitably leads to irresolvable conflicts among these
principles, while those who favor ethical pluralism argue that the multifaceted
nature of the moral life requires a reliance on a plurality of principles.

The disputes over which – and how many – general principles should govern
moral reasoning obviously have enormous implications for business ethics. Business
ethics is supposed to provide the business manager with a method of evaluating
the morality of business practices. How can it do this when there is little agreement
over how reasoning about the morality of business practices should proceed? In
business ethics one form of moral pluralism has been advanced by Velasquez et al.
(1995), and Velasquez (2001), who have argued that there are four irreducibly
distinct kinds of moral principles – utilitarianism, moral rights, justice, and caring
– each of which identifies four different kinds of moral considerations, and all
of which must be taken into account when the business manager reasons about
the morality of particular or general issues. Although adapted by many business
ethicists, their approach has been criticized because, it is claimed, it is based on
the wrong set of moral principles (Brady and Dunn, 1995). DeGeorge (1999)
and Brady (1990) proposed pluralist approaches to business ethics focused on two
kinds of moral principles – utilitarianism and a Kantian-based deontology – while

Boatright (1999) proposed an approach based on three kinds of moral principles – utilitarianism, Kantian-based rights, and justice. A monist approach to business ethics based on Kant was recently proposed by Bowie (1999), but others, such as Elfstrom (1991) have argued in favor of a modified utilitarian approach to business ethics. Such disputes over the very foundations of moral reasoning are bound at the very least to leave the business manager confused, perplexed and frustrated. Some (De George, 1999) have argued that the diversity of approaches is not a bad thing since all the approaches "converge" on "the same moral conclusions with respect to the morality of the practice or act." Others have simply concluded that business ethics, at least as conceived within the traditional model of moral reasoning, does not meet the real needs of business people (Pamental, 1991; Stark, 1993).

In the standard conception of moral reasoning, establishing the supreme moral principles requires a kind of moral reasoning that is very different from that which could establish lower level judgments. Moral reasoning aimed at determining moral judgment at the lower levels proceeds by subsuming these under some higher more general moral judgment. But there are no higher moral judgments under which one might subsume the topmost principles. What kind of moral reasoning, then, might be used to determine these topmost principles? One view – popular among analytic philosophers of the middle twentieth century who were influenced by then-current views of science – holds that the most adequate general moral principles are those that account for the broadest range of those intuitive moral judgments that, after due consideration, we remain convinced are correct. (Urmson, (1974–5); Rawls, (1971). On this view, such intuitive moral judgments are thought of as "data" that should be "explained" by general moral principles in the way that a general scientific theory explains the more particular laws and observations that are implied by the theory. The kinetic-molecular theory of heat, for example, developed in the late nineteenth and early twentieth centuries, explained the laws relating pressure and temperature as well as observations of Brownian movement, and did so in a way that the earlier caloric-fluid theory could not, prompting the rejection of the caloric theory as mistaken and the adoption of the kinetic theory as more adequate. In an analogous way, it has been held, a moral theory can be shown to be adequate by showing that it explains our most deeply held intuitive judgments about what types of actions are right and wrong, the explanation proceeding by showing that these judgments are implied by the theory. Moral reasoning aimed at disproving a candidate for a topmost moral principle would proceed by producing intuitive judgments that serve as counter examples against the principle; while moral reasoning aimed at supporting a topmost moral principle would consist of showing that a suitably broad range of judgments implied by a topmost principle are consistent with our moral intuitions. For example, critics of utilitarianism have argued that utilitarianism must be mistaken because it does not account for some of our most compelling moral intuitions about justice and moral rights, while utilitarians have countered that utilitarianism, if properly modified (e.g., as rule utilitarianism) can account for our intuitions about justice and rights, as well as for a very broad range of our other basic moral intuitions. This general method of determining the topmost general principles of morality has been given the term "reflective equilibrium" by Rawls who wrote "There is a definite if limited class of facts against which conjectured principles can be checked, namely our considered judgments in reflective equilibrium" (Rawls, 1971). Judgments are in reflective equilibrium when they have been compared with what one believes are the most reasonable moral principles, and when reasonable accommodations to the judgments or the principles have been made, either by revising the judgments so they are consistent with the principles, or by altering the principles so as to bring them into line with the judgments. Rawls argued that by relying on a hypothetical reconstruction of social contract bargaining ("the original position"), one could derive a set of moral rules or principles that were consistent with one's considered judgments in reflective equilibrium. Rawls' methodological claims have been extremely influential in business ethics. Donaldson (1989), and Green (1994), for example, have argued that the Rawlsian methodology should be used to establish mid-level moral principles for business.

In spite of the recent popularity of determining the topmost general principles of morality by an appeal to considered judgments, the approach remains controversial. Critics have pointed out that our moral convictions are the outcome of a number of distorting historical influences that makes them unreliable criteria against which to test our moral theories (Brandt, 1979). Singer, for example, notes that our moral convictions derive "from discarded religious systems, from warped views of sex and bodily functions, or from customs necessary for the survival of the group in social and economic circumstances that now lie in the distant past" (Singer, 1974). To claim, then, that business ethics should be based on an appeal to "considered judgments" may be recommending that managers rely on criteria that are historically conditioned and morally distorted.

Whatever the outcome of this debate, it is clear that an appeal to considered judgments is not the only possible method of proving or disproving the supreme principles of ethics. Some ethicists have tried to establish their topmost principles by very different forms of reasoning. Kant seems, at one time at least, to have believed that his own candidate for a topmost principle, the categorical imperative, could be established by thinking about the requirements of human autonomy (Kant, 1964 [1785]). Earlier, natural law theorists argued that the topmost principles can be established by thinking about the requirements of human nature. More recently Gewirth (1967) has argued that the topmost principles can be established by thinking about the general requirements of moral action. Habermas has argued that they can be established by thinking about the requirements of human communication (Habermas, 1990). These examples suggest that another general way of determining the topmost principles of morality is to identify essential elements of the moral life, and then attempting to identify the general rules that must be recognized if those essential elements are to be possible.

Yet another view about how the supreme moral principles should be established has been advanced by some so-called intuitionists and some moral sense theorists. These have argued that the topmost principles of ethics are known by some kind of immediate apprehension that does not involve any kind of moral reasoning. On some interpretations, Aristotle and Aquinas can be read as holding such a theory since they both held that the faculty of "synderesis" grasped the topmost principles without relying on discursive reasoning. In the twentieth century, Ross (1930) advanced the claim that the principles of ethics are known by intuition. According to Ross moral knowledge arises when one notices that a particular feature of a concrete situation (e.g., the fact that I harmed someone) affects the morality of one's actions in that situation. Then, by an intuitive induction we realize that the property must affect the morality of all actions with that same property in any situation, and thus we come to know a general principle of morality. Each of these general principles, Ross held, give rise to merely "prima facie" obligations, and they must be weighed together with other general principles to determine what morality requires. Critics of Ross and other intuitionists have argued that intuitionism implies that things have moral properties or features, and that humans have a special faculty or sense that can somehow perceive these moral properties or features. Both of these assumptions are controversial.

Finally, it should be noted that some have questioned whether reasoning has any role at all to play in establishing moral principles. Hume (1740), for example, held that "reason is and ought to be the slave of the passions," by which he meant that reasoning always assumes the presence of a desire and can only determine the best means for satisfying given desires, being unable, therefore, to establish desires or ends on its own. In this view, moral reasoning cannot establish any moral principles because moral reasoning cannot establish any desires or passions. The only role of moral reasoning – indeed of all practical reasoning – is to determine the most effective or efficient means of satisfying those desires or passions that we already have.

An important related issue that has significant implications for moral reasoning is the so-called "is-ought thesis." The is-ought thesis holds that there is an unbridgeable logical gap between claims about what ought to be the case, and claims about what is the case. The gap is such that from claims expressing only what is the case, one cannot reason to claims about what ought to be the case. Sometimes the thesis is expressed as the view that from factual or descriptive claims alone, no normative or prescriptive claims follow. Hume (1740) is generally taken to have been the first to have asserted the thesis when he remarked that moralists often move almost imperceptibly from factual statements about what is the case to claims about what ought to be the case without justifying this move although it is of the last consequence. Hume asserts that a reason should be given, for what seems altogether inconceivable, how this new relation can be a deduction from others, which are entirely different from it.

The is-ought claim has been held to be especially damaging to naturalist theories of ethics. Naturalist theories of ethics hold that the topmost moral judgments are principles that identify some set of non-moral (i.e., natural) features or properties, $P_1. \ldots P_n$, that all and only morally right or morally good objects have. It is difficult to see how naturalist theories could be justified if the is-ought gap is accepted, since then from the fact that an object has the non-moral features, $P_1. \ldots P_n$, it would not follow that the object has any moral properties, unless one assumes some logically prior unjustified moral judgment to the effect that whatever has $P_1. \ldots P_n$ has those moral properties. But then this logically prior moral judgment would have to be justified, and how could it be justified unless one assumes another logically prior but unjustified moral judgment, etc. In short, naturalism is forced to rely on an unjustified moral judgment, and so the is-ought gap is often held to be a fatal objection to naturalism. The is-ought gap is also significant for reasoning that aims at bringing particular cases under more general rules. If the is-ought gap is real, then it is clear that moral reasoning that results in a moral judgment must, of necessity, appeal to prior moral judgments. Moral reasoning, that is, can never proceed from factual premises alone to any moral conclusions.

The is-ought thesis has had significant implications for business ethics, particularly in the way research in business ethics has been structured. Research in business ethics has tended to remain divided between two approaches: the normative approaches usually adopted by philosophers in liberal arts departments, and the empirical approaches usually taken by social scientists in business schools (Trevino and Weaver, 1994). Underlying the two approaches are assumptions about the value-laden nature of the normative approach proper to moral philosophy on the one hand, and the (ideally) value-free nature of the empirical approaches proper to social science research. The is-ought gap, it has been argued, implies that these two approaches "cannot be conceptually integrated" into a single theoretical approach (Donaldson, 1994) and so business ethics is doomed forever to be parceled into two fields divided by the is-ought gap.

But the is-ought thesis has not been accepted by all business ethicists (Werhane, 1994; Velasquez, 1996). The is-ought thesis assumes, obviously, that it is possible to distinguish adequately between factual or descriptive claims on the one hand, and normative or prescriptive claims on the other. But efforts to draw such a distinction have not been persuasive. To begin with, there is no obvious way of making the distinction on purely grammatical grounds. Some statements that intuitively, at least, seem as if they should count as normative statements are expressed with the verb "is" and seem to be descriptions ("Gonzales is kind." "Smith is fair."). While some statements that intuitively seem to be descriptive are nevertheless expressed with the verb "ought" ("It ought to rain tonight."). Some have suggested drawing the distinction by relying on a list of normative words such as "good," "right," "obligation," "duties," "rights," "kind," "fair," etc. With such a list in hand one can stipulate that normative claims are those that use one or more of the normative words, while descriptive claims are those that do not. But many of the normative words on such lists seem to occur in descriptive claims ("Jones has a right to speak."). Other ways of attempting to draw the distinction (such as the claim that descriptive claims are those that describe the existence of factual states of affairs or events) seem circular since they make use of the very concepts (e.g., "describe," "factual") that need to be explained.

But even if the difficulties involved in trying to distinguish factual from normative claims are set aside, the is-ought thesis encounters other significant problems. Searle (1964), for example, has argued that the thesis cannot be correct because there are clear counter examples to the thesis. In particular, he argues, there is a large group of institutional facts that are purely descriptive, yet which, by themselves, logically imply normative or prescriptive claims. The fact, for example, that an English speaker sincerely uttered the words, "I promise to do X," implies that that person promised to do X, and this in turn logically implies that the person put herself under an obligation to do what she promised, which then logically implies that, all things being equal, she ought to do what she promised. These implications hold, Searle argues, because it is "constitutive" of the institution of promising that when one promises one puts oneself under an obligation to do what one promises to do, and putting oneself under an obligation to do something, by definition implies that, all things being equal, one ought to do it. Searle's argument has been the subject of considerable controversy (Hudson, 1969).

Searle's argument is particularly relevant to business ethics because business is conducted within a network of interlocking institutions. Business contracts and practices, business organizations, and, more generally, the political and economic institutions within which businesses operate, are all institutions. If Searle is right, business institutions, like all social institutions, must be defined in terms of constitutive rights, duties, and obligations to which the business person becomes committed when he or she is engaged in business (Searle, 1995). Sheer descriptions of persons as involved in business activities (e.g., as being "managers" involved in "buying," "selling," or "contracting," for a "business"), then, cannot help but be value-laden and so must be simultaneously descriptive and normative. Indeed, it is arguable that business people are predominantly – and justifiably – guided by the norms that constitute the institutions within which their activities, relationships, and roles are embedded. If so, we should not expect moral reasoning in business to have to appeal to highly abstract moral rules, but should look, rather, at the fine-grained forms of reasoning that lead managers to decide what ought to be done by being attentive to the obligations implicit in the institutions within which they live their business lives.

Challenges to the Standard Conception

Virtue theory

Moral philosophy in general and business ethics in particular have recently seen the revival of virtue ethics, an approach to ethics that rejects the standard view that moral reasoning is based on general rules governing the rightness and wrongness of actions. Virtue ethics, instead, is focused on the character of persons, i.e., on the virtues and vices that make a person good or bad. Virtue theorists who have criticized the standard view's reliance on general rules have argued that in real life people do not decide what they ought to do by consulting a list of rules or principles, and that the moral life is to a large extent a matter of having the proper kinds of feelings and desires and not merely a matter of reasoning with the correct principles. A number of business ethicists have argued that virtue theory should serve as the foundations of business ethics (Solomon, 1992; Morris, 1997; Moberg, 1999).

Although virtue theory is sometimes criticized for having little to say about whether particular actions are right or wrong, this criticism is mistaken. Indeed, it would be strange if virtue theory had nothing to say about what morality requires in human behavior and yet purported to be a theory about how the moral life is to be lived. Virtue theorists insist, however, that judgments about virtue are more basic than judgments about action, i.e., that judgments about what actions are right must be derivative from judgments about what the virtues are. Aristotle, for example, proposed, first, that virtues are expressed or exercised in actions (the temperate man acts temperately and the brave man acts bravely) and, second, that certain kinds of actions develop virtues and others develop vices (repeated temperate acts develop temperance, while repeated cowardly behavior develops cowardliness). Combining these two relationships, a virtue theorist can say that an action (or, by extension, an institution, organization, or policy) is morally right if the action either

1   promotes a virtue, or
2   expresses a virtue

and morally wrong if it either promotes or expresses vice (Smith, 1993). On this model of the relation between virtue and action, moral reasoning is at least in part a matter of considering how behaviors relate both to the promotion and to the exercise of virtues and vices. That is, moral reasoning aims, first, at uncovering the relations between behaviors, institutions, policies, and organizational forms, on the one hand, and the development of virtue and vice on the other. Institutions, behaviors, policies, and organizational forms that hinder the development of virtue or that encourage the development of vice would be judged as immoral and hence to be avoided, while those that promote the virtues while extinguishing vice would be judged as moral and hence to be pursued. Moral reasoning also aims, second, at determining what virtue requires in given circumstances. An important strain of virtue theory, also originating with Aristotle, holds that the virtuous person's judgments about what virtue requires in a given set of circumstance are authoritative; in the final analysis, what the virtuous person believes is right, is right. This view has seemed to some to endorse a form of intuitionism, i.e., the view that at least some of us – presumably those among us who are virtuous – have the ability to recognize without discursive reasoning what virtue requires in a given set of circumstances. However, the claim that right actions are those that the virtuous person knows are right can be interpreted as asserting that the virtuous person has certain cognitive, affective, and perceptual competencies and sensitivities that enable her to reason correctly about what ought to be done in a given set of circumstances. Her judgments can be relied on, then, because she has the competencies required to render these judgments. Still, virtue theory leaves unclear the reasoning processes by which a person with virtue is supposed to discern the right action.

Moreover, a special form of moral reasoning is obviously needed to determine what the virtues are. On this issue (how one determines what the virtues are) there is little consensus. Aristotle, for example, claimed that the virtues are excellences that represent the full development of a human being's rational and nonrational capacities. Determining what the virtues are, then, would entail determining what a fully developed adult human being would be like and what his or her rational and nonrational capacities would be like. On this view of the virtues, moral reasoning aimed at identifying the virtues would proceed by appealing to a view of what the ideally perfect human being would be like, and determine the virtues by reference to this ideal. Many ethicists, for obvious reasons, have rejected this perfectionist approach. A different approach adopted by some virtue theorists is to conceptualize the virtues as competencies that enable one to achieve certain goods. MacIntyre (1981), for example, has argued that the virtues are those acquired characteristics that enable persons to achieve the "goods internal to practices." Yet another approach is that of Pincoffs (1986) who defines the virtues as dispositions that are "generally desirable" because they make a person good at dealing with situations that are typical of the conditions that human life frequently and typically sets before us, "conditions, that is, under which human beings must (given the nature of the physical world and of human nature and human association) live." Each of these approaches, obviously, would imply distinct methods of reasoning about what the virtues are.

Particularists

A second important challenge to the standard approach to moral reasoning – i.e., the approach that assumes that moral reasoning consists of subsuming particular cases under general rules – is a criticism brought by so-called Particularists who, like virtue theorists, hold that moral reasoning should not be conceptualized as relying on general rules. Particularists argue, in fact, that general rules or principles cannot serve as useful guides for reasoning about what one ought to do in a particular situation because each situation has its own contextually significant details and these details, different from one situation to the next, have a bearing on what morality requires in the situation (Dancy, 1993). Some argue that the situational demands of friendship, love, or loyalty often override the claims of impartial moral principles (Blum, 1980). Consequently, moral reasoning cannot be a matter of subsuming particular cases under general principles because particular cases differ from each other too much to make the appeal to general principles useful. Instead, Particularists claim, moral reasoning about what one ought to do in a particular situation must proceed by scrutinizing the particular details of the situation and making a decision that is based on one's judgment about which particular details are morally relevant and which have a decisive bearing on the morality of the situation. Moral principles and moral rules can play a heuristic role in moral reasoning by reminding us of the considerations that have previously been significant in the kind of situation we may be contemplating and so they can lead us to be attentive to and alert for the presence of those considerations in the present situation. But any of the myriad particular features of the situation, and the complexities created by their interrelations, may overwhelm the significance of considerations that had previously seemed decisive in the kind of situation now being contemplated. In previous situations, for example, I may have realized that it was wrong to lie, but now, in my present situation, I may see that if I tell the truth I will not only deeply hurt you, but will also push you into seriously harming someone else. Dienhart (1995) has advocated such an approach in business ethics, arguing that moral reasoning in business ethics should not be "rule governed," but should be much more like the reasoning by which a doctor decides to treat an illness in one way rather than another.

Recently, some ethicists have called attention to an ancient form of moral reasoning that is quite different from subsuming particular cases under general laws and that is quite amenable to the claims of Particularists. This is casuistry, a form of moral reasoning that dominated moral theorizing for several centuries, particularly in the late medieval and early modern period (Jonsen and Toulmin, 1988). The term "casuistry" derives from the Latin word *casus*, meaning "case" and refers to a method of moral reasoning that appeals to particular cases – not general rules – to determine what morality requires. Casuistry proceeds by adverting to previously settled moral judgments about specific cases or specific issues, and determining the morality of new cases or issues by noting how these new cases are analogous to or different from those that have already been settled. (In some respects, casuistic reasoning is similar to legal reasoning that proceeds by identifying relevant precedents, interpreting them, and attempting to apply the precedents to new cases by noting how the new cases are similar to or different from the settled precedents.) A key idea is the view that the detailed circumstances of a case determine its moral properties, so that two actions that are otherwise quite similar, may have different moral properties because they are embedded in different circumstances. Thomas Aquinas (1273), for example, wrote: "The human act ought to vary according to diverse conditions of persons, time, and other circumstances: this is the entire matter of morality."

Casuistic reasoning emerged as a systematic form of reasoning in the handbooks that clergymen used in the middle ages to help them discern what was and was not sinful, and in the large textbooks of moral theology developed in the later middle ages by Roman Catholic theologians who attempted to collect and systematize the moral judgments of these earlier traditions. Casuistry flourished in Europe from about the thirteenth through the seventeenth century. During the heyday of casuistry, numerous theologians wrote lengthy works describing hundreds of cases and indicating the moral judgments that various well-known moralists had made about these cases. One of the longest of these works, by Antonius Diana, included over 20,000 cases and extended over ten volumes.

A form of casuistry made its reappearance in the 1970s when business ethicists began to emphasize the dissection and analysis of particular cases, and several cases became classics such as the Ford Pinto case, the Johnson & Johnson Tylenol case, and the Love Canal case. Some ethicists have suggested that business ethics should devote itself to collecting and systematizing such cases. In their view, moral reasoning should be taught by acquainting students with these cases so as to develop their moral judgment and so as to enable them to discern how the business situations in which they later find themselves are similar to or different from these cases. But it is not clear that such a new form of casuistry is really possible. In the older tradition of casuistry, the views and judgments of the moral theologian – who was, generally, part of the Church's clergy – were perceived as being authoritative. Such an authoritative status is absent from the judgments made by contemporary ethicists.

Conclusion

The two main forms of moral reasoning briefly reviewed above – moral reasoning as the subsumption of particular cases under general rules, and moral reasoning as the exercise of judgment about particulars without reliance on general rules – have significant implications both for the theory and the practice of business ethics. Enough has been said about the theoretical implications, but perhaps a bit more should be added in conclusion about the implications for certain practices: training in and teaching of business ethics. Numerous companies have instituted business ethics programs that attempt to provide employees with training in business ethics and virtually all business schools now require their students to take courses in business ethics. On the traditional conception of moral reasoning, such corporate programs and school courses should attempt to introduce participants to the general moral rules that embody the requirements of morality, and should, perhaps, provide some practice in the use of these rules by discussing particular business cases to which the rules can be applied. On the other hand, the non-rule conception of moral reasoning implies that ethics training in companies, as well as business school courses in ethics, should focus only on the discussion of particular business cases with a view to developing the judgment of participants and with a view toward building a repertoire of cases that participants can use as paradigmatic models for deciding future cases in which they may become involved. Both approaches have become common. It is unclear which, if either, will predominate.

References

Aquinas, T. 1273: *Summa Theologiae*, trans. (1947) by Fathers of the English Dominican Province. New York: Benziger Brothers.

Aristotle, c. 350 BC: *Nicomachean Ethics*, trans. W. D. Ross, in *The Complete Works of Aristotle*, vol. 2, Princeton, NJ: Princeton University Press.

Blum, L. 1980: *Friendship, Altruism, and Morality*. London: Routledge and Kegan Paul.

Boatright, J. 1999: *Ethics and the Conduct of Business*. Englewood Cliffs, NJ: Prentice Hall.

Bowie, N. 1999: *Business Ethics: A Kantian Perspective*. Oxford: Blackwell.

Brady, F. N. 1990: *Ethical Managing: Rules and Results*. New York: MacMillan.

Brady, F. N. and Dunn, C. P. 1995: Business meta-ethics. *Business Ethics Quarterly*, 5, 385–98.

Brandt, R. 1979: *A Theory of the Good and the Right*. Oxford: Clarendon Press.

Dancy, J. 1993: *Moral Reasons*. Oxford: Blackwell.

De George, R. 1999: *Business Ethics*, 3rd edn., New York: MacMillan.

Dienhart, J. 1995: Rationality, ethical codes, and an egalitarian justification of ethical expertise, *Business Ethics Quarterly*, 5, 419–50.

Donaldson, T. 1989: *The Ethics of International Business*. New York: Oxford.

Donaldson, T. 1994: When integration fails: the logic of prescription and description in business ethics, *Business Ethics Quarterly*, 4, 157–69.

Elfstrom, G. 1991: *Moral Issues and Multinational Corporations*. New York: St. Martin's Press.

Finnis, J. 1983: *Fundamentals of Ethics*. Washington, D.C.: Georgetown University Press.

Gensler, H. J. 1996: *Formal Ethics*. New York: Routledge.

Gewirth, A. 1967: Categorical consistency in ethics, *Philosophical Quarterly*, 17, 289–99.

Gewirth, A. 1987: The golden rule rationalized, *Midwest Studies in Philosophy*, 3, 133–44.

Green, R. 1994: *The Ethical Manager*. New York: MacMillan.

Habermas, J. 1990: *Moral Consciousness and Communicative Action*. Cambridge, MA: MIT Press.

Hare, R. M. 1975: Abortion and the golden rule, *Philosophy and Public Affairs*, 3, 201–22.

Hudson, W. D. 1969: ed., *The Is/Ought Question*. London: Macmillan.

Hume, D. 1740: *A Treatise of Human Nature*. L. A. Selby-Bigge ed., Oxford: Clarendon Press, 2nd edn., 1978.

Jonsen, A. and Toulmin, S. 1988: *The Abuse of Casuistry: A History of Moral Reasoning*. Berkeley, CA: University of California Press.

Kant, I. 1964 [1785]: *Groundwork of the Metaphysics of Morals*. Trans. H. J. Paton, New York: Harper & Row.

MacIntyre, A. 1981: *After Virtue*. Notre Dame, IN: University of Notre Dame Press.

Mill, J. S. 1957 [1861]: *Utilitarianism*. Indianapolis, Bobbs-Merrill Company, Inc.

Moberg, D. 1999: The Big Five and organizational virtue. *Business Ethics Quarterly*, 9, 245–72.

Morris, T. V. 1997: *If Aristotle Ran General Motors*. New York: Henry Hold & Co.

Nagel, T. 1979: The fragmentation of value, in *Mortal Questions*. Cambridge: Cambridge University Press, 126–42.

Pamental, G. L. 1991: The course in business ethics: Why don't the philosophers give business students what they need? *Business Ethics Quarterly*, 1, 385–93.

Pincoffs, E. L. 1986: *Quandaries and Virtues*. Lawrence, Kansas: University Press of Kansas.

Rawls, J. 1971: *A Theory of Justice*. Cambridge, MA: Harvard University Press.

Ross, W. D. 1930: *The Right and the Good*. Oxford: Oxford University Press.

Searle, J. 1964: How to derive "ought" from "is" *Philosophical Review*, 73, 43–58

Searle, J. 1995: *The Construction of Social Reality*. New York: Basic Books.

Singer, P. 1974: Sidgwick and reflective equilibrium, *Monist*, 58, 490–517.

Smith, J. 1993: Moral character and abortion, in J. G. Habert (ed.), *Doing and Being*. New York: Macmillan, 442–56.

Solomon, R. C. 1992: *Ethics and Excellence: Cooperation and Integrity in Business*. New York: Oxford University Press.

Stark, A. 1993: What's the matter with business ethics?. *Harvard Business Review*, 71, 38–48.

Stoker, M. 1990: *Plural and Conflicting Values*. Oxford: Oxford University Press.

Trevino, L. K. and Weaver, G. R. 1994: Business ETHICS/BUSINESS ethics: One field or two? *Business Ethics Quarterly*, 4, 113–28.

Urmson, J. O. 1974–5: A defense of intuitionism. *Proceedings of the Aristotelian Society*, 75, 111–20.

Velasquez, M. 1996: Business ethics, the social sciences, and moral philosophy. *Social Justice Research*, 8, 324–35.

Velasquez, M. 2001: *Business Ethics: Concepts and Cases*. 5th edn, Upper Saddle River, NJ: Prentice Hall.

Velasquez, M., Cavanagh, J. and Moberg, D. 1995: Making business ethics practical. *Business Ethics Quarterly*, 5, 399–418.

Wattles, J. 1996: *The Golden Rule*. Oxford: Oxford University Press.

Werhane, P. 1994: The normative/descriptive distinction in methodologies of business ethics. *Business Ethics Quarterly*, 4, 175–80.

Chapter 6

Teaching and Learning Ethics by the Case Method

Kenneth E. Goodpaster

A Philosopher's Odyssey

When I joined the Harvard Business School faculty in 1980, a wayward philosopher seeking to connect ethical theory with management education, I confronted an enormous intellectual and cultural gap. I discovered that philosophers were trained to think differently from professional managers. They usually *zigged* when managers *zagged*. They *ascended* the ladder of reflection toward premises and assumptions when managers *descended* the ladder toward pragmatics and action; they often insisted on *examining* a goal or purpose while managers often cared more about *implementing* it.

The effect was, at first, exasperating. Both the substance and the style of my training ran counter to the distinctive practical orientation of business administration. Nevertheless, I was convinced that philosophy – specifically *moral* philosophy or *ethics* – had as much to offer as to gain from a "joint venture" with management education.

On the *gain* side, there was the practice-oriented pedagogy of the case method. Moral philosophy in the twentieth century had been preoccupied with conceptual analysis. Questions about the meanings of terms like "right" and "good" had dominated the philosophical landscape to the exclusion of questions about what *actions* are right and what *things* are good. Conceptual analysis had run amok in many ways and a return to "applied" ethics (that would-be redundancy) was needed.

What philosophy had to *offer* was an inheritance and a talent. The inheritance was a body of thought about the nature of ethics and the human condition that had developed over more than two millennia. The talent was an eye and an ear for distinguishing cogent reasoning from its counterfeits. At a time when the ethical aspects of professional management were coming under increasing scrutiny, this seemed like a valuable resource.

Learning aimed at integrating ethics and management education called for a different pedagogy. Professor Donald Schön of MIT once suggested an image that may have special meaning in this context:

> In the varied topography of professional practice, there is a high, hard ground which overlooks a swamp. On the high ground, manageable problems lend themselves to solution through the use of research-based theory and technique. In the swampy lowlands, problems are messy and confusing and incapable of technical solution. The irony of this situation is that the problems of the high ground tend to be relatively unimportant to individuals or to society at large, however great their technical interest may be, while in the swamp lie the problems of greatest human concern. The practitioner is confronted with a choice. Shall he remain on the high ground where he can solve relatively unimportant problems according to his standards of rigor, or shall he descend to the swamp of important problems and non-rigorous inquiry?

I found myself departing the high ground and entering the swamp. In the process, I came to believe that if the field of business ethics were to have a future, a new kind of discipline would have to be formed that did not yet exist. A generation of educators was needed that could think and teach using the skills of management education *and* the reflectiveness of moral philosophy at the same time.

On the advice of several Harvard colleagues, therefore, I learned business policy by the case method. Never mind that I was on the instructor's side of the desk. I considered myself a learner. I had to relinquish my "expertise" to learn. It was like starting a second career after having become established in a first. But my students and faculty colleagues helped.

I learned the hard way and the only way: *from teaching and from practice.* At first, I could not appreciate the so-called administrative point of view – how competent managers think about problems; the way they identify issues, formulate and implement strategy, generate action plans. This appreciation was neither part of my experience nor part of my background in moral philosophy. I had to walk in the moccasins of the general manager. I had to puzzle over the strategic, organizational, and interpersonal challenges that general managers face. And I had to do it *case by case.*

I gained a new respect for the vocation of the manager, charting a course amidst the uncertainties of physical events and human nature: trying to motivate others, remaining loyal to providers of resources, setting goals, imposing new structures, monitoring progress and performance, achieving purpose through cooperation and the exercise of authority. I listened and I learned how different was the mind of the manager from the mind of the philosopher. Not better or worse. *Different.*

There were challenges on the other side of the desk too. My first classes in business ethics, using the case method, were no small challenge to my students. On some days, looks of glazed incomprehension were a relief from looks of irritation. What had Plato or John Stuart Mill to do with this marketing strategy and these accounting practices? What was the point of comparing and contrasting utilitarian and social contract theories of justice? But they learned, often in spite of their professor, that questioning *ends* was healthy and that questioning *means* to ends was healthy too; that moral reasoning was more than shooting from the hip; and that their fellow students were actually following certain tried and true patterns in the way they joined their realism with their idealism.

The "joint venture" eventually began to happen. It happened as I acknowledged that the frameworks and concepts that are the stock-in-trade of philosophy often blush in the face of the complexity and concreteness of management decisions. What was needed was an ethical *point of view*, not an ethical *algorithm*. I had believed this many years ago, but had forgotten it. I began to change, to think differently. Outer dialogues became inner dialogues. A case method teacher had joined the philosopher in me, and slowly the case method had become my philosophy of moral education.

Can Ethics be Taught?

Some questions have staying power, and this question from Plato's dialogue, the *Meno*, is certainly one of them: "Can you tell me, Socrates, whether virtue is acquired by teaching or by practice; or if neither by teaching nor practice, then whether it comes to man by nature or in what other way?" (Plato, 1949). It is a question that invites us to probe not one, but two profound ideas in tandem: teaching and virtue. In this essay, I will follow Plato's classical lead, as I explore the meaning of the case method (a learner-centered form of teaching) in the context of business ethics (an organizational and commercial opportunity for virtue).

Teaching is perhaps less mysterious when it is not practical, just as *virtue* is less mysterious when the challenge does not include passing it on. We understand reasonably well how to communicate information and intellectual skills in an educational environment (information about history or skills like computer programming or factoring in algebra). And we understand reasonably well that ethics is about cultivating the moral point of view (and habits of the heart such as prudence, courage, benevolence, and fairness). But when we move education into the ethical arena, or ethics into the educational arena, our understanding seems to weaken.

I propose to discuss not just the case method in isolation – others have done this with distinction; see Lynn (1999), plus Christensen (1987), Andrews (1954) and the classic article by Gragg (1940). Nor do I propose to discuss the field of business ethics in general, something I have done on several previous occasions (Goodpaster, 1997a,b,c,d; 2000a,b,c). Instead, my focus will be on *the case method as a form of pedagogy particularly suited to the subject matter of business ethics*. If the answer to the question of Socrates is that ethics *cannot* be taught, it will not be for lack of trying the most promising (Socratic) pedagogy available: the case method.

In this section, I shall sketch some key features of the case method in action. In later sections, the focus will be on the power of the case method as a pedagogy for ethics.

What is the case method – in aspiration and in action?

The term "case study" is used differently in different contexts. It can mean an anecdote or a clipping from the *Wall Street Journal* used by a professor to illustrate an idea discussed in the classroom (a "case in point"). It can mean a report on a topic or an event describing the empirical results of a study of that topic or event (a "study"). It can mean a summary description of the issue, arguments, and verdict of a judicial proceeding (Harvard Law School "cases"). Or it can mean a narrative designed and written to provide learners with an occasion for engaging one another in a dynamic classroom environment (Harvard Business School "case method"). This essay is about the pedagogy surrounding the last-mentioned meaning of "case" or "case study."

In the words of a classic essay on the case method by Charles I. Gragg (1940):

> A case typically is a record of a business situation that *actually* has been faced by business executives, together with surrounding facts, opinions, and prejudices upon which executive decisions had to depend. These real and particularized cases are presented to students for considered analysis, open discussion, and final decision as to the type of action that should be taken.

The idea behind the case method in the *ethical* arena is to offer the learner a vicarious decision-making opportunity so that both moral and managerial judgment can be exercised, indeed actively *practiced*. For this reason, cases are sometimes presented in sequenced parts to simulate decisions in one part (e.g., the "A" case) that give rise to new decisions in subsequent parts (e.g., the "B," and "C" cases). To quote Gragg (1940) again:

> The outstanding virtue of the case system is that it is suited to inspiring activity, under realistic conditions, on the part of the students; it takes them out of the role of passive absorbers and makes them partners in the joint process of learning and furthering learning.

Given this understanding of the "virtue of the case system," the role of the instructor in the process is crucial. For the instructor guides the special "partnership" in the classroom using various techniques, among them structured questioning, instructor feedback, role playing, breakout team activities, and written case analysis assignments. More recently, Internet technology has enhanced case method teaching and learning through threaded discussions in "virtual" classrooms.

Structured questioning The Socratic character of the case method is nowhere more evident than in the structured questioning that the instructor brings to the material for the day. Questions must be aimed at eliciting the learners' analysis of the important problems, the key decision maker, and a defense of the preferred course of action. Questions can be addressed to *specific* students in the class, especially at the opening of the discussion, which eventually widens out to *any* participant with a comment on the topic at hand. These "first tier" questions are followed up by questions that probe deeper or seek to clarify the student's meaning. Typically, questions will have either a diagnostic or a therapeutic backdrop. That is, the class will seek either to understand more fully the nature of the presenting problem or will explore a solution in the form of a sequence of action steps. Sometimes the instructor will want to elicit more detail from students about the circumstances in the case – and this will call for "When?" "Where?" "What?" and "Who?" questions. At other times, the instructor will be looking more for explanations or justifications – escalating the conversation using "Why?" questions. A thoughtful outline of the various paths of questioning to be explored during the discussion period is important preparation for structured questioning.

Instructor feedback Instructor responses to the learner after a question has been posed and answered are critical variables in case method discussion. Feedback can have several purposes, among them clarification, assessment, reinforcement, and transition. Re-phrasing a student's comment in order to clarify it – always inviting the student to accept or reject the re-phrasing – can be an effective tool in guiding discussion. Sometimes it can exhibit *more starkly* the implications of the student's remarks, leading to more energetic engagement from the rest of the group. ("You said we should *discipline* Mr. West. Do you really mean *fire* him?") Feedback can also involve assessing a student's remark, applauding it for insight or pointing out that it is inconsistent with certain facts in the case. Using a chalkboard, flip chart, or overhead transparency to record visually the unfolding of the discussion provides another opportunity for feedback. Students notice whether and how their comments are recorded as affirmations of their relevance and significance. Feedback can also provide the instructor an opportunity to shift the focus of the discussion or to segue to another topic entirely. ("In the wake of that comment, I think we can now shift from our diagnosis of the problem to an action plan . . .")

Role playing Addressing structured questions and feedback to individuals or sub-groups in the class by casting them into *roles* can be a very effective discussion tool. ("I'd like the left side of the room to take the shareholders' point of view on this management decision, and the right side of the room to play the role of the customers who are looking for more safety features in the product.") Role playing leads the students to take on points of view they might not have appreciated during their preparation of the case, and it models a kind of stakeholder awareness that instructors usually want to encourage, especially in ethics (see the next section, page 124).

Breakout team activities Often small-group breakout activities can energize case discussion and enhance learning, especially when the class is sizable (25–75). Students have more opportunity to speak in small groups, learn team-building and representation skills, and simulate real-life decision making. ("Let's break into five groups, each charged with the following two questions as the product liability jury was in the case study; then report back to the full class after 20 minutes.") The instructor will benefit greatly from silently listening in on the small-group discussions, often discerning student behaviors that are different from those in the full class.

Written case analysis assignments Individual student learning and feedback opportunities are best provided through written case analysis assignments. These need not be lengthy assignments (3–5 pages often suffice), but they provide a window for the instructor on student progress and a gateway for intervention if remedial study is needed.

Threaded discussions in "virtual" classrooms During the mid-1990s, on-line technology became more widely available, which allows for asynchronous, threaded discussions among students (and between students and instructors) outside the physical and temporal confines of the classroom. This technology, while perhaps less personal than classroom communication, makes it possible for interactive discussion to continue "outside of class" (usually before the time of the next class). For large classes in which "air time" for student participation is relatively scarce, and especially for students who for various reasons are less verbally active in the regular classroom, the virtual classroom provides a convenient enhancement to case method learning.

The above-mentioned features of case method interaction between instructor and learner illustrate the *dynamics* of this pedagogy, beyond the written document (the "case") that provides the essential substrate for the process. A good case method instructor who researches and writes cases for classroom use will also prepare a second document – called a *teaching note* – not for the student audience, but for other instructors considering the case for *their* classes (Goodpaster and Nash, 1998).

The teaching note: Slowing down time

Teaching notes can take many forms, but typically they are pedagogical essays, several pages in length, which contain an abstract of the case or case series in question, learning objectives, specific teaching questions and sub-questions with observations about the direction of discussion. Some teaching notes also include suggestions about classroom process, timing and case preparation, design layouts for chalkboards or flip charts that help organize the discussion, and summary bullet points for the instructor to use in winding up the case discussion.

The function of the teaching note is to provide a reflective guide for instructors who might wish to include the case (or cases) in question within their courses. There can, of course, be more than one teaching note for a given case, especially if the case has versatility in the curriculum. Teaching notes serve as formal reminders of the spirit of case method pedagogy as it empowers (with an "inside view") teachers who might be new to the specific facts of a given case narrative.

Teaching notes help put into practice one of the principal learning opportunities afforded by the case method: *slowing down time*. Comedian George Carlin, commenting on the paradoxes of our time in history, once remarked that "we have bigger houses and smaller families; more conveniences, but less time; we have more degrees, but less sense; more knowledge, but less judgment; more experts, but more problems; more medicine, but less wellness."

We can view the case method as a device for slowing time in a decision-making situation, so that learners are able to build habits of discernment otherwise hindered by the sheer velocity of business life. Like a football team viewing and discussing videotapes in slow motion after key games, management students prepare for their futures by practicing on realistic decision situations with minimal urgency.

Properly *processed* in the classroom, cases offer learners the opportunity to think through the details of a decision situation slowly, "try out" ideas on their peers, and debate the merits of decisions and action plans. This means that learners must expect and be responsible for the kind of *preparation* necessary for such a process. These learners are most often professionals, such as MBA students, but they can also be younger (high school, college) or older (life-long learners).

Limitations of case method pedagogy

Case method pedagogy also has important *limitations*. The classroom and the case study are not replacements for reality and experience. No matter how true-to-life the situations are, they are not decided in a real-life setting. Student decision-makers are subject to no risks from amateurish or unreasoned actions, nor can their conclusions be easily tested by subsequent developments in the business situation. As Gragg (1940) comments, "It is too much to expect that anything except experience can be exactly like experience."

Another limitation is that a case can never present all the facts in a situation. Facts in the narrative must of necessity be selected by the casewriter, who generally has a particular expository purpose in mind. Some "facts" are personal reports of events from interviews with the parties involved, and this can introduce evaluation and possible bias. Some cases use press reports as a source of information but the media sometimes have axes to grind in their accounts of corporate action (or inaction). Neutral and complete factual accounts are virtually impossible in case narratives, but then it is well to remember that real life situations seldom present themselves in factually neutral and complete ways.

In summary, as we view the question "Can ethics be taught?" – mindful of the aspiration and practice of the case method – we see that certain prerequisites must be in place for success:

- Well-written and well-researched case narratives
- Instructional techniques (including new forms of online technology) that encourage active learning by "slowing down time"
- Clear expectations about preparation to learners
- Carefully written teaching notes for the preparation of instructors
- A recognition of the inevitable limitations of the case method

Let us now focus more directly on our principal quarry – the learning of *ethics* through case method pedagogy.

Business Ethics and the Case Method

In the context of business ethics, the case method aims at *moral insight* – the ability to discern right and wrong, good and bad, virtue and vice as they pertain to persons within organizations or organizations within the wider society. Harvard philosopher Josiah Royce defined *the moral insight* in his book *The Religious Aspect of Philosophy* (Royce, 1865):

> The moral insight is the realization of one's neighbor, in the full sense of the word realization; the resolution to treat him unselfishly. But this resolution expresses and belongs to the moment of insight. Passion may cloud the insight after no very long time. It is as impossible for us to avoid the illusion of selfishness in our daily lives, as to escape seeing through the illusion at the moment of insight. We see the reality of our neighbor, that is, we determine to treat him as we do ourselves. But then we go back to daily action, and we feel the heat of hereditary passions, and we straightway forget what we have seen. Our neighbor becomes obscured. He is once more a foreign power. He is unreal. We are again deluded and selfish. This conflict goes on and will go on as long as we live after the manner of men. Moments of insight, with their accompanying resolutions; long stretches of delusion and selfishness: That is our life.

The moral insight lies at the foundation of the Golden Rule, the oldest and most widely shared ethical precept known to us. The moral insight is about reciprocity between self-love and love of "one's neighbor" (or more generally, "stakeholders"). Understanding and appreciating the moral insight as the *aim* of case teaching, then, is essential for linking this *insight* with the *method*.

Also essential is understanding the *attitude* with which the case method instructor pursues the moral insight of the learner. Let us take up this attitudinal point first. Then we shall look at a case method tool for approaching the moral insight.

Teaching ethics with an attitude: Making or doing?

Some years ago, I wrote an article for the *Hastings Center Report* (Goodpaster, 1982) in which I argued that the teaching of ethics was not an attempt to *produce* something, to intervene in the lives of learners for the sake of *results* that can be measured at the end of the process. Instead, I said (and still believe) "the teacher seeks to foster a certain kind of growth, but more as a leader of active inquiry than as a therapist or physician." I concluded:

> The subtle contract between teacher and student, especially in the context of adult ethics education, carries in most instances a provision that might read something like this, if it were ever written down: "The teacher is here to work *with* you, not *on* you." One wonders whether the psychological model of moral development, freighted with the discourse of the laboratory and human subjects, would not undermine the very effort it seeks to foster, a kind of moral version of Heisenberg's Uncertainty Principle. This is not to imply that impartiality and objectivity in student evaluation are impossible or undesirable. But the impartiality of the educator is distinguishable from the detachment of the experimenter – and the teacher's effectiveness can be lost by not paying heed to that distinction (Goodpaster, 1982).

The convictions defended in this passage are born of years of personal experience teaching ethics by conventional methods at the University of Notre Dame, and then by the case method at both the Harvard Business School and the University of St. Thomas. The role of the educator in the context of the case method is implied in the Latin roots of the word *educate*, i.e., to *lead out, to elicit*. The wisdom and ethical awareness being sought lie *in the learner*, and it is the mission of the instructor to lead it out. Wisdom "can't be told" in Gragg's memorable phrase, because it does not reside in the instructor to be *conveyed* by some mechanism (like *telling*) to the learner.

Case method pedagogy and moral epistemology

For many philosophers, some of whom are strangers to the case method in the context of ethics education, the foregoing observations are not free of controversy. An occupational hazard of philosophy teaching may be a posture that emphasizes content and rigor, minimizing the importance of a learner-centered process. For this reason, we philosophers are well advised to recall the eloquent reflection of William James in his 1891 essay entitled "The Moral Philosopher and the Moral Life."

> The philosopher is just like the rest of us non-philosophers, so far as we are just and sympathetic instinctively, and so far as we are open to the voice of complaint. His function is in fact indistinguishable from that of the best kind of statesman at the present day. His books upon ethics, therefore, so far as they truly touch the moral

life, must more and more ally themselves with a literature which is confessedly tentative and suggestive rather than dogmatic, – I mean with novels and dramas of the deeper sort, with sermons, with books on statecraft and philanthropy and social and economic reform. Treated in this way, ethical treatises may be voluminous and luminous as well; but they never can be final, except in their abstractest and vaguest features; and they must more and more abandon the old-fashioned, clear-cut, and would-be "scientific" form (James, 1962 [1891]).

An attentive observer in a successful case method ethics classroom, therefore, would see that "what's going on" is less often dogmatic presenting and more often questioning aimed at *forming habits that lead to moral insight*. Critical thinking in ethics is essential, of course, but our understanding of critical thinking must be compatible with the circumstantial realities of human decision makers. For all decisions seem in the end to be a matter of *balancing* by the parties involved. This is a philosophical point, not an accidental side constraint. Inevitably, it means an approach to moral knowledge that is *pluralistic*, that permits several basic methods or principles to be in tension or conflict with one another.

Some fear that the ultimate destination of such a pluralistic approach is some form of relativism or subjectivism. But this is certainly not evident and does not follow from the absence of a moral framework based on a single principle. We must not fall into the trap of identifying moral *pluralism* with moral *relativism*. Moral pluralism is the view that (singular) decision procedures or algorithms are not available to resolve moral arguments. Moral relativism is the view that moral argument is hopelessly fated to lead us in diverse directions, and consequently that a common vision, a moral community, is impossible. The two are not the same, conceptually or practically. One can, and probably should, embrace pluralism with discipline and reject its relativistic counterfeit.

As James implies, studying on a case-by-case basis the challenges of decision making under conditions of uncertainty and personal and institutional imperfection can raise difficult questions for philosophers. Try as they might to achieve positions variously described as archangelic, original, and ideal, decision makers whose problems set the agenda in applied ethics usually "can't get there from here." Neither can the rest of us. But there are some ways to be practical about the limitations of ethical theory.

The CAT scan

An approach to an ethics case that avoids both too much and too little analytical rigor involves doing what I call a "CAT Scan" – and I thank the Centre for Multimedia Development (CMD) for their contribution to the execution of this idea. A *case analysis template*, a matrix for the ethical analysis of cases, is described (and displayed) in *Figure 6.1*. When learners are presented with an administrative situation calling for analysis and judgment, certain questions suggest themselves naturally as an initial inventory:

"C.A.T. Scan" [*Case Analysis Template*]				
CASE ANALYSIS STEPS (5 D's) ↓	INTEREST-BASED OUTLOOK	RIGHTS-BASED OUTLOOK	DUTY-BASED OUTLOOK	VIRTUE-BASED OUTLOOK
DESCRIBE	How did the situation come about? What are the key presenting issues? Who are the key individuals and groups affected by the situation, the *stakeholders*?			
	Identify interests.	Identify rights.	Identify duties.	Identify virtues.
DISCERN	What is the most significant of the "presenting issues" – the one that might lie underneath it all? And who are the core stakeholders involved in the case?			
	Are there conflicting interests with respect to this issue, and how basic are they?	Are there rights in conflict with interests or with other rights? Are some weightier than others?	Does duty come into the picture – and are there tensions with rights or interests? Can I prioritize?	Is character an issue in this case – habits that bring us to this point or that will be reinforced later?
DISPLAY	What are the principal realistic *options* available to the decision maker(s) in this case, including possible branching among sub-options – leading to a set of action plans?			
DECIDE	What is my *considered judgment* on the best option to take from those listed above?			
DEFEND	Which of the avenues predominates in my choice of options above, and can I give *good reasons* for preferring the ethical priorities I have adopted in this case that are consistent with other such cases? What would an imaginary jury of the four "voices" decide and why? What is my moral framework?			

Figure 6.1 Case analysis template ("C.A.T. Scan")

- Are there ethically significant *issues* in this case and do they call for a decision?
- Do I understand the *genesis* of the problems in the case – how they came to be?
- Can I *discern* amidst the sometimes complex issues in the case situation those that are the keys to the resolution of all the others? Is there a most *salient* moral challenge?
- What are several realistic *alternatives* or options from which the decision maker in the case must choose in responding to the most salient challenge?

How does each option look through the principal normative lenses of ethical reasoning?
- What is my recommended *decision* and my suggested *action plan* for implementing it?
- Can I give others and myself a reasonable *justification* for the selection of this alternative or option from among those available? If each normative lens represents a moral "voice," are the voices in harmony or are they in discord?
- If harmony, does this fit with my moral common sense?
- If discord, which "voice" should prevail or override? Can I explain why?
- Am I prepared to see this *kind* of resolution in similar cases when the normative lenses appear to be in conflict?

To apply the above inventory of questions more directly and to make them easier to remember, we can organize them first into a five-step case analysis sequence (the "*5 D's*"):

- *Describe* – the key factual elements of the situation
- *Discern* – the most significant ethical issues at stake
- *Display* – the main options available to the decision maker
- *Decide* – among the options and offer a plan of action
- *Defend* – your decision and your moral framework

These "Ds" order the case analysis process from beginning to end, naming the *rows* of an analytical matrix or template. The *columns* of the matrix are based on what I have elsewhere called the four principal normative lenses (or "avenues") leading to the moral insight (Goodpaster, 1998).

A comprehensive review of the many ways in which philosophers, past and present, have identified the principal normative lenses of ethics is beyond the scope of this essay. It is possible, however, to sketch briefly the recurrent normative views that have been proposed.

Interest-based avenues One of the most influential types of ethical reasoning, at least in the modern period, is *interest-based*. The fundamental idea here is that the moral assessment of actions and policies depends solely on their practical consequences, and that the only consequences that really matter are the interests of the parties affected (usually human beings). *On this view, ethics is all about harms and benefits to identifiable parties.* Moral common sense is governed by *a single dominant objective*, maximizing net expectable utility (happiness, satisfaction, well-being, pleasure). Critical thinking, on this type of view, amounts to testing our ethical instincts and rules of thumb against the yardstick of social costs and benefits. (Problems and questions regarding interest-based thinking are several: How does one *measure* utility or interest satisfaction? For *whom* does one measure it (self, group, humankind, beyond)? What about the *tyranny of the majority* in the calculation?)

Rights-based avenues A second influential type of thinking is *rights-based*. The central idea here is that moral common sense is to be governed not (or not only) by interest satisfaction, but by rights protection. And the relevant rights are of two broad kinds: rights to fair distribution of opportunities and wealth (contractarianism), and rights to basic freedoms or liberties (libertarianism). Fair distribution is often explained as a condition that obtains when all individuals are accorded equal respect and equal voice in social arrangements. Basic liberties are often explained in terms of individuals' opportunities for self-development, work rewards, and freedoms including religion and speech. (Problems and questions regarding this avenue include: Is there a trade-off between equality and liberty when it comes to rights? Does rights-based thinking lead to *tyrannies of minorities* that are as bad as tyrannies of majorities? Is this type of thinking excessively focused on individuals and their entitlements without sufficient attention to larger communities and the *responsibilities* of individuals to such larger wholes?)

Duty-based avenues *Duty-based* thinking is perhaps the least unified and well-defined. The governing ethical idea is *duty* or *responsibility* not so much to other *individuals* as to *communities* of individuals. Critical thinking depends ultimately on individuals conforming to the legitimate norms of a healthy community. Ethics is about playing one's role as part of a larger whole, either a web of relationships (like the family) or a community (communitarianism). This line of thinking was implicit in John F. Kennedy's inaugural address: "Ask not what your country can do for you, ask what you can do for your country." In management, duty-based thinking appears in appeals to principles like fiduciary obligation. (Problems and questions regarding this type of thinking include the concern that individualism might get lost in a kind of collectivism (under a socialist or communitarian banner). Also, how are our various duties to be prioritized when they come into conflict?)

Virtue-based avenues In *virtue-based* thinking actions and policies are subjected to scrutiny not on the basis of their *consequences* (for individuals or for communities), but on the basis of their *genesis* – the degree to which they flow from or reinforce a virtue or positive trait of character. The traditional short list of basic (or "cardinal") virtues includes prudence, temperance, courage, and justice. "Love, and do what you will," Augustine is supposed to have said, indicating that the virtue of love was ethically more basic and more directly practical than attempts at determining "the right thing to do." (Problems or questions associated with the virtue-based thinking include: What are the central virtues and their relative priorities in a postmodern world that does not appear to agree on such matters? Are there timeless character traits that are not culture-bound, so that we can recommend them to anyone, particularly those in leadership roles?)

The resulting case analysis template for preparing and discussing ethics-related cases can then be constructed as displayed in Figure 6.1. (A *blank* version of the template used by students is included as Figure 6.3 on page 138–9. It can be detached and copied for use in class preparation and for case analysis assignments.)

It is important to emphasize that the four "avenues" for ethical reasoning depicted in the template represent what philosophers often call *prima facie* moral guidelines. That is, each "avenue" gives a first approximation to an ethical conclusion, but no one avenue, *by itself*, is ethically definitive. If the application of three or all four avenues gives a positive or a negative assessment for a given option, learners may take this as *a strong case* for or against that option.

If and when avenues *conflict*, however, learners must think through the nature of the conflict – asking whether they are prepared to affirm the positives and override the negatives in comparable cases. Learners are not *encouraged* to conclude in such cases that *moral insight* is unattainable – or that the *moral point of view* is subjective, arbitrary, or self-contradictory. A legitimate conclusion, instead, is that *moral insight* in this case is more elusive and must continue to be sought through further reflection and dialogue.

In "Avenues for Ethical Reasoning in Management," (Goodpaster, 1998) the idea of the *moral point of view* was introduced as a perspective that "governs and disciplines what we take to be the central virtues . . . good and bad reasons, sound and unsound arguments, principles, intuitions." The *moral point of view* was further described as "a mental and emotional standpoint from which all persons have a special dignity or worth, from which the Golden Rule gets its force, from which words like 'ought,' 'duty,' and 'virtue' derive their meaning."

As the instructor works with cases, applying each of the four avenues of ethical reasoning, he or she must remember that the ultimate purpose of the analysis is *to seek the insight of the moral point of view* in the case situation. Each avenue represents an important *voice* in the conversation – so important that one should be uncomfortable when the voices are not unanimous.

An imaginary jury

Instructors might imagine this process within each learner as analogous to a *jury* of deliberative voices from which the learner seeks a verdict. The jury includes interest-based, rights-based, duty-based, and virtue-based voices. Each hopes that his or her jury will speak with unanimity and strong conviction.

The class as a whole is a kind of jury also, with the voices belonging to each of the learners. And as with a more conventional jury in the context of judicial proceedings, case method instructors are dealing with ordinary human beings, not gods. Consequently, they may expect different levels of dispassionate reflection, with appropriate diversity in their approaches to ethical conclusions.

Now most of us do not believe that a jury is immune from error and misjudgment – that what a jury says must, even if unanimous, be correct *just because the jury said so*. But many (if not most) of us *do* believe that the jury system is the best systematic alternative we have for reaching a fair and just outcome. As the judgments of juries are usually our best approximations to *justice* in matters of *law* – the voices represented in the four avenues are our best approximations to the *moral point of view* in matters of applied *ethics*.

Searching out the insight provided by the *moral point of view* is no small task, partly because the voices involved may not always agree, but also because decision makers can "fall back" into other tempting ways of thinking, using *surrogates* for ethical reflection rather than the real thing. Such surrogates include personal self-interest, preoccupation with market competition, existing law and regulation, or any one of the four avenues taken alone without input from the others. Thus the case method instructor must, as part of his or her teaching plan, include questions like these, aimed at eliciting from each of the learners the perspectives of the imaginary jury:

- Whose interests are at stake for each of the decision maker's realistic options in this case?
- Are there legitimate rights that need attention associated with each option?
- What duties does the decision maker have and to whom?
- What virtues or character traits would be reinforced by alternative options available to the decision maker (including traits of individuals and policy precedents for the organization)?
- Which option available is *most responsive* to the four avenues we have identified?

Is there a "normative bias" in the use of this approach to teaching and learning ethics by the case method? To some extent, yes, although "bias" need not be the operative word. "Conviction" may be a better word. Value-neutral education is a myth and always has been, despite post-modern attempts to embrace it. Real education (whether by the case method or not) inevitably conveys ethical content, by omission or commission. Emory University president James T. Laney put it nicely some years ago:

> In many academic disciplines, there has been a retreat from the attempt to relate values and wisdom to what is being taught. Not long ago, Bernard Williams, the noted British philosopher, observed that philosophers have been trying all this century to get rid of the dreadful idea that philosophy ought to be edifying. Philosophers are not the only ones to appreciate the force of that statement. . . . How can society survive if education does not attend to those qualities which it requires for its very perpetuation? (Laney, 1985)

Good business ethics case studies are carefully researched true narratives of managerial challenges in value-laden situations. They represent the stuff of the moral life in business. Some present situations that may seem impossible to resolve; but they can at least serve the purpose of showing how such dilemmas might be avoided through better management. Cases provide an essential empirical basis for normative and conceptual inquiry. They can be used as dynamic tools to test our generalizations and our moral frameworks, just as our generalizations and our moral frameworks can be used to test our judgment in individual cases. John Rawls refers to this as "reflective equilibrium."

In summary, the case method as it relates to business ethics calls for analytical tools that are philosophically rigorous but epistemologically realistic as well. The case method instructor in the ethics arena needs to understand the Socratic character of the interaction more practically than other instructors.

Let us now turn to the third part of our discussion, the place of the case method in the business school curriculum. Case method teaching and learning requires a curricular setting that is friendly to this pedagogy. There must be resources and incentives for linking cases into modules, modules into courses, and for putting curricular unity into course sequences. This does not mean that a business school curriculum needs to be fully dedicated only to case method teaching – even in ethics. But it does mean that support for teaching ethics by case method is essential if students (and faculty) are not to get conflicting messages.

Ethics, Cases, and the Curriculum

Efforts were made at many academic institutions during the 1970s and 1980s by management and philosophy departments to "team teach" business ethics. Implicit in these efforts was a belief that the two sides of the house – management and ethics – needed somehow to be joined. Most of these efforts met with limited success, however, because the integration that was needed was simply *reassigned* to the students rather than *modeled* by the faculty. The marriage of management and moral philosophy would take more than this if it were not to end as so many marriages do today.

I am convinced that a deeper kind of integration is needed. The natural tendency in our society of professionals is to call in the experts when we experience some degree of dissonance over a problem. When the problem is how to relate ethics to business decision making, that tendency leads us to call in ethics specialists much as we would call in specialists in international relations when faced with a question about the US balance of trade. But in business ethics, it does not work that way. The field of ethics does not lend itself to an "external application," despite the best efforts of philosophers to rise to the occasion. A better way is for teachers of business administration to learn some moral philosophy and for moral philosophers to learn some business administration. In this way, the educator can avoid the problem described in an old Latin aphorism: "Nemo dat quod non habet" ("Nobody gives what he/she doesn't have").

Curricular support for joining management education and ethics education manifests itself institutionally in two broad arenas:

(a) integration *within* the curriculum, and

(b) emphasis from what we might call the *"extra-curriculum."*

Ethics within the curriculum: A strategy

A curricular strategy that involves teaching ethics by the case method (Figure 6.2) must start with a commitment by administration and faculty to the importance of the task. Without such a commitment, any strategy is doomed to failure. At the University of St. Thomas, administrators and faculty sought (and succeeded) in 1990 to formulate a mission-like document, which we called a "Preamble," that articulated the institution's commitment to the importance of ethics in the curriculum:

Business education is commonly aimed at the knowledge needed to perform effectively and efficiently in the business world. We at the University of St. Thomas are committed to that objective and more: encouraging serious consideration and application of ethical values in business decision making.

Since business ethics can mean different things to different people, we want to specify the assumptions that guide our efforts. Responsibility for one's actions and respect for the dignity of others are fundamental, both for the content of our approach to ethics and for the process by which we teach it. In this approach, dogmatism is as inappropriate as relativism.

Our emphasis, therefore, is on the importance of dialogue for developing mature moral judgment both personally and in group decision making. In our view, this maturity includes the exercise of certain virtues in the workplace, such as honesty, fairness, empathy, promise keeping, prudence, courage, and concern for the common good. It also includes

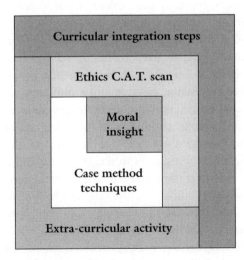

Figure 6.2 Teaching and learning ethics by the case method

interaction between the cognitive and emotional dimensions of conscience (i.e., both "head" and "heart") and the need for congruence between judgment and action. We believe such moral development is a life-long process.

Our goal in the Graduate School of Business and in the Division of Business is to encourage this development in the context of sound policies and practices. We affirm the legitimacy and centrality of moral values in economic decision-making because without them, business relationships and strong communities are impossible.

This statement has served the institution well for over a decade now, providing the "North" on our curricular compass when occasionally we lost our way in either the graduate or the undergraduate schools of business. In the spirit of this "Preamble," there is a *curricular strategy* for the integration of business ethics into these two schools – a strategy that avoids the false dilemma of "Should we have a special course or should ethics be in every course?" This strategy consists of four principal steps in a cycle, each called for by the step preceding and each leading to the step following:

1 *Initiation,* an introductory module or "half-course" to foster a common language among students in addressing ethical aspects of business
2 *Inclusion* of ethics cases and readings in the main functional courses in the curriculum, e.g., marketing, finance, accounting, management, business law and entrepreneurship.
3 *Consolidation* of functional applications of ethics in the business capstone, and
4 *Feedback* from alumni of the program to improve methods and teaching materials for the next generation of students, returning us to the initiatory stage

We *initiate* through a deliberately incomplete, required module at both graduate and undergraduate levels. *Inclusion* is sought through course design workshops with departments, including Marketing, Finance, Accounting, Management, Business Law, and Entrepreneurship. The goal of working with each of the departments is to develop specific cases and readings in the core offerings of each department, linking to the required initiation module and reinforcing students' understanding of the relevance of ethical thinking to their chosen area of specialization in business. One of the notable advantages of including ethics in the curriculum using the case method is that it can enable the teacher to add ethical themes into an already content-packed course, permitting the analysis of conventional business problems that also have significant ethical dimensions. We might call this "curricular multi-tasking."

Consolidation is implemented by working with the capstone course faculty. The hope is to offer the students who are completing the business curriculum in the capstone course a significant exposure to ways of blending strategic and ethical considerations in strategic decision making.

Feedback includes

(a) holding alumni workshops, and
(b) tapping graduates (after they have had substantial business experience) for contributions to ethics-related case development.

This represents a generous investment on their part in future St. Thomas students, and it completes the circle, bringing us back to initiation again as we constantly revitalize the opening module.

The initiatory module offers a set of cases and readings aimed at joining ethical reflection to business decision making. Several criteria guide the selection and organization of these materials: *topical relevance* to the modern manager, *curricular relevance* to the required core courses that will follow, and *conceptual relevance* to applied ethics.

Topically, the idea is to examine current and significant management challenges such as product safety, honesty in marketing, environmental protection, and international business in diverse cultures. From the perspective of *curricular* relevance, the course materials display breadth and richness of a different kind. The principal subject areas in the curriculum should be represented: management (human resources, operations, strategy), marketing, finance, accounting, entrepreneurship and business law. The third criterion – *conceptual* relevance in applied ethics – draws attention to several levels at which ethical concepts can be applied to business activity: the level of the individual (managerial decisions and virtues), the level of the organization (policy formulation and implementation), and the level of the society as a whole (democratic capitalism nationally and globally). Other conceptual questions in the background include: What is the moral point of view? What avenues are available for making responsible decisions? Do ethical principles and values transcend cultural boundaries?

The search for *excellence* in such a course calls for a team effort by the faculty. The *flow* of the course, after some introductory material, goes from "Ethics and the Individual," to "Ethics and the Organization," to "Ethics and Capitalism as a System." In each of these parts of the course – and thus at each of these three levels of analysis – instructors and learners examine cases and readings with attention not only to "stakeholder" thinking but also virtue-based (or culture-based) thinking. Course objectives are:

- to enhance learner awareness of the importance of ethical values for individual and organizational effectiveness;
- to stimulate a positive attitude in learners toward incorporating virtue-based and stakeholder analysis throughout business decision making; and
- to provide a process for thinking through the economic and noneconomic implications of strategies and implementation plans in realistic business situations.

Ethical awareness and sound moral judgment are not, of course, substitutes for basic business skills in the functional areas (marketing, finance, accounting, etc.). But it is becoming increasingly clear, that the exercise of basic managerial skills in an atmosphere of uncritical moral and social premises leads not only to expanding external regulation and adversarialism, but to a widespread and reasonable lack of trust in institutional forms of all kinds: economic, political, academic, and even religious.

Students need to engage in case method dialogue, allowing their preparation, energy, and willingness to learn from peers to produce genuine moral insight. They can then take what they have learned and carry it into each of the courses that make up their business curriculum. Ultimately, students must be *challenged* to go beyond specific issues and courses to develop a responsible business philosophy of their own.

The extra-curriculum

Beyond the regular curriculum itself, wrapped around it in concentric circles as it were, there can be many "extra-curricular" activities that support a *culture of relevance* for ethics and the case method. In addition to core courses, there are elective courses, guest speakers, colloquia, alumni seminars, and various internet-based enhancements to learning.

Elective courses   Making all ethics-related courses in the curriculum *required* courses is probably unwise, never mind that it would be politically impossible in most colleges and universities. The menu of elective courses in a business curriculum that relate in various ways to business ethics (e.g., a seminar on *Spirituality and Management* or a *Great Books* seminar for graduate students and alumni or a *Case Research* practicum) carries an important message to teachers and learners alike about the importance the institution assigns to the ethics agenda.

Guest speakers   Regular guest speakers addressing ethics-related themes are also a powerful signal of an institution's commitment, especially if the audience is "town and gown," i.e., not only faculty and students, but also businesspersons in the college or university community.

Colloquia   Another type of extra-curricular integration of ethics – and case method learning – is the systematic dialogue of colloquia. Colloquia can involve student participants and/or faculty participants and/or executives. Individual and panel presentations can include prepared papers or case studies.

Alumni seminars   While alumni are natural participants in both guest speaker events and colloquia, events held especially for alumni provide an opportunity for both alumni and their *alma mater* to share important information. Lifelong learning for alumni is increasingly valuable to them, of course, but less noticed is an *institution's* need for lifelong learning by sharing the experiences of its alumni, often in the form of case studies. Without the latter information, an institution risks lack of currency and eventually irrelevance in its professional education programs.

Internet Assisted Learning Virtual classrooms were mentioned earlier in this essay as new techniques for case method learning. Other e-learning opportunities that relate to an institution's "extra-curriculum" include internet-based *case studies* and distance learning case method *courses* in ethics (among other subjects). Internet-based case studies, often available on CD-ROMs, provide more than conventional case text. They also provide audio-visual examples of case facts and hyperlinks to relevant case information on various internet sites. Distance learning case method courses in ethics are a very recent development, but they will be a growing pedagogical form. Geographical dispersion and asynchronous delivery can be seen as limitations on the case method – but they can also provide new opportunities. A case discussion in ethics is never richer, for example, than when the participants come from different cultural backgrounds, as the internet makes possible. In a new distance course that this writer has recently developed, the "*CAT Scan*" (discussed above) has been automated as a learning tool for participants and as a way for instructors to regularly monitor participants' understanding of ethics case material.

In summary, the case method is most effective in the ethics arena if it is supported and used widely in an institution. This reinforces the expectations of learners and permits quality control on cases and classroom process. But the responsibility for ethics in the business school curriculum must be borne by the entire business faculty, not outsourced or handled by one or two specialists or "gurus." The risk of both outsourcing (e.g., from a philosophy department) and special "gurus" is the risk of *compartmentalization*. Compartmentalization means that ethical issues that arise in other parts of the business curriculum are "referred to the experts," sending the wrong message to students as future ethical decision makers.

Summary and conclusions

I have portrayed teaching and learning ethics by the case method as an activity which, when undertaken with certain epistemological, analytical, and curricular convictions, provides a powerful approach to professional education. Joining learner-centered techniques with philosophical analysis (the "CAT Scan"), the case method offers as clear an answer as possible to the question that spurred our inquiry at the outset: "Can you tell me, Socrates, whether virtue is acquired by teaching or by practice; or if neither by teaching nor practice, then whether it comes to man by nature or in what other way?" The answer seems to be this: "Virtue is acquired by teaching *and* by practice, assuming an honest desire by all parties to seek moral insight."

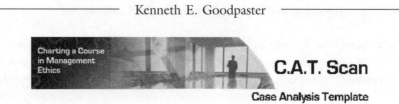

C.A.T. Scan

Case Analysis Template

Type your answers to each question below the red text in each table cell.

Aspects of the Moral Point of View (Avenues = ethical basis)	Interests	Rights	Duties	Virtues
Case Analysis Steps (5 D's sequence)				
Describe Identify the facts.	How did the situation come about? *Type answer here.*			
	What are the key presenting issues? *Type answer here.*			
	Who are the key individuals and groups affected by the situation (i.e., the stakeholders)? *Type answer here.*			
	Who is the key decision maker? *Type answer here.*			
	Identify interests. Are there interests involved? If yes, identify further. Make a list. *Start list here.*	Identify rights. Are there rights involved? If yes, whose are they? Make a list. *Start list here.*	Identify duties. Are there duties involved? If yes, identify further. Make a list. *Start list here.*	Identify virtues. Are there precedents? If yes, wht are they? Make a list. *Start list here.*

Aspects of the Moral Point of View (Avenues = ethical basis)	Interests	Rights	Duties	Virtues
Discern Identify the ethical issues. Select the issue to debate.	What are the three most significant of the "presenting issues" – the one that might lie underneath it all? Describe which issue is the most important. *Type answer here.*			
	Are there conflicting interests with respect to this issue, and how basic are they? Can you rate them in order of importance? *Type answer here.*	Are there rights in conflict with interests or with other rights? Are some weightier than others? *Type answer here.*	Does duty come into the picture – and are there tensions with rights or interests? Can I prioritize these claims? *Type answer here.*	Is character an issue in this case – are there habits that bring us to this point or that will be reinforced later? *Type answer here.*
Display Based on facts and ethical issues, identify options you can consider.	What are the principal realistic options available to the decision maker(s) in this case, including possible branching among sub options – leading to an array of action sequences or plans? *Type answer here.*			
Decide Based on all the options, choose one and create a plan of action to implement it.	What, finally, is my considered judgment on the best option to take from those listed above? The Moral Point of View is here joined to the Administrative or Managerial Point of View. *Type answer here.*			
Defend Justify your choice from the perspective of each avenue.	Which of the avenues predominates in my choice of options above, and can I give good reasons for preferring the ethical priorities I have adopted in this case that are consistent with other such cases? *Type answer here.*			

Figure 6.3 Case analysis template (blank version used by students)

References

Andrews, K. R. 1954: The role of the instructor in the case method. In Malcolm P. McNair, (ed.), *The Case Method at the Harvard Business School*. New York: McGraw-Hill.

Christensen, C. R. with Hansen, A. J. 1987: *Teaching and the Case Method*. Boston: Harvard Business School Press.

Goodpaster, K. E. 1982: Is teaching ethics Making or Doing? *Hastings Center Report*, Vol. 12, No. 1 February 1982. © 1982 by the *Institute of Society, Ethics and the Life Sciences*. This article appeared in tandem with *"A Psychologist Looks at the Teaching of Ethics"* by James R. Rest.

Goodpaster, K. E. 1985: An agenda for Applied Ethics. In *Social Responsibility: Business, Journalism, Law, Medicine*, Volume XI, Lexington, VA: Washington and Lee University.

Goodpaster, K. 1997a: Business ethics. In *Encyclopaedia of Management and Dictionary of Business Ethics*, Oxford: Blackwell Publishers.

Goodpaster, K. 1997b: Teleopathy. In *Encyclopaedia of Management and Dictionary of Business Ethics*, Oxford: Blackwell Publishers.

Goodpaster, K. 1997c: Principle of moral projection. In *Encyclopaedia of Management and Dictionary of Business Ethics*, Oxford: Blackwell Publishers.

Goodpaster, K. 1997d: Stakeholder paradox. In *Encyclopaedia of Management and Dictionary of Business Ethics*, Oxford: Blackwell Publishers.

Goodpaster, K. E. 1998: Avenues for ethical analysis in management. In K. Goodpaster and L. Nash, *Policies and Persons* 3rd edn, McGraw-Hill.

Goodpaster, K. 2000a: Business ethics. In *Encyclopaedia of Ethics*, 2nd edn, Govland Publications.

Goodpaster, K. 2000b: Stakeholder analysis. In *Encyclopaedia of Ethics*, 2nd edn, Govland Publications.

Goodpaster, K. 2000c: Business ethics. In *Oxford Companion to Christian Thought*, Oxford University Press.

Goodpaster, K. and Nash, L. 1998: *Policies and Persons* 3rd edn, McGraw-Hill.

Gragg, C. I. 1940: Because wisdom can't be told, *Harvard Alumni Bulletin*, October 19.

James, W. 1962: *Essays in Faith and Morals*, Cleveland and NY: Meridian. Originally Published in 1891.

Laney, J. T. 1985: The education of the heart, *Harvard Magazine,* September–October 23–4.

Lynn, Jr., L. E. 1999: *Teaching and Learning with Cases: A Guidebook*. London: Chatham House Publishers, London.

Plato 1949: *Meno*, Indianapolis: The Bobbs Merrill Co. Inc.

Royce, J. 1865: *The Religious Aspect of Philosophy*. First Published in 1865. Reprinted 1965 by Harper & Row, Publishers. 155.

Further Reading

Brisin, T. 1995: Active learning in applied ethics instruction. *Journal on Excellence in College Teaching*, 6, No. 3, 161–7.

Campbell, E. 1997: Connecting the ethics of teaching and moral education. *Journal of Teacher Education*, 48 (4), 255–63.

Lundeberg, M. A. ed., 2000: *Who Learns What from Cases and How?: The Research Base for Teaching and Learning with Cases.*

Stevens, B. 1996: Teaching communication with ethics-based cases. *Business Communication Quarterly*, 59 (3), 5–15.

Websites

For useful articles on case method teaching and sample cases from the *Teaching Resource Center* at the University of Virginia, visit http://www.virginia.edu/~trc/casemeth.htm

http://www.agecon.uga.edu/~wacra/wacra.htm *World Association for Case Method Research & Application* offers a comprehensive site for case method educators, based in Needham, Massachusetts.

http://www.stanford.edu/class/ee353/case.htm provides a nice statement from a *Stanford University* course on the nature of the case method.

http://www.abo.fi/instut/hied/case.htm gives a very good online source of links to case method sites and current events related to the case method from *Higher Education Development International.*

Part II
Ethical Issues in
the Practice of Business

Chapter 7

Ethical Issues in Accounting

Mary Beth Armstrong

Accounting is an art, not a science. It requires significant judgments and assumptions and ten accountants, given a complex set of circumstances, will probably arrive at several different net income or taxable income figures. Accounting involves gathering, classifying, summarizing, and reporting financial information about an entity to interested users such as stockholders, creditors, potential investors and creditors, governments, and other stakeholders. In addition, accounting involves the very systems that gather and transform the information, and it involves decision making about the future based on the information. Accounting has been called the "language of business" and, because of its pervasiveness, it affects the lives of individuals in all sectors of our society.

Accountants perform many functions in the private and public sectors. One broad classification of accountants is based on their employment status. Managerial accountants work within businesses and not-for-profit organizations, while public accountants are employed by accounting firms or other organizations that serve various clients. Academic accountants work for colleges and universities and governmental accountants work in the public sector. In reality, the lines between these categories are sometimes fuzzy. Nevertheless, the categories are helpful in a discussion of professional responsibilities and ethics because functions performed, and therefore ethical responsibilities, differ among each of the categories mentioned. Also, within each broad category, performance of different functions creates different sets of responsibilities. Therefore, the following discussion of ethical responsibilities in accounting utilizes these sub-headings: Managerial accounting is divided into internal accounting functions and financial reporting functions. Public accounting is divided into consulting services, tax services, and auditing. Ethical issues relating to academic accountants and governmental accountants are not specifically addressed.

Ethical considerations in accounting tend to be a blend of business ethics issues and professional ethics issues. In particular, accountants must juggle the interests of many stakeholder groups while carrying out their professional responsibilities.

A profession is characterized by at least the following four attributes: expertise, monopoly, public interest, and self-regulation. Expertise is special knowledge of a theoretic, academic nature. One distinguishing feature of the expertise is that it requires the exercise of professional judgment, not just the application of technical rules. The monopoly status is usually a license granted by the state that restricts practice of the expertise to licensees. The public interest is essentially a promise made by the profession to society that its members will benefit, not harm, society. The promise to act in the public interest is at the heart of every profession and is typically codified in their code of ethics. Codes of ethics, therefore, serve to identify how members of a particular profession must conduct themselves if the public interest is to be preserved. Self-regulation is a privilege granted to a profession to regulate its members. The profession, therefore, has a duty to self-regulate. If society perceives that a particular profession is lax in regulating its own members, they tend to withdraw the privilege by increasing governmental regulations and litigation.

The profession of accounting is experiencing a bit of a conundrum in recent years. The only function performed by accountants that requires a license is the attest function (primarily the audit and review of financial statements). The license granted by the state is the Certified Public Accountant (CPA) certificate and only currently licensed CPAs may audit the financial statements of enterprises. Twenty years ago auditing accounted for almost 70 percent of CPA firms' revenue. By the dawn of the year 2000 it had declined to about 35 percent. Part of that change in the mix of services performed by CPAs is due to competitive pressures within the auditing branch of the profession, and part of it is due to external competitive pressures, technological changes, and new opportunities for CPAs to expand into new territory. The result has been a profound change in the culture found in CPA firms, to be discussed below, and a change in emphasis from "professional concerns" (e.g., the public interest) to "business concerns" (e.g., increasing market share). Indeed, even a casual reading of business literature can detect a shift in emphasis. Twenty years ago, or more, reference was made to "the accounting profession." Today, one is more likely to encounter the terms, "the accounting industry" or "the business of accounting."

In the next section, we will look specifically at ethical issues in managerial accounting, followed by a section on issues in public accounting. A separate section is devoted to auditor independence, followed by a section on the role of regulators and standard setters. Finally, we conclude by discussing the need to keep grounded in unchanging values and virtues in the midst of a dynamic and challenging business environment.

Ethical Issues in Management Accounting

In general, the ethical issues faced by accountants in industry are similar to those faced by any professional group (e.g., engineers) working within a corporate setting. They often boil down to a conflict between professional standards and corporate expectations. Accountants are often corporate executives or members of middle management and, as such, are part of a management team striving to meet corporate goals and objectives. But they are also members of a profession, with distinct professional standards. Often the same individual can fulfill the expectations and responsibilities of both roles without conflict. But inevitably conflict does arise and the accountant must make tough choices. We will look at the nature of those choices for two sub-groups of managerial accountants, those who perform internal accounting functions and those responsible for financial reporting for external users of financial information.

Internal accounting functions

Financial executives and managers are often part of an entity's management team. Merchant (1996) divides management processes into three categories: determining organizational mission and goals, strategy formulation, and management controls. The latter group, management controls, is further subdivided into "results" controls, "action" controls, and personnel/culture controls. Results controls include setting performance targets (planning and budgeting), measuring and evaluating performance, and providing rewards and punishments. Action controls include prevention of physical losses, pre-action reviews and oversight, and action accountability such as internal auditing and codes of conduct. Personnel/culture controls consist of management practices designed to enhance employees' internal motivations to perform well and to establish organizational cultures that draw out and reinforce desired performance. Obviously, all of these management processes raise ethical issues, but most of them are not confined to the accounting domain, but are the concerns of the larger field, business ethics. Therefore, in this section we limit our remarks to three topics particularly associated with accountants: budgeting (or performance targets), internal auditing, and internal reporting.

Performance targets, such as budgets, are usually negotiated between employees and their superiors. Such negotiations inevitably lead to targets that are easier to achieve than would have been the case if superiors with perfect information had imposed them. In other words, slack is introduced into the system because of information asymmetry. Employees often benefit from creating budget slack because they are protected from unforeseen contingencies (bad luck) and because meeting targets, or exceeding them, often triggers performance-based rewards. The obvious downside to such a system includes the creation of a culture of "gamesmanship" and dishonesty that clearly violate the tenants of objectivity and integrity required by the codes of conduct of both the Institute of Management Accountants (IMA) and Financial Executives Institute (FEI). While the slack-creating employees may benefit, the slack is often costly to other employees and the company itself, and therefore stockholders of the company. Since companies use budgets and performance targets to allocate scarce resources, such as money and personnel, the decision-making process is distorted by slack and optimum allocation may be compromised.

Another problem with slack is that it creates "easy" targets and thus encourages complacency and inefficiencies. In the budgeting process managers fear reporting profits too far in excess of their targets because doing so will often result in a more difficult target next year. Thus, managers may make unnecessary expenditures to eliminate the profit or save it for future years.

Merchant and Van der Stede (2000, pp. 157–9) argue that creating slack is a rational response within a results-control setting. They do not view slack as a distortion but as a means for employees to protect themselves from the downside potential of an uncertain future. "This protection from risk is particularly valuable in firms that treat the budget forecasts as 'promises' or 'commitments' from the manager to the corporation, as is common."

The potential dysfunctional consequences of a rigid, tight budgetary control style require employees and managers to protect themselves from the downside risk of missing targets and the stigma attached (and often long-term negative consequences) to under-achievers. In other words, rules made for a level playing field should not be applied to a playing field that isn't level.

Of course, the same protective purpose could be achieved in a "legitimate" way if companies used more flexible performance standards. Unfortunately, employees have little or no say in the structuring of performance standards.

Budget slack may sometimes be necessary to address the imbalance of power in a hierarchical organization. Perceptions of evaluation unfairness are probably greatest when a large part of the bonus is determined in a subjective way.

Merchant and Van der Stede also point out that slack is an integral and accepted part of an organization's budget negotiation process. It is the norm and many top managers may have made it to the top precisely because they were good slack negotiators. Indeed, superiors may actually want their subordinates to create slack because they also benefit from it. "When higher-level targets are consolidations of subordinates' targets, superiors enjoy the same reduction in risk and increase in the expected values of their rewards as the slack creators themselves."

Finally, empirical research suggests that moderate levels of slack may actually improve performance and only "too much" or "too little" may be counterproductive.

When creation of slack is widespread and the practice is encouraged, with arguably beneficial outcomes, is the result an institutionalization of a culture of deceit, or is it simply a community establishing its own acceptable behavioral norms? This author gives more weight to the arguments of Merchant and Van der Stede, viewing the corporate setting as a small community within the larger business environment. Communitarian theories of ethics show how "common morality" is embedded in communal living in the context of particular historical traditions and instituted practices. Within the community (e.g., business) setting, a type of common morality in reflective equilibrium with shared moral ideals emerges through moral discussion and open debate. It is different from moral relativism that asserts that all moral discourse is merely the endorsement of personal preferences. Nor would this kind of common morality allow mindless and unquestioning conformity to groupthink, or the abandonment of moral ideals. Nevertheless, it is not based on a belief that some universal moral system should guide all human endeavors.

Internal auditing is the second internal accounting function to be discussed. Internal auditors have traditionally been company employees who perform operational audits (as opposed to financial statement audits performed by public accountants) and who report their findings directly to the Audit Committee of the Board of Directors or to senior management. Lemon and Wallace (2000) address five ethical themes involving internal auditors:

1 Organizational structure
2 Loyalty to the internal auditing function relative to the entity
3 Means of obtaining independence
4 Competition issues involved in development, promotion, and retention
5 Conformity pressures that relate to the institutional context in which internal auditing operates

Each of these themes is briefly summarized next.

Not all organizations have internal auditing departments, although all entities are responsible for maintaining internal accounting controls by the Foreign Corrupt Practices Act. Two phenomena of the last two decades affected the establishment and retention decisions about the internal auditing function in entities: leveraged buy-outs of the 1980s and outsourcing of the 1990s. Leveraged buy-outs were often accompanied by extreme cost cutting to facilitate the resultant debt burden. Eliminating internal auditing departments was one way to cut costs. Also, they argued, since managers are now also owners, incentives exist for self-policing and internal auditors are no longer necessary.

In the early 1990s, corporate America found itself in a recession and fighting bitterly to stay afloat. Costs were again slashed and employees – often middle managers – were laid off. Any "unnecessary" activity was eliminated. Many additional companies got rid of their entire internal auditing departments and then "outsourced" the internal audit function from an external vendor, usually a public accounting firm, and often the company's external auditor.

The propriety of such outsourcing arrangements has been questioned by a number of authors and speakers, including Michael Sutton, when he was Chief Accountant at the SEC (Sutton, 1997). The primary problems associated with outsourcing the internal audit function are as follows (Lemon and Wallace, 2000, p. 193):

• Loss of entity-specific expertise
• Lack of an integrally linked internal auditing group as a facet of the entity's control structure
• Role definitions of external and internal auditors conflict (i.e., public interest vs. loyalty to management)

- Shift in emphasis from internal to external audit activities
- Risk on external audit integrity (i.e., auditing ones own work by external auditors)

The second issue relating to internal auditing is loyalty. To whom should internal auditors be loyal? As Lemon and Wallace point out (2000, p. 195), "internal auditing is in a rather unique role of being defined as a service *to* management yet undeniably operating as a check *on* management." An added complexity emerges when management requests help from internal auditors with various management activities. For example, the controller may view the internal auditors as able to help with the company's internal control structure since internal auditors have expertise in that area. But if the internal auditors help design the system, how can they later give assurances on the adequacy of that same system? Internal auditors are supposed to decline management and operating responsibilities and to only recommend, not design or implement. When they do decline, their loyalty to the organization may be called into question. In addition, internal auditors should report directly to the Audit Committee or Board of Directors without management present. Again, they may be perceived as "disloyal" when doing so.

Independence for internal auditors has a different meaning than it does for external auditors (to be discussed below) because internal auditors are employed by the organizations they serve. In addition, internal auditors' compensation packages often include stock options, whose value is a function of the company's performance. Therefore, reporting links and assurance of access to the Board of Directors is critical to maintain internal auditors' objectivity and independence. In short, if the internal auditors report to financial management, their effectiveness is strained. Ideally, they would report directly to the Audit Committee of the Board of Directors to be free from management's control. In addition, issues of centralization or decentralization arise. With decentralized audit functions, branch loyalty might trump loyalty to the audit function. But in centralized situations, internal audit staff may be required to travel to various branches as a large part of their job responsibility, calling into question quality of life issues.

Competition for talent and the desire for management trainees to work throughout an organization may lead to rotational programs where internal auditing is viewed as a sort of training ground for operating management. The problem with such programs is they signal a lack of a career path within internal auditing itself and may create conflicts of interest for those leaving or returning to operating duties. Auditors should never audit their own work.

The "conformity pressures" described by Lemon and Wallace (2000, p. 198) really have to do with allegiances to outside organizations and their standards. Many internal auditors are Certified Public Accountants and members of both the AICPA and the Institute of Internal Auditors (IIA). Yet the guidance given by these organizations is conflicting. Interpretation 102–3 of the AICPA *Code of Professional Conduct* states: "In dealing with his or her employer's external accountant, a member [e.g., internal auditor] must be candid and not knowingly misrepresent facts or knowingly fail to disclose material facts." Internal auditors, however, view external auditors in much the same way external auditors view regulators: that whistleblowing breaks the confidential nature of the audit process and may lead to less candor by auditees and less overall effectiveness. Therefore, the IIA's guidance suggests that the internal auditor maintain confidentiality and "walk" if corrective action is not taken.

The next section deals with external financial reporting. But accountants in industry also report performance measures internally. "Earnings management," therefore, is a term that can apply both to internal reporting of budget targets or external reporting of overall corporate performance. Managers can accomplish earnings management through either accounting methods or operating methods. Accounting methods involve manipulation of the measurement process by using flexibility available in choosing accounting methods, or formulating accounting assumptions, or modifying accounting judgments. Operating methods involve altering operating decisions such as the timing of discretionary expenditures or requiring employees to work overtime, or speeding up shipments of goods. Merchant and Van der Stede (2000, pp. 162–3) report that most people view accounting methods of earnings management as unethical, while they pardon most of the operating methods. In other words, "operating methods of managing earnings, which often have significant real costs to the firm, are viewed as ethical while cosmetic, accrual-affecting accounting methods are condemned." They suggest that clearer standards for judging accounting performance (various accounting rules) exist than for judging managerial performance. Therefore, they conclude "many people use clarity of standards or laws as a basis for reaching an ethical conclusion." Another reason most people might view accounting methods of earnings management as unethical is because they believe such management somehow distorts the "truth" about earnings. Since accounting is an art, requiring judgments about estimates and assumptions, accountants of good will might come to different conclusions. "True" earnings, therefore, probably don't exist. Nevertheless, changing assumptions and estimates for the sole purpose of managing reported earnings, without some underlying, business justification, is probably what most people really have in mind when they condemn such actions as unethical. However, operating methods of managing earnings can be equally or more unethical, especially when the harm created to one stakeholder group (e.g., future investors) greatly outweighs the benefit to other stakeholder groups (e.g., present stockholders). This might be the case, for example, when needed maintenance and repairs are postponed solely to enhance present earnings, causing much larger expenditures for repairs in the future.

External financial reporting

Accountants in industry are also responsible for preparing financial information to be used by investors, creditors, and other legitimate stakeholders of the organization. They are responsible for preparing financial statements in accordance with rules promulgated by standard setters. The rules are often detailed, complex, and collectively known as Generally Accepted Accounting Principles (GAAP). At the same time these accountants are under enormous pressure to meet market expectations with regard to financial forecasts. Industry analysts often examine a particular company, and then predict future earnings. The stock market reacts to those predictions and forms expectations. When the predicted earnings level is not met, the market reaction can be immediate and devastating. In a speech before the New York University Center for Law and Business, Arthur Levitt, then Chairman of the SEC, cited an incident (1998, 3) where "one major U.S. company . . . failed to meet its so-called 'numbers' by one penny, and lost more than six percent of its stock value in one day." The pressure on the entire organization to meet predictions is enormous, and the accountant is expected to be a "team player" in helping the organization reach its goals. The result is predictable; a host of "tricks" are employed to help smooth earnings.

Chairman Levitt, in his September 1998 speech, stated,

> Our accounting principles weren't meant to be a straitjacket. Accountants are wise enough to know they cannot anticipate every business structure, or every new and innovative transaction, so they develop principles that allow for flexibility to adapt to changing circumstances. That's why the highest standards of objectivity, integrity, and judgment can't be the exception. They must be the rule.

He identified five abuses or "trickery" to achieve earnings management:

1 "Big bath" restructuring charges
2 Creative acquisition accounting
3 "Cookie jar" reserves
4 "Immaterial" misapplications of accounting principles
5 The premature recognition of revenue

He promised that the SEC would be particularly vigilant in monitoring these abuses but also called on the accounting community and SEC registrants to withstand the pressures to "make the numbers." One means of helping management accountants understand their obligations in this regard might be a code of conduct for management accountants.

Code of conduct for management accountants

The IMA is an organization whose members are primarily accountants in industry. Their code of conduct addresses the fact that management accountants have multiple responsibilities; to the public, to their profession, to the organizations they serve, and to themselves. The code does not explicitly state that members' responsibilities to the public or to their profession trump responsibilities to their employer, but it certainly hints at such a priority. The code addresses four broad principles; competence, confidentiality, integrity, and objectivity. It then concludes with a discussion of how to resolve an ethical conflict. In that regard it admonishes that management accountants, when faced with significant ethical issues, should bring the matter to the attention of their supervisors and, if the problem persists, to continually higher levels in the organization. They also caution, "Except where legally prescribed, communication of such problems to authorities or individuals not employed or engaged by the organization is not considered appropriate" (IMA, 1997). This seeming prohibition against external whistleblowing is contradicted later in the same code where, after advising the member to consult an attorney, the code states, "If the ethical conflict still exists after exhausting all levels of internal review, there may be no other recourse on significant matters than to resign from the organization and to submit an informative memorandum. . . . After resignation, depending on the nature of the ethical conflict, it may also be appropriate to notify other parties" (IMA, 1997). Note that the act of whistleblowing is considered by the IMA to be an extreme measure, a course of action of last resort, only available to accountants who have resigned in protest first.

Ethical Issues in Public Accounting

Accountants in public accounting are usually CPAs or working to become CPAs. Public accountants perform a variety of functions, chief among them are consulting, tax preparation and advising, and auditing. While CPAs almost always have multiple responsibilities, the emphasis shifts when they perform different functions. In general, when performing consulting services the CPA's primary responsibility is to the client (just as the physician's primary responsibility is to his/her patient). In tax practice, the CPA has dual responsibilities to the client and to the tax system. The tax practitioner is acknowledged to be an advocate for the client when representing the client before the IRS, but the tax practitioner also has responsibilities to foster increased public compliance with and confidence in the tax system. When performing audits, CPAs are hired, fired, and paid by the client they audit, but their primary obligation is to the users of the financial statements.

Twenty-five to thirty years ago most mid-size to large CPA firms were primarily engaged in the audit function, followed by tax, and consulting was almost an ancillary service. The culture of these firms was dominated by the audit function and responsibility to the public interest was widely understood. Academic accountants were usually also CPAs and instilled a certain culture of professionalism in their students, and the firms later reinforced and nurtured that culture. In today's CPA firms, however, the culture is much more mixed. Not only has the mix of services shifted to where auditing is less dominant, the functions performed by the consultants are much more varied than before. Consulting experts are often not CPAs at all, but computer experts or actuaries or any other type of expert needed by a large consulting firm. They come from much more varied backgrounds. Thus the corporate culture, or office culture, in today's accounting firms has changed and is less likely to exhibit the same public interest focus as in earlier years. It is much more difficult, in today's environment, for CPAs to understand where their primary responsibilities lie. We will examine the ethical issues relating to each of these functions in turn.

Consulting

When performing consulting services, CPAs are held to the same general standards of care that apply to all services: they must undertake only those professional services they can reasonably expect to complete with competence; they must exercise due professional care; they must adequately plan and supervise their services; and they must obtain sufficient relevant data to afford a reasonable basis for their conclusions and recommendations (AICPA, 1992, Rule 201). In addition, they must establish an "understanding with the client" about the scope, nature, and limitations of the engagement, keep the client informed of any conflicts of interest that might occur or significant reservations concerning the engagement and significant findings or events, and serve the client's interest by seeking to accomplish the terms of the "understanding with client," consistent with integrity and objectivity (AICPA, 1988, SRTP 1).

Tax

Tax practitioners give tax advice and help with tax planning, prepare tax returns, and represent clients before the IRS or in tax court. They have responsibilities both to their clients, for whom they are advocates, and to the tax system. Rawls (1955) distinguishes between two kinds of rules: those that define a practice and those that facilitate achieving some objective. Armstrong and Robison (1998) argue that tax rules fall in the first of Rawls' categories, while financial reporting rules fall in the second. Thus, tax rules are like the rules in baseball, where no objective exists outside the rules and the rules themselves define right behavior. A strict adherence to the rules is required, where the rules are explicit, but "loopholing" is allowed where the rules are silent. In baseball, "gray" areas (e.g., is the runner safe or out?) are decided by the umpire. The Treasury Department, American Bar Association, and American Institute of Certified Public Accountants (AICPA) have the same standard for tax practitioners whose client has a "gray" area in tax: the "realistic possibility" standard. Essentially, the tax practitioner must ask, about any particular tax issue, "does it have a realistic possibility of being upheld if challenged?" In other words, the tax practitioner, after appropriate research and consultation, must judge whether there is a realistic possibility (defined by the Treasury Department as a one-in-three likelihood) that the tax court (umpire), knowing all the facts and circumstances, would allow the tax treatment. If so – go for it! It is a huge game, like baseball, and all taxpayers are free to minimize their taxes within the letter of the law. Judge Learned Hand said something similar in *Commissioner v. Newman* [159 F. 2d 848 (CA-2, 1947)]:

> Over and over again courts have said there is nothing sinister in so arranging one's affairs as to keep taxes as low as possible. Everybody does so, rich or poor, and all do right, for nobody owes any public duty to pay more than the law demands: taxes are enforced extractions, not voluntary contributions. To demand more in the name of morals is mere cant.

Other standards for tax practitioners are given in the Treasury Department's Circular 230 and the AICPA's *Statements on Standards for Tax Services*.

Audit

Auditors examine the financial statements of entities and render their expert opinion concerning the fairness of those statements, in accordance with GAAP. Auditors are required to follow professional auditing standards, known as Generally Accepted Auditing Standards (GAAS), which are promulgated by the Auditing Standards Board of the AICPA. The auditors' opinion on the financial statements is intended to add credibility to those statements and thus the auditors' role in a free-market economy is to aid in achieving the optimum allocation of scarce financial resources. Information is required for investors and creditors to make informed decisions, and the better the information, the more timely and credible it is, the better the allocation choices will be.

There are several problems with the system, as we now know it in the USA, not the least of which is the inherent conflict of interest among the audit participants. The auditee's management hires, pays, and fires the auditor, yet the auditor is essentially attesting to the fairness of management's representations about its own stewardship. All the while, the auditor's primary responsibility is toward the users of the financial information being audited. It is somewhat analogous to butchers hiring their own meat inspectors, with the power to set their prices and fire them if they do not like the inspection reports issued.

In spite of the structural conflict-of-interests problem, the system has worked well for over half a century, largely because of the professional culture pervading in auditing firms. But, in recent years, that very culture has come under attack for a variety of reasons including the decreased emphasis on auditing, the increased variety of functions performed by CPAs, restructuring of firms along industry lines instead of along traditional functions (audit, tax, consulting), and increased competitive pressures. A number of authors have suggested solutions to the structural problem, including governmental audits, an audit "tax" to fund audits, audits bought by large institutional investors instead of the companies themselves, a "tenure" system for auditors, mandatory periodic rotation of auditors, and others.

In 1994, the Public Oversight Board (POB) of the SEC Practice Section of the AICPA issued a report titled "Strengthening the Professionalism of the Independent Auditor." The report offered a number of suggestions to improve the profession, but the chief observation was that the Board of Directors, as the representative of the shareholders, should be the client, not corporate management. Boards, they said, "particularly independent directors, and auditors are, or should be, natural allies in protecting shareholder interests." Further, they recommended that Audit Committees of the Board should:

- expect the auditor to express independent judgments about the appropriateness, not just acceptability, of the accounting principles used and the clarity of financial disclosures
- hear directly from the auditors on whether management's choices of accounting principles are conservative, moderate, or extreme and whether those principles chosen are common practices or minority practices
- be informed of the auditor's reasoning in determining the appropriateness of accounting principles, disclosures, and estimates
- review the auditor's fees to insure they are appropriate for the services rendered
- meet with the auditors, at least annually, without management present.

The remainder of the 1990s witnessed a dramatic increase in the structure, power, and effectiveness of audit committees. In response to the POB's recommendations and to Arthur Levitt's 1998 speech, the New York Stock Exchange and National Association of Securities Dealers created a Blue Ribbon Committee on Improving the Effectiveness of Corporate Audit Committees. The Committee issued its recommendations in early 1999 and, by December of that year, a number of self-regulatory bodies and the SEC issued new rules implementing their recommendations. The stock exchanges' rules cover the corporate governance areas addressed by the Committee, namely, audit committee independence, qualifications, composition, and charter. The Auditing Standards Board of the AICPA required new communications about annual and quarterly financial reporting. The SEC's rules require timely quarterly reviews by auditors as well as disclosure about audit committees in companies' annual proxy statements.

In addition to the issue of who the audit client is, another pervasive problem in the auditing function is the expansion of non-audit (consulting) services for audit clients. Clearly, there is a potential for loss of independence if auditors and their corporate clients create a mutuality of interests through large consulting arrangements or multiple consulting arrangements. Critics of auditors doing consulting point out that there is a fundamental conflict of interest when auditors do consulting for their audit clients because the "client" is management for a consulting engagement and is the Board of Directors/investors when doing audit engagements. The existence of this conflict of interests impairs auditor independence. In addition, auditors may end up auditing their own work, or the consulting engagement may be a higher priority to the firm than the audit because of its sheer size, or that the pressure on audit staff to sell additional consulting services to their audit clients reduces their effectiveness. It is pretty hard to convince the company's controller of the need for a certain audit adjustment while simultaneously trying to sell the controller a new service. The pressure to sell comes from firms' compensation arrangements that reward audit partners for new services brought into the firm. Promotions below the partner level are also affected by one's ability to market new services.

Others counter these arguments by pointing to a number of empirical studies, which have failed to show actual impairments to audits because of consulting services. They also argue that the auditor is often in the best position to know the client's needs and serve them, and in doing so the audit function may actually be improved. The issue is being hotly debated in the profession, but while the debate goes on the SEC continues to add pressure. The result is that by the year 2000 each of the largest five accounting firms (the "Big 5") had moved, in one way or another, toward divesting itself of its consulting division.

The term "expectations gap" was coined to describe another major issue in the auditing function. The expectations gap is the difference between what the public expects of auditors and what auditors themselves see as their proper role with respect to detection of fraud and prediction of business failures. To address the expectations gap, the accounting profession has issued new auditing standards giving guidance about evaluating internal controls, providing early warning of a company's financial difficulties, designing the audit to provide reasonable assurance of detecting material fraud, and improving communication to financial statement users and audit committees. In spite of all these efforts, the expectations gap persists. Over the past twenty-five years, a number of blue-ribbon panel recommendations have been issued calling for companies to report on their internal control structures and for auditors to audit those reports. It wasn't until the mid-1990s that the profession publicly supported having reports on internal controls. There is no question that financial fraud is closely linked to the strength of a company's internal control system. Auditors have the technical ability to evaluate internal controls, and reporting on such an evaluation seems to be a logical extension of the financial statement audit and a way to force companies to follow the auditors' suggestions for improving internal controls. Improved internal controls lead to less financial fraud and a narrowing of the expectations gap. However, mandatory reporting on a company's internal control system would have to be required by the SEC and no movement in that direction is on the near horizon. When the DOW next falls, and companies fall prey to an economic downturn, pressures to improve "the bottom line" will increase proportionately. It is during such times that bankruptcies increase, incidents of fraud are uncovered, and Congress holds hearings to determine, "where were the auditors?" Probably not until then will the climate be ripe for the SEC to mandate reporting on internal controls.

As long as the economy is still robust, another ethical issue faces auditors: lack of appropriate experience in audit personnel. The auditing profession, indeed public accounting in general, has a high level of turnover for a variety of reasons, and the problem is exacerbated when demand for employees is especially strong throughout the economy. While large numbers of brand new auditors are hired out of colleges and universities every year, only a small percentage of those new hires stay with the firms long enough to celebrate their fifth anniversary. Even though each audit team includes a partner in charge of the audit, as well as other seasoned staff, inexperienced trainees who simply lack the ability to make professional judgments required of the work inevitably perform the bulk of the work. Warnings have come recently from a number of sources, including the SEC, that young, inexperienced staff must have adequate levels of supervision for audits to be effective.

MacIntyre (1984) discusses virtues as the means to achieving internal goods of a practice, such as accounting. The internal goods of accounting would be improvements in the art itself. For example, an improved way to portray in financial statements the economic reality of compensatory stock options granted to corporate employees, or an improvement in auditing techniques that leads to a greater level of assurance offered to users of financial statements. In other words, continuous improvements in the art of accounting and auditing lead to excellence, and the road to excellence requires exercise of virtues.

The AICPA has named several virtues necessary to achieve excellence: independence (when providing audit or other attest services), integrity, objectivity, due care, concern for the public interest, and confidentiality. Other authors would add to this list the virtues of professional skepticism, trustworthiness, and others. The point is, as a profession we know what it takes to achieve excellence, but without a strong culture of professionalism reinforcing the need for these virtues, we are easily distracted by the pursuit of external goods such as wealth, increase in market share, and others.

Independence

Because independence is so important to the attest function and because of recent developments in the profession, a separate section is devoted to this important topic. The principles section of the AICPA *Code of Professional Conduct* (1992, ET Section 55) describes independence as precluding relationships that may appear to impair a member's objectivity in rendering attestation services. It further states, "a member who provides auditing and other attestation services should be independent in fact and appearance." Three items of interest should be noted about ET Section 55:

1 Independence is applicable only to CPAs in public practice, and then only when they perform auditing or other attestation services (not tax or consulting).
2 Independence deals with relationships.
3 Independence has two facets – "in fact" and "in appearance."

The first item is significant because less than half of the members of the AICPA are in public practice, and less than half of those perform any attest services. Therefore, less than 25 percent of the AICPA members need to concern themselves with independence. Nevertheless, Interpretations and Rulings under Rule 101 (Independence) comprise over 60 percent of the enforceable part of the AICPA code. A casual observer might conclude that such heavy emphasis on independence is due to the fact that it is the most important attribute of CPAs. This author would disagree with that conclusion. Independence is indeed important, but objectivity and integrity are equally important, if not more so. The reason CPAs must not enter into forbidden relationships is so their objectivity will not be impaired or their integrity tempted. Why then, is there such a heavy emphasis on independence in the code? Because objectivity is described as a "state of mind" and integrity as "an element of character." Neither a state of mind nor an element of character can be seen, so rules about them are difficult to enforce.

Independence, however, has to do with relationships, which can be seen. Therefore the AICPA goes to great lengths to describe all the relationships that are forbidden and some of the relationships that might be allowed. The result is a forest of detailed, confusing, and sometimes unfathomable restrictions that the average CPA does not comprehend. For example, if one of the partners in an audit firm has a brother-in-law who is a member of the board of directors of a client audited by that partner's office, independence is impaired if the brother-in-law is the partner's sister's husband, but independence is not impaired if the brother-in-law is the partner's spouse's brother.

Although the Principles section of the AICPA code addresses independence in fact and independence in appearance, the Principles section is "educational" in nature. That is, it is not enforceable. The Rules section of the Code, including Interpretations and Rulings, is enforceable. In the Rules section the AICPA appears to draw bright lines between allowed and not-allowed relationships. Thus, they seem to be eliminating professional judgment and the whole concept of independence in appearance.

Independence Standards Board (ISB)

Because of the problems associated with the independence rules as defined in the Code of Professional Conduct, and because of an apparent lack of active enforcement on a wide-scale basis, the SEC put pressure on the AICPA to create the ISB in 1997. The ISB is an independent organization charged with examining auditor independence from the ground up. One of their earliest tasks was to create a "conceptual framework" for independence so the rules would not be of an *ad hoc* nature but would be consistent. Much of the work of the ISB is still not formalized but, by August 2000, they did issue one pronouncement requiring auditors to discuss their independence and relationships that might bear on independence with their clients' Audit Committees or Boards of Directors. They issued another pronouncement relaxing independence rules relating to the audit of mutual funds and related entities, and issued a third pronouncement concerning safeguards audit firms should implement when their professionals quit the audit firm and join audit clients as employees of those clients.

The ISB has issued a number of discussion memoranda concerning other issues related to independence. One theme that seems to run through their deliberations is a return to the use of professional judgment to determine if an auditor or firm is independent. They do that by enumerating certain "bright lines" whose violations are clear cases of independence impairment. But staying within the lines does not necessarily guarantee independence. Instead, the ISB would require processes in place in each firm whereby certain situations are examined, on a case-by-case basis, and a designated group who must document their deliberations and bases for conclusions makes a determination about independence. The processes would be monitored during the firms' peer reviews.

PricewaterhouseCoopers (PwC)

Before the ISB completed any significant work on reformulating independence rules, the profession was rocked by an independence scandal. PwC, one of the "Big 5" accounting firms, was found to have over 8000 violations of independence rules. The PwC case started in 1997 with a SEC investigation of the Tampa, Florida office of Coopers & Lybrand, one of the PwC "legacy" firms (the other was Price Waterhouse). Because of independence violations found in Tampa, and other issues, in January, 1999 the SEC ordered a firm-wide investigation. All members of the firm, 36,170 professionals, were required to do a self-analysis of their relationships with clients and to send their confirmations to an outside firm, who performed a random sample study of the results. In total, 1885 individuals reported 8064 violations. In the vast majority of the cases, the individuals involved had no contact with the client whose stock they, or a spouse, held and often the violations were related to mutual fund families. In most cases, the violator worked in one office of the firm but owned stock in a client audited by another office of the firm and the violator was unaware s/he owned a client's stock. Only 184 of the violations, involving 52 different clients, were considered "client service infractions" where the violator actually worked on the audit or in some other capacity for the audit client. The SEC investigated each of those cases and decided the infraction did not jeopardize the audit. In other words, the SEC, after investigating the facts, decided to process the public filings of the clients in their ordinary course. The vast majority of the infractions were due to a less-than-thorough review of the firm's independence lists by the individuals involved. Nevertheless, the SEC strongly suggested that a few of PwC's large audit clients find new auditors, and they did so. After the results of the study, PwC invested close to $50 million in a new system of tracking firm members' holdings and matching them with clients (as opposed to giving the lists to firm members to self-check) and in educating all firm members in the independence rules.

By June 2000, each of the other large auditing firms agreed to take part in a voluntary program reviewing their independence compliance. In addition, the SEC proposed changes in their independence rules that would significantly reduce the number of audit firm employees and their family members whose investments in audit clients would impair an auditor's independence. The changes would also identify certain non-audit services that would impair independence if performed for an audit client. In addition, a limited exception would be provided to accounting firms for inadvertent independence violations if the firm has quality controls in place and the violation is corrected promptly. Further, companies would disclose in their annual proxy statements certain information about non-audit services provided by their auditors during the last fiscal year. The majority of the SEC's proposed changes became effective in January 2001.

The real tragedy of the PwC case is the reduction in public confidence in the whole accounting profession because of headlines detailing over 8000 independence violations in one of the profession's most prestigious firms. What the public doesn't realize is that most of those violations did not affect independence in fact (indeed, often the individual violator neither worked on the audit nor knew the stock belonged to an audit client) nor did it violate independence in appearance until the financial press reported the news. What were violated were myriad technical rules. The objectivity of the auditors on the audit teams examining the clients' financial statements was probably never threatened, in spite of the 8064 technical violations. This does not excuse, however, the obvious low priority paid to the details of the independence rules and to making sure there were no violations of them. It does indicate that the time is more than ripe for a re-examination of the independence rules. In early 2001, the AICPA issued an exposure draft of proposed changes in its independence rules, similar to the new SEC independence rules.

The next section examines the role played by regulators and standard setters in a self-regulated profession, such as accounting.

The Roles of Regulators and Standard Setters

It is not always clear where the boundaries lie between self-regulation and governmental regulation. For example, in 1988 the Tax Division of the AICPA wrote eight *Statements on Responsibilities in Tax Practice* (SRTP). They clearly state that the SRTPs are "educational in nature" and violations of them do not constitute a violation of the *Code of Professional Conduct*. Nevertheless, some states incorporated the SRTPs into their regulations by name (e.g., Florida) while other states' regulations required licensees to comply with "all applicable professional standards," presumably including the SRTPs (e.g., California). Thus, a California or Florida CPA could have found him or herself disciplined for violating an AICPA tax standard that clearly stated it was only educational in nature. In October 2000, the AICPA acknowledged this difficulty and replaced the SRTPs with *Statements of Standards for Tax Services* (SSTS), which are mandatory (i.e., violation of the new SSTSs constitutes a violation of the code of conduct).

Because they share common objectives with regard to the public interest, the accounting profession, regulators (e.g., SEC and state Boards of Accountancy), and standard setters (e.g., Financial Accounting Standards Board (FASB), Auditing Standards Board) need to cooperate with each other to achieve their common goals. Unfortunately, the working relationships among these groups are sometimes strained, to the detriment of all involved. In 1994 Walter Schuetze, then Chief Accountant at the SEC, accused large auditing firms of being "cheerleaders for their clients" because the senior partners in the six largest auditing firms jointly signed a letter to the FASB objecting to proposed changes in standards relating to accounting for stock options granted to corporate employees. While large firms certainly should communicate their views on proposed accounting standards, those communications should not come jointly from the Big 5. Joint letters create the impression that the senior partners and the firms they represent are trying to impress the FASB with clout rather than sound reasoning.

Standard setters should be committed to addressing and resolving issues on a timely basis. A number of times, the SEC has demonstrated impatience with the FASB and has promulgated its own accounting rules to spur on or prod the standard setters to address important issues faster. In particular, the FASB needs to be more aggressive in bringing issues forward for discussion.

The SEC is charged with enforcing accounting and auditing standards, not establishing them. The SEC should be a standard setter of last resort, acting only if the profession is unable or unwilling to do so in a timely manner, but even then the SEC should follow due process. For example, the FASB established the Emerging Issues Task Force (EITF) in 1984 to help it identify emerging accounting issues. Often, as a result of discussing an issue, the EITF reaches a general consensus and the FASB probably does not need to address the issue. On other occasions, the inability of the EITF to reach a consensus may be clear evidence that the FASB needs to address the issue. In one instance the chief accountant of the SEC added detailed guidance on accounting for restructuring charges to the minutes of an EITF meeting even though the EITF had not reached a consensus on that guidance and it had not been stated at the meeting.

What is needed, but sometimes is clearly missing, is an attitude of mutual respect and cooperation among the accountants themselves, the standard setters, and the regulators, for the sake of the public interest.

Keeping Grounded in a Dynamic Environment

The world around us, including the business environment, is changing at a dizzying speed. The profession of accounting is not immune to its dynamic environment. Large CPA firms no longer even identify themselves as such, but refer to themselves as "professional service providers." Alternative practice structures have emerged where the parent entity is often a publicly traded corporation. Services once exclusively performed by CPA firms are now provided by other entities, while CPA firms are branching into previously forbidden territories. Fee arrangements differ; entities are forming new, strategic alliances rarely heard of just a decade or two before. In short, it is not my grandfather's (or even father's) accounting profession. How does a profession remain grounded in its core beliefs, values, and virtues when undergoing such profound and rapid changes? How do we know if we are throwing out just the bath water, or the baby, too?

In 1997, the AICPA began a two-year project to examine the accounting profession and form a vision of its future. This "vision project" involved discussions and brainstorming with CPAs all over the country. Approximately 3400 CPAs spent over 21,000 hours identifying both challenges and opportunities for the profession in the year 2011. The results were captured in a database of core values, core services, core competencies, and significant issues for the future. Core values were identified by the participants in the project:

1 Continuing education and life-long learning
2 Competence
3 Integrity
4 Attuned to broad business issues
5 Objectivity

In addition, the individuals who brought this enormous amount of material together identified certain underlying themes. The themes were identified as essential for CPAs to make the vision a reality and are reflected in the following "overarching messages for the profession":

1 The only constant is change at an unprecedented pace
2 Moving up the economic value chain
3 Protect the public interest
4 Leverage diversity of experience and thought
5 Coping with an increasing rate of change
6 Leaders or followers

Observe that the 3400 CPAs who contributed to the vision project in their forums and otherwise, did not identify the public interest or independence as core values. It was only at the end of the project that the "overarching message" of protecting the public interest was added. Over the years, a number of authors have asked whether accounting is more of a profession or more of a business because, clearly, the two overlap a great deal. But the distinguishing mark of a profession, that which sets it apart from other businesses, is the promise to act in the public interest. Apparently CPAs, in recent years, have forgotten that or never learned it. On a brighter note, the CPAs involved in the vision project clearly understood that integrity and objectivity are what we are about and necessary for us to succeed at what we do. The AICPA is comprised of members in public accounting, industry, government, and education and all segments of the profession took part in the vision project. The core attributes of integrity and objectivity are equally important for all accountants, no matter what specific function they perform.

References

AICPA (American Institute of Certified Public Accountants). 1988: *Statements on Responsibility in Tax Practice.* New York: AICPA.

AICPA (American Institute of Certified Public Accountants). 1991: *Statements on Standards in Consulting Services.* New York: AICPA.

AICPA (American Institute of Certified Public Accountants). 1992: *Code of Professional Conduct as Amended 14 January 1992.* New York: AICPA.

AICPA (American Institute of Certified Public Accountants). 2000: *Statements on Standards for Tax Services.* New York: AICPA.

Armstrong, M. B. and Robison, J. 1998: Ethics in taxation. *Journal of Accounting, Ethics, & Public Policy,* 1 (4), Fall, 535–57.

Institute of Management Accountants. 1997: *Standards of Ethical Conduct for Practitioners of Management Accounting and Financial Management.* Montvale, NJ: IMA.

Lemon, W. M. and Wallace, W. A. 2000: Ethical issues facing internal auditors and their profession. *Research on Accounting Ethics,* 6, 189–203.

Levitt, A. 1998: *The Numbers Game.* New York University: Center for Law and Business. 28 September 1–8.

MacIntyre, A. 1984: *After Virtue.* Notre Dame, IN: University of Notre Dame Press.

Merchant, K. S. 1996: *Management Control Systems: Text and Cases.* Englewood Cliffs, NJ: Prentice-Hall.

Merchant, K. S. and Van der Stede, W. A. 2000: Ethical issues related to "Results-Oriented" management control systems. *Research on Accounting Ethics,* 6, 153–69.

Rawls, J. 1955: Two concepts of rules. *Philosophical Review,* 64, 3–32.

Sutton, M. H. 1997: Auditor independence: The challenge of fact and appearance. *Accounting Horizons,* 11 (2), March, 86–91.

Chapter 8

Marketing Ethics at the Millennium: Review, Reflections, and Recommendations

Patrick E. Murphy

Marketing ethics came of age in the 1990s. Substantial attention was devoted to the topic in the academic and business press during the last decade. It was no longer uncommon to see journal articles that examined theoretical foundations or empirical results on this topic. The field moved from what was earlier believed as the oxymoron stage to one of academic legitimacy. This movement occurred over a relatively short period of time.

The first articles on ethical issues in marketing appeared in the 1960s and were, for the most part, philosophical essays (Murphy and Laczniak, 1981). The early empirical work dealing with the decision-making process tended to be lacking in a theoretical foundation. The research tradition in marketing ethics continued in the 1970s with modest work on the subject. In the 1980s, a major research thrust was devoted to examining ethics in marketing; for a summary of this literature, see Leigh and Murphy (1999). Laczniak (1993) observed that the state of marketing ethics research at that time was increasingly characterized as having broader coverage, greater academic visibility and a developing theoretical and empirical foundation. Since these reviews appear to have accurately captured the status of marketing ethics, the focus here is almost exclusively on research and practice in marketing over the last decade.

Before moving to the outline of the chapter, a brief characterization of marketing ethics is necessary. This field is a subset of business ethics and deals with the systematic study of how moral standards are applied to marketing decisions, behaviors and institutions. In essence, marketing ethics examines moral issues faced by marketing managers and organizations. A long list of topics fall under the rubric of marketing ethics. Some of the most prevalent are: product safety and liability, advertising truthfulness and honesty, fairness in pricing, power within the channels of distribution, privacy in Internet and database marketing, and forthrightness in selling.

This paper begins with a short background on the research progress in the 1990s and moves to a discussion of positive trends in the study of marketing ethics. The third section examines some not so positive trends and then discusses methods of resolving ethical challenges in marketing. Lastly, the paper addresses responsible marketing practice and concludes with areas of needed research emphasis in marketing.

Four books appeared during this time period that were devoted to marketing ethics. Laczniak and Murphy (1993) wrote a ten-chapter book examining the ethical aspects of a range of marketing decisions including marketing research, the marketing mix variables and international issues applying a strong philosophical ethics base. Smith and Quelch's (1993) text featured a compilation of over twenty Harvard cases, readings from the business press and overview articles on all the major areas of marketing. Chonko (1995) employed a conflict and decision-making lens to his standard treatment of ethical issues in marketing. Schlegelmilch's (1998) book differed from the others in that his was positioned as an international marketing ethics text. He devoted eight chapters to ethical issues in marketing, included four cases and eight published journal articles as background reading. Taken together, these works helped establish the legitimacy of the field, but only spawned a small number of courses on the topic.

Scholarly attention in marketing journals on ethics was sustained and assisted by several targeted efforts. Nine articles have appeared in the *Journal of Marketing*, arguably the leading journal in marketing, from 1989 to date, specifically devoted to ethics. Three were co-authored by Shelby Hunt and his doctoral students or colleagues, and two were co-authored by Craig Smith. Other specialty-oriented marketing journals devoted one or more special issues to ethics during this time. For example, the *Journal of Public Policy and Marketing* featured a special section on marketing ethics in the Spring 1993 issue containing three articles and an overview piece by the section editor, Gene Laczniak. In the Fall 1998 issue, the *Journal of Public Policy and Marketing* published a series of reaction papers to the Pontifical Council's *Ethics in Advertising* document. The *European Journal of Marketing* published a special issue in 1996 on marketing and social responsibility (Volume 30, Number 5) with the six articles evenly split between those on ethics and social/environmental responsibility.

Not surprisingly, the journal paying by far the most attention in the 1990s to marketing ethics was *Journal of Business Ethics*. On three separate occasions, special issues were devoted to this topic. The first appeared in the April 1991 issue and included seven papers from a conference chaired at DePaul University by Robert Pitts. The second was guest edited by Anusorn Singhapakdi and Scott Vitell on international marketing ethics featuring nine articles in the January 1999 issue. The February 2000 issue contained seven papers that were revised from presentations given at the Marketing Exchange Colloquium held in Vienna during the Summer 1998. Numerous other articles on various facets of marketing ethics have been published in the past dozen years. In fact, one of the four *Journal of Business Ethics* sections is marketing (others being theoretical foundations, work and international management) and its editor is Scott Vitell.

Positive Trends

Among the positive developments in marketing ethics during recent years has been a recognition of the distinction between normative, descriptive and analytical work in the field (Brenkert, 1999). Normative (or prescriptive) ethics deals with formulating and defending basic moral norms, while descriptive ethics deals with the scientific study of ethics by social scientists with popular and business press treatments of marketing issues. Analytical marketing ethics, as envisioned by Brenkert (1999), includes works that examine basic ethical marketing concepts and norms, and why marketers ought to be worried about being moral (p. 187). This writer would classify some of these efforts as normative. The distinction between empirical and conceptual is a common delineation of ethics research and one that has led to significant controversy (especially in the pages of *Business Ethics Quarterly*), but will not be explicitly examined here.

Normative marketing ethics

The traditional normative ethical theories of utilitarianism and right/duty-based ethics have received some discussion in recent years (Nantel and Weeks, 1996; Murphy, 1997). However, major new theoretical paradigms appeared during the 1990s in marketing. Robin and Reidenbach (1993) propose an ethical philosophy for marketing that is characterized by bounded moral relativism and relies heavily on descriptive ethics. Thompson (1995) offers a contextualist model of marketing ethics based on the work of Kohlberg and Gilligan, and claims that adopting a more caring orientation for marketing is an opportunity to be an ethical innovator in the organization. Drawing on the European tradition of dialogic idealism, Nill and Schultz (1997) contend that solving ethical issues in marketing is related not so much to opportunity as will. That is, when stakeholders enter into a dialogue to resolve common dilemmas, more positive outcomes are probable. Most recently, integrative social contracts theory has been proposed as providing a coherent framework for resolving ethical issues that arise across multiple communities and cultures (Dunfee et al. 1999). Since each of these theoretical proposals emanate from different philosophical traditions, they have broadened the normative base for marketing ethics.

One normative ethical theory that has received substantial attention during the 1990s is virtue/character ethics. Williams and Murphy (1990) elaborated on the applicability of virtue ethics with its Aristotlean roots to marketing mix variables and, using this theory, contrasted Johnson & Johnson handling of the Tylenol crisis with Nestle's strategy for selling infant formula in less developed countries. Hartman and Beck-Dudley (1999) proposed a framework to integrate virtue ethics into marketing theory and demonstrated its applicability in case study. Murphy (1999) advocated five core virtues: integrity, fairness, trust, respect and empathy as especially relevant for marketing in a multi-cultural and multinational context. While difficult to operationalize, the focus on virtue/character is viewed as a theory that can inform marketing since individual judgment is important in making proper ethical decisions.

Theory testing in marketing ethics

Several articles appeared in the major marketing journals during the 1990s testing normative theories in a marketing context. One theory that received substantial attention is Kohlberg's theory of cognitive moral development (CMD). Goolsby and Hunt (1992) introduced it to the marketing field and found that

(a) marketing practitioners are similar to other professional groups on the CMD scale
(b) highly educated female marketers score highest on CMD, and
(c) those marketers most advanced in moral reasoning also exhibit socially responsible attitudes and behavior.

Fraedrich and Ferrell (1992) questioned CMD's appropriateness for marketing ethics research since they found 85 percent of their respondents did not use a consistent philosophical theory in work and nonwork situations. They further elaborated on this point of view in a subsequent article (Fraedrich et al. 1994).

Additional empirical investigation examined several traditional and recent theoretical precepts in marketing. Hunt and Vasquez-Parraga's (1993) findings suggest decisions to either discipline or reward salespeople's behavior are guided primarily by the inherent rightness or wrongness (deontological considerations) and only secondarily by consequences (teleological factors) (p. 78). Morgan and Hunt (1994) studied the virtues of commitment and trust in relationship marketing and determined that keys to relationship building were maintaining high corporate standards, communicating actively with partners and avoiding malevolent behavior. Finally, Sparks and Hunt (1998) examined ethical sensitivity among a sample of marketing researchers and found that those who exhibited greater ethical sensitivity were socialized into the research profession by learning the ethical norms.

Descriptive marketing ethics

Several major articles in marketing ethics were not theory-based, but examined ongoing ethical issues dealing with market segmentation and targeting, dangerous products and unethical behavior in the marketplace. Both Smith and Cooper-Martin (1997) and Brenkert (1998a, b) noted that targeting vulnerable consumers is often viewed as an unethical marketing activity. Brenkert (1998b) discussed the marketing of PowerMaster malt liquor to inner-city African Americans and concluded that marketers must accept moral responsibility both for their targeting strategies as well as a collective impact of the combined marketing efforts aimed at that segment. Smith and Cooper-Martin (1997) empirically examined the question of harmful products aimed at vulnerable segments in two studies and found that both targeting as well as product harm raised ethical concerns. Taking a broader viewpoint, Brenkert (1998a) challenges marketing programs that target vulnerable (defined as physically, cognitively, motivationally and socially) consumers to treat them fairly. He proposes the doctrine of targeted consumer liability patterned after the product liability doctrine as a method of accountability.

The question of unethical behavior in marketing has also been a subject of several other articles in recent years. In studying a national sample of sales managers, Bellizzi and Hite (1989) found that harsher disciplinary action occurred when the salespeople were poor performers and involved in unethical behavior. Mascarenhas (1995) focused on unethical behavior of higher level marketing executives and proposed ten propositions that challenge marketing executives to go beyond legal and attributional responsibilities to approportional responsibilities of commitment to consumers they serve (p. 43). Bishop (2000) presents a moral defense of image advertising (that some critics view as unethical) and concludes that it is basically an ethical technique that does not undermine several types of autonomy. Many additional works in the special issues of the *Journal of Business Ethics* noted above examine a multitude of issues in descriptive marketing ethics.

Not So Positive Trends

While there is substantial good news to report on the recent trends in marketing ethics research and practice, several troubling trends have also surfaced. Four are discussed here: student samples, scenario-based research, cross-cultural studies and testing narrow theoretical propositions.

Student Samples

A longstanding question in the academic marketing field is: are students real people? In the context of marketing manager (as opposed to consumer) ethics, this writer believes the answer is clearly no. It should be noted that student samples are a problem in much social science research, often because of expediency. The focus should be on the marketing manager/executive, who is the decision maker, and few students have held meaningful positions in the business world. Therefore, they appear to be suspect respondents and the external validity of studies that use exclusively student subjects for research in marketing ethics must be questioned. In some instances, MBA students or executive MBA students (who have had substantial experience and are currently employed) may be utilized effectively in ethics research. However, they should be used cautiously and, ideally, with a practitioner sample. While some academics argue their acceptability for scale validation – (students were selected for use in this study because there is a long history of using CMD measures with students and because national norms are established for them (Robin et al., 1996, p. 500) – they should be used cautiously in marketing ethics research. Sparks and Hunt (1998) studied both students with practitioners and their conclusions were largely drawn from the managers' sample.

Scenario-based research

Many articles dealing with ethical issues in marketing over the years have effectively used scenarios to set up realistic situations to which respondents can react. However, some researchers in marketing ethics utilize too many or too few scenarios; in one instance, twenty were presented. Expecting anyone to respond meaningfully to this many situations is unrealistic. Others vary one particular scenario and draw conclusions from it. While this approach makes for a "cleaner" experiment or survey, it places too much emphasis on one situation that may be contrived or unusual. A related practice is continuing to use scenarios developed many years ago. Assuredly, valid measures need to be used and there is value in replication. Experimentation with scenarios that reflect recent events impacting the practice of marketing such as online selling, research on the web, privacy concerns and so on are needed in marketing ethics research.

Cross-cultural research

In the figuratively shrinking world of the late twentieth and early twenty-first centuries, marketing is increasingly global. As mentioned previously, the January 1999 issue of *Journal of Business Ethics* was devoted entirely to international marketing ethics. Researchers in the marketing field have begun to collaborate with foreign-based colleagues to examine ethical questions of interest in multiple countries. Such comparisons can be valuable. However, small sample studies from two or three countries often yield conflicting and confusing findings. Furthermore, findings that consumers or salespeople or managers operate from somewhat different ethical bases on which to make decisions tend to be commonsensical.

Cross-cultural research could be less atheoretical. Too often studies set out to test hypotheses that are obvious and/or trivial and any failure to find support is generally a failing of method rather than theory. Inadequate conceptualization is a big drawback, followed closely by methodological rigor. In the future, greater efforts should be made by empirical researchers in marketing ethics to design cross-cultural studies that extend our understanding of consumers, markets or companies rather than confirm Hofstede's values typology or undertake advertising strategy comparisons in different countries of brand evaluations. Since the differences between cultures appear to be lessening and marketers are attempting to address global needs, finding areas of commonality and ethical agreement would seem to be more beneficial than identifying often trivial differences between cultures.

Testing narrow theoretical propositions

Theory testing is essential in marketing ethics as in other fields. The 1990s saw a major increase in this type of research within marketing ethics. The theory most often tested is the Hunt and Vitell (1986) model with many papers appearing in the last fifteen years. While it is quite difficult to operationalize generalized theories and models, some marketing scholars have been content to investigate such narrow propositions and theories that the outcome of their work is marginalized. The field of marketing ethics seems increasingly to be using the same narrow lens that has characterized much of the consumer behavior research over a prolonged period. Many of the issues in marketing ethics are murky and hard to operationalize, but should not be trivialized. The work of marketing ethics can impact the practice of marketing if researchers keep in mind that they are not engaged in just a narrow academic exercise. In fact, too many authors are unwilling to extrapolate beyond the data and add meaningful implications of their work. This shortcoming contributes to the marginalization of their research.

Reversing these trends

Taken singly or together these not so favorable trends do not undermine marketing ethics scholarship or the desire to make marketing more ethical. At the expense of sounding trite, all these areas are in need of increased emphasis on quality rather than quantity. Judicious and reasoned use of student samples in studying reactions to advertising or selling efforts aimed at teens and young adults is appropriate. Comparisons of managers' reactions of new vs. time tested scenarios can make a contribution. Cross-cultural research that helps understand similarities rather than differences should be undertaken. Finally, theory testing must go on, but answers to larger, rather than smaller, questions should be sought.

Resolving Ethical Challenges in Marketing

Improving the status of ethics in marketing for the future, especially in a global world, will require substantial effort on a number of fronts. Ones examined here are regulation, organizational leadership, social responsibility, and candid communication – these headings are adapted from Shultz and Holbrook (1999).

Regulation

Several ethical issues facing marketing appear to be sufficiently intractable that some type of governmental regulation will be needed to find solutions for them. One is the area of bribery and corruption. The US Foreign Corrupt Practices Act, enacted in 1977, places constraints on US based corporations regarding bribery. While this topic is one that is often discussed in a business ethics context (DeGeorge, 1993; Donaldson, 1996), it can be viewed as a marketing ethics issue because sales or marketing executives are frequently the ones placed in a position of whether to offer a bribe. The OECD in 1999 instituted guidelines for companies operating in member countries but only 21 countries have complied to date; see oecd.org/daf/nocorruption/instruments.htm. Dunfee et al. (1999) examined bribery in detail and contended that an ethical solution can be found. A major effort to put pressure on governments to reduce bribery and corruption is Transparency International's Bribe Payers Index and Corruption Perceptions Index, (CPI) (transparency.org) Despite these initiatives, it appears that the long-term solution will take the efforts of individual country governments and major organizations such as the EU and OECD to make them work.

A second area where regulation is likely the preferred outcome is in product counterfeiting. Some would not describe this as an ethical issue, since counterfeiting is stealing and against the law in many places. Yet, the issue is examined in an ethical context. Products like software, watches, jeans, and perfumes are ones often associated with counterfeit activity (Chaudhry and Walsh, 1996). Furthermore, aircraft parts, pharmaceuticals, and infant formula are products where lower quality can definitely impact a consumer's safety. Some governments have chosen to crack down on this practice, but as marketing firms rush to expand to China (ranked in a tie with four others in 58th place on CPI) and other parts of the developing world, this issue will continue to be one for which a solution will be elusive.

Third, the phenomenal growth of the use of the internet and online commerce has brought out a number of ethical concerns including privacy, security and jurisdiction. This writer and others (Caudill and Murphy, 2000; Culnan, 2000) have identified privacy as an ethical and public policy concern. The EU was far ahead of the USA in identifying privacy as a consumer issue and issued a directive in 1995 on the subject. Both philosophical and practical differences in the way privacy is viewed in the EU and the USA are important to understand (Scheibal and Gladstone, 2000). Only recently was a compromise resolution between the USA and the EU achieved (Caudill and Murphy, 2000). In the USA, the Federal Trade Commission has taken a leadership position in setting industry guidelines for privacy and commercial transactions. Many believe that self-regulation is the answer, but the international scope of the issue makes both regulation and self-regulation difficult. As the USA now has a new President and Congress, some regulatory action is likely.

Organizational leadership

Ethics at the organizational level obviously has a pronounced impact on decisions made in marketing. Leadership at the corporate and marketing level set the ethical climate for the firm. Researchers have proposed or found this linkage (Ferrell et al., 1989; Hunt et al., 1989) and a recently published paper concluded: informal culture was found to have a direct relationship to ethical decision making. The relationship of formal policies, however, was largely an indirect one . . . (Leigh and Murphy 1999, p. 69). A study of salespeople and their propensity to engage in lying concluded that ethics codes and ethics clarity do have an effect on behavior (Ross and Robertson, 2000, p. 436). Rallapalli (1999) proposed a global code of ethics for marketing and identified moral reasoning, organizational ethical climate, level of economic development and cultural dimensions as factors that may impede the adoption of such a code. Organizational factors such as size (MNC or SME), culture/climate and presence or absence of ethics statements need further investigation as to their influence on marketing actions.

Three companies have exhibited the type of organizational leadership advocated by these researchers. Probably the best known corporate statement on ethics is the Johnson & Johnson Credo. The Tylenol incident is the known incident of a company following its ethical values. What is not as well known is that the Credo is translated into many languages, framed reprints are prominently displayed in most offices and it is evaluated bi-annually via a questionnaire that asks managerial support for every line of the Credo. A second illustration is Levi Strauss & Company. The firm has multiple ethics statements and exhibited leadership with its Global Sourcing & Operating Guidelines. They offer detailed guidance in working with worldwide suppliers. (For more information on the company's ethics statements, see Murphy (1998, pp. 130–9).) A third firm offering its employees direction with respect to ethics is United Technologies. The company has developed nine separate booklets on ethical issues facing its managers and workers. Of particular relevance to marketing is the one on Gathering Competitive Information. This is an area of growing strategic importance for companies and few offer the level of specificity offered by United Technologies. These firms are not alone in exhibiting leadership with their corporate stance on ethics, but marketing managers do need moral and real support.

Social responsibility

The relationship between ethics and social responsibility is one that is often discussed, but sometimes interpreted differently. For our purposes, ethics deals with issues pertaining to the organization and its stakeholders in day to day business transactions. Social responsibility refers to a company's posture relative to the community (either narrowly or broadly defined). Ethics tends to be more internal in orientation, while social responsibility is more external, but the orientation is not an absolute one. Ethics usually deals at the individual manager level, while social responsibility is associated with the corporate/organizational level.

Some view ethics in marketing as being synonymous with social responsibility. Many companies that are highly ethical also exhibit heightened levels of corporate social responsibility (CSR), but they are not the same. In fact, the term "corporate citizenship" is used now to denote many of the activities that fell under CSR umbrella. Maignan and Ferrell (2000) both operationalized and measured corporate citizenship along four correlated dimensions: economic, legal, ethical and discretionary.

In a recently published anthology, *Handbook of Marketing and Society*, Bloom and Gundlach (2001) feature twenty-two papers that examine all facets of marketing's role in society. Two papers in the volume directly address CSR. Smith (2001) proposes a model of consumer influence (in terms of special interest groups and boycotts) on CSR. Drumwright and Murphy (2001) coined the term "corporate societal marketing" to describe a range of ten activities that have economic and non-economic objectives and influence social welfare. Table 8.1 depicts the forms and dimensions of corporate societal marketing. The scope of these activities is growing and when they are combined with an integrated communications program, many additional hybrid forms may result. These programs sometimes are controversial and the ethical challenges in terms of micro and macro ethical issues to corporate societal marketing are outlined. For instance, American Express (AmEx) has been heavily criticized for two of its cause-related marketing campaigns, "Charge Against Hunger" and "Statue of Liberty," because far more was spent on advertising the initiative than was given to the causes. In conclusion, social responsibility within marketing appears to have evolved into a more sophisticated, less philanthropic and more cautious venture from here onwards.

Candid communication

A common theme in both business and marketing ethics is the importance of communication to reduce unethical behavior or the perception of it. This communication should be both internal and external. In my survey of codes of ethics (Murphy, 1995), it was rather surprising that nearly half of all codes remain as internal documents only. One surmises that an ethics code that is just for internal purposes is rather legalistic or meant to cover legal bases rather than as an aspirational document. In the conclusion of their empirical study of salespeople, Ross and Robertson (2000, p. 436) drew several implications for practitioners and stated: "The most important of these is the communication of ethical clarity."

Table 8.1 Corporate societal marketing: Forms and dimensions

Form	Emphasis given economic objectives	Employee involvement	Types of resources deployed	Budget source
Traditional philanthropy	Low	Low	Money	Philanthropy
Strategic philanthropy	Moderate	Low	Money, in-kind gifts	Philanthropy
Sponsorships	Moderate to high	Low to moderate	Money, in-kind gifts, volunteer support	Marketing
Advertising with a social dimension	Moderate to high	Low	Advertising expertise and expenditures	Marketing
Cause-related marketing	Moderate to high	Low	Advertising expertise and expenditures, money	Marketing
Licensing agreements	High	None	Contractual fees, co-branding support	Corporate, marketing
Social alliances	Low to moderate	Low to high	Advertising expertise and expenditures, personal selling, special events, in-kind gifts, money, professional expertise, volunteer support	Marketing, sales, philanthropy, community relations, corporate
Traditional volunteerism	Low	High	Volunteer support	Community relations
Strategic volunteerism	Moderate	High	Volunteer support, professional expertise, advertising	Community relations, marketing, human resources
Enterprises	Low to high	Low to high	Professional expertise from varied company functions	Corporate, marketing

Source: Drumwright and Murphy (2001, p. 166), Reprinted by permission of the author.

Since marketing is at the forefront of a firm's external communication, discussion of ethical issues should not be a foreign concept. Going forward, the necessity for clear and candid communication to surmount ethical problems seems mandatory. In fact, Enderle (1998) proposes practicing honest communication as one of four ethical guidelines for marketing in a global context. He sees this as a precept that can be universalized across societies. A word to describe more openness in communication and decision making that is frequently used in Europe is "transparency." Further examination of what factors lead to candor/openness/transparency in marketing is needed.

Responsible Marketing Practice

Despite substantial academic efforts to explain and influence ethical behavior in marketing, the business press continues to contain very frequent articles on a litany of marketing transgressions including slotting fees in the retail sector, product safety with automobile and SUV tires and prescription drugs, advertising and promotional activities of the movie industry and others, the marketing practices of cigarettes, firearms and other dangerous products and rampant negative advertising by politicians virtually at all levels and all parties in the recently concluded election. Rather than criticize the well-known and well-chronicled ethical inadequacies of industry's marketing arm, this section of the paper proposes two positive approaches that marketing practitioners could embrace to create a more ethical organization.

Responsible marketing

The practice of ethical or responsible marketing is an objective of many (if not most) marketing organizations. Five specific examples are examined here as illustrative of what companies can and are accomplishing. It should be added that these firms, like virtually all others, are not ethically pure, but do depict what can happen with a responsible approach to an ethical issue.

The first company is International Business Machines (IBM) and their response to the privacy problems that databases and the Internet have spawned. In early 1999, when the uproar over Internet privacy was reaching a fever pitch, IBM informed all of the companies on whose web sites IBM advertised that they must have published privacy policies within ninety days or IBM would pull its advertising. At the time, IBM was the second largest advertiser on the web and only 30 percent of the 800 firms had such a policy at the time.

Another organization that has acted responsibly in dealing with the privacy issue is AmEx. AmEx was one of the first US-based companies in compliance with the strict EU Directive on Privacy because its cardholder lists are never sold to third parties. In 2000, the company launched a major print advertising campaign using the familiar tag line, "Do you know me?" (Recall the long-running campaign featuring sports and TV stars.) The company promises anonymity online. This is a good illustration of the ethical purity point because of the aforementioned criticism of AmEx's cause-related marketing programs.

A third is the Co-operative Bank headquartered in Manchester, England. The bank developed its Ethical Policy in the early 1990s and updated it in 1995 as part of an overall program on ethical banking. Based on extensive consumer research indicating that over 80 percent felt banks should have a clear ethical policy, the Co-operative bank embarked on a repositioning program that high-lighted these policies in their products, advertising and company communications. Some of the controversial social issues directly addressed in this policy pertain to human rights, armament exports, tobacco manufacture, animal experimentation, fur trade, and blood sports. The bank continues with the policy today and has seen significant gain in its market position since introducing it.

e-Bay is a fourth example of an organization practicing responsible marketing. The CEO, Margaret Whitman, outlined the company's thinking in an interview published in the *Wall Street Journal* on e-Bay's decision not to carry certain prod-ucts in the firm's online auction. She responded to the interviewer as follows:

> It's an issue that we think about a lot. As you know, in February of last year we did eliminate the entire firearms category. Two weeks ago or 10 days ago we eliminated the alcohol category and the tobacco category. There are items in those categories that are absolutely perfectly legal such as antique firearms. Obviously assault weapons and bazookas and rocket launchers are not. But all of those have appeared on e-Bay at one time or another.
>
> With firearms, we felt the Internet was not the appropriate venue, because you could never be completely sure about who the purchaser of the firearm was. That was a very unpopular decision with our 2,000 firearms dealers. Yet we felt we had to make the decision in favor of the entire community. Had a gun been bought through e-Bay and been used in a very visible killing or shooting that would have been a horrible thing for e-Bay and for the entire community.
>
> With alcohol and tobacco, there's myriad complex governmental rules and regula-tions surrounding those two categories. We felt it was almost impossible to deal with all that on the site. It was the easiest and cleanest thing to do. Again, there are a number of sellers of those categories who are not happy with e-Bay. But we felt the risk to the community was higher in allowing those categories than to take them down (Anders, 1999, p. R68).

Other firms from controversial industries have taken steps recently to engage in responsible marketing. For example, Harrah's chain of casinos recently introduced a "Code of Commitment" dealing with marketing and advertising activities that will forbid advertising in media aimed at teenagers and avoid messages that stipulate that gambling is a rite of passage (Binkley, 2000). The firm has trumpeted an award they received for "responsible gaming" in full page color ads in major newspapers. Hollywood studios have recently been chastised for their continuing efforts at marketing violence and adult rated movies at children. In light of the criticism leveled at them by the FTC and the media, the TV networks and studios are sponsoring PSAs that are intended to address violence not only in the media but in everyday life. Even the much maligned cigarette industry appears to be turning over a new leaf in consciously marketing cigarettes at adult-only populations in the wake of the November 1998 master settlement agreement with the industry an 46 attorneys general (Jarvis, 2000).

Marketing ethics statements

This writer has examined and written about corporate ethics statements previously (Murphy, 1995, 1998). From recent work in this area, it is somewhat surprising that marketing issues do not find themselves incorporated fully into company codes and other statements. In a survey of large firms, most have clear guidelines on gift giving (94 percent of respondents checked this category), selling practices (62 percent) and competitive intelligence (61 percent). However, product safety and advertising (both 31 percent) were the least addressed areas within a code (Murphy, 2000). It might be added that the number for advertising may be high in that very few codes explicitly mention advertising issues in them. One of the few is Target (formerly Dayton Hudson). What is surprising is that the consumer packaged goods companies and other marketers like automobiles, cosmetics and sports shoe sellers spend millions aimed at consumers and yet make no mention of advertising in their company codes. The corporate marketing world seems to need much more guidance regarding acceptable conduct.

Academic Research in Marketing Ethics

The future of marketing ethics scholarship could be enhanced in several ways: greater integration with business ethics, stakeholder analysis in marketing, more case analysis and ethics' role in marketing and society. Several specific areas in need of scholarly research within marketing ethics in the first decade of the twenty-first century are also delineated.

Greater integration with business ethics

While the record of scholarly treatment of marketing ethics in the last decade is impressive in many respects, this has been accomplished largely by the efforts of marketing professors writing on this topic. Modest headway, frankly, has been made in getting those philosophers who do the bulk of writing in business ethics to understand the scope of marketing ethics. This lack of integration has been most noticeable in business ethics texts. Historically, these texts have focused primarily on advertising and only discussed marketing as a secondary issue. For instance, Boylan's (2001) book only contains a section on advertising and makes no mention of marketing. Dienhart (2000) labels his section advertising and marketing. Boatright in his latest edition (2000) reduced his marketing, advertising and product safety coverage from two chapters to one.

Among the most popular business ethics texts, the news is more promising. DeGeorge (1999) has a major chapter on marketing, truth and advertising and Donaldson and Werhane (1999) include a case and three articles in their marketing section. Beauchamp and Bowie's latest edition (2001) "Marketing and Disclosure" section features ten readings and seven cases. It should be noted that none of the marketing ethics texts have been revised and only one appeared in the last five years.

Stakeholder analysis in marketing

The stakeholder concept is central to an understanding of ethics in any organization. This notion is very similar to the concept of "publics" introduced by Kotler many years ago in the marketing literature. Based on the pioneering work of Freeman and extended by Goodpaster – both reprinted in Beauchamp and Bowie (2001) – significant work in stakeholder analysis has been undertaken in the management literature.

Currently, stakeholders are frequently mentioned in marketing principles books and in classroom discussions. Substantial research has been conducted addressing stakeholder impact in business ethics, but little conceptual or empirical examination on the relative impact of various stakeholders on marketing activities has occurred. This writer and colleagues (O'Sullivan and Murphy, 1998; Laczniak et al., 1999), drawing on the initial formulation by Carroll and Buchholtz (1999), distinguished between primary (direct contractual relationship), indirect (arms-length or infrequent relationship) and secondary (distant relationship) stakeholders in the sports field. This approach could and should be extended to other marketing relationships. Furthermore, almost no discussion (beyond the Caux Principles) has centered on competitors in this increasingly competitive world and what level of stakeholder relationship (if any) that marketing organizations have with them.

Case analysis

If we academics are preparing future marketing managers to be sensitive to ethical issues and address them effectively, it will likely require substantial case analysis discussion and written evaluation. Without such attention, these managers might react as McCoy (1997) in one of the most thought-provoking articles ever written on business ethics: "Real moral dilemmas are ambiguous, and many of us hike right through them, unaware that they exist" (p. 58). In recent years, little systematic efforts at marketing ethics case writing has occurred. Since Craig Smith left Harvard a decade ago and John Quelch also departed for the London Business School, no one has taken the mantle at HBS to engage in marketing ethics case writing. (Some of the cases in Smith and Quelch (1993) are still useful today, but many of them are now dated. Smith has published some recent cases on his own.) The lack of good marketing ethics cases is obvious when one peruses the business ethics texts featuring issues that occurred ten to fifteen years ago.

Several proposals might be considered to solve the problem of the lack of new and appropriate marketing ethics cases. First, this writer and others have had modest success in getting MBA students to write cases based on their experiences that can be used for subsequent classes. Second, marketing academics should team with philosophers to jointly write cases. An illustration is the "Natural Cereals Case" – reprinted in Dienhart (2000) – that Norman Bowie and I co-authored as part of the Arthur Andersen ethics program. Third, those interested in publishing such cases should consider the *Case Research Journal* so that they are available to others. Finally, philosophers or marketing ethicists might consider writing an "ethics overlay" (consisting of a few questions and a short teaching note with answers/discussion points) to existing marketing cases so that faculty members who would like to incorporate ethics into the case, but at the moment feel unprepared to raise ethics topics with their students, could do so.

Ethics role in marketing and society

Marketing ethics as a subfield of marketing generally is viewed as falling under the umbrella of marketing and society. Ethical issues are often closely associated with legal ones (Gundlach and Murphy, 1993) and the public policy process is invoked when marketers cross the line from unethical to illegal behavior. Research is needed on the interface between ethical and societal and public policy questions. In a major examination of marketing's contribution to society, Wilkie and Moore (1999) employ a classic utilitarian analysis by identifying the benefits and criticisms of the aggregate marketing system. The criticisms and problems they identified (Figure 6 on p. 214) provide a list of topics that are often identified with marketing ethics such as the values of the marketing system, consumer rights, product safety and liability, high-pressure personal selling, fairness in pricing, bribery, etc. Marketing scholars could help set an agenda for delineating the areas of overlap and distinctiveness within the business and society field.

Important research topics in marketing ethics

Without the benefit of a crystal ball and with the distinct possibility that these issues may not turn out to be the most salient ones, this writer offers the following challenges to scholarly researchers in marketing to investigate these important issues to the field. Both conceptual and empirical work is necessary on the following topics.

Online privacy and security One of the biggest impediments to growth in online marketing is the prospect that consumers and businesses may not trust it. Privacy issues have been noted previously here and studied by a number of researchers. The ongoing debate between self-regulatory activities vs. targeted regulation such as the Children's Online Privacy Protection Act passed in late 1998 needs objective study by the academy. Research implications include a better understanding of the cost and benefits, rights of buyers and sellers and how the "ethic of the mean" from virtue ethics might be accomplished without chilling regulation.

Power and responsibility in the channel An ongoing issue in marketing is the power of larger firms relative to consumers and smaller organizations. The power-responsibility equilibrium states that if powerful organizations do not assume their commensurate social responsibility, they are destined to lose power (usually through regulatory activities). The issue of slotting fees prevalent in the supermarket industry is directly related to the power of the retailer in that channel. Furthermore, the recent spate of mergers throughout the world like AOL-Time-Warner, DiamlerChrysler, Pepsi and Quaker, Unilever and Ben and Jerry's mean that cross-marketing opportunities are many and that companies can be connected with consumers in a myriad of ways. Researchers in marketing need to examine not only the pervasiveness of these efforts and their impacts on consumers but also what new ethical abuses may arise.

Environmental marketing The natural environment continues present challenges to marketing decision makers and public policy officials. Whether consumers will take the long term view regarding their product choices and their disposability remains an open question. Although we hear less of the "disposable society" arguments today and fewer criticisms of environmental appeals (at least in the USA), growing landfill problems and several types of pollution continue to plague most countries. Researchers have examined consumer attitudes and values relative to the environment, but a renewed research thrust appears necessary. The natural environment as a "stakeholder" is only infrequently mentioned in academic research or case analyses. In addition, what companies are associated with best practices and can they be emulated elsewhere?

Core values for global marketing Several attempts have been made in developing core values for responsible business and marketing practices throughout the world. Some include the Caux, CERES and Sullivan Principles. Other efforts have been made in garment and sweatshop principles that business corporations should follow. Researchers should study these existing general documents and also company ones like Levi's Global Sourcing and Operating Guidelines. Both a business and educational benefit may result in developing core values that businesses might follow and that marketing educators might communicate to their students. One such attempt was made by this writer (Murphy, 1999) to develop core virtues for international marketing. This is one of many starting points and could be expanded upon and improved.

Marketing's role in promoting societal issues/causes Marketing principles and practices are increasingly applied to a panoply of causes from AIDS, drug use, education, politics, racism and many others. If marketing is to be effective in promoting the greater good, it must be undertaken ethically. This is not always the case and it is unclear as to who should monitor these societal marketing efforts that may be undertaken by corporations, governments and not-for profit-organizations. The 2000 elections in the USA brought cries of unethical negative advertising and soft money promotion or defamation of many candidates. This issue may result in a public policy solution. However, marketing's role in improving, if not solving, social problems and promoting social causes will be less effective if ethical abuses are not examined more closely by researchers.

Conclusion

This paper has attempted to provide a status report on marketing ethics at the turn of the century. The temptation is always to give an incomplete grade. However, on balance, my preference would be to give the field a B grade with an opportunity to improve. Despite a few troubling developments, the field has matured and gained in stature. Much work remains to be done by serious scholars and practitioners if marketing ethics is ever going to gain the credibility of some of our competing business disciplines that have a stronger record of professional accountability and evaluation. However, it is this writer's assessment that we in marketing are up to the challenge.

Acknowledgment

The author wants to thank Norman Bowie, Georges Enderle, Gene Laczniak and Craig Smith for their helpful comments on an earlier draft.

References

Anders, G. 1999: The auctioneer. *The Wall Street Journal*, 22 November, R68.

Beauchamp, T. L. and Bowie, N. E. 2001: *Ethical Theory and Business.* Upper Saddle River, NJ: Prentice Hall, Inc.

Bellizzi, J. A. and Hite, R. E. 1989: Supervising unethical salesforce behavior. *Journal of Marketing*, 53, 36–47.

Binkley, C. 2000: Harrah's new code to restrict marketing. *The Wall Street Journal*, 19 October, B16.

Bishop, J. D. 2000: Is self-identity image advertising ethical? *Business Ethics Quarterly*, 10, 371–98.

Bloom, P. N. and Gundlach, G. T. (eds). 2001: *Handbook of Marketing and Society.* Thousand Oaks, CA: Sage Publications.

Boatright, J. R. 2000: *Ethics and the Conduct of Business.* Upper Saddle River, NJ: Prentice Hall, Inc.

Boylan, M. 2001: *Business Ethics.* Upper Saddle River, NJ: Prentice Hall Inc.

Brenkert, G. G. 1998a: Marketing and the vulnerable. *Business Ethics Quarterly,* The Ruffin Series, Special Issue No. 1, 7–20.

Brenkert, G. G. 1998b: Marketing to inner-city blacks: Powermaster and moral responsibility. *Business Ethics Quarterly,* 8, 1–18.

Brenkert, G. G. 1999: Marketing ethics. In R. E. Frederick (ed.). *A Companion to Business Ethics.* Malden, MA: Blackwell Publishers Ltd, 178–93.

Carroll, A. B. and Buchholtz, A. K. 1999: *Business and Society: Ethics and Stakeholder Management.* Florence, KY: South-Western College Publishing.

Caudill, E. M. and Murphy, P. E. 2000: Consumer online privacy: Legal and ethical issues. *Journal of Public Policy and Marketing,* 19, 7–19.

Chaudhry, P. E. and Walsh, M. G. 1996: The privacy paradox persists. *Columbia Journal of World Business,* 31, 34–48.

Chonko, L. B. 1995: *Ethical Decision Making in Marketing.* Thousand Oaks, CA: Sage Publications.

Culnan, M. J. 2000: Protecting privacy online: Is self-regulation working? *Journal of Public Policy and Marketing,* 19, 20–6.

DeGeorge, R. T. 1993: *Competing with Integrity in International Business.* New York, NY: Oxford University Press.

DeGeorge, R. T. 1999: *Business Ethics.* Upper Saddle River, NJ: Prentice Hall.

Dienhart, J. W. 2000: *Business, Institutions, and Ethics.* New York, NY: Oxford University Press, Inc.

Donaldson, T. 1996: Values in tension: Ethics away from home. *Harvard Business Review,* September/October, 48–62.

Donaldson, T. and Werhane, P. H. 1999: *Ethical Issues in Business: A Philosophical Approach.* Upper Saddle River, NJ: Prentice Hall Inc.

Drumwright, M. E. and Murphy, P. E. 2001: Corporate societal marketing. In P. N. Bloom and G. T. Gundlach (eds). *Handbook of Marketing and Society.* Thousand Oaks, CA: Sage Publications, 162–83.

Dunfee, T. W., Smith, N. C. and Ross Jr. W. T. 1999: Social contracts and marketing ethics. *Journal of Marketing,* 63, 14–32.

Enderle, G. 1998: A framework for international marketing ethics: Preliminary considerations and emerging perspectives. *Journal of Human Values,* 4 (1), 25–43.

Ferrell, O. C., Gresham, L. G. and Fraedrich, J. 1989: A synthesis of ethical decision models for marketing. *Journal of Macromarketing,* 9, 55–64.

Fraedrich, J. and Ferrell, O. C. 1992: Cognitive consistency of marketing managers in ethics situations. *Journal of the Academy of Marketing Science,* 20, 245–52.

Fraedrich, J., Thorne, D. M. and Ferrell, O. C. 1994: Assessing the application of cognitive moral development theory to business ethics. *Journal of Business Ethics,* 13, 829–38.

Goolsby, J. R. and Hunt, S. D. 1992: Cognitive moral development and marketing. *Journal of Marketing,* 56, 55–68.

Gundlach, G. T. and Murphy, P. E. 1993: Ethical and legal foundations of regional marketing exchanges. *Journal of Marketing,* 57 October, 35–46.

Hartman, C. L. and Beck-Dudley, C. L. 1999: Marketing strategies and the search for virtue: A case analysis of the Body Shop, International. *Journal of Business Ethics*, 20, 249–63.

Hunt, S. D. and Vasquez-Parraga, A. Z. 1993: Organizational consequences, marketing ethics, and salesforce supervision. *Journal of Marketing Research*, February, 78–90.

Hunt, S. D. and Vitell, S. 1986: A general theory of marketing ethics. *Journal of Macromarketing*, 6, 5–16.

Hunt, S. D., Wood, V. R. and Chonko, L. B. 1989: Corporate ethical values and organizational commitment in marketing. *Journal of Marketing*, 53, 79–90.

Jarvis, S. 2000: Filtered cigarettes: How tobacco companies market two years after government deal. *Marketing News*, 20 November, 9.

Laczniak, G. R. 1993: Marketing ethics: Onward toward greater expectations. *Journal of Public Policy & Marketing*, 12, 91–6.

Laczniak, G. R. and Murphy, P. E. 1993: *Ethical Marketing Decisions: The Higher Road*. Upper Saddle River, NJ: Prentice Hall Inc.

Laczniak, G. R., Burton, R. and Murphy P. E. 1999: Sports marketing ethics in today's marketplace. *Sports Marketing Quarterly*, 8, 43–53.

Leigh, J. H. and Murphy, P. E. 1999: The role of formal policies and informal culture on ethical decision making by marketing managers. In J. N. Sheth and A. Parvatiyar (eds). *Research in Marketing*. Stanford, CT: Jai Press Inc, 69–100.

McCoy, B. H. 1997: The parable of the sadhu. *Harvard Business Review*, May/June, 54–6, 58–60, 62, 64.

Maignan, I. and Ferrell, O. C. 2000: Measuring corporate citizenship in two countries: The case of the United States and France. *Journal of Business Ethics*, 23, 283–97.

Mascarenhas, O. A. J. 1995: Exonerating unethical marketing executive behaviors: A diagnostic framework. *Journal of Marketing*, 59, 43–57.

Morgan, R. M. and Hunt, S. D. 1994: The commitment-trust theory of relationship marketing. *Journal of Marketing*, 58, 20–38.

Murphy, P. E. 1995: Corporate ethics statements: Current status and future prospects. *Journal of Business Ethics*, 14, 727–40.

Murphy, P. E. 1997: *Ethics in marketing: A global view*. Presented at VII Coloquio De Etica Empresarial Y Economica, Barcelona, Spain, 23 October.

Murphy, P. E. 1998: *Eighty Exemplary Ethics Statements*. Notre Dame, IN: University of Notre Dame Press.

Murphy, P. E. 1999: Character and virtue ethics in international marketing: An agenda for managers, researchers and educators. *Journal of Business Ethics*, 18, 107–24.

Murphy, P. E. 2000: Corporate ethics statements: An update. In O. F. Williams (ed.). *Global Codes of Conduct*. Notre Dame, IN: University of Notre Dame Press, 295–304.

Murphy, P. E. and Laczniak, G. R. 1981: Marketing ethics: A review with implications for managers, educators and researchers. In B. M. Enis and K. Roering (eds). *Review of Marketing 1981*. Chicago, IL: American Marketing Association, 251–66.

Nantel, J. and Weeks, W. 1996: Marketing ethics: Is there more to it than the utilitarian approach? *European Journal of Marketing*, 30, 9–19.

Nill, A. and Shultz, C. 1997: Cross cultural marketing ethics and the emergence of dialogic idealism as a decision marketing model. *Journal of Macromarketing*, 17, 4–19.

O'Sullivan, P. and Murphy, P. E. 1998: Ambush marketing: The ethical issues. *Psychology & Marketing*, 15, 349–66.

Rallapalli, K. C. 1999: A paradigm for development and promulgation of a global code of marketing ethics. *Journal of Business Ethics*, 18, 125–37.

Robin, D. P. and Reidenbach, R. E. 1993: Searching for a place to stand: Toward a workable ethical philosophy for marketing. *Journal of Public Policy and Marketing*, 12, 97–105.

Robin, D. P., Gordon, G., Jordan, C. and Reidenbach, R. E. 1996: The empirical performance of cognitive moral development in predicting behavioral intent. *Business Ethics Quarterly*, 6, 493–516.

Ross, W. T. and Robertson, D. C. 2000: Lying: The impact of decision context. *Business Ethics Quarterly*, 10, 409–40.

Scheibal, W. J. and Gladstone, J. A. 2000: Privacy on the net: Europe changes the rules. *Business Horizons*, May–June, 13–18.

Schlegelmilch, B. 1998: *Marketing Ethics: An International Perspective*. London, UK: International Thomson Business Press.

Shultz, C. J. and Holbrook, M. B. 1999: Marketing and the tragedy of the commons: A synthesis, commentary, and analysis for action. *Journal of Public Policy & Marketing*, 18, 218–29.

Smith, N. C. 2001: Changes in corporate practices in response to public interest advocacy and actions. In P. N. Bloom and G. T. Gundlach (eds). *Handbook of Marketing and Society*. Thousand Oaks, CA: Sage Publications, 140–61.

Smith, N. C. and Cooper-Martin, E. 1997: Ethics and target marketing: The role of product harm and consumer vulnerability. *Journal of Marketing*, 61, 1–20.

Smith, N. C. and Quelch, J. A. 1993: *Ethics in Marketing*. Homewood, IL: Irwin.

Sparks, J. R. and Hunt, S. D. 1998: Marketing research ethical sensitivity: Conceptualization, measurement, and exploratory investigation. *Journal of Marketing*, 62, 92–109.

Thompson, C. J. 1995: A contextualist proposal for the conceptualization and study on marketing ethics. *Journal of Public Policy and Marketing*, 14, 177–91.

Wilkie, W. L. and Moore, E. S. 1999: Marketing's contributions to society. *Journal of Marketing*, 63, 198–218.

Williams, O. F. and Murphy, P. E. 1990: The ethics of virtue: A moral theory for marketing. *Journal of Macromarketing*, 10, 19–29.

Chapter 9

Ethical Issues in Selling and Advertising

Thomas L. Carson

Introduction

This paper addresses moral questions common to advertising and sales: questions concerning lying, deception, and withholding information.

Advertising

I explain the laws concerning deceptive advertising and argue that deceptive advertising is *prima facie* wrong because it harms consumers, competitors, and the social fabric. The benefit to the advertiser is almost never an adequate justification for deceptive advertising. I also argue that deceptive advertising is wrong because those who practice it violate consistency requirements for morality – the golden rule and the categorical imperative.

Sales

The ethics of sales is an important, but neglected, topic in business ethics. Approximately 10 percent of the US workforce is involved in sales. In addition, most of us occasionally sell major holdings such as used cars and real estate. Because sales were long governed by the principle of *caveat emptor*, discussions of the ethics of sales usually focus on the ethics of withholding information and the question "what sort of information is a salesperson obligated to reveal to customers?" One of the best treatments of this topic is David Holley's (1993) paper "A Moral Evaluation of Sales Practices." I explain his theory, propose several criticisms, and formulate what I take to be a more plausible theory about the duties of salespeople. My theory avoids the objections I raise against Holley and yields intuitively plausible results when applied to cases. I also defend my theory by appeal to the golden rule and offer a defense of the version of the golden rule to which I appeal.

Preliminaries: A conceptual roadmap

We need to distinguish between lying, deception, withholding information, and concealing information. Roughly, deception is intentionally causing someone to have false beliefs. Standard dictionary definitions of lying say that a lie is a false statement intended to deceive others. The *Oxford English Dictionary* defines a lie as: "a false statement made with the intent to deceive." *Webster's* (1963) gives the following definition of the verb "to lie": "to make an untrue statement with intent to deceive." (We might want to add a third condition to this definition and say that, for a false statement to be a lie, the person who makes it must know or believe that it is false. The third condition makes a difference in cases in which someone attempts to deceive another person by means of a false statement that he mistakenly believes to be true. Nothing in the present paper turns on this issue.) Lying arguably requires the intent to deceive others – I express my doubts about this in Carson (1988) – but lies that do not succeed in causing others to have false beliefs are not instances of deception. The word "deception" implies success, but lying is often unsuccessful in causing deception. A further difference between lying and deception is that, while a lie must be a false statement, deception needn't involve false statements; true statements can be deceptive and many forms of deception do not involve making statements of any sort. Thus, many instances of deception do not constitute lying.

Withholding information does not constitute deception. It is not a case of *causing* someone to have false beliefs; it is merely a case of failing to correct false beliefs or incomplete information. On the other hand, actively concealing information usually constitutes deception.

Deception in Advertising

Deceptive advertising and the law

In the United States the laws concerning deceptive advertising are administered by the Federal Trade Commission (FTC) and state consumer protection agencies. The FTC has jurisdiction only in cases of ads that in some way cross state lines. Local ads that do not cross state lines fall under the jurisdiction of state consumer protection agencies. In addition, the Federal Lanham Trademark Act allows businesses that have been harmed by misrepresentations of other sellers to sue for damages (Preston, 1994, pp. 9, 47, 97; Preston, 1998, p. 63). Lanham suits are a significant deterrent to deceptive advertising. Since advertising does not require a license or membership in any professional organization such as the bar association, industry or professional codes of ethics have very limited power to discourage deceptive advertising. Professional codes of ethics for advertisers lack the force of codes of ethics for the law and medicine; there is nothing comparable to disbarment proceedings in advertising (Preston, 1994, p. 176).

Since most states follow the FTC, it is sufficient for our purposes to describe the FTC standards for regulating and defining deceptive advertising. The FTC prohibits deceptive advertising. Advertisers who are found guilty of deceptive advertising are required to discontinue the deceptive ads. Ordinarily, no penalties are imposed unless the advertiser continues the deceptive ads, but the FTC sometimes fines advertisers for ads that contain explicit falsities when the falsity is judged to be obvious and deliberate (Preston, 1994, pp. 10, 41). By contrast, suits in Lanham courts subject advertisers to substantial civil penalties.

The FTC Standards for deception

The FTC defines the deceptiveness of an ad in terms of the likelihood of its misleading reasonable consumers (misleading consumers who act *reasonably*):

> The Commission believes that to be deceptive the representation, omission or practice must be likely to mislead reasonable consumers under the circumstances. The test is whether the consumer's interpretation or reaction is reasonable (FTC Statement, 1983).

In many cases, the FTC judges whether ads are deceptive without going to the trouble and expense of testing consumer responses to them. When it studies consumer responses, the FTC looks to see whether ads convey false claims about the products in question (a claim is conveyed if consumers take the ad to be making or implying that claim). The FTC usually judges an ad to be deceptive if it conveys a false claim to 20–25 percent or more of the target audience; the FTC usually judges ads to be not deceptive if they do not convey any false claims to 20–25 percent or more of the target audience (Preston, 1994, p. 13). This figure is not a standard that the FTC uses in making decisions. Rather, it describes what is typically done. How the FTC rules depends, in part, on the extent of the harm that the deception is likely to cause consumers.

It is possible for an ad to convey a false claim to someone without misleading her. Suppose that I take an ad to be claiming that X, where X is a false statement. The ad conveys to me the claim that X, but I am not misled unless I believe that X is true. I am not misled if I think that X is false. The FTC usually takes the fact that an ad conveys a false claim to 20–25 percent or more of the target audience to be evidence that it is likely to mislead consumers who act reasonably.

Lanham Courts tend to apply stricter criteria for deceptiveness. Ads that convey false claims to 15 percent or more of the target audience are usually found to be deceptive by Lanham courts (Preston, 1994, p. 13).

Several features of the FTC definition of deception stand out. First, the FTC regards an ad as deceptive only if the deception in question is "material" to consumer behavior.

> [T]he representation or practice must be a "material" one. The basic question is whether the act or practice is likely to affect the consumer's conduct or decision with regard to a product or service . . . the Commission will find deception if there is a representation, omission or practice that is likely to mislead the consumer acting reasonably in the circumstances, to the consumer's detriment (FTC Statement, 1983).

An ad that caused many reasonable consumers to have false beliefs would not be considered deceptive if the FTC judged that it was unlikely to affect consumers' behavior.

Second, an ad can be deceptive even if all of its explicit claims are true. An ad that is literally true might be deceptive in virtue of implying a false claim. For example, a TV commercial for Baggies contained the following demonstration. Sandwiches were wrapped in Baggies and a competing brand of sandwich wrap. Both were placed under water. Baggies kept the sandwiches dry and the competing brand did not. Everything shown and claimed in the ad was true, but the commercial was still judged to be deceptive by the FTC. It implied or conveyed the false claim that Baggies were better at keeping sandwiches fresh than the other brand. In fact, both brands of sandwich bags have pores that let in air. Baggies are not superior to the other brand for ordinary purposes, since sandwiches are not ordinarily stored under water (Preston, 1994, p. 37). Ads that appeal to demonstrations or studies can be deceptive, even if all the statements they make about the demonstrations or studies are literally true. For example, an ad for Black Flag Roach Killer presented a demonstration in which Black Flag killed roaches while "the other leading brand" failed to kill them. This ad was very misleading because the demonstration used roaches that had been bred to be resistant to the type of poison used by the competitor (Preston, 1994, p. 41).

Third, ads that contain false statements are not necessarily considered deceptive. Some ads contain obviously false and exaggerated claims for the sake of humor. An Isuzu TV ad showed a speeded up film clip of Joe Isuzu driving his car and claimed that he was going more than 500 m.p.h. Such ads are not deceptive because they are not likely to mislead very many consumers.

Fourth, deception as defined by the FTC doesn't require that the advertiser intends to mislead consumers. It is a "no fault concept" in that intention and blameworthiness are not assumed and, ordinarily, advertisers are not subject to any punishment for their first violation of the law (Preston, 1994, p. 133). In this respect, the FTC's definition of deception differs from the ordinary language concept of deception (which seems to require the intent to mislead others).

Fifth, if an ad is directed at a specific audience or group, then the FTC judges the deceptiveness or non-deceptiveness of the ad relative to that audience.

When representations or sales practices are targeted to a specific audience, such as children, the elderly, or the terminally ill, the Commission determines the effect of the practice on a reasonable member of that group (FTC Statement, 1983, III).

Sixth, the FTC Policy Statement on Deception defines deception in terms of the likelihood of misleading consumers who act *reasonably*. The FTC usually takes evidence that an ad conveys false claims to 20–25 percent or more of its target audience to be evidence that the ad is likely to mislead members of the target audience who act reasonably. Even if an ad causes people to be misled on account of their own inattention, carelessness, or stupidity, it can still be considered deceptive if it misleads a sufficient percentage of its target audience (Preston, 1994, p. 13). The FTC Statement specifically allows that consumers who are acting reasonably sometimes read only parts of written ads and sometimes fail to appreciate the importance of qualifications included in advertisements. The FTC takes its charge to be to protect any group of people that is large enough to constitute an important public interest (Preston, 1994, pp. 13, 131–3).

Preston's criticisms of the FTC

Preston, claims that, in practice, the FTC permits many deceptive ads that are harmful to consumers and ought to be prohibited. What the FTC regards as harmless puffery is often harmful deception that ought to be prohibited. Preston claims that, in the case of puffery, the FTC fails to enforce its own standards prohibiting any ads that mislead a significant percentage of the population.

Puffery includes bald or bare claims to the affect that a certain product is the best when there is no basis for those claims, e.g., Goodyear's claim that it makes the best tires in the world, "Nestle's makes the very best chocolate," and "Nobody gets the dirt out like Hoover" (Preston, 1998, p. 54). The FTC maintains that such ads are meaningless and do not influence consumer decisions. However, according to Preston, such claims are often meaningful, false, and deceptive. Preston claims that the FTC takes an *a priori* approach to puffery and doesn't do nearly enough to investigate actual consumer behavior and beliefs. He cites two studies examining consumer response to typical puffery in advertising, e.g., "Minute rice gives you perfect rice every time," "Coke is it," and "Ford has a better idea." Well over 20 percent of the respondents regarded these claims as "completely true" and a majority regarded them as at least "partly true" (Preston, 1998, pp. 80–1).

The legal loopholes that permit puffery harm consumers who trust advertising (Preston, 1998, p. 103). To a lesser extent, these loopholes also harm those who distrust advertising (Preston, 1998, pp. 105–6). Given that advertising is deceptive, it is best not to be trusting, but people should be able to trust and rely on advertising. The law should aim to make it the case that all advertising can be trusted and relied on. Preston claims that this would benefit both consumers and advertisers (Preston, 1994, p. 222; 1998, pp. 106–13).

Preston claims that many standard cases of puffery are not only misleading, but false and fraudulent. Any statement implies that the speaker knows a basis for claiming it to be true. It is dishonest to claim that a certain product is "the best" when you have no basis for making this claim (Preston, 1998, p. 96). If advertisers had good reasons for claiming that their products are the best they would surely provide them. It is reasonable to assume that advertisers who make bare unsubstantiated claims that their product is the best, have no basis for their claims. Thus, claims to the affect that some product is the best are typically false and fraudulent (Preston, 1998, pp. 97–8).

According to Preston, the actions of advertisers contradict their claim (and the FTC's claim) that puffery is meaningless. Advertisers tell the FTC that puffery is meaningless and ineffectual, but, at the same time, they claim to their clients that puffery is an effective form of advertising; no one is interested in paying money for ads that leave the public completely unmoved (Preston, 1998, pp. 84–5, 110). Advertisers clearly think that consumers rely on puffs or they wouldn't use them (Preston, 1994, p. 181). Since advertisers invite trust and reliance, they can't claim that the public shouldn't trust their ads because the ads are meaningless (Preston, 1994, pp. 187–8).

Preston claims that the overriding cause of puffery is advertisers' need to differentiate their products from those of competitors, when, in fact, there is often very little difference between competing brands that are heavily advertised. Advertisers need to claim that their brands are unique and better than other brands in certain significant respects. Since it is often (or usually) the case there are no significant differences between competing brands, it is difficult to make claims about one's own brand that are both true and significant (Preston, 1994, pp. 58, 207). For example, there are no significant differences between different brands of aspirin (all aspirin has the same chemical formula). Nonetheless, Bayer ads claim that "Bayer is the world's best aspirin."

Why deceptive advertising is wrong

Deceptive ads harm consumers by causing them to have false beliefs about the nature of the products advertised and thereby cause some consumers to make different purchasing decisions than they would have made otherwise. For example, deceptive claims about the features of a car might cause someone to purchase a car that is unsuitable for her needs. Consumers are harmed if deceptive advertising causes them to spend more money for a brand name product than a generic brand that works just as a well. If the products in question are inexpensive the harm to any given consumer is small, but the aggregate harm to the society as a whole can still be considerable (Carson et al., 1985, p. 100; Preston, 1994, p. 177).

Many consumers were harmed by ads for Sears's Kenmore dishwasher that falsely claimed that it could completely clean dishes, pots and pans "without prior rinsing or scraping." Since they acted on the basis of false claims, many who purchased the Kenmore dishwasher presumably would have preferred not to purchase it had they not been deceived. Some people with perfectly good dishwashers purchased the Kenmore because they wanted a dishwasher that didn't require any prior rinsing or scraping. These people wasted their money. The Sears ads were apparently successful, since the Kenmore dishwasher gained an increased market share. Thus, the ad also harmed Sears's competitors. Sears clearly knew that the claim made by the ad was false. Tests that Sears ran indicated that the dishwasher would not clean the dishes unless they were first rinsed and scraped. The owner's manual instructed people to rinse and scrape the dishes prior to putting them in the dishwasher! (Preston, 1994, pp. 16–18).

Listerine Mouthwash was long advertised as strong (bad tasting) mouthwash "that kills millions of germs which can cause colds on contact." Listerine kills germs, but germs don't cause colds (colds are caused by viruses). These ads harmed many consumers. Many were led to spend more money for Listerine than they otherwise would have spent on mouthwash. Many who spent money on Listerine and endured its bad taste would not have used mouthwash at all (or as often) had they not been deceived by the ads. The ads also harmed Listerine's competitors who lost market share (Beauchamp, 1983, pp. 65–74).

Deceptive advertising can be harmful to people's health. During the past 20 years, many foods such as stick margarine were advertised and prominently labeled as being low in cholesterol (and therefore healthy). Many consumers eat these products thinking that they are healthy for their hearts when, in fact, they are very high in saturated fats. (All saturated fats pose a serious risk for heart disease.) Cholesterol is saturated fat from animal sources. Saturated fats from non-animal sources, e.g., palm oil, contain no cholesterol, but they are just as harmful as cholesterol. These facts are now widely known, but they were not commonly known twenty years ago. At least in the past, many people were misled.

A person's true interests are determined by the decisions she would make were she fully informed and rational – to the extent that an ad gives me false beliefs about what I am buying it has the potential to harm me. To the extent that deceptive advertising succeeds and causes people to make purchases that they would not have made otherwise, it harms competing businesses by reducing their sales.

Deceptive advertising is also harmful in that it lowers the general level of trust and truthfulness essential for a flourishing society and economy. The law alone cannot secure the level of honesty and trust in business necessary for people to be sufficiently willing to enter into mutually beneficial market transactions. In order for this to be the case, most people must voluntarily adhere to norms of honesty on moral grounds. No legal system can effectively police or deter rampant universal dishonesty in business. The legal system doesn't have the means to prosecute all business people. Consumer protection laws could not function effectively if all businesses practiced deception. If people were honest only because they feared getting caught the economy would soon cease to function. (On the importance of trust see Bok (1979); on the importance of trust in business see DeGeorge (1982, p. 6) and Bowie (1982, pp. 61–4).)

In response to the argument that deception harms the social fabric, it might be objected that the *moderate* level of distrust fostered by advertising is desirable. Advertising helps to foster a healthy skepticism not only for the claims of other advertisers, but for the claims of politicians and government officials as well. A certain measure of distrust of others is prudent and advertising sometimes helps to instill this distrust. However, these considerations cannot justify deceptive advertising. One cannot justify unethical conduct on the grounds that it helps to warn others to be on guard against conduct of that very sort. A mugger cannot justify his actions on the ground that he causes people to be more cautious about where and how they travel. Similarly, a politician cannot justify lying to the public on the grounds that doing so will help instill a prudent distrust of politicians in the average person.

Because deceptive advertising harms consumers, competitors, and the social fabric, there is a presumption for thinking that it is morally wrong. Are there any conceivable justifications for deceptive advertising that might override this presumption? What about the benefits to the advertiser? Can a company justify deceptive advertising on the ground that the company and its various stake-holders benefit from it? This is *possible*. But such cases are very rare. In any given case, it is unlikely that the benefits derived by the seller outweigh the harms to others; deception not only harms consumers, it also harms competing sellers and diminishes the trust essential for a flourishing economy. Consider a case in which deception provides great benefits to a corporation and its employees and shareholders. A company that is on the verge of bankruptcy might be able to stay in business by deceiving the public about its products. Economic necessity is only very rarely an adequate moral justification for deceptive practices. A firm that needs to deceive the public about the nature of its goods or services in order to stay in business is of doubtful value to society – the resources it utilizes could be put to better use in some other way (on a very similar point see page 201). In the normal course of things, the benefit to the advertiser is likely to be counter-balanced by the harm to (honest) competitors and their employees and shareholders – to say nothing about harm to consumers and the social fabric. In cases in which one appeals to "economic necessity" as a justification for deceptive advertising the deception benefits the seller and harms buyers. We should remember that in such cases the alternative (or an alternative) is a *mutually beneficial* transaction between the buyer and some other seller who does not deceive the buyer.

Advertisers who practice deception violate the golden rule. They, themselves, are consumers and are not willing to have others deceive them in the marketplace or base their own economic decisions on false beliefs. As advertisers, they want consumers to trust advertising and give credence to the claims of advertising. They cannot be willing to have all advertisers practice deception; if deception in advertising were a universal practice, few people would trust advertising and it would be very difficult to gain an advantage by means of deceptive advertising (see pages 199 and 204 for more on the golden rule.)

In almost exactly the same way deceptive advertising fails to satisfy the requirements of Kant's categorical imperative. The universal law version of the categorical imperative says that we must be willing to have everyone else follow the same principles that we act on. Kant (1993, p. 30) writes:

> Act only according to that maxim whereby you can at the same time will that it should become a universal law. . . . Act as if the maxim of your action were to become through your will a universal law of nature.

To be willing that the maxim of one's act be a universal law of nature means that one is willing to have everyone else in the universe follow the same principle that one follows in the action in question. Suppose that I create and run a deceptive ad for my own personal gain. Can I will that everyone else or every other advertiser make it a policy to do the same? Presumably not. In my own economic decisions I want to act on the basis of true information. Further, since I hope to profit by deceptive ads, I want the public to be trusting of advertising. If all advertisers engaged in deception the public would be less trusting. Those who intentionally engage in deceptive advertising treacherously invite others to trust and rely on their ads and at the same time betray that trust. If deceptive advertising were a universal practice, few people would trust advertising and no one could gain an advantage by means of deceptive advertising. I cannot will that all other advertisers follow the same principles (maxims) that I follow. I want to make a special exception for myself. (On the "self-defeatingness" of immoral business practices if their maxims were universally followed see Bowie and Duska, (1990, pp. 47–8).)

Deception and Withholding Information in Sales

The common-law principle of caveat emptor

According to the common-law principle of *caveat emptor*, sellers are not required to inform prospective buyers about the properties of the goods they sell. Under *caveat emptor*, sales and contracts to sell are legally enforceable even if the seller fails to inform the buyer of serious defects in the goods that are sold. Buyers, themselves, are responsible for determining the quality of the goods they purchase. In addition, English common-law sometimes called for the enforcement of sales in cases in which sellers made false or misleading statements about the goods they sold (Atiyah, 1979, pp. 464–5).

Currently, all US states, operate under the Uniform Commercial Code of 1968. Section 2–313 of the Code defines the notion of sellers' warranties (Preston, 1975, p. 52). The Code provides that all factual affirmations or statements about the goods being sold are warranties. This means that sales are not valid or legally enforceable if the seller makes false statements about the goods s/he is selling. The American legal system has developed the concept of an "implied" (as opposed to an express or explicit) warranty. Implied warranties are a significant limitation on the principle of *caveat emptor*. According to the Uniform Commercial Code, any transaction carries with it the following implied warranties: 1) that the seller owns the goods he is selling and 2) that the goods are "merchantable," i.e., suitable for the purposes for which they are sold (Preston, 1975, pp. 56–7). The implied warranty of merchantability does not apply to defects when the buyer inspects the goods and reasonable inspection ought to have revealed the defects. However, a buyer's failure to inspect doesn't negate implied warranties, unless the buyer refuses the seller's demand that she inspect. Implied warranties can be expressly disclaimed by such statements as "all warranties express or implied are hereby disclaimed." Such disclaimers of warranty are often made by used car dealers (Preston, 1975, pp. 59–60). Many local ordinances require that people who sell real estate inform buyers about all known serious defects of the property they sell. These ordinances are also a significant limitation on the traditional principle of *caveat emptor*.

Deceptive sales practices also fall under the purview of the FTC. The FTC prohibits deceptive sales practices [practices likely to materially mislead reasonable consumers] (FTC Statement, 1983).

Many salespeople take complying with the law to be an acceptable moral standard for their conduct and claim that they have no moral duty to provide buyers with information about the goods they sell, except for that information which the law requires for an enforceable sale.

Holley's theory

Holley's theory is based on his concept of a "voluntary" or "mutually beneficial" market exchange (Holley uses the terms "voluntary exchange" and "mutually beneficial exchange" interchangeably). He says that a voluntary exchange occurs "only if" the following conditions are met (he takes his conditions to be *necessary* conditions for an acceptable exchange):

1 Both buyer and seller understand what they are giving up and what they are receiving in return.
2 Neither buyer nor seller is compelled to enter into the exchange as a result of coercion, severely restricted alternatives, or other constraints on the ability to choose.
3 Both buyer and seller are able at the time of the exchange to make rational judgments about its costs and benefits (Holley, 1993, p. 463).

These three conditions admit of degrees of satisfaction. An ideal exchange is an exchange involving people who are fully informed, fully rational, and "enter into the exchange entirely of their own volition" (Holley, 1993, p. 464). The conditions for an ideal exchange are seldom, if ever, met in practice. However, Holley claims that it is still possible to have an "acceptable exchange" if the parties are "adequately informed, rational and free from compulsion" (Holley, 1993, p. 464).

According to Holley, "the primary duty of salespeople to customers is to avoid undermining the conditions of an acceptable exchange" (Holley, 1993, p. 464). He makes it clear that, on his view, acts of omission (as well as acts of commission) can undermine the conditions of an acceptable exchange (Holley, 1993, p. 464).

Because of the complexity of many goods and services, customers often lack information necessary for an acceptable exchange. Careful examination of products will not necessarily reveal problems or defects. According to Holley, *caveat emptor* is not acceptable as a moral principle, because customers often lack information necessary for an acceptable exchange. In such cases, salespeople are morally obligated to give information to the buyer. The question then is: *what kind of information* do salespeople need to provide buyers, to insure that the buyer is adequately informed? Holley attempts to answer this question in the following passage in which he appeals to the golden rule:

> Determining exactly how much information needs to be provided is not always clear-cut. We must in general rely on our assessments of what a reasonable person would want to know. As a practical guide, a salesperson might consider, "What would I want to know, if I were considering buying this product"? (Holley, 1993, p. 467)

This principle is very demanding, perhaps more demanding than Holley realizes. Presumably, most reasonable people would *want* to know *a great deal* about the things they are thinking of buying. They might want to know *everything* relevant to the decision whether or not to buy something – more on this point shortly.

Criticisms of Holley

First, when time does not permit it, a salesperson cannot be morally obligated to provide all information necessary to ensure that the customer is adequately informed (all the information that a reasonable person would *want* to know if she were in the buyer's position). In many cases, reasonable customers would *want* to know a great deal of information. Often salespeople simply don't have the time to give all customers all the information Holley deems necessary for an acceptable exchange. Salespeople don't always know all the information that the buyer needs for an acceptable exchange. It cannot be a person's duty to do what is impossible – the statement that someone *ought* to do a certain act implies that she *can* do that act. Further, in many cases, salespeople don't know enough about the buyer's state of knowledge to know what information the buyer needs in order to be adequately informed. A salesperson might know that the buyer needs certain information in order to be adequately informed but not know whether or not the buyer possesses that information. One might reply that salespeople *should* know all the information necessary for an adequate exchange. However, on examination, this is not a plausible view. A salesperson in a large retail store cannot be expected to be knowledgeable about every product he sells. Often, it is impossible for realtors and used car salesman to know much about the condition of the houses and cars they sell or the likelihood that they will need expensive repairs.

Second, Holley's theory implies that a salesperson in a store would be obligated to inform customers that a particular piece of merchandise in her store sells for less at a competing store if she knows this to be the case. (Presumably, she would *want* to know where she can get it for the lowest price, were she herself considering buying the product.) Not only do salespeople have no duty to provide this kind of information, (ordinarily) it would be wrong for them to do so.

Third, Holley's theory seems to yield unacceptable consequences in cases in which the buyer's alternatives are severely constrained. Suppose that a person with a very modest income attempts to buy a house in a small town. Her options are severely constrained, since there is only one house for sale in her price range. According to Holley, there can't be an acceptable exchange in such cases, because condition 2 is not satisfied. However, it's not clear what he thinks sellers ought to do in such cases. The seller can't be expected to remove these constraints by giving the buyer money or building more homes in town. Holley's view seems to imply that it would be wrong for anyone to sell or rent housing to such a person. This result is unacceptable.

Towards a more plausible theory about the ethics of sales

I believe that salespeople have the following moral duties regarding the disclosure of information when dealing with *rational adult consumers* (cases involving children or adults who are not fully rational raise special problems that I will not try to deal with here):

1   Salespeople should provide buyers with safety warnings and precautions about the goods they sell. [Sometimes it is enough for salespeople to call attention to written warnings and precautions that come with the goods and services in question. These warnings are unnecessary if the buyers already understand the dangers or precautions in question.]
2   Salespeople should refrain from lying and deception in their dealings with customers.
3   As much as their knowledge and time constraints permit, salespeople should fully answer questions about the products and services they sell. They should answer questions forthrightly and not evade questions or withhold information that has been asked for (even if this makes it less likely that they will make a successful sale). Salespeople are obligated to answer questions about the goods and services they, themselves, sell. However, they are justified in refusing to

answer questions that would require them to reveal information about what their competitors are selling. They are not obligated to answer questions about competing goods and services or give information about other sellers.

4   Salespeople should not try to "steer" customers towards purchases that they have reason to think will prove to be harmful to customers (financial harm counts) or that customers will come to regret.

These are *prima facie* duties that can conflict with other duties and are sometimes overridden by other duties. A *prima facie* duty is one's actual duty, other things being equal; it is an actual duty in the absence of conflicting duties of greater or equal importance – see Ross (1930, pp. 18–20, 28, 46; 1939, pp. 83–6) and Ewing (1948, p. 186). For example, my *prima facie* duty to keep promises is my actual duty in the absence of conflicting duties of equal or greater importance. 1–4 is a *minimal list* of the duties of salespeople concerning the disclosure of information. I believe that the following are also *prima facie* duties of salespeople, but I am much less certain that these principles can be justified:

5   Salespeople should not sell customers goods or services they have reason to think will prove to be harmful to customers or that the customers will come to regret later, without giving the customers their reasons for thinking that this is the case. [This duty does not hold if the seller has good reasons to think that the customer already possesses the information in question.]

6   Salespeople should not sell items they know to be defective or of poor quality without alerting customers to this. [This duty does not hold if the buyer can be reasonably expected to know about poor quality of what he is buying.]

I have what I take to be strong arguments for 1–4, but I'm not so sure that I can justify 5 and 6. I believe that reasonable people can disagree about 5 and 6. (I have very little to say about 5 or 6 in the present paper. See Carson (2001) for a discussion of arguments for 5 and 6.)

There are some important connections between duties 2, 4, and 6. Lying and deception in sales are not confined to lying to or deceiving customers about the goods one sells. Many salespeople misrepresent their own motives to customers/clients. Almost all salespeople invite the trust of customers/clients and claim, implicitly or explicitly, to be acting in the interests of customers/clients. Salespeople often ask customers to defer to their judgment about what is best for them. For most salespeople, gaining the trust of customers or clients is essential for success. Many salespeople are *not* interested in helping customers in the way they represent themselves as being. A salesperson who misrepresents her motives and intentions to customers violates principle 2. This simultaneous inviting and betrayal of trust is a kind of treachery. In ordinary cases, rules against lying and deception alone prohibit salespeople from steering customers towards goods or services they have reason to think will be bad for them. It is difficult to steer someone in this way without lying or deception, e.g., saying that you believe that a certain product is best for someone when you don't believe this to be the case. Similar remarks apply to selling defective goods. Often it is impossible to do this without lying to or deceiving customers. In practice, most or many violations of rules 4 and 6 are also violations of rule 2.

A justification for my theory

1–4 yield intuitively plausible results in concrete cases and avoid all of the objections I raised against Holley. I also justify 1–4 by appeal to the golden rule.

Taken together, 1–4 give us an intuitively plausible theory about the duties of salespeople regarding the disclosure of information; they give more acceptable results in actual cases than Holley's theory. 1–4 can account for cases in which the conduct of salespeople seems clearly wrong, e.g., cases of lying, deception, and steering customers into harmful decisions. Unlike Holley's theory, 1–4 do not make unreasonable demands on salespeople. They don't require that salespeople provide information that they don't have or spend more time with customers than they can spend. Nor do they require salespeople to divulge information about the virtues of what their competitors are selling.

In addition, my theory explains why different kinds of salespeople have different kinds of duties to their customers. For example, ordinarily, realtors have a duty to provide much more information to customers than sales clerks who sell inexpensive items in gift stores. My theory explains this difference in terms of the following:

1   the realtor's greater knowledge and expertise
2   the much greater amount of time the realtor can devote to the customer
3   the greater importance of the purchase of a home than the purchase of a small gift and the greater potential for harm or benefit to the buyer, and (in some cases)
4   implicit or explicit claims by the realtor to be acting on behalf of prospective home buyers (clerks in stores rarely make such claims).

The golden rule   I think that the golden rule is most plausibly construed as a consistency principle (those who violate the golden rule are guilty of inconsistency). The following version of the golden rule can be justified:

> GR: Consistency requires that if you think that it would be morally permissible for someone to do a certain act to another person, then you must consent to someone else doing the same act to you in relevantly similar circumstances.

How the golden rule supports my theory   Given this version of the golden rule, any rational and consistent moral judge who makes judgments about the moral obligations of salespeople will have to accept 1–4 as *prima facie* duties. Consider each duty in turn:

1   All of us have reason to fear the hazards about us in the world; we depend on others to warn us of those hazards. Few people would survive to adulthood were it not for the warnings of others about such things as oncoming cars, live electric wires, and approaching tornadoes. No one who values her own life can honestly say that she is willing to have others fail to warn her of dangers.

2   Like everyone else, a salesperson needs correct information in order to act effectively to achieve her goals and advance her interests. She is not willing to act on the basis of false beliefs. Consequently, she is not willing to have others deceive her or lie to her about matters relevant to her decisions in the market-place. She is not willing to have members of other professions (such as law and medicine) make it a policy to deceive her or lie to her whenever they can gain financially from doing so.

3   Salespeople have questions about the goods and services they themselves buy. They can't say that they are willing to have others evade or refuse to answer those questions. We want our questions to be answered by salespeople or else we wouldn't ask them. We are not willing to have salespeople evade or refrain from answering our questions. [Digression. Principle 3 permits salespeople to refuse to answer questions that would force them to provide information about their competitors. Why should we say *this*? Why not say instead that salespeople are obligated to answer *all questions* that customers ask? The answer is as follows: A salesperson's actions affect *both* her customers and her employer. In applying the golden rule to this issue she can't simply ask what kind of information she would want were she in the customer's position (Holley poses the question in just this way; see page 196). 3 can probably be improved upon, but it is a decent first approximation. A disinterested person who was not trying to give preference to the interests of salespeople, employers, or customers could endorse 3 as a policy for salespeople to follow. We can and must recognize the legitimacy of employers' demands for loyalty. The role of being an advocate or agent for someone who is selling things is legitimate within certain bounds – almost all of us are willing to have real estate agents work for us. A rational person could consent to the idea that everyone follow principles such as 3.]

4   All of us are capable of being manipulated by others into doing things that harm us, especially in cases in which others are more knowledgeable than we are. No one can consent to the idea that other people (or salespeople) should manipulate us into doing things that harm us whenever doing so is to their own advantage. Salespeople who claim that it would be permissible for them to make it a policy to deceive customers, fail to warn them about dangers, evade their questions, or manipulate them into doing things that are harmful to them whenever doing so is advantageous to them are inconsistent because they are not willing to have others do the same to them.

They must allow that 1–4 are *prima facie* moral duties.

1–4 are only *prima facie duties*. The golden rule can account for the cases in which 1–4 are overridden by other more important duties. For example, we would be willing to have other people violate 1–4 if doing so were necessary in order to save the life of an innocent person. In practice, violating 1, 2, 3, or 4 is permissible only in very rare cases. The financial interests of salespeople seldom justify violations of 1, 2, 3, or 4. The fact that a salesperson can make more money by violating 1, 2, 3, or 4 would not justify her in violating 1, 2, 3 or 4 unless she has very pressing financial obligations that she cannot meet otherwise. Often salespeople need to meet certain minimum sales quotas to avoid being fired (Oakes, 1990, p. 86). Suppose that a salesperson needs to make it a policy to violate 1–4 in order to meet her sales quotas and keep her job. Would this justify her in violating 1–4? *Possibly.* But, in order for this to be the case, the following conditions would have to be met: a) she has important moral obligations such as feeding and housing her family that require her to be employed (needing money to keep one's family in an expensive house or take them to Disney World wouldn't justify violating 1–4) and b) she can't find another job that would enable her to meet her obligations without violating 1–4 (or other equally important duties). Those salespeople who can't keep their jobs or make an adequate income without violating 1–4 should seek other lines of employment.

A defense of the version of the golden rule employed earlier

My argument is as follows:

1   Consistency requires that if you think that it would be morally permissible for someone to do a certain act to another person, then you must grant that it would be morally permissible for someone to do that same act to you in relevantly similar circumstances.
2   Consistency requires that if you think that it would be morally permissible for someone to do a certain act to you in certain circumstances, then you must *consent* to him/her doing that act to you in those circumstances.

Therefore,

> GR. Consistency requires that if you think that it would be morally permissible for someone to do a certain act to another person, then you must consent to someone doing the same act to you in relevantly similar circumstances. [You are inconsistent if you think that it would be morally permissible for someone to do a certain act to another person, but do not consent to someone doing the same act to you in relevantly similar circumstances.] (This argument follows that given by Gensler (1986, pp. 89–90).)

This argument is valid, i.e., the conclusion follows from the premises, and both its premises are true. Both premises are consistency requirements. Premise 1 addresses questions about the consistency of a person's different moral beliefs. Premise 2 addresses questions about whether a person's moral beliefs are consistent with her attitudes and actions. Our attitudes and actions can be either consistent or inconsistent with the moral judgments we accept.

Premise 1 Premise 1 follows from, or is a narrower version of, the universalizability principle (UP). The UP can be stated as follows:

> Consistency requires that, if one makes a moral judgment about a particular case, then one must make the same moral judgment about any similar case, unless there is a morally relevant difference between the cases.

Premise 1 is a principle of consistency for judgments about the moral permissibility of actions. The UP, by contrast, is a principle of consistency for *any kind of moral judgment*, including judgments about what things are good and bad.

Premise 2 How shall we understand what is meant by "consenting to" something? For our present purposes, we should not take consenting to something to be the same as desiring it or trying to bring it about. My thinking that it is morally permissible for you to beat me at chess does not commit me to desiring that you beat me, nor does it commit me to playing so as to allow you to beat me. Consenting to an action is more like not objecting to it, not criticizing, not resenting, the other person for doing it. If I think that it is permissible for you to beat me at chess then I cannot object to your beating me (Gensler, 1996, pp. 63–4). I am inconsistent if I object to your doing something that I take to be morally permissible. If I claim that it is permissible for someone to do something to another person, then, on pain of inconsistency, I cannot object if someone else does the same thing to me in relevantly similar circumstances. The gist of my application of the golden rule to sales is that since we *do object* to salespeople doing such things as lying to us, deceiving us, failing to answer our questions, we cannot consistently say that it is morally permissible for them to *do* these things.

Examples

I will discuss several cases to illustrate and clarify my theory.

Example A I am selling a used car that I know has bad brakes; this is one of the reasons I am selling the car. You don't ask me any questions about the car and I sell it to you without informing you of the problem with the brakes.

Example B I am selling a used car that starts poorly in cold weather. You arrange to look at the car early in the morning on a very cold day. I don't own a garage so the car is out in the cold. With difficulty, I start it up and drive it for thirty minutes shortly before you look at it and then cover the car with snow to make it seem as if it hasn't been driven. The engine is still hot when you come and the car starts up immediately. You then purchase the car remarking that you need a car that starts well in the cold to get to work, since you don't have a garage.

Example C While working as a salesperson I feign a friendly concern for a customer's interests. I say "I will try to help you find the product that is best suited for your needs. I don't want you to spend any more money than you need to. Take as much time as you need." The customer believes me, but she is deceived. In fact, I couldn't care less about her welfare. I only want to sell her the highest priced item I can as quickly as I can. I don't like the customer: indeed, I am contemptuous of her.

In example A, I violate duty 1 and put the buyer and other motorists, passengers, and pedestrians at risk. In example B, I violate duties 2 and 5. In example C, I violate duty 2. In the absence of conflicting obligations that are at least as important as the duties I violate, my actions in examples A–C are morally wrong.

Example D: A Longer Case [true story] In 1980, I received a one-year Fellowship from The National Endowment for the Humanities. The fellowship paid for my salary, but not my fringe benefits. Someone in the benefits office of my university told me that I had the option of continuing my health insurance through the university, if I paid for the premiums out of my own pocket. I told the benefits person that this was a lousy deal and that I could do better by going to a private insurance company. I went to the office of Prudential Insurance agent Mr. A. O. "Ed" Mokarem. I told him that I was looking for a one-year medical insurance policy to cover me during the period of the fellowship and that I planned to resume my university policy when I returned to teaching. (The university provided this policy free of charge to all faculty who were teaching.) He showed me a comparable Prudential policy that cost about half as much as the university's policy. He explained the policy to me. I asked him to fill out the forms so that I could purchase the policy. He then told me that there was a potential problem I should consider. He said roughly the following:

> You will want to return to your free university policy next year when you return to teaching. The Prudential policy is a one-year terminal policy. If you develop any serious medical problems during the next year, Prudential will probably consider you "uninsurable" and will not be willing to sell you health insurance in the future. If you buy the Prudential policy, you may encounter the same problems with your university policy. Since you will be dropping this policy *voluntarily*, they will have the right to underwrite your application for re-enrollment. If you develop a serious health problem during the next year, their underwriting decision could be "Total Rejection," imposing some waivers and/or exclusions, or (at best) subjecting your coverage to the "pre-existing conditions clause," which would not cover any pre-existing conditions until you have been covered under the new policy for at least a year.

If I left my current health insurance for a year, I risked developing a costly medical condition for which no one would be willing to insure me. That would have been a very foolish risk to take. So, I thanked him very much and, swallowing my pride, went back to renew my health insurance coverage through the university. I never bought any insurance from Mr. Mokarem and never had occasion to send him any business.

I have discussed this case with numerous classes through the years. It usually generates a lively discussion. Most of my students do not think that Mr. Mokarem was morally obligated to do what he did, but they don't think that what he did was wrong either – they regard his actions as supererogatory or above and beyond the call of duty.

My view about example D   On my theory, this is a difficult case to assess. If 1–4 are a salesperson's only duties concerning the disclosure of information, then Mr. Mokarem was not obligated to inform me as he did. (In this case, the information in question was information about a *competing product* – the university's health insurance policy.) If 5 is a *prima facie* duty of salespeople, then (assuming that he had no conflicting moral duties of greater or equal importance) it was his duty, all things considered, to inform me as he did. Since I am uncertain that 5 can be justified, I'm not sure whether or not Mr. Mokarem was obligated to do what he did or whether his actions were supererogatory. This case illustrates part of what is at stake in the question of whether 5 is a *prima facie* duty of salespeople.

Acknowledgments

Thanks to Ivan Preston for his very generous and helpful advice and criticisms. Everyone interested in these topics should read his work. The second half of this paper is based on my paper "Deception and Withholding Information in Sales" (Carson, 2001). That paper gives a more detailed and nuanced treatment of moral issues in sales than the present paper. I thank *Business Ethics Quarterly* for permission to use include material from that paper here. I also thank the journal for its policy of giving authors the copyrights for their articles.

References

Atiyah, P. S. 1979: *The Rise and Fall of Freedom of Contract.* Oxford: The Clarendon Press.
Beauchamp, T. 1983: *Case Studies in Business, Society, and Ethics.* Englewood Cliffs, NJ: Prentice Hall.
Bok, S. 1979: *Lying: Moral Choice in Public and Private Life.* New York: Vintage Books.
Bowie, N. 1982: *Business Ethics.* Englewood Cliffs, NJ: Prentice Hall Inc.
Bowie, N. and Duska, R. 1990: *Business Ethics,* 2nd edn. Englewood Cliffs, NJ: Prentice Hall.

Carson, T. 1988: On the definition of lying: a reply to jones and revisions. *Journal of Business Ethics*, 7, 509–14.

Carson, T. 1993: Second thoughts on bluffing. *Business Ethics Guarterly*. 3, 317–41.

Carson, T. 2001: Deception and withholding information in sales *Business Ethics Quarterly*. 11 (2), April, 275–306.

Carson, T., Wokutch, R. and Cox, J. 1985: An ethical analysis of deception in advertising. *Journal of Business Ethics*. 4, 93–104.

DeGeorge, R. 1982: *Business Ethics*, 1st edn. New York: MacMillan.

Ewing, A. C. 1948: *The definition of good*. London: Routledge and Kegan Paul.

FTC policy statement on deception. 1983 – still current. Available on the Web at: http.://www.ftc.gov/bcp/guides/guides.htm then click on FTC Policy Statement on Deception.

Gensler, H. 1986: A Kantian argument against abortion. *Philosophical Studies*, 49, 83–98.

Gensler, H. 1996: *Formal Ethics*. New York: Routledge.

Holley, D. 1993: A moral evaluation of sales practices. In Tom Beauchamp and Norman Bowie, eds. *Ethical Theory and Business*, 4th edn 462–72. Englewood Cliffs, NJ: Prentice Hall.

Kant, I. 1993: *Grounding for the Metaphysics of Morals*. James Ellington, trans., 3rd edn. Indianapolis: Hackett.

Oakes, G. 1990: *The Soul of the Salesman*. Atlantic Highlands, NJ: Humanities Press.

Oxford English Dictionary, 2nd edn. 1989. Oxford: Oxford University Press.

Preston, I. 1975: *The Great American Blow-up: Puffery in Advertising and Selling*. Madison: University of Wisconsin Press.

Preston, I. 1994: *The Tangled Web They Weave: Truth, Falsity, and Advertisers*. Madison: University of Wisconsin Press.

Preston, I. 1998: Puffery and other "loophole" claims: How the law's "don't ask don't tell" policy condones fraudulent falsity in advertising. *Journal of Law and Commerce*. 18, 49–114.

Ross, W. D. 1930: *The Right and the Good*. Oxford: Oxford University Press.

Ross, W. D. 1939: *The Foundations of Ethics*. Oxford: Oxford University Press.

Webster's Third New International Dictionary of the English Language. 1963. Springfield, Mass.: G. and C. Merriam Company.

———— Chapter 10 ————

Ethical Issues in Financial Services

Ronald F. Duska and James J. Clarke

"Some turn every quality or art into a means of getting wealth; this they conceive to be the end, and to the promotion of the end they think all things must contribute."
Aristotle, *Politics*, Bk. 1, Ch. 9. 1258a 13–14

"The unfettered love of money is the root of all evil". Such a claim, which got revised into "Money is the root of all evil", exaggerated as it is, reflects an ethical bias against money and money markets, and, by extension, finance and financial services that permeates many, if not most, cultures' thinking. Western philosophical culture, particularly as exemplified in Aristotle, defines the very notion of liberal as being free from concerns about money. Aristotle claims that it is all right to study wealth getting, but "to be engaged in it practically is illiberal and irksome." Further, he maintains that

> [w]ealth getting that results from exchange is justly censured; for it is unnatural, and a mode by which men gain from one another. The most hated sort of wealth getting, and with the greatest reason, is usury, which makes a gain out of money itself, and not from the natural object of it. For money was intended to be used in exchange, but not to increase at interest (Aristotle, *Politics* Bk 1, Ch 11, 1258b10–11 and *Politics*, Bk. 1, Ch. 10. 1258b 1).

Major religions, such as Christianity and Islam, at one or another point in their histories, followed this lead of Aristotle and maintained prohibitions against usury, i.e. the loaning of money at interest. Consequently, from the perspective of western culture, the notion that there could be ethics in financial services is at least problematic if not downright oxymoronic.

Such an ethical indictment of the financial services industry carries over in the views of contemporary popular culture. Recent non-fiction best sellers such as *Liar's Poker* and *Serpent on the Rock* present us with a picture of cultures in the financial world rife with exploitation, manipulation, fraud and excess. Novels, such as *Bonfire of the Vanities* and motion pictures such as *Wall Street, Other People's Money, Barbarians at the Gate,* and *Boiler Room* among numerous others, portray the "Masters of the Universe", the investment bankers, arbitrageurs, the take over companies and stock brokers as the incarnation of evil. A new TV series, *Bull*, portrays life on Wall Street as life in a vicious, dog eat dog world, where the pursuit of big money is the overriding driving force. Individuals such as Ivan Boesky and Michael Milken become icons and exemplars of unethical behavior. Insurance companies – such as Metropolitan Life, Prudential and New York Life – are found guilty of market misconduct in their sales practices, misrepresenting and unnecessarily replacing life insurance policies to the detriment of their clients for the sake of a heavily front end loaded commission. Class action suits against the companies are settled for billions of dollars. In short, popular culture and recent events give us a picture in which the financial services industry appears essentially corrupt and unethical.

However, this essay will try to show that such a picture is seriously distorted, and that ethics in the financial services industry is not only present, but also necessary. A critique depending on Aristotle's view of money would be seriously flawed because it would fail to take into account the extent to which money itself and money markets have become of significant instrumental worth to society by aiding the production and distribution of goods. Certainly if a culture turns the pursuit of money, an instrumental good, into the ultimate goal of human beings, such a culture would be ethically corrupt. That is the moral of the story of King Midas. Nevertheless, the invention of money and the conversion of it into a commodity itself, to be used for the purchase of a multitude of other goods, was a boon to the human race, and properly utilized and constrained, financial markets, which facilitate the exchange of money, have an abidingly important and positive impact on society.

For the purposes of this essay, we stipulate that ethics is a normative enterprise that analyzes and evaluates not only individual actions and types of action, but also practices, institutions, and systems. In that we follow the lead of Aristotle and John Stuart Mill, who remind us that human beings are social animals, and that the fulfillment of their appropriate ends, which is the goal of ethical behavior, can only take place in a society whose structures either help or hinder individual fulfillment (Aristotle, *Politics*, Bk 1, Chapter 2, 1253a1–35; Mill, 1957 [1861]). Hence, Aristotle and Mill, tell us that a complete ethical analysis requires the analysis and evaluation of the institutions and systems of a society to see if they contribute to or frustrate individuals' fulfillment.

Using such a broad scope requires that the ethics of financial services analyze and evaluate not only individual actions in the financial services industry, such as churning or stock manipulation, but also the entire financial system, including financial markets, financial institutions, and financial instruments. From a macro point of view, a system that benefits people is ethically preferable to systems that do not provide as many benefits for people. From a micro point of view, within the financial system itself, ethical issues such as insider trading, greenmail, de-mutualization or rebating in insurance, surface frequently and their resolution depends on understanding these practices in the context of the highly complex nature of the financial environment. Thus, to help us evaluate the system (the macro view) and the practices within the system (the micro view) it is important to begin with basic definitions, and develop a conceptual vision of how the system interconnects.

If a system is large, of course, individuals get reduced to ciphers, and their individual wants and desires play little or no role in assuring the development of equilibrium and efficiency. Given the ends of efficiency and equilibrium, individual propensities are necessarily sacrificed. Is such sacrifice justified? Yes, but solely for the sake of efficiency, an efficiency which is itself justified by something like an invisible hand argument, which assures that such efficiency will provide benefits for society in general, the greatest good for the greatest number. For the system to be justified it must provide a rising tide which lifts all boats, and do it with some semblance of fairness.

The Financial System

Financial systems mirror the complexities of a nation's economic system and its level of economic development, development being a normative term that implies a desirable end point. We will focus on the financial system of the United States where economic development is advanced, and the financial markets, instruments, and institutions set the benchmark for the rest of the world.

Financial markets are the bedrock of the financial system. Their purpose is to allocate savings efficiently to parties who use funds for investment in real assets or financial assets. An optimal allocation function will channel savings to the most productive use of those savings. In the US system the mediator in the allocation process is price, and price in a financial system is usually described in terms of an interest rate. Efficiency of allocation is critical to assure adequate capital formation and economic growth in a modern economy. System efficiency is achieved when the price reflected in the market is an equilibrium price; that is, a market clearing price. If dis-equilibrium exists, rapid adjustment to a new equilibrium is guaranteed. Efficiency will occur more readily if the number of buyers and sellers is large; both parties to a transaction easily obtain information; and transaction costs are kept to a minimum.

Types of financial markets

Financial markets can be categorized according to time or according to their purpose.

Markets according to time   Categorizing financial markets according to time allows us to divide them into money markets and capital markets. Money markets trade in securities with original maturity of one year or less; whereas capital markets trade in securities with maturity greater than one year. Time is not arbitrary, but rather reflects the accounting cycle. Therefore transactions occurring within the accounting cycle, usually for cash management motives, are satisfied through money markets. These money market transactions involve the buying and selling of:

1   US Treasury bills, the largest and most important money market
2   Federal funds, which involve inter-bank borrowing and lending, and are a critical channel for monetary policy
3   commercial paper, short-term debt issued by financial and non financial corporations, and
4   eurodollars, the market for short-term dollar deposits outside the US.

These markets are primarily institutional, since individual investors are less likely to deal directly in the money market. Rather individuals' cash management transactions are facilitated through a bank or a mutual fund.

Capital markets, whose securities have maturity greater than a year, include three broad areas – the bond, the mortgage and the stock market. The bond market includes the sale of government, corporate, municipal and international bonds. The largest and most important bond market is the US Treasury market, since US Treasury interest rates on government bonds are the reference for security valuation both domestically and internationally. This makes the Treasury bond and note market critically important around the world. The mortgage market involves the financing of residential and commercial real estate, while equity markets involve trading in common and preferred stock.

Markets according to purpose   Markets are also divided according to the purpose of the transaction, whether that is raising new capital or the exchange of existing instruments. Transactions carried on to raise new capital for a corporation or government occur in what is called a primary market or new issue market. Transactions that exchange existing investments occur in what is called a secondary market.

Capital generation   Capital generation may be facilitated in a number of ways. Securities may be:

1   issued through an auction process, as is the case with Treasury securities
2   privately placed to a small group of sophisticated investors, as is the case with many corporate bond issues
3   issued through a rights offering to existing stockholders, or
4   facilitated by an underwriter or investment banker.

The best test of efficiency in primary markets is the net cost of the capital the market generates. The lower the cost of the capital, the more efficient the allocation of financial resources.

Each method of capital generation is susceptible to a variety of ethically questionable activities, on numerous levels, ranging from manipulation, misuse of inside information, fraud, misrepresentation, to bribery, over or under-evaluation of assets, high pressure sales, etc.

Security exchange Most people are not as familiar with primary market activity as they are with secondary markets that are constantly referenced in the daily media. Secondary markets are either exchanges, like the New York Stock Exchange (NYSE) or over-the-counter markets. Exchanges use the auction process for price discovery, determining price through the interaction of buyers and sellers. Any exchange, be it the NYSE or the Chicago Mercantile Exchange (CME), involves

1   a physical location
2   a set of rules governing trading, operations and behavior, and
3   members who have purchased the right to conduct transactions.

The over-the-counter (OTC) market deals with a greater volume of trading investments than the exchanges do with their auction process. Foreign exchange, which is the largest financial market, trades OTC. US Treasury notes, bonds and bills are traded OTC. The majority of corporate and municipal bond transactions occur OTC, as do the trading in mortgage and asset backed securities. The common stock of many prominent and recognizable companies is traded on the NYSE, but the majority of equities are traded on The National Association of Security Dealers (NASD) systems. For example, prominent companies such as Microsoft and Cisco Systems are traded over the counter.

The OTC systems are made up of dealers, who stand ready to make a market in a particular financial asset, and brokers, who assist customers in trading. A dealer, as opposed to a broker, carries inventory. A dealer, usually through an electronic network, posts bid and ask prices. The dealer will purchase securities at the bid price and sell securities at the ask price. The difference is referred to as the spread and is how a dealer is compensated for the trade.

Any exchange is susceptible to the temptation of one of the parties to profit at the expense of the other. Consequently rules are in place governing what constitutes fair trading. These rules constitute some of the ethical rules governing those who conduct market exchanges. For example, the US OTC market is regulated by a code of ethics established by the National Association of Security Dealers. (NASD is a private organization, one of whose functions is to encourage ethical practices by its members.) The rules specified in the codes reinforce what are usually common sense intuitions about what is ethically acceptable behavior and what is not. If one promises to sell a customer a security at a certain price, it is unethical to renege on that promise because a later customer offers to pay a higher price. Ethics demands one keep one's word. It is unethical for a broker to give out information about a company, whose stock he is selling, which is colored to make the stock look more attractive. Perhaps the most important ethical principle among brokers and dealers is "Your word is your bond." Absent adherence to that rule, it is likely the system would break down.

Financial instruments and institutions

Financial markets are at the heart of the financial system since they provide the infrastructure for issuing and trading securities, but there are two other critical components in the system, financial instruments and financial institutions.

Financial instruments are the securities that are traded. They are identified by either a time or contractual reference. As we have seen, classified according to time, money market securities are those having original maturity of one year or less while capital market instruments are those with a maturity of more than a year. Classified according to contractual reference, financial instruments are either debt or equity claims.

Debt claims usually provide the owner with a periodic return, called a coupon interest payment, and the return of principal at the end of the contract. Examples of debt claims include the fixed income securities such as bonds and mortgages, along with money market securities and life and long term care insurance policies and annuities. The chief ethical issue in this domain will involve the responsibility to honor contracts.

Common and preferred stock are two examples of equity claims. Equity claims imply ownership, whereas debt holders have no claim to ownership. If a company is dissolved, debt holders have first legal claim on the assets. Whereas debt claims mature, most equity claims are perpetuities, and whereas debt claims come with fixed obligations as to periodic or coupon return and the return of principal, most equity claims make no fixed promise as to future cash flows. Common stock, the most familiar equity claim, may pay the owner or investor a periodic return in the form of dividends, but there is no fixed or legal obligation to make the payment.

Along with financial instruments, there are the financial institutions, the portal for the average person to participate in the financial system, which help those people exchange those instruments. Financial institutions include, but are not limited to, banks, securities dealers and brokers, pension funds, accounting firms, mutual fund companies and insurance companies. Such institutions are an integral part of the financial system in that they facilitate the activity of exchange.

From the 1930s to the 1990s, US financial institutions were neatly compartmentalized, with each type of institution having a specific function in the overall workings of the financial system. The landmark law that created the compartmentalization was the Glass–Steagall Act (or Banking Act) of 1933, which was passed by Congress as a reaction to bank failures and the perceived responsibility of banks for the Great Depression and the general market failures of the time. The Glass-Steagall Act confined banking services to making loans and taking deposits, while insurance services were relegated to insurance companies, and home lending to savings and loans. Banks were also prohibited from assisting their large corporate customers in purchasing corporate stock and reselling it in the open market. In the 1990s the clear demarcation of financial institutions began to get muddied. Passage of the Financial Services Modernization Act (The Gramm–Leach–Bliley Act) in 1999 has ushered in a new chapter in US financial history, some of the implications of which are still not clear.

Financial intermediaries Financial institutions are often referred to as financial intermediaries. In a world of direct finance, where borrowers and lenders interact using primary securities, there is no need for financial institutions, but direct finance creates problems that intermediaries can help resolve. There are three types of intermediation – of denomination, maturity and risk.

Intermediation of denomination and maturity occurs because very often borrowers and lenders have different desires with respect to the dollar amount of a transaction and the maturity of the loan or the investment. A financial institution, such as a bank, can easily allow depositors to save in any convenient amount and then package the saving and accommodate a lender's desires. With respect to maturity, the intermediator can guarantee a saver one time frame, say six months, and simultaneously make a loan for a different length of time, say two years.

Financial institutions also engage in risk intermediation. The typical household saver is risk adverse and they would have difficulty dealing directly with a borrower. In such a situation, the bank provides a secure and risk free way for money to be transferred from the saver to the borrower, while simultaneously controlling the risk of the transaction. Insurance companies are risk intermediators in a different way. They create pools of risk adverse people so that they can insure themselves against catastrophic events that would ruin them financially.

Besides functioning as intermediaries, financial institutions facilitate exchange by acting as depository, contractual, or investment institutions. Commercial banks and thrifts, including credit unions, are the chief depository institutions, where the major source of funds is deposits sold to savers, and the major use of funds is loans to borrowers. Contractual institutions include insurance companies and pension funds where the source of funding is premiums paid to obtain various types of insurance policies or pension contributions which create annuities guaranteed by a structured contract. Investment institutions are comprised of investment companies, primarily mutual funds and broker dealers

To sum up: the financial system is the complex array of financial markets, securities, and institutions that interact in facilitating the movement of capital among savers and borrowers. That financial system is also used for mediation of risk among parties. In the best possible model, this is all accomplished in a very efficient and, hopefully, ethical manner.

The Ethics of the Market System

In the light of the above, the following seems clear. Financial markets are a critical component of a modern developed economy, that is, they are the fundamental element of the free market or capitalist system. Historically, they have lead to the highest overall standard of living in history. In short, they are instrumentally beneficial in helping bring about material conditions for the good life of society.

That being the case, it is interesting to note to what extent, even the religious opposition to the free market system mentioned in the opening paragraph, has abated. In 1991, in the encyclical *Centesimus Annus*, Pope John Paul II (1995, p. 489) states, "It would appear that on the level of individual nations and of international relations, the free market is the most efficient instrument for utilizing resources and effectively responding to needs." It seems clear, then, that the free market economy, and the financial system that facilitates it have become almost universally recognized as instrumentally beneficial for society. Not only that, but it benefits society and participation in it, in some ways, can now be viewed as a noble calling (Novak, 1996). So if the market and its instruments are not abused, it is a least ethically acceptable from a macro point of view.

Ethical practices within the system

Still, we need to examine the various types of behavior within the system from a micro point of view. There are financial services practices generally recognized as unethical like fraud, stock manipulation and churning. There are also practices in financial dealings whose ethical acceptability is questionable. Questions can be raised about the following sorts of practices. Is insider trading really wrong? If so, what exactly is wrong with it? How much disclosure is necessary in sales of financial instruments? How much disclosure is necessary in financial statements that show the financial strengths and weaknesses of a company? Should mutual fund managers put themselves in unwarranted conflict of interest situations by engaging in private purchases of stocks their company trades in? Should banks be able to sell insurance and investment products, and does such a capability create unnecessary conflicts of interest for them? Should accountants do consulting for firms they audit? Is day trading merely legalized gambling? Should law firms and accounting firms join together into multi-disciplinary estate planning teams? Is it fair for mutual insurance companies to demutualize? What should the limits of privacy be in the credit industry? What climate should be created so that those interests of the broker do not conflict with those of his client? Do we need fee based advising only, or is commissioned based selling with an agent's responsibility to give a client the best possible advice? Are financial service personnel professionals or simply sales people, and what are their responsibilities as such?

A litany of unethical practices

Deception and fraud The ethical rules in the market place, even the market place of money, that individuals should follow, are fairly straightforward. Market transactions between individuals ought to be carried on without using others and without engaging in deception or fraud in accordance with one's role. However, human beings, being what they are, they will, for a variety of reasons fall short of fulfilling their responsibilities or what is worse greedily and selfishly use others for their own gain. What follows is a list of ethically problematic ways of behaving in the financial services industry.

Ways of being deceitful or dishonest in the financial services industry include misrepresenting the financial product, including deceptive illustrations of possible returns, concealing of risk factors, withholding full disclosure, misrepresenting one's ability, and other activities. Fraud is a legal concept and has specific meanings in specific instances, but generally involves "intentional misrepresentation, concealment, or omission of the truth for the purpose of deception or manipulation to the detriment of a person or organization" (Downes and Goodman, 1985, p. 148). Beyond deception and fraud, there are other ways of using a client, particularly in exchange situations, but possibly elsewhere, which involve coercing or manipulating the client, by fear mongering or other means.

A central concern in financial services arises from conflicts of interest. There is conflicting interest when either the broker or agent's interest is served by selling a product that the client does not need or which is inferior to another product, typically a product that provides less remuneration to the sales person. There is also conflict when an agent has two clients, and service to one will be detrimental to the other. If the interests in conflict are the interests of the agent against those of the client, professionalism demands that the agent subordinate his or her interests to those of the client. When the interests in conflict are those of two parties, both of whom the agent serves, solutions are more complex.

There are particularly difficult conflict of interest situations for accounting firms arising from providing external audit function for a publicly held firm while simultaneously selling consulting services to the same firm. Also, the audit function has inherent conflicts balancing confidentiality to the client and their duty to inform the public of possible illegal practices. The SEC has historically been concerned about the latter problem, but it is the mixing of auditing and consulting that concerns the SEC at the present time.

Financial planners routinely run into conflicts between the interests of their clients and the structure of fees for their services. There is an interesting juxtaposition in the field between fee-only planners and planners that sell product. A fee-only planner charges for their advice, but receives no commission from the client's implementation of that advice. Most planners are not fee-only, but rather do not overtly charge for their advice, but are remunerated through a commission on the implementation of that advice. This creates an interesting dilemma – does my advice purely service the needs of the client or do I shade my advice depending on the structure of a fee schedule?

There are numerous examples of potential unethical practices in money management and investment banking, for example, money managers who trade personally in the securities their firms hold in portfolio. A manager with large holdings in a security can easily influence the price of that security as they buy and sell; therefore why not enter the market for a personal transaction before placing the firm's transaction. Investment bankers have ample opportunities to engage in practices that are either clearly a conflict of interest, and often illegal, or border on a conflict of interest. Free riding and withholding securities from the public in an initial public offering is illegal, but the temptation to compromise this rule is powerful when the issue is "hot"; that is everyone knows the price will increase once the security begins to trade in the secondary market. In December 2000, the SEC commenced an investigation against three prominent investment banking firms for selectively providing shares of "hot" IPOs to certain clients. The investigation centers on a "quid pro quo" arrangement where the client is charged higher fees for other services in exchange for IPO shares that will surely rise in value.

Another unethical practice which occurs in the financial services industry would be scalping securities: for example an investment advisor who buys a security before recommending it, then selling out after the price has risen based on the recommendation. The most prominent case occurred in the 1980s involving the *Wall Street Journal*'s "Heard on the Street" column. This column is widely read and carefully followed by investors. The articles are very specific and often list companies and recommendations. The author was accused of tipping off certain individuals about the contents of articles before they were published.

Cornering the market is obviously unethical and often illegal, especially when it is in direct violation of government regulations, as was the well-publicized case against Salomon Brothers in 1991. Salomon was one of the major primary dealers in US government securities. These dealers bid in the auctions for Treasury bills, notes and bonds. The government has regulations concerning the percentage of successful bids that may go to individual firms, but firms may also bid for their customers. In one auction in early 1991, Salomon received over 80 percent of the offering under the pretense that a sizeable amount of the bids were for customers. In the subsequent investigation, Salomon was charged with illegal activity, but there was also evidence to suggest that Salomon had used agreements with customers that technically may not have been illegal, but surely bordered on the unethical given the intent of the government rules.

Companies can get involved in activities such as: illegal dividend payments, where "dividend payments come out of capital surplus or that make the company insolvent" (Downes and Goodman, 1985, p. 174); incestuous share dealing – buying and selling of shares in each other's companies to create a tax or other financial advantage (Downes and Goodman, 1985, p. 175); compensation design, where they set up alternative forms of payment to allow agents to avoid rebating violations; discrimination in hiring and promoting; misrepresentation to new hires; invasion of privacy; and dubious claim settlement policies.

In insurance sales, there is needless replacement, and defective illustrations, which have been the basis of billion dollar lawsuits against Prudential, New York Life and Metropolitan Life, among others. Brokers and agents get involved in churning accounts that benefit the agents at the expense of the clients. For broker/ dealers, there is insistence on suitability rules, which demands you know and act on behalf of the best interests of the client you are selling to. There is the prohibition for financial planners and for those with control over clients' monies, either as trustees or brokers or advisers against commingling those funds with the financial service agent's.

For those on the exchanges, there is insider trading, which is as the name implies, involves trading on the basis of inside information, which is viewed as unfair to other traders who do not have the information. It makes for an unequal playing field. There is free riding, in the form of withholding a new securities issue to resell later at a higher price, or in the form of buying and selling in rapid order without putting up money for the sale.

In arbitrage, there is Greenmail, which is "payment by a takeover target to a potential acquirer, usually to buy back acquired shares at a premium. In exchange, the acquirer agrees not to pursue the takeover bid further" (Downes and Goodman, 1985, p. 164). Gun jumping involves trading securities based on information before it becomes public, or soliciting buy orders in an under-writing before the SEC registration is complete (Downes and Goodman, 1985, p. 165).

Finally, there are prohibitions against schemes such as pyramiding that build on non-existing values, such as a Ponzi Scheme, rigging the market, manipulation, or running ahead i.e. an analyst buying a stock before making the recommendation to buy to his or her client (Downes and Goodman, 1985, p. 352).

Most of these unethical practices have in common, if not downright deception, the use of one's customers or clients for the benefit of the financial service professional. There is neither time nor room to deal with all of these issues, but this litany should help us begin to understand the tremendous range of possible conflicts of interest and outright possibilities of fraud in financial interaction. What can be done to avoid such problems?

Basic ethical principles

We have just provided a list of only some of the types of ethical misbehavior to occur in the financial services industry. Given the huge diversity of issues what is the practical way to approach them? First, it would seem useful to come up with some general principles to follow. Second, it would be helpful to examine the various kinds of regulation governing financial services. Finally, it would seem helpful to examine how to make the environment more susceptible to ethical behavior.

Our experience show there are two valuable and overarching ethical principles that can be applied to the majority of issues in financial services:

1 avoid deception and fraud, and
2 honor your commitments.

What follows will be a brief discussion of how these two principles can be used to resolve a number of the ethical issues financial service professionals face.

The avoidance of deception and fraud Economists have developed the notion of an ideal market exchange as a transaction in which two autonomous individuals, with full information, agree to transfer goods. Ideally there is perfect information about the worth of what is being given and received in return. Such an exchange, freely entered into with full information, should maximize satisfaction on both sides. Not only is there satisfaction on both sides, the expansion of such market behavior to all – agreements of exchange made freely and honored, leads to the overall improvement of each trader's lot and benefits the entire society.

When the conditions of an ideal trade, which includes the freedom of the participants, and full knowledge of the pertinent details of the product, are met we have what is often called informed consent. Consent cannot be presumed if one is either forced into an exchange or lacks adequate knowledge of the product one is bargaining for.

However real financial markets are not ideal. In real financial markets consumers are often closer to ignorance than perfect knowledge. That makes them vulnerable to the unethical machinations, which if they were to become widespread, would lead to the general demise of the health of the financial market itself.

Clearly deception undermines the "ideal exchange model." Deception leads to the deceived party getting something different and usually less valuable than it expected. The mutual satisfaction disappears. A financial system fraught with deception and fraud where one could not rely on others to honor their commitments would be an inherently unstable as well as an economically inefficient society. Hence, the acceptance of practices that utilize deception and fraud along with not honoring one's word would lead to undermining the market.

Empirical observations provide us with multiple examples of such failures. Many economies founder because of graft and corruption, bribery, extortion, and failure to abide by one's word. In fact, it is this exact environment that permeates Russia and stifles its successful transition into a modern economic state. The reason for such failure is clear. Any rational person would be foolish to deal with a country, company or person who is deceptive and unreliable. Rational and ethical financial dealing requires people be able to trust those with whom they are dealing to be honest and abide by their commitments, even if abiding by those commitments is disadvantageous to them.

Still, because of the temptation to pursue one's interest at the expense of another, financial markets are full of examples of dishonest dealings. An agent tells a client that an insurance policy is a savings plan so as to make the sale and obtain the commission. A broker tells the client for whom a low-risk investment is suitable, that a high-risk investment will meet the client's needs so as to make the sale. A financial officer gives the credit manager at a bank an inaccurate picture of the receivables of the company to secure a loan he assumes the bank would not approve if it had the true picture. All of these misrepresentations at the expense of the client (or at least without the informed consent of the client) to benefit the agent are essentially situations where one person is used for the benefit of another, by being led to believe something other than the truth. That is the essence of lying, using another to benefit oneself.

But some of the most interesting cases of unethical behavior in the world of finance are not those of outright misrepresentation. A more subtle way of circumventing ideal exchange is through failure to disclose pertinent information. Often agents defend failure to disclose by saying "Not disclosing isn't lying, it's just not telling." But such a rationalization misses the point. Any action of deliberately withholding information to get another to act contrary to the way she would if she had that information has the same deceptive structure and consequence as the overt lie. Such action doesn't allow for informed choice.

However, deciding how much to disclose is not easy. Effective salespersons are always reluctant to put negative thoughts in a buyer's mind. Pointing out the possible unsuitable features of a stock, its risk, or a variable annuity, its lower return on investment when tied to a life insurance policy, jeopardizes the sale. Aggressive intermediaries are reluctant to disclose downsides of their products. Should one disclose the downside of a product and if so how much?

The characterization of lying given above shows an approach that is helpful in determining how much to disclose. "Whenever a person is tempted not to disclose some information, that person should ask why he is not disclosing." If an agent is withholding information because of fear of losing the sale if the client knows the whole story, the agent is manipulating that client. When stock brokers, financial planners or insurance agents claim that their customers don't need all the information that is given to them, they are often rationalizing and some care needs to be taken to determine if that really is the case.

Of course, the factor that makes the issue of disclosure critical is the asymmetry of knowledge. As we have seen, in financial markets clients are often closer to ignorance than perfect knowledge and hence are entitled to enough disclosure to give informed consent. Given the complexity of financial products, the seller or financial advisor usually has far greater understanding of the financial instrument than the buyer, especially when the buyer is an individual rather than an institution. Where there is asymmetry of knowledge, there is a dependency relationship where the person with less knowledge is vulnerable to the person with more knowledge. In an ethical world, such a vulnerable person is entitled to disclosure that will allow informed consent.

Such dependency relationships reflect a need for a special ethical approach that permeates the world of financial markets, the world of fiduciary relationships and/or agent/principal relationships, where the client depends on the expertise, honesty and good will of the agent, broker or adviser. Such a dependency relationship puts an added responsibility on the fiduciary or agent. Fiduciaries and agents have, by virtue of their relationship with their clients, an ethical responsibility to look out for the best interest of their client. Technically, a Fiduciary is "a person, company, or association holding assets in trust for a beneficiary. The fiduciary is charged with the responsibility of investing the money wisely for the beneficiary's benefit." An agent is "an individual authorized by another person, called the principal, to act in the latter's behalf in transactions involving a third party" (Downes and Goodman, 1985, p. 12). Thus, beyond being honest, the agent or trustee has an ethical obligation to look out for the client's best interest.

The responsibility to look out for a client's interests comes because the agent or fiduciary has taken it upon herself to play a certain role in the financial services industry. Hence the responsibility arises because one has made a commitment as an agent, a broker, an accountant, a banker or a planner.

The financial intermediary is more than a mere salesperson. There are specific roles that need to be played in the financial markets and those roles carry specific responsibilities. In committing to those roles, the financial service professional commits to those consequent responsibilities. A banker has different responsibilities from an accountant, who has different responsibilities from a broker or a mutual fund manager. But to the extent they took on those jobs, they committed to the responsibilities of those jobs.

Types of Roles in Financial Markets

A number of roles have evolved to make markets more efficient. We need the creators of products and marketers of the products as well as the intermediaries. We have brokers, agents and dealers whose role is to sell. We need accountants to keep track of the exchanges and their worth. We also need accountants to give a true picture of the financial status of companies. We need auditors to attest to the accuracy or the truth of the financial statements of the companies being audited. While a broker's and agent's primary role is to make financial instruments or products available to consumers, given the complexity of the financial products available today, they often need to take on the role of an advisor. Bankers play multiple roles in the financial system. They give advice to savers, make decisions on loans, and act as fiduciaries in the trust function. An emergent role in the financial services system is that of a mutual fund manager. Finally, CEOs of financial institutions have a role to maximize profit for their shareholders, and some would argue, balance that over against the interests of all the other stakeholders.

Regulatory procedures

Given such a diversity of roles, it is clear that a device is necessary to spell out the obligations that arise from the assumption of such roles. There are two means of regulating, either self-policing or through state or federal laws. People in groups that regulate themselves view themselves as professionals, and develop codes of ethics which spell out the responsibilities those professionals have to their clients.

Professionalism

Recognizing the importance of being a person of one's word, numerous people in the financial services industry have encouraged the development of a professional attitude among participants in the industry. If we look at the older paradigms of professions such as the medical, legal and teaching profession, we see that what is characteristic of those professions is the reliance of the patient, client or student on the expertise of the doctor, lawyer or teacher as well as the respective pro-fessional's concern for the well-being of the patient, client or student. In the financial market, where profit seeking is so prominent, and where the principle of enlightened self-interest is such a motivating factor, and products and instruments are so complicated, it becomes necessary to insist in some circumstances that people put their lives and or fortunes in other people's hands. Having a client's welfare in their hands makes it imperative that professionals look out for the best interest of those clients, even at the expense of the professional who has the expertise.

Insurance agents, financial planners, estate planners, brokers, dealers, accountants, mutual fund managers, valuation specialists, bankers, and all other financial services personnel, are experts who have others dependent on them for their well-being. They need to look on themselves as professionals, and on the requirement to look out for the best interest of their client's, (or of the public, as in the case of the accountant/auditor) as an ethical requirement. In short, while sales people sell, financial service professionals, even in selling, provide a service for their clients and it is incumbent on them that that service is in the client's best interests.

Thus, most professional codes of ethics require that transactions be carried out with integrity, fairness, competence, objectivity, professionalism, diligence and respect for clients' confidences. Those are characteristics usually demanded of professionals by the financial services industry's many codes of ethics, which govern the behavior of financial planners, accountants, tax attorneys, bankers, valuation specialists and others. In short, the codes of the professional organizations provide an excellent example of sets of ethical rules governing individual behavior.

The Legal Environment

We could argue that self-regulation required by professional codes will lead to ethical business, and indeed it will have some effect. But the call for professionalism in the financial services marketplace with its shift of attitude toward an insistence on ethics has not taken place by itself. Human nature being what it is there will always be the necessity of government regulation, in short laws. Laws tend to codify common morality or popular custom and add the extra incentive of stipulated punishment for misbehavior. When a law based on an ethical rule is stipulated and enforced a penalty is imposed on the violator. In this way, society can legislate the most important aspects of morality.

There is a framework for indicating acceptable behavior within the financial system. Unfortunately, it is fragmented, consisting of legal statutes, voluntary compliance standards, self regulated associations, regulatory standards, and codes of ethics. Financial markets and institutions went through difficult times in the late 1920s and early 1930s. Markets collapsed, fortunes were lost and public confidence was eroded. Much of the blame was placed on internal abuses, including rampant speculation, unfounded optimism supported by brokers and dealers, and a general disregard for common sense and prudence. The 1933 and 1934 Security Acts were the first serious attempt at bringing order to the financial markets. The 1933 Act applied to the primary market, that is, the markets responsible for raising capital; the 1934 Act attempted to regulate the secondary market, that is, the trading of existing securities. Legislation has evolved since the 1930s in an attempt to strengthen the integrity of market transactions and to force full disclosure in all transactions. The initial responsibility for enforcement falls on the Securities and Exchange Commission, and the regulators of the banking and insurance industries.

But, by the late 1930s, the intent of the 1933 and 1934 legislation was being channeled into self-regulation by the various players in the market. The New York Stock Exchange took a lead in this area, lobbying Congress to allow internal standards and enforcement to meet the goals of the 1933 and 1934 Securities Acts. The New York Stock Exchange is member owned and managed, including what is referred to as "Member Firm Regulation."

The Exchange believes that self-regulation is good business and that effective supervision is essential to the successful operation of every broker/dealer. This system of self-regulation, which Congress endorsed, begins with broker/dealer firms and places heavy reliance of their adherence to rules of conduct and the exercise of effective supervision and control over all operations and personnel. The Exchange plays a role in the process as the SEC appointed Designated Examining Authority for most of its member firms. The Exchange maintains an extensive system for monitoring and regulating the activities of members. Finally, it has the responsibility to investigate and prosecute violators of Exchange rules and the Securities and Exchange Act of 1934 and the rules thereunder.

All other exchanges have the same member firm system of self-regulation. In 1937, Congress passed the Maloney Act, providing for the establishment of national securities associations to supervise the OTC securities market. The OTC or dealer markets are primarily regulated by the NASD Regulation, Inc. (NASDR), which was established in 1996 as a separate, independent subsidiary of the NASD. NASDR was created as a part of an unprecedented restructuring of NASD, a major feature of which was to separate the regulation of the broker/dealer professional from the operation of the NASDAQ Stock Market. Up until 1996, the regulatory arm of the OTC markets was within the general organizational structure of the NASD and the NASDAQ market. The new structure is a positive step in self-regulation. A board composed of a 50/50 mix of public representation and industry professionals provides the governance of NASDR. This is another interesting innovation on the part of NASD.

During the last decade, banks have become prominent in the sale and marketing of securities. This has created new challenges for regulators and new ethical issues. The prime investment or savings products banks have traditionally sold are deposit instruments, the majority of which are insured by the Federal Deposit Insurance Corporation (FDIC). As banks sell non-deposit products the challenge is to make certain that customers understand to which products FDIC insurance applies. Bank regulators have been promulgating additional rules and regulations to augment current broker/dealer rules when the transaction occurs through a bank.

There is plenty of evidence of regulator and internal control over the behavior of individuals responsible for the marketing and sales of securities and insurance. Most organizations within their self-regulatory structures have attempted to focus on "codes of conduct". The American Institute of Certified Public Accountants, The Institute of Management Accountants, The American Bankers Association, The Association for Investment Management and Research, The Certified Financial Planner Board of Standards, the International Association for Financial Planning, The American Institute for Chartered Property Casualty Underwriters, The Society of Financial Service Professionals, formerly the American Society of Chartered Life Underwriters, and many other professional groups in the financial service industry have codes of ethics, which lay out principles and rules of proper behavior.

What is interesting is the attempt to blend codes and regulations together. There are numerous examples. Arthur Levitt of the SEC recently encouraged the AICPA to strengthen its code governing conflicts of interest. But, one of the industry groups which is especially interesting in the mutual fund managers group is the Investment Company Institute, the national association of the US investment company industry. It has published "An Investment Company Director's Guide to Oversight of Codes of Ethics and Personal Investing." The 1940 Investment Company Act reflects congressional recognition of the delicate fiduciary nature of an investment advisory relationship as well as intent to address any potential conflicts of interest that might inhibit an investment advisor's ability to render disinterested advice to its clients.

Congress, the SEC and the mutual fund industry recognized the need to reconcile these fiduciary obligations with personal investing practices. The SEC's Rule 17j–1, requires that all investment companies and their advisers adopt codes of ethics and procedures designed to detect and prevent inappropriate personal investing. This is a very positive sign in the area of money management since the mutual fund industry has become prominent and highly visible in the financial system landscape, and for them to address these complex issues through a formalized code of ethics is encouraging.

Institutional Barriers to Ethical Behavior
in the Financial Services

We have seen that there are unethical practices and that the self-regulating of the various professions as well as the laws have been utilized to improve ethical behavior in the financial services industry. But is there anything else that can be done?

First, there must be recognition of the unethical activities taking place. Then, it is imperative that financial services professionals commit to, as most of their codes insist they do, putting the best interests of their clients first, and develop a strong enough character to withstand temptation. But, beyond that, there are other practical ways to encourage or enable ethical behavior.

One of the most common procedures being developed is the separation of the sales function from the advisor function. Fee-only planners are an example of this model. A wall between the activity of selling and advising would go a long way in cleaning up powerful temptations facing brokers and agents, but the resistance from the agents and brokers is strong, both because of the tradition of commission for sales and the high remuneration tied to those sales.

What is also critical for encouraging ethical behavior is to reduce, as much as possible, the pressures created by the corporate culture of the market place. A marketplace that measures success almost exclusively by profit creates pressure on companies and their managers to succeed whatever it takes. Their companies, who are in turn forced by the demands of profitability to act in ways they see as unethical, often force financial service professionals. For example, captive agents in insurance are asked to sell variable annuities that they think are unsuitable. The companies produce the annuities to stay competitive. The competitive forces pressure managers, and agents are pressured to go along with their managers. Basic ethical attitudes must be compromised to do one's job.

The view that business should be concerned with profits no matter what the cost filters through the organization to the financial service professionals. Such a view needs to be replaced by a view that business should be compatible with the other values of society. The financial market system needs to concur that the business environment should not be an environment where there is a split between the personal ethical attitudes and the attitudes governing one's business life. Rather, the corporate culture, the business milieu should be one that supports personal "integrity" along with profitability.

Most of the professional codes in financial services require integrity. Usually, we think of the person of "integrity" as one who is truthful, and that is certainly one meaning. But there is a fuller meaning of "integrity" where integrity means a quality whereby one's life is unified, where there is a sort of "wholeness." Such wholeness requires a culture where people can work in an environment that doesn't cause them to violate their "conscience", and which promotes their flourishing. A milieu such as Solomon Brothers pictured in *Liar's Poker* must give way to a view of enlightened self-interest concerned with the best interests of those the corporation serves.

In short, a new perspective is needed. Business culture needs to be seen as a place where there is a sense of responsibility for the creation of goods and services. Financial service agents need to view themselves as agents who bring value to their clients' lives. An agent who is told to forget about the good of the client, either straight-out or subtly, cannot justify his behavior by telling himself he is helping the client. He knows he is simply lining his and the manager's pockets at the expense of the client. A professional will find such a manager's sales pushes morally repugnant and a threat to his own integrity.

For early ethicists, such as Plato and Aristotle, individual human flourishing was the main concern of ethics and setting up of a culture or environment where such flourishing was possible was the main task of societal regulation. From their perspective, human beings are part of nature like everything else, and just as plants cannot flourish unless they have an environment of rich soil, so human beings cannot flourish unless their environment is rich soil. Honesty and trust and cooperation and caring are part of a rich robust human life. To live among people who lie, are untrustworthy and who do not care for one another is to live in a sort of human hell. To enter such an environment daily has a debilitating effect, and if one capitulates to that environment, one necessarily diminishes oneself.

Managers in the financial services industry and elsewhere, whose *sole* driving force is maximizing profits, are creating a business climate, in the name of "profit maximization" that will force employees to sacrifice some of their integrity. The growing pressure for businesses to be ethical in the sense of creating value is just the opposite. It is a pressure to create a business climate or culture where the honest, caring, right thing is the thing expected. And, there are those who argue, such an environment will coincidentally lead to more profit.

Ethics has become important in the culture of the financial services market. A strong view that the purpose of business activities in general and financial services in particular is the creation of value for the consumer, will make it possible that ethics in the financial services industry will not only exist, but flourish.

References

Aristotle, *Politics.*

Downes J. and Goodman, J. 1985: *Money's Complete Guide to Personal Finance and investment Terms.* Barron's Educational Series, Woodbury, New York.

John Paul II, 1995: *Centesimus Annus.* Quoted in *On Moral Business,* edited by Max Stackhouse et al., William B. Eerdmans Publishing Company, Grand Rapids, Michigan, 489.

Mill, J. S. 1957: *Utilitarianism.* Indianapolis: Bobbs Merill Co. Inc. First published in 1861.

Novak, M. 1996: *Business as a Calling: Work and the Examined Life,* Free Press, New York.

Chapter 11

Ethical Issues in
Human Resources

Daryl Koehn

In the past, business ethicists have offered static analyses of workplace ethics. Working within a Kantian or quasi-religious framework, they have argued for a variety of employee rights – e.g., a right to work, a right to privacy, a right to be paid in accordance with comparable worth, a right not to be the victim of discrimination. These analyses appeal to some supposedly timeless fundamental rights, such as the right to be respected or the right to be treated justly. Particular rights are merely instantiations of these more general fundamental rights. Like the fundamental right to respect, these particular rights are accorded a timeless status – e.g., people always have an inviolable right to privacy or a right to work.

This mode of analysis is weak in several respects. First, the analysis ignores the extent to which rights are always somewhat partially context-dependent. It makes little sense to posit a right to some service if, at the present time, no provider in the world has the skill to provide this service. If there is no correlative duty on someone in particular to honor this claim to some service, treatment, privilege or freedom, then the claim is not an enforceable one and, therefore, does not qualify as a right. Second, the analysis overlooks the historical character of many of these rights. As Hannah Arendt has shown, the elevation of work into a respectable activity is of relatively recent origin. Many ancient Greeks saw work as antithetical to the good life, a life requiring leisure (Arendt, 1998). These early Greeks would not have insisted upon a right to work.

It is time for business ethicists to adopt a more dynamic approach to rights, especially employee workplace rights. This article examines employee rights in light of their history and their enforceability and in light of major changes occurring in the US and world economy. Closer examination of certain key rights raises doubts as to whether they qualify as true rights. If these "rights" exist at all, they exist in a far more circumscribed form than many theorists have realized.

Right to Work

Various ethicists have contended that people have a right to work. People have a right to self-respect (Kant, 1964). Insofar as work is a major source of people's self-respect and dignity (Meyers, 1988), the right to self-respect entails the right to work.

But matters are not as simple as this derivation of a right to work would suggest. People frequently are alienated from their work. Far from being a source of self-respect, work may be demeaning. In the former Soviet Union, workers made products that absolutely no one wanted. Although the Soviets posited and enforced a right to work, guaranteeing all adults a job, the jobs were pointless. People did earn money, but, by and large, they did not earn self-respect through work.

Even if we were to grant that work is a source of self-respect, we clearly must add some qualifiers concerning the type of work we are discussing. The Jews who provided slave labor for the Nazis certainly worked hard. Yet, this intensive labor was not in any way self-ennobling. Although we might try to salvage the notion of a right to work by stipulating that the work must be voluntarily undertaken and must be meaningful, this qualifying caveat will not solve the problem of degrading work. The Jews who worked for Schindler did so wilingly. They begged him for jobs, choosing to do repetitive factory work over trying to escape or dying in a death camp. Having a job in Schindler's factory was extremely meaningful – it meant the difference between staying alive and perishing in a concentration camp. Here, then, we have a case in which work was both chosen and meaningful but nevertheless did not generate self-respect.

In part, the problem lies with the nature of work and labor. During the Middle Ages, work and labor displaced action as the primary form of human activity (Arendt, 1998). In the classical era, only action was thought to be a form of self-definition. A man or woman was known by her deeds. In fact, the Greek historians Herodotos and Thucydides saw themselves as showcasing and preserving the memorable deeds of those who acted especially virtuously (or viciously) during wartime and peace. The Greeks and Romans believed that it was our deeds, not our jobs, that define us because our actions originate in us. Unlike animals who move in accordance with instinct, we shape our lives through our choices, which put certain chains of events into motion. That explains why funeral elegies allude to the character of the dead person and his or her character-defining acts. No one is remembered for his or her job competence. Our humanity reveals and fulfills itself through deeds, not through the repetitive motions of labor nor through adherence to certain job specifications.

From the classical point of view, action is intrinsically more satisfying to human beings than a job ever is or could be. When we act, we both learn who we are and what it means to have and to display virtues such as courage, moderation, or justice. The individual agent does not invent these virtues. These virtues are akin to pre-existing forms or typologies well-known to members of the community. Others can see our virtue and recognize it as such. Even the vicious have some inkling of courage. Shakespeare's villain, Iago, is jealous of Othello. For Iago, Othello is little more than a savage. Still, Othello has acted far more splendidly than Iago ever has or ever will. Othello has the visible courage Iago, who always operates in the darkness and shadows, lacks. At some level, Iago knows himself to be inferior.

When we act, we implicitly are conforming ourselves (or failing to conform ourselves) to an order or typology of human excellence. On the one hand, there is a creative element to action insofar as we discover important dimensions of our character and humanity through acting. On the other hand, action is a practice of conforming ourselves to this objective order of recognized excellences.

Work or labor, by contrast, does not involve conforming oneself to an order of excellence. People invent all sorts of silly tasks and then impose these chores on themselves or others. It is hard to find meaning in work because work has an element of arbitrariness – of sheer busy-ness – that action never has. Since work does not entail conforming to an external and meaningful order to excellence, work cannot provide the valuable insight and meaning people crave. That is why work typically does not provide self-respect. The working self has no external order against which to measure its accomplishments and to find and to feel itself worthy or unworthy.

Work can, and does, become a source of self-respect the more it approximates to action. The entrepreneur who takes risks earns respect for her courage. Founding a company requires a huge amount of self-discipline and moderation as well. The founder must be wise in the ways of men and women if she is to inspire her employees and to co-ordinate their various efforts. Such leadership is always understood as action, not as work or labor. And with good reason: in this sort of case, the entrepreneur is originating a whole series of actions and knows that she is making a name for herself (be that good or bad). The stakes are very high and very personal in a way that they never are for the "working stiff" (note how revealing our language is: the working man or woman is as good as dead!). Put differently: only those who have bought into the ethically suspect ideology of the Protestant work ethic and who believe that busy work *per se* is valuable will believe in a right to work based upon the notion that work is a source of self-respect.

If work is alienating or deadening, then the displacement of action in favor of work is a trend that is itself ethically suspect. Since we have rights to things that are considered good (e.g., a right to free speech), it is doubtful whether there could be a *right* to work if work is intrinsically demeaning. Indeed, talk of such a right is profoundly misleading. It makes it sound as if people do not need to *act* to find meaning and a sense of self-worth. Instead, all they need is for someone else to honor their right to work and to give them a job.

This last comment points to a second problem with the notion of a right to work, a problem that becomes especially acute in the rapidly evolving world economy. For every right, there must be a correlative duty upon someone else in particular to honor this right and to make it effective. This duty must be discharge-able. Thus, if I have a right to freely associate with others, you and everyone else has a duty not to interfere with my attempts to form voluntary associations. In this example, the duty is a negative one, a duty of non-interference. In other cases, the correlative duty is a positive one. If I have a right to welfare benefits, then someone else has a duty to provide these benefits. If there were a right to work, it might be interpreted as entailing a positive or negative duty. In the negative sense, a right to work would impose a duty on everyone else not to interfere with my attempts to find and secure work. Almost no one would deny the existence of such a duty, although one may doubt whether it makes much sense to speak of a right to work in this sort of case. In today's world, people need to work to live. Since all living things have an instinct and drive to stay alive, people are going to seek work, regardless of what others do or say. When business ethicists argue for a right to work, they are placing the stronger, positive interpretation on the notion. They are claiming that people have a right to work and that someone else has a positive duty to provide this work. (The individual presumably remains free to decline the job offer if he prefers to paint or to write a book instead of, say, harvesting hay). But now we come up against the key question: On whom exactly does this duty devolve in today's economy?

There are three candidates: government, business, and unions. Does the government have a duty to provide work to all able adults? We must specify which government we mean. Today we have an extremely mobile labor force that freely crosses national borders to obtain jobs. Large numbers of Mexicans work in the USA, both legally and illegally. Germany is home to hundreds of thousands of Gästarbeiter (primarily Turks). Austria has 800,000 refugees from the former Yugoslavia, many of whom work in that country. If the entire international labor force has a right to work (and they must have such a right, if the right derives from a generic, timeless, absolute, universal human duty to respect individuals), does the US government owe every member of this force a job? Or must we look to the EU to generate work for every worker within Europe, while the USA must provide jobs for all North Americans? Even wealthy countries would find it difficult to create jobs for such a large constituency.

And what about jobs for Africans or Nicaraguans? It is not plausible to argue that every national government owes jobs to its own citizens because third world governments are typically extremely poor or incompetent. Such governments are in no position to provide work for all of their adult citizens. And, if a duty is not enforceable, the correlative right does not exist. It is simply empty and thus does not qualify as a right or enforceable claim by one party against another.

Nor does history give us much reason to think that governments will be very successful in creating work for their constituencies, regardless of how we choose to define this notion. When the US government tried to foster the electric car industry, it spent millions, betting on the wrong technology. Examples of misplaced governmental bets abound. Governmental efforts to create markets or jobs tend instead to create an entrenched constituency, making it difficult for the government to respond to market signals and to switch to new technologies or to abandon ineffective approaches. In the past, when the government has succeeded in creating jobs, critics have gone on the offensive, charging that the jobs are not "good" jobs. When the city of New York created work for welfare recipients whom it had forced off the welfare rolls, critics cited the dead end nature of these jobs and accused the city of exploiting the poor with a view to getting cheap labor.

If there were a right to meaningful work, governments would be ethically bound to invent "good" or "satisfying" jobs. But, as we have just seen, this duty is unenforceable. Moreover, people's tastes differ. One person's dream job will be another's nightmare position. Those individuals who do enjoy their jobs usually have either created their position through action (which can be fulfilling) or have a vocation that they support by means of a job on the side. In both of these cases, the individuals have assumed full responsibility for acting to discover and to fulfill their vocation. The government will never be in a position to discover people's vocations or to bestow meaningful jobs upon them. By definition, finding a vocation is something individuals must do for themselves. Perhaps this fact explains why studies have shown that over time an individual's happiness remains more or less constant. External circumstances can change. The person may be promoted, win the lottery, or suffer a debilitating accident. In the short run, these external events affect people's perceived level of happiness. In the long run, though, people revert to the same level of happiness they had prior to the external event. Self-respect and happiness alike depend crucially upon the extent to which the individual has shouldered the responsibility to initiate actions designed to discover meaning. Advocating a right to work distracts people from assuming this crucial responsibility.

Therefore, there is, and can be, no duty on the government to provide a soul-satisfying job. There is a second reason why such a duty is unenforceable for the foreseeable future. Before it could embark upon a major program of job creation, members of the government would have to agree upon a vision of the government's role in the labor markets. Given the diverse and opposing ideas concerning such a role not only within the US legislative bodies but also within the coalition governments common in Europe and other countries such as Israel and Australia, it is not very likely that a sustainable consensus on this matter will be forthcoming. A temporary consensus might emerge occasionally. An intermittent consensus, though, is not sufficient to ground a duty. Duties do not flicker in and out of existence. So, on this score, too, there can be no right to work.

There are two additional relevant points. Many European governments are allied with trade unions. Consequently, these governments focus less on providing new jobs and more on maintaining existing jobs. The high structural unemployment in Europe is due, in part, to regulations and policies that protect whole industries and, in part, to generous welfare benefits. One might say that these governments implicitly are committed to people's right *not* to work. Second, while the US federal and state governments currently enjoy budget surpluses, the major shift toward e-commerce may reduce government tax monies in the future. E-commerce is not taxed at the present, and there does not appear to be much interest in or support for imposing an e-commerce tax. As consumers do more of their shopping on the web instead of in stores (average number of visits per consumer to malls are down substantially in the late 1990s;) e-commerce revenues have more than doubled each of the past few years), states will suffer a loss of sales tax revenue. Unless governments levy a specific tax earmarked for governmental job creation (which is unlikely given the many politicians and voters against tax increases and in favor of limited government intervention in labor markets), they may not have the money to fund an ambitious jobs creation program. Since there can be no duty to spend money one does not have and cannot raise, individuals employees have no right to have the government create a job for them.

Perhaps, though, the duty to generate jobs falls not upon the government but upon big business. Is this assertion plausible? For several decades, economies every-where have been experiencing disintermediation – the loss of the middleman. People have discovered that the computer is not only a computational tool but also a communication device for telegraphing their desires and concerns. Consumers (including businesses that consume the products and services of other businesses) are using the internet to gather competitive information and to make purchases. The development of e-commerce is accelerating the trend toward disintermedia-tion, threatening many venerable institutions. Consumers no longer have to buy stocks through brokers. They can trade stocks directly via electronic exchanges. Multi-level marketing companies are making it possible for consumers to place orders directly with headquarters, enabling consumers to avoid having to buy through company representatives. It is just a matter of time before consumers can buy insurance and other products directly from the company, again circum-venting the independent agent who used to be the channel of distribution. This disintermediation, coupled with re-engineering in the early 1990s, has resulted in the loss of many middle management jobs. These jobs may not be gone forever, but they certainly are gone for the immediately foreseeable future.

Disintermediation simultaneously is putting downward pressure on prices. Using shopping robots, consumers and business buyers alike easily can surf the web for the best price on a consumer good or on some raw material. E-commerce is standardizing product offerings, making price comparisons even easier. This down-ward pressure has forced businesses to monitor costs closely in order to remain competitive. Businesses that wish to remain profitable cannot simply create jobs for people if

1   there are no tasks for these folks to perform; and
2   the jobs do not lead to increases in productivity sufficient to offset the increase in costs.

If creating a job will lead to high productivity gains, the business will be moti-vated by self-interest to hire someone to do the task. However, businesses are not bound by any duty to create jobs if doing so means committing economic suicide. Of course, one might argue that businesses have a duty to hire people when it makes economic sense to do so. But, in that case, talk of duty to hire employees and of the correlative right to work is superfluous. The supposed duty to hire people has no binding force if businesses are going to hire people anyway out of self-interest.

Ironically, the fact that businesses are not bound to provide workers with jobs may be the greatest source of jobs and the most significant force encouraging people to fulfill themselves through action rather than through mere work. Many of the middle managers laid off during the early 1990s founded their own small businesses. Since small businesses are the primary engine of job growth throughout the world, the layoffs very likely created more jobs than were lost. Those who have had the thrill and pleasure of founding a business have resisted returning to large corporations. "Going corporate" is seen as a form of slavery, as a relinquishing of new-found freedom. These self-employed agents do not favor a right to work because they have no interest in the jobs they would be offered by corporate America. They do not need a right to work in order to have self-respect. They derive their self-respect from the best source – self-disciplined and courageous action undertaken with a view to finding what is most meaningful in life.

If businesses and government do not have a duty to create jobs, any such ethical duty must devolve upon the third candidate: unions. Since unions do not them-selves create jobs, the unions could only have a duty to create jobs in a qualified sense. They might have a duty to try to force businesses to create jobs by staging strikes or slowdowns. However, these activities require power. Union membership has dropped precipitately over the past two decades, resulting in a loss of clout. Unions do not have the requisite power, and there can be no duty if there is no ability to discharge the duty. The trend toward disintermediation is diminishing union power still further. Jobs are disappearing and being replaced by piecework. Corporations are using the internet to hire people to do specific tasks. Independent contractors list their skills on the web, and corporations then bid out the work on the web and choose the best provider. In many cases, the company never meets the contractor and knows little about the party. Employer-employee relationships are becoming more transactional. These employee-contractors usually do not want an intermediary party – a union or an agent – representing them.

Unions have a credibility problem when they talk about a right to work. Some unions have a history of pushing for closed shops. These unions do not believe in a right to work grounded in people's right to be respected; they believe that one has a right to work only if one joins and helps to finance these particular unions. Furthermore, when unionized companies have downsized in the past, union leaders have willingly sacrificed the jobs of more junior workers in order to preserve their jobs and those of more senior workers. In these unions' eyes, some workers appar-ently have more of a right to work than other workers. That, though, is equivalent to admitting that not even unions believe in a right to work. For, if there were such a right, it would be absolute and universal, not relative to seniority.

Given that there is no party who is or could be bound by a correlative duty to create work, there is no right to work. Another important point about correlative duties: individuals could have a right to work only if they have an ethical duty to be trainable. Are individuals bound by an enforceable duty to be trainable to perform a job created by someone else? Clearly not. Some people simply do not want to hold jobs, preferring to scrape along as best they can. Artists may prefer to put their energy into developing artistic skills instead of training for a job. Housewives may opt to raise children, finding the action of loving and developing another human being infinitely preferable to holding a job.

Furthermore, if businesses did have a duty to provide jobs, they certainly would not be bound to preserve obsolete jobs. In the new economy, jobs change very quickly. Today's workers can expect to hold five or six jobs over the course of a lifetime. At best, a firm would have a duty to train people to fulfill the new jobs. But, again, some people simply do not want to learn new tasks. When IBM reorganized in the 1980s, a fair number of employees took early retirement, saying they were not interested in going through yet another reorganization. If individuals do not have any desire to learn new skills, they will not be trainable. And, if they are not trainable, the company clearly has no duty to provide them with a job.

In other cases, adults have habits that are not conducive to keeping a job. Some people are drug addicts and are too addled to hold down any job. When General Motors laid off workers in Flint, Michigan, some of the former auto-workers found alternative jobs in the fastfood industry but could not stomach the punishing pace of their new jobs and quit. While many welfare mothers have been glad for the chance to enter the workforce, others have not been able to keep a job because they lack the discipline to keep regular hours. In the past, they could keep irregular hours and have developed a habit of doing so. By definition, habits are hard to break. Given that many jobs are not especially fulfilling, out of work individuals have little incentive to alter their habits and to become trainable. Yet, if individuals are not trainable, they can have no right to work.

A final thought concerning the enforceability of a duty to provide meaningful work: if there is an *employee* right to work, then there surely must be a *corporate* right to have employees perform in a responsible and accountable fashion. The more business ethicists emphasize the *employee* right to work, the more this *corporate* right to accountable performance seems to fade in to the background. In the absence of any discussion of offsetting or correlative corporate rights, the alleged employee right to meaningful work appears implausible and maybe somewhat dangerous.

Consider the difficulties companies are now facing in managing the growing number of millionaire employees. More than 4.6 million families were worth more than $1 million by the end of 1998. This number represents more than 5 percent of all US families, with the majority of millionaires concentrated in the high-tech and financial industries. Approximately one-third of all of Microsoft's employees are millionaires. More mainstream companies like Wal-Mart and Citigroup also have their share of millionaires. At Citigroup, roughly 1500 people make over $1 million in cash each year (Wetlaufer, 2000). Given that these millionaires do not need to work and can quit their job if they do not feel satisfied, they constitute a kind of test case for the existence of a right to meaningful work. For, of all groups, they are in the best position to assert such a right and to successfully pressure corporations to honor it.

Indeed, faced with the challenge of managing wealthy employees, some corporate executives have begun to argue that workers – or, at least, these highfliers – should be provided with challenging and satisfying work. Sycamore Networks presently operates as five "mini-companies." The activities of each company are reviewed weekly or even daily and regular feedback is given to employees. As the CEO Dan Smith puts it, "People should always know what they're working on and why, and they should always be in a position to understand how their work makes a difference and feel its immediacy? That's true whether they're millionaires or not, but it's more important when people need reasons to come to work every morning" (Wetlaufer, 2000). Firms have become more entrepreneurial in an effort to attract and keep the millionaire employees who enjoy taking on grand challenges and who claim to derive their self-respect from tackling new projects. At Priceline.com, the company spins off each new business opportunity in order to give top talent a chance to launch a product and to take some risk. These changes, initiated to retain millionaire employees, inevitably alter the entire culture, creating (in theory) more meaningful work for employees at all levels.

Yet, catering to these highfliers' insistence that they have a right to meaningful work while neglecting the rights of the corporation has created a false impression that the entire ethical onus falls upon the corporate employer. The employer's correlative right to receive a good performance is trampled in the dust. These wealthy and pampered employees who flaunt their ability to quit whenever they choose or to switch jobs with ease often lack interest in the work, regardless of how challenging it is. If the work happens to bore them, they may feel justified in doing a sloppy job or dumping the project into a co-worker's lap. Since they can move on, these millionaire employees typically do not feel accountable – and frequently are not held responsible by a management afraid of alienating highfliers – for the messes they create. It devolves upon their successors to sort out matters, to soothe the ruffled feathers of customers, to renegotiate poorly written contracts, and to re-design products thrown together in a haphazard, thoughtless fashion.

One can well understand why corporations and the fellow employees of these millionaires view the millionaires' alleged right to meaningful work with a high degree of suspicion. Any talk about an employee's right to (meaningful) work needs to be accompanied by a discussion of these same employees' responsibility to act accountably, and by an analysis of the larger corporate and social culture in which employees work and which they help to create through their actions and attitudes. Although many employees have increasing leverage to assert and enforce a right to meaningful work, it does not follow that the resulting culture will automatically be either ethically or fiscally sound.

Right to Privacy

An employee right to privacy, like the right to meaningful work, has been derived from the right to be respected. To the extent that ethicists have regarded the right to self-respect as absolute, they have tended to view the right to privacy as similarly unconditional. They reason that individuals need an inviolable space in order to have dignity, a precondition of self-respect. On this standard view, it is not ethical for employers to require employees to take drug tests or job candidates to take a polygraph test as a condition of employment.

Such arguments ignore several key facts. First, privacy has not always been seen as an unqualified good. The Greek word for private – *idiotes* – is the source of our term "idiotic." Ancient Greeks saw the private realm as a circumscribed realm that could never be a source of identity or self-respect. Actions develop character, in part, by giving rise to praise and blame. Actions must occur in the public realm where they are visible to other people who judge these deeds. Privacy as such became valued only in the nineteenth century as people sought to protect themselves from attempts by the social body and corporate institutions to press for conformity or to manipulate their identity. Louis Brandeis first coined the idea of a "right to privacy" in a case involving a company who had lifted a woman's picture from a newspaper and then used that picture to advertise its product. Brandeis was worried that people would lose control over their identity if others could, so to speak, confiscate that identity and use it for their own purposes.

This mini-history suggests that the idea of privacy is related in complicated ways to the notion of identity. We are not entitled to claim that privacy is absolutely good, positing an unconditional right to self-respect and then deriving privacy from this supposed right. Instead, we must carefully consider the role privacy plays in character development, public discourse, and identity. Moreover, privacy must be conceived relationally. No piece of information about a person is intrinsically private. My neighbor has no claim to have access to my financial records, but my accountant does have such a claim. A recent graduate need not share his transcript with her dentist, but the accounting firm that is considering hiring her presumably does have a right to see whether she took the college courses in accounting she claims to have taken. To insist that some fact about a person is justifiably, or rightfully, private means that this person is entitled to refuse to share this fact with someone else in particular (Brenkert, 1988).

In addition technological, economic, and political changes also are forcing a reconsideration of what falls under the rubric of an employee's supposed right to privacy. In the past, privacy issues centered upon the question of how much employers were entitled to know about the character, personality, preferences and habits of employees. Privacy advocates argued that employers could ask questions about employee's traits only to the extent these traits were relevant to the employee's job. Thus, an airline is entitled to investigate whether a pilot actually had his license and whether he was, in fact, doing the training necessary to maintain his flying skills but the airline could not legitimately ask about or investigate the pilot's sex life.

New developments are threatening this firewall ethicists have tried to erect around employee's privacy. Today, employee privacy centers less on questions of disclosure and more on issues connected with the monitoring of employee movements and communications and with the searching of employee computer files and workspace. US courts have held that workers' right to privacy in the workplace is less extensive than the right to privacy in their homes. According to these rulings, employees have a right to privacy only if they can reasonably expect to be free from search and seizure. If the worker has no reasonable expectation of privacy, then no such right exists. As a result of this ruling, companies have begun to adopt policies telling employees that their e-mail may be scrutinized.

By implementing these policies, the company lowers the expectation of privacy in advance (Rosen, 2000). Consequently, we are witnessing something of a race to the bottom, as companies assert an increasingly expansive right to monitor and search employees in an effort to be able to sustain a legal claim that monitored employees have no reasonable expectation to privacy with respect to their e-mails, filing cabinets, locked drawers, etc. On the one hand, this trend is troubling. Is nothing sacrosanct? Surely an employee has a right to privacy in the bathroom, regardless of whether the company has announced that it may monitor bathroom usage. On the other hand, it is hard to see how an employee's identity is threatened when the company examines the use the employee has been making of corporate assets such as email or company letterhead. Character is a large part of identity. Knowing whether an employee is the sort of person to make fraudulent use of corporate assets does not destroy identity; it establishes both the character and identity of the party. If so, the employee has no right to privacy rooted in a need to preserve identity.

Ironically, it is the ever-expanding domain of alleged employee rights that is imperiling any employee right to privacy. If employees have an ethical and legal right to a secure workplace and to be free from sexual harassment, then companies are legally liable if an employee is assaulted on company premises or is sexually harassed by a fellow employee. Companies are legitimately concerned that, if they do not monitor employee e-mails with a view to identifying employees who post sexist or pornographic notes, the company will be sued for tolerating a hostile workplace. The companies err on the side of draconian measures because cyber communications seem to persist forever on hard drives, backup tapes, and servers. Lawyers subpoena these drives and tapes, increasing the chance that they will find evidence that some employee downloaded pornographic pictures or sent an offensive e-mail within the corporation. In this technological and legal environment, companies are understandably concerned about the possibility of expensive adverse legal judgments.

It is naive to assert an employee right to privacy without taking into account both the company's rights and the changing technological and legal realities faced by companies. For example, one might argue that companies have a right to do business without having to be continually afraid that they will be ambushed by a lawsuit brought about by a thoughtless or corrupt employee's inappropriate behavior. If so, an employee's right to privacy may prove to be considerably more circumscribed than some ethicists seem to think. Furthermore, even if one were to grant the existence of an employee right to privacy, the extent of such a right will need to be continually re-thought in light of technological developments and legal rulings.

Right to be Paid One's Comparable Worth

In 1963, Congress passed the Equal Pay Act (EPA). This act stipulates that men and women must be paid the same wages for jobs that involve "equal skill, effort, and responsibility." Since no two jobs are exactly identical, the law has been the subject of numerous court challenges. The courts have ruled that the EPA is applicable to employees who perform substantially the same, although not necessarily identical, work. Receiving the same compensation for substantially the same work is relatively uncontroversial and has been enshrined as a legal employee right. When critics complain about a lack of pay equity, they usually are appealing to a more suspect right – the right to be paid in accordance with comparable worth. US courts have not endorsed this right.

The principle of comparable worth states that the value of an employee's labor should not be determined by market forces. It should be calculated instead in light of the job's intrinsic value. Jobs having the same intrinsic value should be paid the same, regardless of market conditions. On this view, we should not rely on market forces to correctly determine what people's labor is truly worth because the labor market is plagued by gender-based discrimination. This discrimination is not correctable by market forces for several reasons. Some institutions (the government) and corporations (monopolies) are immune to market forces. In addition, sexist employers may well be willing to pay (in the form of lost sales due to consumer boycotts or of a reduced inability to attract good workers) for the "privilege" of discriminating against women. Given that the labor market is not self-correcting, we should foster pay equity by doing job studies to ascertain the intrinsic value of a wide variety of jobs and then require that employees be paid their objectively determined comparable worth. These studies should evaluate job content by rating the skill, effort, and level of responsibility required by each job.

Is this principle of comparable worth defensible? Does every worker have a right to be paid what some job study determines that he or she is worth? Does such a right make sense in our changing economy? The pay equity issue clearly touches upon a nerve. In some polls, employees have listed fair pay as the number one corporate ethics issue. But it is unclear how employees understand "fairness." They clearly do not want mere equality. For equality could be achieved by lowering the compensation of those who are supposedly overpaid. Instead, when allegedly underpaid people talk about comparable worth, they envision that they will be paid the higher, "correct" level of compensation received by peers. (Note the ironic tension: proponents of comparable worth contend that the labor market is unable to assign correct compensation yet they rely upon the market to determine the correct compensation for comparable jobs).

The right to be paid one's comparable worth is rooted in a perception that one has been slighted, especially in relation to others. There is thus always a danger that believers in a right to comparable worth will wind up fanning the flames of resentment. Any appeal to or unleashing of resentment is dangerous. As the not so distant past experiences of the Eastern Europeans, Russians and the Chinese show, simmering resentment can explode in rage at the propertied classes, managers, officials, ethnic minorities or whoever else is a handy scapegoat.

Asserting a right to comparable worth is especially tricky because proponents typically leave unspecified how a number of crucial interests are to be resolved. For example, who is to assess the job evaluators who are to "objectively" assess the value of work? If women are widely underpaid as a result of systematic discrimination, this bias against women presumably exists even among the job evaluators. Is the intrinsic value of a job to be determined only by women? How then will one avoid the charge that one is unfairly discriminating against male evaluators?

In cases where the jobs occupied by women are paid lower than the supposedly comparable positions occupied by men, how will we know when the pay differential is due to discrimination and not to other factors? The determinants of pay are many and complex. Critics of comparable worth have argued that, when these other factors are taken into account, pay differentials between men and women disappear entirely or are, at least, greatly reduced. Consider these factors:

- *Firm size* Employees of small firms usually are paid less than workers in large firms. Some evidence suggests that women prefer to work in smaller, more intimate firms (Hartman, 1998).
- *Industry* Accountants and engineers working for hightech companies often earn more than their counterparts employed by more established or "Rust Belt" firms. If we look only at the level of skill, effort and responsibility involved in a job, we will completely overlook the substantial salary variations attributable to differences among industries. Indeed, in some industries, women are paid more than men. A 2000 survey showed that, in advertising, female executives have an average annual salary of $275,000, while male executives average $253,100. Women in occupational therapy average $39,312, which is $7384 more than men make. Female physicians on average earn $65,208; their male counterparts average $64,800 (*New York Times*, "Pay equity, in some places", 9 July 2000, Business section, p. 6).
- *Fringe benefits* Although one job may appear to pay less than another, appearances frequently are misleading. A woman may decide to accept a lower

salary at a firm that offers more of the benefits that women typically find attractive – e.g., adoption assistance, childcare, flexible hours, health coverage for dependents, coverage of fertility treatments, elder care, tuition benefits. Fringe benefits take all kinds of forms, making it exceedingly difficult to assign a dollar value to the jobs comparable worth advocates would have us compare.

- *Intrinsic satisfaction and psychic compensation* Some people select jobs for which they feel they have a calling. Others take jobs that provide a high level of social status or a great sense of achievement or that involve a wide variety of stimulating tasks (Hartman, 1998). Still others may choose a lesser paying job because it offers them more freedom, autonomy or flexibility or because they like their sympathetic boss. Women may be willing to forego some compensation in return for the privilege of working at home or for being able to arrange their schedules to better suit their families' needs. Many women work to make ends meet but gain greater satisfaction from being at home with their children. Comparable worth proponents typically overlook the wide array of psychic satisfactions – itself a form of compensation – that figure into a decision as to whether to take a particular job.

- *Hours worked* Comparisons among jobs are notoriously tricky because it is difficult to know what counts as salary or compensation and to insure that one is, in fact, comparing apples with apples. Fringe benefits need to be included (see above). Overtime earnings probably should be considered when calculating compensation. These earnings vary substantially by industry and can skew job comparisons. The length of time of the employment contract needs to be looked at as well. Many women teach. Teachers typically are on a nine-month contract. On the one hand, it is misleading to compare a nine-month salary with monies earned over a full year. On the other hand, not all teachers may be able to find work during the summer. How do we distinguish among the two classes of teachers when calculating comparable worth?

The aforementioned factors have been widely discussed in the comparable worth literature. I mention them to illustrate the difficulties associated with any attempt to determine what would truly constitute an individual's comparable worth. If we cannot ascertain comparable worth of an individual's job, then that person has no right to be paid his or her comparable worth. We have no right to anything to which we cannot assign any meaningful content.

As was noted in the introduction, rights are always somewhat context dependent. Yet comparable worth proponents consistently fail to assess the context in which any supposed right to comparable worth would exist. They overlook the various factors coming into play as the economy becomes more global and as an increasing amount of commerce is done via internet startups. Like the above factors, these new factors make it difficult to prove that differences in pay between men and women are due to discrimination against women. They also make talk about an acontextual right to comparable worth untenable.

Consider these factors:

- *Job switching* Some studies have shown that employees who switch jobs frequently wind up with higher salaries and pensions in the long run. In today's tight labor market, where many firms are competing for the same employees, job-hopping employees can negotiate very rich compensation packages for themselves. Of course, leaving jobs often means drifting apart from former co-workers. If, as some feminists assert, women value relationships more than men, then women may choose to forego job changes and increased salaries in return for being able to develop and maintain deeper and more lasting work relationships.

- *Job security* If feminists are right and if women feel a strong ethical imperative to care for their children and family members, women may be less willing than men to risk changing jobs, even in a tight labor market. If more frequent, risky job switches lead to higher average salaries, we would expect women's salaries to lag behind men's.

- *Willingness to relocate* Discussions of comparable worth overlook what is clearly a huge factor in salary differentials in today's economy – the willingness to relocate. As companies become more global, they are transferring employees around the world. Even companies that rely upon the local labor force still use expatriates in a variety of roles. To the extent that women have a distinctive ethic of caring and favor relationship-maintenance over autonomy, we would expect fewer women to relocate and to see slower promotions for women. Since companies know that working abroad can be stressful, they frequently pay a premium or bonus to expatriates and reward expatriates with promotions upon their return. Although women who are unwilling to relocate will not reap this bonus, it does not follow that they are victims of discrimination or that they ethically deserve the same salaries and bonuses as those men and women who do choose to relocate.

- *Willingness to assume substantial risks* A willingness to assume substantial risks is another huge factor in today's high-tech world. Many have become rich by developing start-up companies and then by exercising their lucrative stock options or by selling these companies. Entrepreneurs work exceptionally long hours and travel extensively, pitching their company to venture capitalists, meeting with potential customers, and brainstorming with fellow founders or employees. The sacrifice of time is enormous, and the risks are major. The company's products may fail to catch on; the venture capital may dry up; the stock market may punish the company's stock as part of a sell-off in a particular sector. Since the wealth and income of startup founders/employees typically is in the form of stock or stock options, people can see their income and any life savings they have sunk into the venture evaporate over night. The market rewards people for taking such risks, and it seems fair that it does so. People should receive some reward for taking risks others have not been willing to assume. Many women with dependents may prefer the steady income stream of a safe, less risky job with shorter hours and less stress. Comparable worth calculations are misleading because they never take into account the existence of a risk premium, a gross oversight in today's economy. These calculations focus only on skill, effort and responsibility.

- *Willingness to defer earnings* Many workers, especially younger ones, willingly accept lower earnings in the present in return for larger future earnings. In the past, women have opted for jobs (e.g., teacher, social worker, caregivers) that may pay more than what is earned by entrepreneurs at the beginning of their career but that have far less upside earnings potential. So, again, comparing men's and women's salaries will be extremely misleading unless one somehow corrects for this difference in chosen career trajectories.

These "new economy" factors likely are affecting the relative compensation received by men and women. If we are to speak in a non-misleading way about comparable worth, we must assess these factors, not merely matters such as the skill, effort and responsibility involved in a particular job. This calculation will be immensely complicated, and it may well be impossible. Some factors might seem, at first blush, to track together – e.g., an entrepreneurial willingness to take risk and the willingness to defer earnings. However, there is anecdotal evidence suggesting that some people are very willing to defer earnings for a short period of time yet are quite unwilling to assume substantial risks over the longer haul. Since people's attitudes toward work are exceedingly complicated, it will prove nigh impossible to make the sort of generalizations necessary for modeling meaningful, non-misleading comparable worth calculations. Such a calculation might have been possible during the feudal era or early industrial age when the variety of jobs was relatively limited and when jobs were easy to describe. Today there is just too much noise in the data to yield meaningful results. If a non-misleading calculation of comparable worth cannot be done, there can be no right to comparable worth. Perhaps such calculations should not even be attempted, given that they almost certainly will result in injustice as the work choices made by individuals are grossly over-simplified and misrepresented.

There is a final difficulty with comparative worth arguments – the problem of a correlative, enforceable duty. Advocates of a right to be paid in accordance with one's comparable worth assume that some party is able to fund the increases in salaries required to underwrite pay equity. Estimates of the dollar amount needed range from $2 billion to $150 billion. Who exactly bears the duty of paying these many billions of dollars?

There are two candidates: individual businesses or the government. Since those who are asserting the right to comparable worth treat this right as an absolute claim that must be respected regardless of the cost, I will assume that the higher figure of $150 billion is the correct one. Could businesses come up with this amount of money? In 1999, the US private sector spent $108 billion on computers and $164 billion on industrial equipment (Kukewicz, 2000). If there were a right to comparable worth, the private sector would have to halve its computer budget and spend two-thirds less on industrial equipment to underwrite pay equity. If we assume that at least some companies have acceptable compensation arrangements, it follows that the $150 billion burden will fall on only a portion of the private sector. This staggering figure would likely prove even greater than comparable worth proponents let on because the companies would need a fairly elaborate administrative mechanism to measure supposed pay inequities and to administer the changes. The burden would bankrupt some companies, especially the smaller firms favored by women. Asserting a right to employee comparable worth is equivalent to positing an ethical duty for companies to commit financial suicide. While companies can be expected to pay their share of taxes and to dispose of waste properly, they have no ethical duty to self-destruct, particularly if going out of business hurts the women whom comparable worth advocates are trying to help.

Companies that managed to stay in business would be rendered less competitive than foreign companies that did not have to cut back on investment in computers and industrial equipment. These companies, too, might be driven to lay off workers, including the more marginal or part-time workers who so often are women. Even if the companies paid for pay equity over a few years, the cost would still be substantial. Unlike market-based wage increases tied to productivity, comparable worth calculations never factor in productivity. These calculations only look at the employee's skill level, effort and responsibility. If two people have substantially the same skills and level of responsibility and if they exert similar effort, then they are alleged to have equal worth, even if one person is actually far more productive than the other (i.e., puts effort to better use). We cannot count, therefore, on any productivity gains to fund pay equity programs. On the contrary, companies may well experience a productivity loss because the administrative mechanism to establish, refine, monitor, and defend such an elaborate pay program will be non-productive asset.

Any major pay equity initiative to benefit women employees would come at the expense of other stakeholders. In particular, shareholders would see the value of their corporate shares decline, perhaps precipitately. Since many employees are now shareholders, they might well find that their retirement nest eggs have shrunk dramatically. The losses women employees experience in their corporate portfolio might outweigh any pay equity increase they would gain. The right to comparable worth might prove to be a right to suffer financial losses, which is clearly not what proponents have in mind.

Perhaps, then, the government has a duty to devise, administer and fund a pay equity program. The government might pay for such a program by spending surplus monies or by raising corporate or individual income taxes. Since the US is currently running a large surplus (estimated at $224 billion for the year 2000), now would seem to be a perfect time to fund an expensive pay equity program. However, whether or not the government has a duty to pay for this program clearly depends upon which other rights are asserted. The Social Security system is running out of money. Potential and actual retirees who have funded the system have not only a legal right but also an ethical right to have Social Security saved and to have the commitments made by the government over the past decades honored.

The supposed right to comparable worth is on far shakier ground than this right of retirees. While we cannot even compute comparable worth, we certainly can calculate what employees have paid into Social Security and the value of promised benefits. If the surplus is to be spent, it is only fair that it be used to honor the most credible of rights. The surplus option, therefore, does not yield any governmental duty to pay for salary equity and so does not support any right to comparable worth. If the government were to assess corporate income taxes to pay for the program, the result would be the same as requiring businesses to fund it – likely bankruptcy for some smaller companies, less competitiveness, and higher unemployment for women.

That leaves the personal income tax option. If we believe that women are already underpaid, it seems rather perverse to tax their current income to fund a future pay increase. Federal programs tend to be self-perpetuating, so it is likely that a portion of women's higher future earnings will go to fund more pay equity studies and the administrative apparatus for calculating and lobbying for pay equity. Women might well end up being worse off if a pay equity personal income tax were instituted. Let us assume an across the board pay equity personal income tax of 1 percent. Assume as well that the underpaid woman is married. She makes $40,000 a year as a public school teacher; her husband is earning $150,000 as a midlevel banking executive. The woman pays a pay equity tax of $400; the husband pays $1500 for a family total of $1900. Pay equity calculations show that the woman should be making $41,000 per year, so she receives a $1000 a year before-tax increase. Although the woman is now making more money, she and her husband have $900 less money than they did before.

We could limit the pay equity tax to men so as to avoid lowering women's earnings still further. Doing so, though, would not solve the problem of dual income families. In the above example, the family would still lose a net $500 if a 1 percent pay equity tax were limited only to men. Moreover, a single sex tax would raise many questions of fairness and would face a stiff legal challenge. It is doubtful whether the government has an ethical duty to flaunt its own constitution to fund a questionable right to comparable worth.

It appears, then, that no party has a duty to fund a pay equity scheme. If there is no such duty, then there is no right to comparable worth.

Conclusion

Many employee rights are theoretically suspect. Supposed rights, such as the right to meaningful work, to privacy and to be paid one's comparable worth, cannot be derived merely by appealing to an employee's right to be respected. A right does not exist if and when there is no specific correlative, enforceable, and dischargeable duty to honor this claim incumbent on a specific, identifiable party. Furthermore, any employee rights must be balanced against corporate rights and considered in light of developing technology, changes in the economy, and the legal liabilities faced by corporations. Finally, employee rights must be considered as a whole, for these rights are often in tension with each other. When this more nuanced approach is taken, employee rights are seen to be dubious or, at least, far more circumscribed than many theorists realize.

References

Arendt, H. 1998: *The Human Condition*. Chicago: University of Chicago Press.

Brenkert, G. 1988: Privacy, polygraphs and work. In T. Beauchamp and N. Bowie, *Ethical Theory and Business*. Englewood Cliffs, NJ: Prentice Hall, 280–6.

Hartman, L. 1998: *Perspectives in Business Ethics*. Chicago: Irwin McGraw-Hill.

Kant, I. 1964: *Groundwork of the Metaphysics of Morals*. New York: Harper Collins.

Kukewicz, W. 2000: Washington has no right to a run a surplus. *Wall Street Journal*. 10 July A34.

Meyers, D. T. 1988: Work and self-respect. In T. Beauchamp and N. Bowie, *Ethical Theory and Business*. Englewood Cliffs, NJ: Prentice Hall, 275–9.

Rosen, J. 2000: *The Unwanted Gaze*. New York: Random House.

Wetlaufer, S. 2000: Who wants to manage a millionaire? *Harvard Business Review*. July–August, 53–8.

Further Reading

Boatright, J. 2000: *Ethics and the Conduct of Business*. Upper Saddle, NJ: Prentice Hall.

Chapter 12

Environmental Responsibility

Joseph R. DesJardins

An adequate account of business' environmental responsibilities must be informed by work from both environmental ethics and business ethics. Environmental ethics provides an account of the ethical responsibilities humans in general have towards the nonhuman natural world. Business ethics helps to determine the role that business should play in fulfilling those responsibilities.

In the first sections of this chapter, I draw from environmental ethics to review a range of responsibilities that humans in general have towards the nonhuman natural world. I present a view that can be described as pluralistic and pragmatic. Humans have a wide variety of environmental responsibilities that cannot be reduced to a single maxim or theory of environmental ethics. I then consider how standard models of corporate social responsibility address such responsibilities. I argue against those who hold that the workings of economic markets, in either the *laissez faire* or regulated variety, can meet those responsibilities over the long term. In the final section, I describe a redesign of business institutions that plausibly can meet both our economic and environmental expectations of business.

Environmental Values and Corporate Social Responsibility

A wide range of public policy issues is identified as "environmental" in both the popular press and in scholarly literature. These include such diverse policy concerns as the conservation of fossil fuels and other natural resources, soil erosion and desertification, preservation of wilderness areas, forests, and wetlands, preservation of endangered species, air and water pollution, agricultural use of pesticides, chemical fertilizers, and genetically modified crops and livestock, moral standing for animals and plants, global warming, the depletion of the ozone layer, biodiversity, urban sprawl, nuclear waste, and population growth.

At least as important from a philosophical perspective is the wide range of values appealed to in defense of various environmental policy prescriptions. Environmental policies are defended by appeal to reasons of prudence, morality, social justice to present generations, social justice to future generations, aesthetics, spirituality and religious conviction, historical and symbolic significance, and economics. Environmental philosophers debate the possibility of reconciling this diversity of environmental values. Moral monists argue that a single principle must ultimately hold sway, while moral pluralists maintain that there can be a plurality of independent values that cannot be reduced to a single unified theory. Environmental pragmatists discount the need to attain a unity of value rationales and, instead, focus on finding agreement on specific policy recommendations. This chapter adopts a pragmatic orientation.

Much work within environmental ethics can be understood in terms of an expanding circle of moral standing. Almost without exception traditional western moral theories are, in the language of environmental ethics, anthropocentric. Such familiar ethical approaches as natural law, ethical egoism, utilitarianism, and Kantian ethics take individual human beings as the paradigmatic and exclusive holder of ethical value. Many environmental issues easily fit within standard anthropocentric ethics and rely on such standard ethical concepts as rights and duties, negligence and liability, equal opportunity, fairness, property rights, and compensatory justice.

As societies confronted a variety of new environmental challenges in recent decades, philosophers began to consider the possibility that the domain of moral considerability was being too narrowly drawn. Disposal of nuclear wastes, for example, forces us to consider responsibilities to generations of human beings not yet living. A variety of other issues, from species extinction to the destruction of ecosystems, raised the possibility that moral standing ought to be extended to nonhuman living beings as well. Animal welfare advocates extend moral standing to at least some animals on the basis of sentience or consciousness. Biocentrists argue that only life itself can provide a non-question begging ground for moral consideration. While anthropocentric ethics allows for ethical responsibilities *regarding* the nonhuman natural world, nonanthropocentric ethicists hold that we have direct moral responsibilities *to* the nonhuman natural world.

To the degree that such arguments are sound, the range of environmental responsibilities can become very extensive. The animal welfare perspective creates strong *prima facie* prohibitions against using animals for food, in research, and in sports and entertainment. The ethical implications of biocentric ethics are even more extensive. Any activity that harms any living being would be *prima facie* wrong.

Another important distinction found within the environmental literature is that between individualistic and holistic approaches to the environment. Most of the ethical theories described above, both anthropocentric and nonanthropocentric, assume that only individual beings can be the holders of ethical value. Individual humans have standing in the case of anthropocentric ethics, individual animals and living beings in the case of various biocentric approaches. In contrast, influenced by the science of ecology, ecocentrists defend an ethical status for such ecological wholes as ecosystems, populations, and species.

Environmental holism generates ethical responsibilities different from, and in some cases conflicting with, individualistic ethics. These implications are best captured in Aldo Leopold's remark from *A Sand County Almanac*: "A thing is right when it tends to preserve the integrity, stability, and beauty of the biotic community. It is wrong when it tends otherwise" (Leopold, 1949, p. 262). Thus ecocentric ethics would place higher value on endangered plants and animals than domesticated animals or livestock. It would value native plants and animals while seeking to eliminate non-native exotic species that threaten the integrity of an ecosystem. Ecocentric ethics would have no in-principle objection to using animals as food, pets, or game. In fact, ecocentric ethics could sanction select- ive hunting and killing as a means to protect ecosystems from overpopulation or from invasion by non-native species. Selective thinning of forest lands by logging could also be compatible with an ecocentric approach, although clear-cut forestry would not. Tree farms and factory farming of livestock, except in so far as they replace or threaten the genetic diversity of native forests and animals, are not an environmental concern to ecocentrists.

Holistic environmental ethics would generate distinct environmental respon- sibilities for business. In some ways, ecocentric approaches offer business greater latitude than individualistic approaches. Using natural objects as resources is not *per se* an ethical issue from the ecocentric perspective. Commercial use of specific natural resources raises few ethical issues as long as ecosystems and species of which they are a part remain biologically diverse and healthy.

Of course, environmental policy issues involve values other than those of moral standing and many of these issues are not easily addressed by concepts such as moral rights and moral considerability. The shift to more holistic approaches to environmentalism helps bring this to the fore. While some have argued for moral standing for such things as ecosystems and species, ecocentric theories are more likely to explain environmental value in non-moral value terms. We might seek to preserve natural and wild spaces, for example, because they are beautiful, awe-inspiring, or majestic. Preserving biological diversity might be sought as an expression of religious or spiritual values. Protecting an endangered species such as the bald eagle or giant sequoia tree is defended as symbolically valuable. Wilderness areas get preserved not because they are moral beings, but for their historical and cultural meaning.

A distinction between instrumental and intrinsic value can help explain the nature of such aesthetic, religious, spiritual, historic, and symbolic values. Philos- ophers sometimes speak as if the value domain is exhausted by the categories of moral value and instrumental value. Some ethicists mistakenly suggest that if something is not an end in itself, not a moral subject, then it is a mere means. Since only autonomous beings are taken to be ends in themselves, the nonhuman natural world is reduced to having only instrumental value. But there are many environmental values that cannot be reduced either to questions of moral standing or mere usefulness.

Objects can be said to have instrumental value when they are valued for their usefulness. Instrumental value is a function of how something is used, and its value is diminished to the degree that its usefulness is diminished. An object's instrumental value can be replaced by another object with equal or more efficient usefulness. Thus, for example, the instrumental value of a dollar bill can be replaced without loss by four quarters. An object is intrinsically valuable, valued in itself, when its value is unique to the object. Intrinsic value cannot be replaced by another object, no matter how similar or useful. Thus, the first dollar bill I earn in my business, framed and mounted over my desk, possesses intrinsic value as a symbol of my start in business. This symbolic value is irreplaceable by four quarters or a different bill. Something of value would be irretrievably lost if this unique bill was destroyed. This value inheres in, or is intrinsic to, the object itself.

Standard moral theory holds that each human being is uniquely valuable in this sense because each human is a moral subject. But there are many environmental issues that do not involve moral value in this sense. The concept of moral standing is stretched beyond recognition in claiming, for example, that a prairie, a mountain, a wetland, a swamp, or the Grand Canyon is a moral subject. But it is equally misguided to conclude that such things are to be valued simply for their usefulness. Many nonhuman natural objects possess intrinsic value and human beings would be doing a harm, not a moral harm but a harm nonetheless, in destroying them.

What are the implications of these reflections for the social responsibility of business? According to what I will call the neoclassical model of corporate social responsibility, perhaps not much. This model holds that business fulfills its social responsibilities when it responds to the demands of the marketplace while obeying the law and respecting minimum moral duties. (It therefore differs from the classical model of corporate social responsibility, which holds that the only responsibility of business is to maximize profits within the law.) Thus, for example, Bowie (1990) has argued that apart from the duties to cause no avoidable harm to humans, to obey the law, and to refrain from unduly influencing environmental legislation, business has no special environmental responsibility. Business may choose, as a matter of supererogation, to do environmental good, but it is otherwise free to pursue profits by responding to the demands of the economic marketplace without any particular regard to environmental responsibilities. In so far as society desires environmental goods, e.g., lowering pollution by increasing the fuel efficiency of automobiles, it is free to express those desires through legislation or within the marketplace. Absent those demands, business has no special environmental responsibilities.

Given that the environmental values just reviewed have a potential for generating significant and wide-ranging ethical responsibilities for all people, it is understandable why some would argue that business has no special environmental obligation. One can reasonably claim that commercial institutions are simply one means by which society pursues its ends. Until and unless society adopts different ends in respect to the ethical treatment of the natural environment, either through the demands of the marketplace or through government regulation, we cannot reasonably require business to do so unilaterally. Until there is some consensus coming out of environmental ethics, it is unreasonable to require business to take on any particular environmental duties. If moral responsibilities are equally binding on all, it would be unfair to single out one institution to bear a disproportionate burden in fulfilling those responsibilities, particularly if taking the lead in pursuing such goals, absent consumer demand, threatens the economic viability of the firm. The problem with this approach, as I shall argue, is that it excludes *a priori* any ethical responsibilities that emerge from those nonmoral intrinsic values found in nature.

Pluralism and Pragmatism: Towards a Consensus on Environmental Responsibilities

I think that some environmental ethicists have been mislead by an over reliance on the Kantian framework of hypothetical and categorical imperatives. On that view, reason can be practical in one of two ways. Instrumental rationality connects means to ends and results in the issuance of hypothetical imperatives. We have a reason to do X, only if we contingently possess the subjective desire for Y, and X is a means to obtain Y. Formal rationality can judge ends only on formalistic grounds, e.g., universalizability, and it results in issuing categorical imperatives. We have a categorical reason to do X only if the maxim implicit in doing X can be universalized. We are thus left with no "rational" way to judge the ends themselves other than the formal criterion of determining if they can be universally prescribed. It should come as no surprise therefore that the only thing good in itself is the good will and thus the only things with moral standing are autonomous human beings. All else is left with mere instrumental, i.e., hypothetical, value.

We will be left with a very impoverished environmentalism if this is the standard by which we determine environmental responsibilities. Perhaps some animals could be brought in under the criterion of autonomy, but the rest of the natural world could be valued only instrumentally and we would be left with what is, at best, a conservationist ethic. In this section, I would like to exploit a richer understanding of practical reason, one with roots in Plato and Aristotle rather than in Kant, that can support a more robust environmentalism. On this view, the *point* of ethics is to provide an answer to the (Socratic) question: How ought we to live? That is, ethics seeks to provide good reasons for doing one thing rather than another, for being one type of person rather than another. We have ethical responsibilities (not categorical obligations in the Kantian sense) when doing one thing rather than another will produce or preserve something of value. To the degree that these values are more than mere subjective preferences, our reasons for acting are more than merely instrumental, hypothetical imperatives. In this sense, the range of environmental values previously reviewed provides us with many good reasons for acting in ways that minimize harm to the natural environment. Some, but not all, of our environmental responsibilities involve moral responsibilities to other human beings. Some, but not all, are morally obligatory. In general, reasonable humans have ethical responsibilities to do that which promotes or preserves intrinsic value.

Philosophical debates will continue over the justification of such values and over the possibility of ever unifying such a plurality of values. The fear of some is that we become ethical relativists if we cannot establish some value hierarchy or algorithmic decision-procedure. But such a quest is ill-advised and unnecessary. It is ill-advised because there are good reasons to celebrate the diversity of environmental values. It is unnecessary because the real problems of relativism may be minimized in others ways. A pragmatic approach to environmental responsibilities can acknowledge and respect a wide diversity of environmental values.

There are reasons not to push too hard for a unification of environmental values. This diversity of values reflects a richness of human experience that should be recognized and respected rather than reduced to homogeneity. If we truly respect diverse cultures and people, we must remain open to the possibility that we can learn from them. To give full equal consideration and respect we must listen to the values of others, incorporate diverse perspectives into our own, and refrain from subsuming divergent views into a single universal worldview.

Respecting a diversity of values also reinforces democratic structures and decision procedures. Democracy is traditionally justified as a political arrangement most compatible with respect for autonomous persons and most likely to contribute, through participatory structures of dialogue and debate, to the development of an informed citizenry and a stable public policy. Pluralism in respect to environmental values is likely to keep more people at the table of public policy discussion, debate, and consensus.

The diversity of environmental values is more a diversity of reasons and explanations than it is a diversity of actions and policies. Norton (1991), for example, has argued that while there is significant divergence among the worldviews of environmentalists, there is a growing convergence on environmental policies and actions. For example, while there is a wide-spread consensus that biological diversity ought to be preserved, there is disagreement on the reasons for doing so. In defense of this policy, appeals are made to the moral status of all living creatures, to ecological stability and integrity, to prudence, to aesthetics, to respect for God's creation, and so forth. In good pragmatic fashion, the difference (in justification) that ceases to make a difference (in policy) can be downplayed.

Important philosophical issues certainly remain to be addressed. Oftentimes a difference in justification does make a major difference in policy, as when holists sanction and animal rights theorists prohibit thinning herds to stabilize populations and ecosystems. The view of practical reason I have introduced does indeed leave open the possibility of irreconcilable ethical conflict and tragedy. An environmental policy can be said to be more reasonable than the alternatives however if a plurality of values support it over the alternatives. Such a policy may not be obligatory (i.e., categorically required), but it is the most reasonable thing to do nonetheless. Proving a practical conclusion beyond this may simply not be possible in ethics. But in the meantime practical decisions need to be made about policy, decisions that sometimes can do irreversible environmental harm and which, therefore, cannot be postponed. Achieving a unity of environmental values is unnecessary for prescribing a wide-range of reasonable and widely-supported environmental policies.

What, then, can we conclude about human responsibilities regarding the natural environment? I would like to suggest four general policy areas in which a consensus of values ("good reasons") leads to reasonable environmental policies. We can say, therefore, that we have strong *prima facie* responsibilities to foster such policies. These four areas concern wastes and pollution, use of natural resources, preservation of environmentally sensitive areas, and preservation of biodiversity.

Pollution can be understood as byproducts of human activities introduced into the biosphere that can harm humans or makes the biosphere less able to sustain life. Clearly, many disputes concerning pollution remain to be resolved. Some are factual and scientific, as debates concerning the atmospheric and climatic effects of an increase in CO_2 pollution demonstrate. Some are ethical and value-based, for example debates concerning the relative harms and benefits of agricultural pesticides. Nevertheless, a strong consensus of environmental values leads us to conclude that pollution must be minimized and, wherever possible, eliminated.

From a strictly prudential perspective, pollution represents wasted resources and poses a threat to human well-being. On self-interested grounds, waste is inefficient and irrational. Pollution can also directly threaten the health and safety of human beings. Some pollution threatens the well-being of future generations, as when we bury nuclear wastes or bring about global climate change. Pollution can produce unforeseen harms to other living creatures, as so eloquently documented in Rachel Carson's (1962) *Silent Spring*. And in many cases, pollution is downright ugly and offensive.

A second area of emerging environmental policy consensus, that concerning the use of natural resources, addresses the opposite end of the business process. All living beings use resources from their environment to sustain life. *That* we use non-human natural objects as resources is not the ethical issue. *Which* objects we use as resources, *how* we use them, *what* we use them for and, most importantly, the *rate at which* they are used do raise important ethical and policy questions. Again, a wide range of values, including but not limited to prudential and moral values, would support a common approach to natural resource use.

A rational resource use policy would favor reliance on renewable resources over nonrenewable resources. Using nonrenewables when renewable alternatives are available is like using capital rather than income for a business' operating expenses. It can be done, but it is an irrational long-term policy. When renewable resources are used, approaches that minimize disruption of ecosystems, e.g., solar and wind generated electricity, should be favored over those that disrupt ecosystems, e.g., hydroelectric dams. When nonrenewables are used, they should be used in ways that are efficient and just. For example, most power plants burn tons of fossil fuels to boil water to create steam to turn electricity-generating turbines. This is an inefficient and wasteful use of a valuable and nonrenewable resource. Technologies exist to separate out many complex molecules from oil and coal, thereby producing cleaner-burning fuels and valuable by-products. Most importantly, using non-renewable resources to increase the creature comforts of a consumerist lifestyle while millions of people live in need of the essentials of food, clean water, health care, and housing is unconscionable.

A rational and just policy for the use of nonrenewable resources would prohibit using them in ways and at rates at which an equal opportunity to benefit from them is denied to others, particularly the least advantaged individuals. Part of this responsibility can be fulfilled by a change in demand. Greater efficiencies in the use of use of resources, particularly nonrenewable energy sources, would contribute significantly to this end. Part of this responsibility can be met on the supply side. The key principle is that both present and future generation humans have a right to an equal opportunity to the benefits derived from nonrenewable natural resources. Increasing the supply of those resources, of those goods and services provided by those resources, or of equally productive substitutes would be ways to meet this responsibility on the supply side. Research and technology aimed at increasing the supply, research and development of alternatives, and a more equitable distribution of present supplies are obvious steps that are consistent with this responsibility.

Preservation of environmentally sensitive natural areas is a third topic in which a plurality of values would find common ground. No reasonable person can expect all open spaces to be preserved from development, nor can we wish to turn every natural area into a human artifact. The challenge is to identify which areas should remain protected from development. Those open areas valued by a variety of perspectives, what we can call environmentally sensitive natural areas, are obvious candidates. Preserving open park space within a highly urbanized area serves environmental, aesthetic, prudential, economic, and psychological goods. Connecting these areas via habitat corridors and trails adds additional value dimensions to such preservation. Preserving rare, majestic, unique landscapes also serves a variety of values. Other natural areas can serve historical, symbolic, and spiritual values in much the way that Muir Woods, Yellowstone, the Everglades for example presently do. Given their function in minimizing threats of floods and purifying water, we have good prudential reasons to preserve wetlands. Preserved wetlands, in turn, also serve as habitat for a variety of plant and animal species, including both endangered plants species and game species of ducks and geese. Preserving a variety of ecosystems (prairies, oak savannas, pine forests, riparian corridors, swamps, and the like) of a size that can be self-sustaining over the long-term serves a variety of values, not the least of which is the educational value for teaching science, ecology, history.

Finally, preserving biological diversity would also be an environmental responsibility supported from a wide variety of value perspectives. Again, there are good prudential reasons, both short and long-term, for preserving biological diversity among both plant and animals species. Lost diversity among crops makes food production more prone to disease and weather-related failures. Plant diversity holds great promise for research into food and medicine production. Biodiversity contributes to healthier ecosystems. It is testimony to the wondrous adaptability of life itself, providing religious, aesthetic, and symbolic inspiration to many.

This section has reviewed four general environmental issues around which a rational consensus can be formed. Based on a variety of widely held and important values, humans can be said to have responsibilities to: minimize or eliminate pollution and waste; conserve natural resources; preserve environmentally sensitive areas; and preserve biological diversity. In the following sections, we turn to how business institutions might best be designed and regulated so that we might fulfill these responsibilities.

The Failure of Market-Based Environmental Policies

Standard models of corporate social responsibility all presuppose the legitimacy of a growth-based, market economy. These views treat market-based solutions as the default position. As long as minimal moral requirements are satisfied, whatever social policy flows from the workings of competitive markets is ethically acceptable. Business needs only obey the law, respect moral minimums, and respond to the demands expressed within the market because efficient markets and economic growth otherwise best serve social goals. Ethical and legal responsibilities function as side-constraints upon the economic goals that follow from the role of business institutions within the neoclassical economic model.

The question of business' environmental responsibilities comes down to the question of whether or not such models of corporate social responsibility can adequately address environmental concerns. Can the environmental responsibilities outlined above be left to the workings of competitive markets or can they be brought within the moral minimum? Will an ethically adequate environmental policy be achieved when such responsibilities function as side-constraints on the goal of economic growth? I believe that an adequate environmental ethic for business is possible only if environmental responsibility functions not as a side-constraint upon normal business activities, but as shaping the very nature of how business is conducted. In short, any view that leaves the fulfillment of environmental responsibilities to the undirected workings of competitive markets will prove inadequate on a variety of ethical grounds.

Standard models of corporate social responsibility can underestimate the range of managerial discretion once the duties of law and the moral minimum are met. What can be lost in these discussions is the very important fact that there are many ways to pursue profits within the side-constraints of law and morality. Such views also assume that economic growth is environmentally and ethically benign. I will argue that it is decidedly not. Business' environmental responsibilities cannot be met without a conscious restructuring of business operations

Consider how a growth-based market-driven economy would address the four policy concerns outlined above. Defenders of the market claim that there are reasonably straightforward economic responses to the problem of pollution. There is an optimal level of pollution, a level at which society judges the risks acceptable given the relative costs. A society could attain cleaner drinking water, for example, if it would be willing to pay more for filtration systems or for the goods and services that create the pollution, e.g., agricultural products and petrochemicals. Of course, when markets fail by externalizing the costs of pollution, the law would be justified through taxation or civil penalties in requiring business to internalize such costs. In turn, this provides business with a greater incentive to reduce pollution since in such a case pollution truly constitutes wasted resources.

Competitive markets also allocate and distribute resources to their most highly valued use. The law of supply and demand, as reflected in the price of commodities, insures that resource use is balanced in such a way that an optimal satisfaction of societal demands is met. Individuals decide for themselves what they most want and these preferences, as expressed by a willingness to pay, determine how resources get used. As the supply of natural resources diminishes, prices rise thereby lowering demand and providing entrepreneurs with the incentive to discover new supplies or adequate substitutes.

Likewise, the law of supply and demand within competitive markets insures that society will have adequate open space. As the supply of parkland, wilderness areas, and open space diminishes, prices will rise, demand will decrease, and these valuable spaces will be left undeveloped. Particularly valued land can also always be legally removed from the market and preserved as public goods if this is what society most wants.

Finally, with some adjustments to the present configuration of property rights, competitive markets can also adequately address species preservation. Market defenders point out that species are threatened as a result of an inadequate system of property rights over them. The population of whales, ocean fisheries, wolves, and so forth, decline whenever they are treated as common property, free to be exploited by whoever gets to them first. An adequate system of private property rights would provide owners with the incentive to protect and preserve the species, just as owners of cattle, chicken, cows, and other domesticated animals protect their property. A similar argument would be made for rare plant species that are threatened only when left unowned as common property. Once again, supply and demand will work to preserve species once their supply has diminished. Highly valued species such as the bald eagle, the blue whale, and the redwood tree can also receive legal protection as a public good.

Such would be the general approach to environmental problems taken by those who assume the legitimacy of competitive markets as public policy instruments.

From the perspective of both the classical model of corporate social responsibility and the modified neoclassical model, business' environmental responsibilities are clear: obey the law and respond to the demands of society as expressed in the marketplace. Market forces will take care of the rest.

Extensive criticisms have been raised against the legitimacy of markets as tools for setting environmental (or any public) policy. A complete review of these would be beyond the scope of this chapter. However, two general challenges to the ethical and environmental legitimacy of such a reliance on markets establish a fairly conclusive case.

Challenge 1

Even the strongest defenders of markets acknowledge the existence of a variety of market failures. Particularly relevant for our concern is the existence of externalities, the textbook example of which is environmental pollution. Since the "costs" of such things as air pollution, groundwater contamination and depletion, soil erosion, and nuclear waste disposal are typically borne by parties "external" to the economic exchange (e.g., people downwind, neighbors, future generations), free market exchanges cannot guarantee optimal results.

A second type of market failure occurs when no markets exist to create a price for important social goods. Endangered species, scenic vistas, rare plants and animals, and biodiversity are just some environmental goods that typically are not traded on open markets (when they are, it often is in ways that seriously threaten their viability as when rhinoceros horns, tiger claws, elephant tusks, and mahogany trees are sold on the black market). Public goods such as clean air and ocean fisheries also have no established market price. The diverse intrinsic values described previously cannot be measured by nor reduced to their exchange value. With no established exchange value, markets fail to guarantee that such goods are preserved and protected.

A third way in which market failures can lead to serious environmental harm involves a distinction between individual decisions and group consequences. Important ethical and policy questions can be missed if we leave policy decisions solely to the outcome of individual decisions. This problem arises for many issues, particularly for health risks involved in environmental concerns such as exposure to workplace chemicals, consuming food treated with pesticides, and drinking water that contains nitrates and chemical residues. As a particular example, consider the decision involved in choosing to drive a low mileage sports utility vehicle.

Driving such vehicles significantly increases the amount of airborne pollutants discharged per mile driven. A 13-mpg SUV will discharge 134 tons of CO_2 over its 124,000 mile lifetime. A 36-mpg compact car will discharge 48 tons over the same distance. If I act as the rationally self-interested individual presupposed by neoclassical economics, I would calculate the benefits of driving an SUV and weigh them against the increased costs and health risks that I face from pollution.

Since the increased risks to me (or to any individual facing such a choice) of *my* driving an SUV rather than a compact are infinitesimally small, my self-interested choice to drive an SUV is reasonable according to market conceptions of individual rationality.

Consider these same facts not from an individual point of view but from the point of view of the population of, say, Los Angeles. Since, as our individual calculation indicated, it can be rational for any individual to choose an SUV, the individualistic approach implicit in market solutions would accept the Los Angeles pollution rate as a rational policy. The overall social result of such individual calculations might be significant increases in pollution and such pollution-related diseases as asthma and allergies. There are a number of alternative policies (e.g., restricting SUV sales, increasing taxes on gasoline, treating SUVs as cars instead of light trucks in calculating CAFE standards) that could address pollution and pollution-related disease. However, these alternatives would only be considered if we examine this question from a social rather than individualistic perspective. Because these are important ethical questions, and because they remain unasked from within market transactions, we must conclude that markets are incomplete (at best) in their approach to the overall social good. In other words, what is good and rational for a collection of individuals is not necessarily what is good and rational for a society.

These three types of market failure raise serious concerns for the ability of economic markets to achieve a sound environmental policy. As a consequence, any account of business' environmental responsibility which thinks that this responsibility will be satisfied simply by leaving business free to respond to market demands will be incomplete at best.

Of course, defenders of market solutions have ready responses to these challenges. Even free market defenders could support regulation that would require business to internalize externalities. Presumably they would support legislation to create shadow prices for unpriced social goods or for exempting such goods from the market, as when national parks and wilderness areas are set aside as public lands. A more adequate system of legal property rights is also often proposed as a response to threats to commonly unowned good such as ocean fisheries and rare animals. The law is also the appropriate mechanism for addressing social goods that are unattainable through individual choice. In short, the law is the obvious remedy for environmental harms resulting from market failures. And, once again, as long as business obeys the law, it is meeting its environmental responsibility when it responds to consumer demand in the marketplace.

But there are good reasons for thinking that such *ad hoc* attempts to repair market failures are environmentally inadequate. First is what I call the first-generation problem. Markets can work to prevent harm only through information supplied by the existence of markets failures. Only when fish populations in the North Atlantic collapsed did we learn that free and open competition among the world's fishing industry for unowned public goods failed to prevent the decimation of cod, swordfish, Atlantic salmon, and lobster populations. That is, we learn about markets failures and thereby prevent harms in the future only by sacrificing the "first-generation" as a means for gaining this information. When public policy involves irreplaceable public goods such as endangered species, rare wilderness areas, and public health and safety, such a reactionary strategy is ill-advised.

But even if we allow government regulation to establish environmental standards for business, we are still faced with the ability of business to influence both government regulation and consumer demand. The neoclassical model limits business' environmental responsibility to obeying the law and responding to consumer demand. On this model, it is government's responsibility to prevent and compensate for market failures. Once market failures are adequately addressed, business need only obey the law and respond to the market. But this assumes that business cannot or does not inappropriately influence the law. "Inappropriate" influence, on this model, is influence aimed not at optimizing the overall good (the goal, after all, of markets) but at protecting the interests of business. An obvious example is the automobile industry's successful lobbying effort to have SUVs treated as trucks rather than as passenger vehicles so that manufacturers can meet corporate automobile fuel efficiency (CAFE) standards established by law.

To his credit, Bowie (1990) recognizes the potential problem here and acknowledges that if business can be said to have any special environmental responsibility it is to refrain from influencing government environmental standards. But just as we must recognize the ability of business to influence government policy, we must recognize the ability to influence consumers. To conclude that business fulfills its environmental responsibility when it responds to the environmental demands of consumers is to underestimate the role that business can play in shaping public opinion. Advertising is a $200 billion a year industry in the USA alone. It is surely disingenuous to claim that business passively responds to consumer desires and that consumers are unaffected by the messages that business conveys. Assuming that business is not going to stop advertising its products or lobbying government, the market-based approach to environmental responsibility that is implicit within both the classical and neoclassical model of corporate social responsibility is inadequate.

Finally, there are good reasons to minimize the range of ethical responsibilities enforced by law. The law functions best when it provides general targets for, and side constraints upon, managerial discretion. The law is a crude tool to use to micromanage managerial decisions. It is preferable, on both economic and moral grounds, to expect business to meet its ethical responsibilities without having these mandated by law.

Challenge 2

A more comprehensive challenge to the ability of markets to set reasonable environmental policy has been raised in the work of Herman Daly and other economists working on sustainable development and ecological economics. Daly

(1996) makes a convincing case for an understanding of economic *development* that transcends the present standard of economic *growth*. There are, Daly argues, biological, physical, and ethical limits to growth, many of which the present world economy is already approaching, if not overshooting. Unless we make significant changes in our understanding of economic activity, unless quite literally we change the way we do business, we will fail to meet some very basic ethical and environmental obligations. According to Daly, we need a major paradigm shift in how we understand economic activity.

We can begin with the standard understanding of economic activity and economic growth found in almost every economics textbook. What is sometimes called the "circular flow model" explains the nature of economic transactions in terms of a flow of resources from businesses to households (Figure 12.1). Business produces goods and services in response to the market demands of households. These goods and services are shipped to households in exchange for payments back to business. These payments are in turn sent back to households in the form of wages, salaries, rents, profits, and interests. Households in exchange for the labor, land, capital and entrepreneurial skills used by business to produce goods and services receive these payments.

Two items are worth noting at this point. First, natural resources are undifferentiated from the other factors of production. On this model, the origin of resources is never explained. They are simply owned by households from which they, like labor, capital, and entrepreneurial skill, can be sold to business. In the words of Julian Simon, "As economists or consumers, we are interested in the particular services that resources yield, not in the resources themselves" (Simon, 1981). Those services can be provided in many ways and by substituting different factors of production. In Simon's terms, resources can therefore be treated as "infinite."

A second observation is that this model treats economic growth as not only the solution to all social ills, but also as boundless. To keep up with population growth, the economy must grow. To provide for a higher standard of living, the

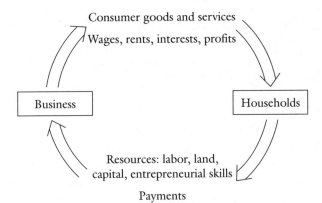

Figure 12.1

economy must grow. To alleviate poverty, hunger, and disease, the economy must grow. The possibility that the economy cannot grow indefinitely is simply not part of this model.

Three points summarize the challenges this model faces into the near future. First, a large percentage of the world population today lives in abject poverty. Current economic arrangements do not provide for the basic needs of hundreds of millions of people. One reasonable estimate is that the 25 percent of the world's population living in industrialized countries consume 80 percent of the world's resources. The current economic paradigm addresses this problem by promoting further economic growth in the "developing" world. Yet the world would require significant economic growth during the next few decades just to meet the basic needs of the other 75 percent of the planet's population. According to some estimates, it would need to grow by a factor of five-to-tenfold over the next fifty years to bring the standard of living of present populations in the developing world into line with the standard of living in the industrialized world.

Second, the world's population during this period will continue to increase significantly, particularly in the most impoverished and already highly populated regions. Even assuming a reduced rate of growth, worldwide population over the next fifty years likely will double, to about eleven billion people. Thus, economic activity to meet the basic needs of the world's population in the near future will need to increase proportionately.

Finally, the only sources for all this economic activity are the natural resources of the earth itself. Many of these resources – clean air, drinkable water, fertile soil, and food – cannot be replaced by the remaining factors of production. We cannot breathe, drink, eat, or grow food on, labor, capital or entrepreneurial skill alone. Because the world's environment is already under stress from current economic activity, the future looks bleak unless major changes take place. Given these realities, we must create an economic system that can provide for the needs of the world's population without destroying the environment in the process. This, according to some, is the role of sustainable economics and sustainable development.

Daly argues that neoclassical economics, with its emphasis on economic growth as the goal of economic policy, will inevitably fail to meet these challenges unless it recognizes that the economy is but a subsystem within earth's biosphere. Economic activity takes place within this biosphere and cannot expand beyond its capacity to sustain life. All the factors that go into production – natural resources, capital, entrepreneurial skill, and labor – ultimately originate in the productive capacity of the earth. In light of this, the entire classical model will prove unstable if resources move through this system at a rate that outpaces the productive capacity of the earth or of the earth's capacity to absorb the wastes and by-products of this production. Thus, we need to develop an economic system that uses resources only at a rate that can be sustained over the long term and that recycles or reuses both the by-products of the production process and the products themselves. A model of such a system, based on the work of Daly, is printed as figure 12.2.

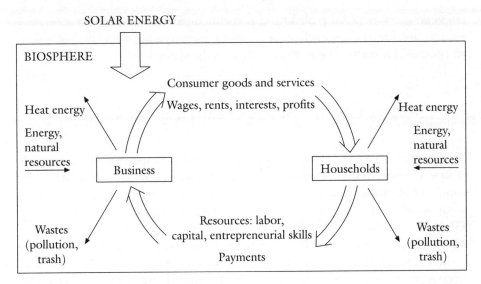

SOLAR ENERGY

BIOSPHERE

Consumer goods and services

Wages, rents, interests, profits

Heat energy

Energy,
natural
resources

Business

Heat energy

Energy,
natural
resources

Households

Wastes
(pollution,
trash)

Resources: labor,
capital, entrepreneurial skills

Payments

Wastes
(pollution,
trash)

Figure 12.2

Figure 12.2 differs from figure 12.1 in several important ways. First, there is a recognition that the economy exists within a finite biosphere that encompasses little more than a few miles-wide ban surrounding the earth's surface. From the first law of thermodynamics (the conservation of matter/energy), we recognize that neither matter nor energy can truly be "created," it can only be transferred from one form to another. Second, energy is lost at every stage of economic activity. Consistent with the second law of thermodynamics (entropy increases within a closed system), the amount of usable energy decreases over time. "Waste energy" leaves the economic system continuously and thus new low entropy energy must constantly flow into the system. Ultimately, the only source for low-entropy energy is the sun. Third, natural resources are no longer treated as an undifferentiated and unexplained factor of production emerging from households. Natural resource come from the biosphere and cannot be created *ex nihilo*. Finally, wastes are produced at each stage of economic activity and these wastes are dumped back into the biosphere.

The conclusion that should be drawn from this new model is relatively simple. Over the long-term, resources and energy cannot be used, nor wastes produced, at rates at which the biosphere cannot replace or absorb them without jeopardizing its ability to sustain (human) life. These are what Daly calls the "biophysical limits to growth" (Daly, 1996, pp. 33–5). The biosphere can produce resources indefinitely, and it can absorb wastes indefinitely, but only at a certain rate and with a certain type of economic activity. This is the goal of sustainable development. Finding this rate and type of economic activity, creating a sustainable business practice, is the ultimate environmental responsibility of business.

Figure 12.2 also provides us with a model for interpreting the four policy areas of environmental consensus presented previously. The consensus for eliminating pollution and wastes, for prudent use of resources, for preserving environmentally sensitive areas and biodiversity can be understood as requiring economic institutions to operate in a sustainable manner within the biosphere.

Business Ethics in the Age of Sustainable Development

Three criteria, the "three pillars of sustainability," are often used to judge sustainable practices. Sustainable development must be economically, environmentally, and socially satisfactory. Economically, sustainable practices must be able, in the words of the World Commission on Environment and Development (an agency of the UN), to meet the "needs of the present without compromising the ability of future generations to meet their own needs." Environmentally, they must do so without harming the ability of the biosphere to sustain life over the long term. Socially, they must address the real needs of people, particularly those hundreds of millions of people who lack adequate food, water, and other necessities. I suggest three similar criteria by which we should judge models of corporate social responsibility. Business ought to be arranged in such a way that it adequately meets the economic expectations of society (i.e., jobs, income, goods and services) in an efficient manner. Business ought also to be arranged in a way that supports, rather than degrades, the ability of the biosphere to sustain life, especially but not exclusively human life, over the long term. Business also ought to be arranged in a way that addresses minimum demands of social justice.

As we begin to consider how business should be restructured in order to meet its environmental responsibilities, it is worth emphasizing a point made previously. We should not underestimate the range of managerial discretion. Business managers, rightfully, enjoy a wide range of decision-making discretion. There are many ways to pursue and attain profitability. We must move away from the view of environmental responsibilities as side-constraints on "the" pursuit of profit, as if there is only one way to pursue profits and ethical responsibilities are a barrier to that. Rather, we must recognize that some avenues to profitability are environmentally risky, others environmentally prudent and sensible. Fortunately, we have some good models for environmentally sustainable business practices.

In *Natural Capitalism*, authors Paul Hawken, Amory Lovins, and Hunter Lovins provide a conceptual model for, and numerous examples of, sustainable business practices (Hawken et al., 1999). While an essay on business ethics perhaps is not the place for a detailed description of specific managerial practices, I will follow their work in sketching some specifics of an environmentally responsible business model.

Natural Capitalism offers four guiding principles for the redesign of business. First, the productivity of natural resources must and can be dramatically increased. This constitutes a further development of what is sometimes called "ecoefficiency." A second principle, called "biomimicry" or "closed-loop design," requires that business be redesigned to model biological processes. Byproducts formerly lost as waste and pollution must be eliminated, reintegrated into the production process, or returned as a benign or beneficial product to the biosphere. Third, traditional models of business as producers of goods should be replaced with a model of business as provider of services. The old economy focuses on producing goods, e.g., light bulbs and carpets, when consumer demand really focuses on services, e.g., illumination and floor-covering. This shift can provide significant incentives for accomplishing the first two goals. Finally, business must reinvest in natural capital. As any introductory textbook in economics or finance teaches, responsible business management requires a reinvestment in productive capital. Because traditional economic models have ignored the origin of natural capital they have neglected to include reinvestment in natural capital as part of prudent business practice. An environmentally responsible business must address this shortcoming.

Both ecoefficiency and biomimicry can be understood in terms of Figure 12.2. Ecoefficient management would discover ways to reduce the rate at which natural resources flow through the economic system. *Natural Capitalism* contains numerous examples in which managerial decisions regarding the design of both products and production methods has increased resources efficiency by a factor of 5, 10, and, in some cases, even 100. The standard growth model of economic development tells us that we can meet the needs of the poorest 75 percent of the world's population by increasing economic growth by a factor of 5–10. Ecoefficent business practices aims for the same end by increasing efficiency, and therefore decreasing resource use, by a factor of 5–10.

Examples of ecoefficiency can be found in many areas of business operations. Business managers must find ways to meet consumer demand with fewer resources. A simple example would be a housing developer who designs a neighborhood with cluster housing, green spaces, habitat corridors, and biking trails instead of the traditional "cookie-cutter" development pattern. Each development pattern can be profitable but one is more environmentally destructive than the other. Energy demand is another particularly apt example for this responsibility. *Natural Capitalism* describes the redesign of an industrial pumping system at Interface Corporation. With an eye towards reducing energy demand, the redesign with larger and straighter pipes resulted in a 92 percent, or 12-fold, energy savings. Energy efficient windows, lighting, motors, and insulation in the design and upgrade of every building would greatly reduce overall energy use while still meeting present production targets.

Ecoefficiency alone is only part of the solution. The principle of biomimicry attempts to eliminate the wastes produced by even ecoefficient production processes. Business managers have a responsibility to seek ways to integrate former wastes back into the production system, transform wastes into biologically beneficial elements or, minimally, to produce wastes at rates no faster than the biosphere can absorb them. An interesting example, taken from the traditionally environmentally destructive coal industry, is SGI International, a leader in the "green coal" industry. SGI has developed a technology that transforms high-sulfur coal into a variety of specialty chemicals, liquids, and fuels. In traditional power plants, coal is simply burned as fuel, producing significant carbon dioxide pollution and, in the case of high-sulfur coal, the sulfuric acid compounds responsible for acid rain. SGI's process gasifies the coal, and separates the gas out (effectively distilling it) into a liquid hydrocarbon, and then further separates it into a variety of distinct chemical products. The process also produces a solid coal product that will burn much cleaner and more efficiently than traditional coal. The remaining non-condensable gases are used to provide over 70 percent of energy requirements for the production process itself. SGI claims that their entire process is 90 percent energy efficient, a 3 to 4-fold increase over traditional coal-fired power plants. The traditional process burns coal to produce energy and pollution, while also destroying highly complex molecules which were created in nature over millions of years. While still producing energy from coal, SGI transforms this process to greatly reduce pollution and create a variety of highly marketable specialty chemicals.

In many ways, challenges of ecoefficiency and biomimicry are challenges of business design. A well-publicized test case of such sustainable design principles is taking place at Ford Motor Company's Rouge River industrial complex. This $2 billion redesign, overseen by environmental architect and designer Will McDonough, will introduce sustainable principles to one of the world's largest industrial complexes. Reinvestment in productive capital is a basic economic responsibility for every business manager. Doing so in the way that Ford intends, in a way that addresses environmental and social concerns as well as economic ones, should be among the ethical responsibilities of every business manager.

The third principle of sustainable business practice may require a greater paradigm shift in business management. Traditional manufacturing aims to produce goods; this new model shifts to providing services. This shift, according to *Natural Capitalism*, will reinforce principles of both ecoefficiency and biomimicry. Traditional economic and managerial models interpret consumer demand as the demand for products, e.g., washing machines, carpets, lights, consumer electronics, air conditioners, cars, computers, and so forth. A service-based economy interprets consumer demand as a demand for services, e.g., for clothes cleaning, floor-covering, illumination, entertainment, cool air, transportation, word processing, and so forth. *Natural Capitalism* provides examples of businesses that have made such a shift in each of these industries. This change produces incentives for product redesigns that create more durable and more easily recyclable products.

Interface Corporation, a major carpet-manufacturing firm from Atlanta, is a well-known innovator in this area. Interface has made a transition from selling carpeting to leasing floor-covering services. On the traditional model, carpet is sold to consumers who, once they become dissatisfied with the color or style or once the carpeting becomes worn, dispose of the carpet in landfills. There is little incentive here to produce long-lasting or easily recyclable carpeting. Once Interface shifted to leasing floor-covering services, incentives are created to produce long-lasting, easily replaceable and recyclable carpets. Interface thereby accepts responsibility for the entire life-cycle of the product it markets. Because they retain ownership and are responsible for maintenance, Interface now produces carpeting that can be easily replaced in sections rather than in its entirety, that is more durable, and that can eventually be remanufactured. Redesigning their carpets and shifting to a service lease has also improved production efficiencies and reduced material and energy costs significantly. Consumers benefit by getting what they truly desire, at lower costs and with fewer burdens.

Finally, business managers have a responsibility to reinvest in natural capital, the one factor of production traditionally ignored in economic and financial analysis. The principle involved in this is simple, but its implementation is a challenge. The principle is that business has a responsibility not to use resources at rates faster than what can be replenished by the biosphere, and especially ought not to destroy the productive capacity of the biosphere itself. The financial analogue is a business that liquidates capital for operating expenses or the household that spends savings as income. The prudential and responsible decision is to use the income generated by capital for living expenses while reserving the capital itself for long-term viability. So, too, with natural capital. We ought to use this capital only at the rate at which it can renew itself.

Because the productive capacity of the biosphere is a true public good and because of the many market failures and incentives for individuals to act irresponsibly in such cases, reinvestment in natural capital is perhaps one business responsibility that should be especially subject to government regulation. Business managers ought to do so, but as individuals operating within competitive markets they cannot be expected to do so. Tax incentives to encourage such investment, and tax penalties for uncompensated resource extraction, is one option.

The roof of the Ford Rouge factory is one simple example of reinvesting in nature. This roof will be covered with ivy-like sedum plants that will not only reduce water run-off and add insulation value but, like all plants, they will also convert carbon dioxide (a major auto-emission pollutant) to oxygen. Tax subsidies for such decisions, especially if there are short-term economic disincentives for doing this, seem a reasonable policy. We already have a model for this in gasoline taxes that are earmarked for highway construction and repair. There is no reason why similar taxes could not be targeted at other industries that treat nature's capital as income and the monies devoted to a reinvestment in nature's capital.

Conclusions

This chapter has provided a blueprint for how we ought to think about business' environmental responsibilities. I have argued for an approach that balances economic considerations with environmental responsibilities. I suggested that competitive markets, even those constrained by law and moral obligation, are unlikely to allow business to meet reasonable environmental responsibilities. Yet strong market conditions are necessary if business is to meet our legitimate economic expectations as well. Reconceiving business' ethical responsibilities in light of the economics of sustainable development provides a model for how business institutions might meet both our environmental and economic expectations.

References

Bowie, N. 1990: Morality, money, and motor cars. In W. M. Hoffman, R. Frederick, and E. Petry (eds) *Business, Ethics, and the Environment*. New York: Quorum Books, 89–97.

Carson, R. 1962: *Silent Spring*. Boston: Houghton Mifflin.

Daly, H. 1996: *Beyond Growth*. Boston: Beacon Press.

Hawken, P., Lovins, A. and Lovins, H. 1999: *Natural Capitalism*. Boston: Little, Brown and Company.

Leopold, A. 1949: *A Sand County Almanac*. New York: Oxford University Press.

Norton, B. 1991: *Toward Unity among Environmentalists*. New York: Oxford University Press.

Simon, J. 1981: *The Ultimate Resource*. Princeton: Princeton University Press.

Further Reading

Constanza, R. (ed.) 1991: *Ecological Economics: The Science and Management of Sustainability*. New York: Columbia University Press.

DeSimone, L. D. and Popoff, F. 1997: *Eco-Efficiency: The Business Link to Sustainable Development*. Cambridge, MA.: The MIT Press.

DesJardins, J. R. 1999: Business's environmental responsibility. In R. Frederick (ed.) *A Companion to Business Ethics*. Malden, MA.: Blackwell Publishers, 280–9.

DesJardins, J. R. 2001: *Environmental Ethics: An Introduction to Environmental Philosophy*. 3rd edn. Belmont, California: Wadsworth Publishing.

Kolk, A. 2000: *Economics of Environmental Management*. Essex, England: Financial Times/ Prentice Hall.

Light, A. and Katz, E. (eds) 1998: *Environmental Pragmatism*. New York: Routledge.

McDonough, W. and Baungart, M. 1998: The next industrial revolution. *Atlantic Monthly*. 284 (4).

Rocky Mountain Institute publications at *www.rmi.org*.

World Business Council on Sustainable Development, *www.wbcsd.org*.

Part III
New Directions

Chapter 13

Ethical Issues in Information Technology

Richard T. DeGeorge

In the transition from the Industrial Age to the Information Age business is being transformed in all its aspects. Computers have changed the way offices are organized and the tasks done. They have changed manufacturing, purchasing, marketing, finance, and management. The ethical issues are therefore not simply issues that are involved in computers and their use and in information technology more broadly, but in the way business is done in the Information Age.

We can distinguish five different kinds of ethical problems connected with information technology:

1 Ethical issues in the use of technology in business
2 Ethical issues in the information technology business
3 Ethical issues dealing with the Internet
4 Ethical issues in e-business
5 Ethical issues resulting from the impact of computers and information technology on society, both nationally and internationally

The five are interrelated.

Lurking behind all of them is the Myth of Amoral Computers and Information Technology. This is the widespread belief that computers and information technology have nothing to do with ethics. Computers, of course, are a type of machine and are not moral beings. But they are developed, programmed, and used by human beings. Nonetheless, "The computer is down" is often taken as a valid excuse, as if no one is to blame for this and no moral blame should be assessed. That there are human beings who are responsible for making sure that the computer is up seems beyond the realm of one's imagination. Similarly, "It's a computer error" seems to exonerate anyone from any responsibility for the error. The myth covers over the fact that those who use computers are responsible for them and for their proper use. Before computers, if there was a billing error, one did not blame the calculator. Yet somehow, what can be attributed to the computer is free of moral evaluation. The result, and part of the myth, is that human beings are relieved of responsibility to the extent that computers are involved. It may be that this is the result of the ordinary person's limited knowledge of the workings of computers and of the feeling that, when something goes wrong, it is not their fault – as well it may not be. But mechanical failures do not exonerate those responsible for their operation to the extent that computer failures do.

Crimes, such as theft and fraud, are as unethical if committed by the use of computers as if they are done any other way. But when done by computer there is no face-to-face encounter, no harm to a seen person, no physical violence. The act takes on an impersonal quality that helps hide responsibility. Unethical hackers, who enter into secured computers owned by corporations or government or other people often say that they intend no harm; they just want to test their skill. And in the process their entry lets those whose sites they violate know that the security measures they have employed are not adequate. Yet these same people would never break into homes or offices to demonstrate that the locks on the doors are not secure. The distance that the computer allows, the anonymity that it makes possible, the element of a game that it sometimes fosters, all help cover over any sense of wrongdoing or the acceptance of responsibility. Nonetheless, surreptitious entry, "cracking" other people's or company's sites, stealing passwords, unleashing viruses are all clearly unethical, even if not seen to be so by some of the perpetrators.

The failure to take responsibility is widespread, from those who write the programs to those who release them commercially before all (or most) of the bugs have been eliminated, to those who use them to serve their customers. Not only hackers but people who would never think of secretly entering fellow workers' offices or going through their files cabinets, think little of looking at their computer files by using a password they have learned or by guessing at it. Entry is from the privacy of one's office, not a physical break. One's search is done seemingly anonymously and no one is physically hurt. Actions in a virtual world or in Cyberspace are not evaluated from a moral point of view the way actions in the physical world are.

Part of the reason for the myth is that computers and information technology have developed so fast that the moral intuitions of the ordinary person and so of society as a whole have not had time to be formed and develop. Information technology necessitates a rethinking of many practices in business – and in society more broadly – that has not yet taken place. Another complementary reason is that, absent the necessary rethinking, laws governing and restraining much unethical activity involving computers and information technology have been slow in coming.

One of the things society has learned from the Industrial Age is that certain business practices that harm many in society are not corrected by the market and require legislation. The challenge in the Information Age is to pass the necessary legislation before the harmful practices become entrenched. But in a democracy, this means that the consciousness of the population has to be raised to demand the legislation – which has been equally slow to develop. Unmasking the Myth of Amoral Computing and Information Technology requires raising public consciousness of the ethical issues raised by computers and IT.

Ethical Issues in the Use of Technology in Business

Since information technology has changed the way business is done, ethical issues arise in all of the areas of business.

One topic that can serve to illustrate a range of issues is privacy, which affects both marketing with respect to consumers and management with respect to employees.

Privacy concerns the limits that one puts on access to oneself. The notion of privacy varies somewhat from society to society, even though the right to privacy is listed as one of the rights in the Universal Declaration of Human Rights. For our purposes, we can focus on personal information privacy and communication privacy.

Computers have made important changes in marketing. It is now possible to compile large databases on consumers, to merge databases, to infer potential information from data acquired. The degree to which the collection and use of information on customers is possible has increased enormously. The collection and compilation of data on customers' credit card use, bank histories, employment records and so on by the large credit companies make possible almost instant credit at department stores and other retail outlets. That is a benefit for many. It comes at the possible cost of individual information privacy.

In 1991, Lotus, together with the credit company Equifax, announced its intent to make available to small businesses information on potential customers who fit a certain profile. The product – Lotus Marketplace: Households – contained information on 80 million families, including name, address, telephone number, and inferred information such as income. When it was announced, privacy groups launched a campaign and Lotus was quickly inundated with over 35,000 letters and emails of protest. It withdrew the product. Nonetheless, the capacity for developing and selling such a product clearly exists, and personal information of a similar type is sold extensively.

Under information privacy, we can group four different but related issues: the collection of personal information, informed consent, confidentiality, and responsibility for errors and harm.

The collection of personal information

To what extent is one's privacy violated by the collection, collation, and selling information about individuals? Is the dissemination of large amounts of information about one, without that individual's knowledge, a violation of one's privacy?

To the extent that one's privacy consists in a state of affairs in which one limits access to oneself, proponents of privacy argue that one's privacy is violated by the practice, since it makes one's vulnerable to access, domination, and possible harm by unknown people, vendors or government. One's medical records, for instance, may be revealed by one's employer to the company's medical insurer, and it may then be sold or used in ways and by persons the employee is not even aware of. Similarly, one's purchases of prescription drugs from pharmacies charged on a credit card, may find their way into a data base compiled on one, accessible by potential employers, by other insurance companies, and by marketers of all types. One may be denied insurance, or employment, or suffer in other ways, sometimes based in inaccurate data.

Less sensitive, perhaps, are one's purchasing habits. Yet these too may reveal more of oneself than an individual making individual purchases wishes or intends to reveal, and may leave the individual open to ridicule, shame, embarrassment or the like. The problem is only exacerbated when the data is mined to infer a variety of things about an individual, which may or may not be accurate.

The collection of such information also makes one vulnerable to harms such as identity theft, in which a third party obtains one's social security number and other identifiable information and then uses them and one's good credit rating to open up new charge accounts and sometimes even to empty the victim's bank account.

The threat of misuse by government of the vast account of information it gathers in a variety of ways is a fear that some have. But legislation seems to be more acceptable in limiting cross-referencing and the use of information gathered by the government for one purpose (such as income tax or census), than is the case for business use of information that businesses gather.

Informed consent

In some areas of life, such as medicine, the doctrine of informed consent is firmly established. In business it is present to a limited extent. In the United States there are various truth in lending laws that mandate that customers be given information about interest rates and sign a form explaining the real rates. Many states also mandate a three-day period during which certain transactions can be rescinded by the customer – for instance real estate purchases and other purchases in which high-pressure sales techniques are often used and to which one may later regret having succumbed.

Yet to be determined in a large number of areas involving computer transactions and the Internet, however, is whether informed consent is ethically appropriate, whether it is implicit, and whether it should be made explicit. One example is the use of credit cards. When one uses a credit card, does one implicitly consent to having the information about one's charges collected and then sold by the credit card company to interested businesses or individuals? The practice is widespread. But it is usually done without the customer's knowledge, and so without his explicit consent. The least that seems appropriate is that such information be included in the credit card agreement that one initially signs. The question of what one consents to in purchases, in mail orders, in subscriptions, and so on, is rarely made explicit. Yet these are the sources of much of the information that is gathered on people. Hence, privacy advocates claim with some justification that the informed consent of customers should be required about what information on them is collected, how it will be used, whether it will be shared or sold and to whom (perhaps by category). At present this is rarely the case.

With respect to public documents – for instance, birth and marriage information – what is the purpose of such records, and is it consistent with that purpose that these records and other public records be placed on the Internet and made readily available to anyone wishing to call up all public records on any individual for any purpose? When one goes to a public records office to see a document one usually is identifiable, and the act is a public act. It also takes time and effort and one's privacy is thereby protected to some extent, even though the information is public. There has been little discussion or debate about making public records widely available, except with respect to drivers' licenses. In this latter case, many people reacted negatively when some states started selling this information to those wishing to buy it. The information was especially sensitive when it included social security numbers, or when the driver's license number was the individual's social security number.

Confidentiality

Like informed consent, sometimes there is a legitimate expectation of confidentiality – for instance in one's interaction with one's doctor. Unless there is confidentiality, one will not reveal one's ills in all the detail necessary for proper diagnosis and treatment. One expects confidentiality with respect to one's dealing with lawyers. What about with one's bank? Here the situation is less clear. People may expect it, but that does not mean that one's transactions are confidential, and often they are not. Like informed consent, the extent to which one's credit card use, one's subscriptions, one's purchases are confidential is minimal. This made little difference before the widespread use of computers and the large databases they make possible. The changing situation raises issues of the possible violation of confidentiality and demands rethinking and clarifying and making explicit which transactions are confidential, which are not, and the degree of confidentiality in any given case.

Responsibility for errors and harm

Until recently those who stole someone else's identity and used that to open charge accounts, get credit cards, and withdraw their bank deposits acted with relative impunity. Such crimes were not pursued vigilantly because they involved no physical harm. Credit card companies limited liability of the person defrauded to $50.00, but the large credit services did little to restore the credit-worthiness of the victims. No party assumed responsibility, even though victims' lives were sometimes turned into nightmares because of the illicit use by someone else of information about them available from computer databases. The crimes and harm were bad enough. The lack of any party accepting responsibility for making the crime possible or for precluding it was and continues to be largely ignored.

Communication privacy raises issues in three separate areas with respect to information technology and employees: e-mail and internet use; surveillance; and records.

E-mail and Internet use

Both of these raise ethical issues related to employees and privacy. In the USA, law protects the Federal mail. People have the knowledge that one's mail, addressed to an individual, is private. Hence it is natural, although a mistake, for employees and the general public to believe that by analogy their e-mail is similarly protected by law. It is not. Legally, whatever is on the computer in a business belongs to the business. This includes e-mail sent by individuals within a company. There are then two ethical issues. The first is the amount of privacy, if any, employees should have, despite the legal doctrine. The second is proper notification of employees of the company's policy.

What does respect for persons imply or demand, if anything, with respect to employees? Should they be allowed any privacy with respect to e-mail? Should they be allowed to use company e-mail for limited personal use, and, if so, should that be considered private? It is usual and reasonable for companies to allow employees to make a limited number of personal calls on the telephone – especially if they have to work late, or an emergency arises, or if they have to be contacted by children or others because of personal circumstances. Such calls are generally considered personal and private. Should a similar policy be extended to the use of e-mail? Exactly how much privacy should be accorded workers is a disputed topic. It is clear that official documents are corporate property and should be accessible to those who need them if the person who generated them is not present. Yet this need not necessitate either the routine or the random scrutiny of employee's e-mail. In some cases, such as in response to a subpoena or a criminal investigation, a company may have to legally turn over e-mail to the proper authorities. There are programs that will search through all e-mail that is sent looking for key words. In some cases the words searched are words of complaint, and the program is used by management to catch disgruntled workers who send disparaging e-mails about the firm or the executives or the sender's boss. The key words to be searched are entered by the executives or those in charge of information technology in the firm. The use of the program is legal; but is it ethical?

Without resolving this debated question, the least that ethics demands is that employees be notified what the proper use of e-mail is in the firm for which they work; whether personal use is allowed and, if so, to what extent; whether e-mail will be routinely read by third parties, or read randomly, or be subject to word-content searches; whether it will be archived; who may have access to it under which specified conditions; and what the penalties are for misuse. Such notification provides the employees with the information they deserve to have so they know the conditions under which they work. To fail to do this, and then to read messages that at least some employees think is private, is to knowingly and willingly deceive them, and not to treat them with the respect they deserve.

A similar problem arises with the use of the Internet. Clearly employees are not paid to spend any significant periods of time browsing the web for their own interests and amusement. Such action would be tantamount to stealing time for which they are paid. Checking the stock market quotations or trading on the Web, searching for information on one's hobby, shopping, or looking at pornography are typical uses of which employers complain. Which are permissible and which not are decisions that each company should make. It might not be unreasonable for a company to allow its employees to spend a few minutes checking, say, stock quotations; and it would not be unreasonable to allow them to use the Internet during their free time. It is also not unreasonable to prohibit access to porno-graphic sites, which can trace the accessing computer back to the company and may generate pornographic spam and other unsolicited and inappropriate ads – all of which may also lead to legal complaints by others of a hostile sexual environment. As with e-mail, there are programs that can track the Web use of any and all employees and there are programs that can monitor use and flag those accessing prohibited sites. Whether companies should use such programs is again a debated issue, and companies have taken different stances. Some trust their employees to make proper use of the Internet and only check when excess use seems to interfere with an individual's work or when there is a complaint by a third party. Some prohibit any personal use of the Internet. Some avoid the problem by not making the Internet available at most workstations. Although ethics requires that employees be treated fairly and with respect, it does not demand any one set of rules of Internet use. As with e-mail, however, ethics does demand that the company's policy be clearly made known to the employees. Penalties should not be imposed for improper use of the Internet without the rules for its proper use being clearly spelled out.

Surveillance

Implicit in our discussion of both e-mail and Internet use has been the ethics of surveillance of employees by employers. Computer technology has made sur-veillance of employees possible in greater detail than previously imaginable. Every keystroke can be recorded, including mistakes, and the speed at which characters are typed – making every activity of an employee at a computer open to surveillance. Cameras, hidden or exposed, can watch every movement of every employee. The technology is available. In such circumstances what rights, if any, to privacy do employees have? To what extent is it appropriate to track their every movement, every keystroke, every action? The answer, of course, depends on the type of activity in which the employee is engaged. If they are money counters at a casino, their every action is appropriately surveyed while they are in the money room counting the day's take. The need for surveillance, even here, however, surely stops with the restroom or the locker room where employees change into their uniforms.

Surveillance is a means of control, and the control should be both appropriate to the task and the surveillance made known to the employee. A camera on a cashier might be considered necessary both to prevent theft by the cashier and to record theft or attempted theft by customers. What is the purpose of surveillance of every keystroke by employees? Does this turn work into sweat shop conditions in which workers are pushed to their limits or is it an effective means to measure productivity and increase efficiency? There may be proper uses of such technology. But they require justification, and should not be used to harass employees. Such surveillance, if used to track output and rate of work does not violate the workers' privacy in the usual sense, although it may intimidate them or inhibit even their appropriate actions for fear of how the record of their action may be interpreted.

Records

No matter how their records are kept – whether on paper or on computer – employees deserve the same amount of confidentiality. Computer records are often not safeguarded to the same extent that paper records are. The privacy of workers – their medical records, their evaluations, and in some firms their salaries – are personal. The personnel record of employees should be available for their inspection to prevent and correct errors; they should be purged periodically of out-of-date material; and they should be kept secure. Purging is often necessitated with paper files because there is only so much room in file cabinets. This is not a problem with computer files, and hence it is an area that deserves careful checking.

Privacy is obviously not the only issue in the use of technology in business. Yet it demonstrates one aspect of the changes being brought by IT in marketing and management, and some of the ethical issues they raise.

Ethical Issues in the Information Technology Business

We can divide the issues we shall be concerned with here into two classes: those that have to do with the responsibility of software and hardware providers; and those that have to do with property.

Under responsibility, we shall deal briefly with responsibility for computers and programs; guarantees and harm; and risk.

Responsibility for computers and computer programs

We have already noted the absence of responsibility as present in the Myth of Amoral Computing and Information Technology. The lack of responsibility carries over into the information technology business. The general public, evidently, is so impressed with the accomplishments of those in the information technology field that they have accepted their excuses for program and hardware failure with little complaint. Customers do not usually accept products that fail with regularity as coming up to the expected state of the art for any product. Yet when operating systems or computer applications fail with some regularity they are accepted as part of the technology. They need not be, and one can raise the issue of the ethical obligation of software providers.

Granted, in any complex program there will be some bugs, or glitches that are unforeseeable. But before being considered marketable, programs should be adequately tested and the vast majority of bugs found and corrected. A once in a thousand year bug is within the level of acceptability. A program that crashes five times a day is not. Developers often issue Beta versions of their programs so that interested people can test the software and report bugs they find. This is an unusual approach to product development, in which customers test products for the developer. But there is nothing unethical about it if the customer knows the conditions under which he is receiving the program. Often the beta version is distributed free, so one gets use of the program early in return for the nuisance of encountering bugs. What is unethical is to distribute versions of a software product that have not been adequately tested and debugged. Frequently the justification for so doing is to beat the competition to the market with a new product. But if all developers were held to the same standard of reliable software, competition would remain without the burden being placed on the consumer. The ethical norm that should be expected and demanded is the kind of reliability that one finds in other products. Lamps, automobiles, TV sets are sometimes defective. But if any of them is produced with a defect and the defect is not simply the result of some mishap and replaced, the item is recalled and fixed properly. Why computer programs are exempt from such standards requires justification that has not been forthcoming.

In both hardware and software, the producers should be held responsible for their products. This leads to warranties and harm. The typical warranty for software is replacement. Replacement of one copy of software that is bug-ridden with an identical program is, of course, of no use. So the warranty does not cover bugs. Sometimes, there is technical assistance available provided by a company to work through problems that a customer may have in installing or using a program. Because of the lack of uniform standards and the complexity of many programs, incompatibility problems are frequent. Hence customers have the need for technical assistance. But if available and included in the price of the product, then it is unreasonable for customers to have to wait on hold on the telephone for an hour or longer for help. Some companies are very good in this regard. Others are not, and it is the terrible ones that raise ethical concern. It is not only bad business but also unethical to treat people in this way.

Warranties for software are typically limited to replacing a defective program with a non-defective one. What the producer considers defective and what the consumer considers defective may vary considerably. The producer writes the warranty and defines the conditions of the sale unilaterally. It is typical that one must break the shrinkwrap around the statement of the conditions of sale to see them, but doing so indicates one's acceptance of them. In some cases one must actually begin installing a program before the conditions appear on the screen and one is informed that one must accept them to proceed. Once again one learns the conditions of sale only after installation of the product has begun. The extent to which customers are stuck with products if they refuse to accept the conditions is often not clear. It should be.

The typical program accepts no responsibility for what it calls "consequent damages." If during the installation of the program the installation fouls up the computer's registry and requires that the operating system be reinstalled, the time and cost involved are borne by the consumer, not the supplier of the product. If the program crashes and destroys other files, if it leads to expensive loss of time and money, this again is borne by the customer.

Guarantees and harm

Most other products are covered in the United States by strict liability laws, under which the producer is responsible for any damage suffered by a consumer from the use, and even often from the misuse, of a product. Strict liability does not extend to computer programs. The rationale for strict liability is that the producer is given an incentive to make the product as safe as possible; the producer is in a better position than the consumer to self-insure by adding a small amount to every sale to cover the cost of possible damages; and defects are likely to be brought to the attention of the producer immediately and repaired as quickly as possible to prevent further suits. The rationale applies as well to computer programs. But strict liability has not been extended to them. One reason may be that the harm done from other products is often physical harm, and harm from computer program failure or defect is rarely of this type and is often minor. Nonetheless, the application of strict liability to computer programs is certainly an issue that deserves discussion it has not received.

The situation is somewhat different when it comes to computer hardware or computer chips that are parts of other hardware. Here the more traditional ethical and legal rules apply the same as in other areas. A new ethical issue in this regard, however, arises from the substitution of software for hardware in a variety of safety-sensitive areas and applications. The problem comes from the difficulty of providing redundancy in software, the way one does with hardware. Typically hardware fails because of some material defect, and another system or even another instance of the same part can take over when something fails. Software often fails because of some mistake in the program, some overlooked possibility, some aspect of the real world that was not built into the model on which the program was based. Having another copy of the same program does not provide redundancy. And having another program that was written according to the same model also does not provide redundancy. Hence those involved in possibly dangerous software applications must ensure safety to the extent possible.

Risk

The first rule of all engineering codes is to hold the safety of the public paramount and this ethical norm applies as well with software and hardware computer applications. Almost all human activities involve some risk – crossing the street, driving or riding in a car or plane or train, being in a building, crossing a bridge, turning on an electrical appliance. What engineers do is make the risk as small as possible. In a car, we know that some cars are safer than others. All must come up to a certain standard. But all can be vehicles of death in certain circumstances. Often one can buy more safety by buying a more expensive, or perhaps a bigger and heavier car. Risk is minimized and thereafter ethics requires that one be informed of the risk one is assuming, that one know how to avoid or minimize the risk, and that one know the alternatives. If the alternative to a less safe car is a more expensive one, one may choose (because of necessity) the less safe but cheaper one.

The same rules apply to computer products and products that use computer chips. Ethically, the risk should be made minimal; users should be informed of the risk; and they should be informed of the alternatives. Consumers are not generally engineers. Hence, the risks should be made clear to the users and purchasers in understandable terms.

The second major area is property, which raises issues of the ownership of programs, copyright and patents, and multiple use by purchaser.

Ownership of programs

Programs are a form of intellectual property. Like other forms of intellectual property they can be copied or stolen or shared, without depriving the original owner of them. But anyone of these does deprive the original owner of his or her exclusive use. When software first began to be developed, most of it was shared with other programmers freely. In this way many people could improve on a program and share the improvements to the benefit of all. Some programmers continue to feel that it is in the best interest of society that software code be open and shared with all interested in improving it. But this is not the general rule. Some code is open and shared. Some software is freeware, that is, available to anyone interested in obtaining it, usually downloading it from the World Wide Web. Some programs are shareware, that is, they are free to copy and use, but if one continues to use them, the user is expected to pay some modest fee for the continued use of the program. Most software is commercial, and covered by some sort of legal protection.

Software is written in a computer language, called the source code or source language. To be used by the computer it must be translated into what is called an object code, or machine language consisting of strings of zeros and ones. For a number of years machine code could not be protected by copyright, but the source code could, even though the latter was translated into the former by a compiler. This anomaly was changed and now both can be protected by copyright. Until fairly recently, software could not be protected by patent. That also has now changed and some software is patentable, providing it meets certain conditions. Software can also be protected by trade secrecy. Protected software is licensed to users. Copyright, patents, and licensing with respect to computer programs are all controversial and involve ethical as well as legal issues.

Who owns a program is at the heart of much controversy. In dealing with programs, as with many areas involving computers, society has found it useful to argue by analogy. What is a program like, and is it enough like whatever analogy is used to apply the same rules as we apply to the analogue?

Programs are in some ways like documents or books in that they contain databases or information. A program of medical information serves a function very comparable to a medical reference book. In some ways, programs are like a machine, in that they do something. A word processing program, for instance, turns a computer into a very fancy typewriter. For purposes of liability, courts have considered whether programs are more like books or more like machines. The same type of reasoning has been applied to copyright and patent protection of software. The analogies are, of course, just that – analogies.

Copyrights and patents

In the case of both copyright and patent the existing statutes have simply been extended to cover software, even though neither is a very good fit. The lack of fit is clear when one looks at the history of the application of each to programs and the difficulties that have arisen. Those who defend the use of existing legislation argue that copyright and patent protection are the only means recognized worldwide and that the introduction of any other new kind of protection would not grant adequate protection world-wide. The counter argument is that every nation faces a similar problem and what is required is a new kind of protection appropriate to software that is agreed upon by all nations at an appropriate international convention.

Copyright originally covered written material and now by extension, pictures, motion pictures, music, etc. Copyright law was recently extended to provide protection for the expression of ideas to seventy years plus the life of an author (ninety-five years for a corporate author). Many software companies claim that software tends to be outdated within four years. Protection for 95 years seems peculiar and not tailor-made for the product. Patents are granted for 17 years from the time the patent is granted or 20 years from the date of application. Patent is granted for inventions, machines or devices that are useful and non-obvious to people skilled in the area in question. They are not granted for ideas, mathematical or scientific formulae or for facts of nature.

Until recently algorithms for programs could not be patented, just as mathematical algorithms cannot be patented. This changed with the *Diamond v. Diehr Supreme Court* decision in 1981. Now some algorithms, which are the general formulae for writing a program, can be patented. This is a much stronger claim to ownership than copyright, since it covers various ways of performing some activity. The rule was that algorithms could be patented if they were included as a necessary part of some virtual machine. Critics claim that the patent office personnel granting patents are not trained in computers sufficiently to know when certain applications are obvious, and are granting patents to many algorithms, hampering the development of new software. This is because developers must now conduct costly patent searches to make sure that what they develop is not already patented. The patents, critics further claim, are held by a relatively small number of firms that have thousands of patents and charge licensing fees for anyone that wishes to use one of their products, even though the developer could develop it itself.

The ethical justification for the protection now available still relies on the claim that patents and copyright provide protection to the developers of socially useful items, and that without such protection there would be little incentive for people or companies to develop new products, since competitors would immediately copy them and sell them at lower prices than the originator, who has to recoup investment and development costs. Whether in fact copyright and patent with respect to software is enhancing or undercutting software development is a debated point. If the latter is the case, then the ethical justification no longer holds.

Whatever means is ultimately determined best for protection of software, it is clear that some sort of protection is necessary and appropriate. Even those who defend the free availability of source code admit this. Operating systems and commercial applications are not the center of debate.

Multiple use by purchaser

It is clear that piracy of music, films, literary works, and programs is unethical. It is stealing. Less clear, however, is what constitutes or what should constitute fair use of products one buys. When VCRs first appeared, some companies claimed that videotaping a program or a movie for one to view later violated copyright rules. The courts ruled otherwise. One cannot only copy such programs, one can also lend the copy to a friend, just as one can lend the copy of a book one buys. Yet one cannot legally lend a copy of an application program to a friend. Arguing by analogy, many claim this is unfair. By analogy when one buys a copy of a book one cannot of course copy and resell it as one's own. But the individual book belongs to the purchaser and he or she may lend it to others, read it to others, and so on.

Those who sell software, however, claim that the analogy does not hold. For they do not sell the program to the purchaser, even though the purchaser may think they do. What they sell is a license to use the program. This, in itself, makes it seem less like the objects that are traditionally covered by copyright. The license, moreover, is spelled out in the material that comes with the commercial program, as we have already noted. Usually the license allows the purchaser to make a backup copy and to use the program on only one machine at a time. If one has both a desktop computer at home and a portable, it can only be used on one machine at a time. Otherwise, a license for two programs should be purchased. Many users find this an indefensible restriction, and one which they flout with impunity. The principle of licensing a program for use on one machine makes sense if, for instance, a company will install a word processing program on a thousand computers in the company. Then it should purchase a license for 1000 users, and the unit price would be lowered accordingly. But not letting an individual user lend a copy of a program to a friend is felt by many to be unreasonable. The practice is widespread, and still computer programming companies flourish. The latter may claim lost sales. But it is difficult to show that those to whom the programs were lent would have bought a copy, and some argue that if they like the product the borrowers tend to become users and so purchase later versions. The law is clear on the issue, even though it is rarely enforced against individual users, since it is so difficult to know who is sharing or borrowing or lending to a friend. This is different, of course, from making available free from one's Web site a commercial program that one has purchased, since that does clearly violate the rights of the producer.

Ethical Issues Dealing with the Internet

The ethical issues we have already seen are repeated, sometimes exacerbated, and new ones arise when we turn to the Internet.

The issue of the violation of privacy is one problem that is exacerbated by the Internet and on the Internet. When we shop in a mall or in a city, no one tracks us, follows us from store to store, notes what we look at for how long, what we buy, what we do not buy. It would be highly unusual for this to happen, and if it did we might rightfully complain, if we were aware of it, to the local policeman that someone was following us. On the Internet, even though we access it from the privacy of our home, our every move can be and often is routinely tracked.

Not only are cookies – small bits of information about our visiting a particular site placed on our computer's hard drive – but advertising businesses, such as Double Click, through the banners displayed on various sites can track us as we move from site to site. The tracking is not disclosed to us as we move from site to site, and so is done surreptitiously, and without any request for consent, much less informed consent. If we enter any personal data on any site, that can then be correlated with the tracking information. That, in turn, can be correlated with information about us in other databases.

The issues of violation of privacy, lack of informed consent and confidentiality, and potential harm all reappear in an exacerbated form.

Property issues similarly reappear. The complaints about the unfairness of patents came to a head with Amazon.com, Inc.'s patent on "one-click" purchasing, when it patented a way to click once instead of twice when a customer places an order. Critics claim that this and other techniques for which patents have been awarded are obvious to programmers who work in the area and that the patents restrict development instead of promoting it, as patents were originally intended to do.

While patents raise one set of property issues, copyright raises another. Sites on the Internet are multimedia, involving sound, graphics, and text, often mixed in new and creative ways. Exactly what combinations can be copyrighted and protected, however, is not clear. Moreover, it is very easy to copy any aspect of what appears on a website, and enforcing protection is extremely difficult.

The ease of copying raises questions of fair use. May one user of a recording of a particular song, for instance, share that with a friend? If one places one's CD music collection on one's website, others can download any item or the whole collection. Now we have an indefinitely large number of users doing this and then making their collections available to anyone else, and downloading from others those pieces they do not already have. No one is selling any of the pieces, and so no one is profiting financially. Yet it is clear that if this becomes widespread, the sale of new material would plummet, as potential buyers copied the recording free from someone on the Web instead of buying it. Unlike allowing a friend to make a copy, one now allows anyone in the world to copy one's recordings without charge. The practice cannot continue indefinitely without taking away the profits that attract those who make the recordings, and so without possibly undermining the music industry. For this reason, as well as because the practice violates copyright law, the practice is unethical. Yet even if made illegal, policing such legislation would be impractical, since there is no central distributor or middleman facilitating the arrangement but potentially millions of individual users.

The issue or piracy or the stealing and selling of commercially produced material seems clearly unethical, although some cultures seem to feel otherwise and claim that intellectual property cannot be owned. The piracy of videotapes in some countries is common. In the near future, when movies can be downloaded on the web as easily as music, the problem will escalate. Whether our notions of fair use, ownership of intellectual property, and the marketing of digitalized products will change remains to be seen.

Other practices are new since the introduction of the Internet. For instance, take a website such as ebay.com, which auctions off almost any kind of item. Who owns the information about the prices and bids on the site? Items auctioned there are also often auctioned on specialized sites. Suppose another webmaster collects all the bids on each individual item and then posts that, advertising that they can get the item from the site with the lowest price for a small fee, saving the purchaser the hours of trying to locate and compare all the different sites. Is this ethical or does the information on each site belong to the owner of that site? The bids are public in the sense that they are open to any viewer to see. But the site surely has a claim on the organization of the contents. To have a third party copy all that information and compile it together with information copied from many other sites is prima facie unethical, yet not illegal, for one cannot copyright constantly changing bids.

The fact that the Internet is global only makes the problems more difficult. Each country can pass laws that it deems appropriate. But unless they are coordinated, and agreements made as to who will prosecute and what the penalties will be, there is often little legal control.

This is evident at present when someone in one country launches a virus that can cause millions of dollars in damage and untold difficulties to users in a great many other countries. Clearly, such destruction of property is unethical. But it is not illegal in every country and when the perpetrator is in such a country it is difficult to prosecute, even if the perpetrator can be found.

Closely related to this are the problems raised by anonymity and by encryption. Anonymity can be achieved by using a variety of different means to prevent visited sites from knowing the real identity of the person visiting or the computer used to visit the site. It can thus be used to protect one's privacy. But using an anonymous server also makes it possible for people to avoid responsibility for their actions – be they fraud, illegal solicitation, hate speech directed at particular people, spamming, and so on. The first use – protecting privacy – is ethical. The second in most instances is not. The problem is how to make possible the first while still keeping people responsible for their actions. Similarly, encryption protects one's privacy by making e-mails and other transmissions very difficult or impossible to intercept in any readable form. Clearly, this is useful in safeguarding all financial transactions – from bank transfers to the use of credit card payments made on the Internet. But strong encryption can also be used by criminals to prevent the government from learning their plans or activities by making surveillance of their transaction with a court order useless. For a number of years, the US government tried to prevent the use of strong encryption without supplying the government with a means of breaking the encryption codes if necessary to carry out surveillance of suspected criminals and terrorists. Businesses, however, complained that the rules put them at a competitive disadvantage because other governments did not have such requirements and stronger encryption was available outside the USA. The rules have been weakened considerably, but the ethical issue remains unresolved.

The possibility of fraud on the Internet is closely associated with the fact that anyone can post anything on the Internet. Disinformation as well as information, partial truths, questionable claims and data all appear as information. Clearly, fraud, misleading statements, deliberate misinformation are unethical. But often there is no way for users to know whether or not what they find on the Internet is information that is accurate and reliable. There is little in the way of authentication of Websites, even of a medical kind, although there are sites that try to list reliable medical sources. There is also a need for being able to verify that the person with whom one is in contact is in fact the person one believes him or her to be, or that the site is a legitimate site.

Various unethical and questionable practices have emerged. One is cybersquatting or the purchasing of domain names that are likely to be chosen by corporations or political candidates, and then charging exorbitant fees for the name. Another is the choosing of a domain name with one key-stoke different from another domain name with the expectation that people will with some frequency type the mistake and be led to the second site, believing they are at the first one. The second site might be a commercial competitor or it might be the site of an opposed political party from the first, or someone with some grudge or complaint against the first, and so on. Although not illegal, the intent is clearly to trade on the user's mistakes and take advantage of that mistake, and so is arguably unethical.

Another set of issues deals with freedom of speech vs. censorship, with children and advertising, and with pornography and children. Although none of these is peculiar to the Internet and comparable issues are found elsewhere, the issues take on a special complexion on the Internet.

Two aspects of freedom of speech vs. censorship make the problem especially important with respect to the Internet. The first is that the international nature of the Internet makes it difficult to control pornography that originates in a great many different countries. From a legal point of view, even if pornography is illegal in one country, it is possible for it not to be illegal to produce in another country and it can be accessed with ease. The second problem has to do with children. Many libraries are struggling with the issue of how they can restrict access of pornography to children and still make it available to consenting adults. Chat rooms and bulletin boards on the Internet in addition pose problems with child predators.

Also problematic is the manipulation of children by advertisers, who often seek and obtain personal information from children who do not realize the full implications of the information they are revealing about themselves and their families.

Ethical Issues in E-Business

Many traditional firms have entered the realm of e-business, and others exist only as e-businesses. Of the latter, Dell and Amazon.com are prime examples. Increasingly important are also B2B or business-to-business sites.

One issue concerns location, and so taxation. Should purchases made on the Internet be taxed the way mail order businesses are taxed in the USA, state by state, with taxes levied only in those states in which the company has a physical presence? What exactly constitutes a physical presence for an e-business, and if the company also has traditional stores, should that count as a physical presence for the e-business, even if no goods are sold or shipped from those locations? What is fair with respect to competition, to the revenues of states and local communities, to consumers? A three-year moratorium on taxation was granted to e-business in the USA, but there is a hot debate between those who hold that taxation will undermine e-business and so produce more harm overall than good, and those who argue that lack of taxation constitutes unfair competition.

Employees in both e-business and in traditional businesses now often work from computers at home. At one point OSHA became concerned about safety of the workplace for such workers. But public reaction was overwhelmingly negative to the idea of government inspectors entering homes and applying OSHA regulations there. Yet what of workman's compensation for injuries at home but while the person is working? Is it fair for companies to be liable and yet to have no control over the conditions for which they will be held liable in case of accident? Is it fair not to have worker's compensation for those who work at home? How much monitoring of those who work at home is appropriate, and how does one fairly check productivity without invading the privacy of an employee's home?

On the Internet, we have already seen the ethical issues in tracking. Yet the preferred method of advertising on the Internet is not broadcast but one-on-one, which requires tailoring one's ads to those with the appropriate interests, income, and needs, and requires having access to the appropriate information about potential customers. Of course, one-on-one marketing is not essential, and e-business would certainly survive without it. Some potential customers want it; others do not, and feel it is an invasion of their privacy. A method that allows for informed consent, with opt-out as the default is arguably the most ethically defensible alternative.

Authenticity of sites, the prevention of fraud, and the security of payments are all issues that pose problems and for which solutions are being sought.

We have already noted problems in the interaction of children and the Internet. Sites that solicit information from children for marketing or other purposes, and that conduct one-on-one marketing to children are ethically suspect. The general rules regarding the ethics of advertising to children in other media apply on the Internet as well. Misleading ads, misrepresentation, and manipulation are all unethical practices.

The general ethical rules of business apply in e-business as well. The new issues are emerging as such business develops.

Ethical Issues Resulting from the Impact of Computers and Information Technology on Society, Both Nationally and Internationally

The social implications of computer technology and the internet are many. We shall briefly deal with only six: technological development; the view of human beings; the changing nature of work; haves and have-nots; democracy and control; and international legal coordination

Technological development

The impact of technology on culture and society is not limited to the use of the computer and to information technology. But these have clearly affected most contemporary societies and will continue to do so. The greatest threat is what can be called the "technological imperative," namely, that whatever is possible to produce technologically will be produced and developed. Are there technologies that should not be developed? Are there limits that should be placed on techno-logical development? If so, what are they, who should determine them and who should enforce them? The scientific community has delayed the development of human cloning. Are there areas in which computer technologists should exercise similar restraints? Should we develop the perfect assassin or the perfect bank robber or the unstoppable robot, if any of these become theoretically possible?

The view of human beings

Norbert Wiener (1954) in *The Human Use of Human Beings* and later Joseph Weizenbaum (1976) in *Computer Power and Human Reason* both raised the issue of what it means to be a human being in the technological age. The Copernican revolution meant that the earth was no longer the center of the universe, shaking the view of human beings as the privileged center of everything; the theory of evolution challenged for some the special place of human beings in nature; the computer is having a similar impact, causing some to wonder whether human beings are simply complicated meat machines and whether eventually we will be out paced and possibly replaced by our own creations. The result is a new challenge to the notion of the dignity and importance of the human person. People tend to become manipulable pawns as it becomes more and more difficult to see what is unique about them that cannot be replaced by a computer. Machines have already to a large extent replaced the drudgery work. Intellectual work is now similarly being taken over more and more by computers, which calculate faster, remember more accurately, and process information at incredible speeds. Computer language more and more slips into ordinary speech as one human function after another is described in computer terms. Wiener described the human use of human beings, and underscored the importance of using computers for human beings. The danger is that computers become more and more dominant and people became subservient to them. The image of individuals who work from home and interact with others only through their computers is an image many find unattractive, if not demeaning. The anarchy of the information age in which no one is in charge, no conductor is orchestrating development, no one controlling harmful applications may yield untold changes in the future that should be morally evaluated.

The changing nature of work

We have already noted some changes brought about by e-business, and some of the possibilities of monitoring and tracking that are changing the workplace. Machines, often run by computers, are increasingly replacing work of a physical type. Robots can do dangerous jobs as well as repetitious ones. The nineteenth century saw the replacement of hand labor by machine labor in the industrial countries. The same trend is presently taking place in the less developed countries. In the Information Age, the processing of information and the application of that information will form the major tasks for workers. We have already touched on worker privacy and the ethics of surveillance. What new rights for workers will emerge, what virtues other than truthfulness and accuracy will be necessary, and how the power and responsibility of management should be balanced in the decentralized corporation all raise ethical issues still too vague to be definitively stated, much less answered.

Haves and have-nots

The issue arises on the national and on the international level. The haves and have nots are not only the rich and the poor, but also the computer literate and the computer illiterate. Just as the ability to read made an important difference in the jobs available during the twentieth century, the ability to use the computer will differentiate jobs, opportunities, and income in the new millennium. There is a growing gap between the young and the old with respect to computer literacy. The challenge is to make the computer and the Internet as easy to use as telephones once were. Voice recognition and commands, as well as instantaneous translations into one's native language of material accessed on the Web are ethical as well as technological imperatives.

Democracy and control

The possibility of direct democracy, with every citizen voting on any issue he or she chooses, is not a distant dream but a real possibility. Is it preferable to indirect democracy in which representatives are elected and charged with passing appropriate legislation? Information is now readily available on most issues, and web sites dedicated to different sides of an issue are common. But few people have the time to pursue even a small portion of the information available, to know how to get it, or to decide what to believe. Disinformation is as common as reliable information.

Democracy may follow the Internet as more and more information becomes available to people and as governments are no longer able to prevent their citizens from learning other opinions and points of view, as well as news about one's own country from other countries. This is the optimistic scenario. The pessimistic one is of government getting greater control over the information about each citizen and using that to control and manipulate them in the manner foreshadowed in Orwell's *1984*. Both are possibilities. The ethical challenge is to prevent the latter and promote the former.

International legal coordination

As the Internet and global business bring people closer together and make national borders permeable and often irrelevant, the issue of national law and international access becomes a growing problem. Controlling the Internet is efficient only to the extent that most, if not all, nations have similar laws that outlaw similar activities – such as child pornography and the spreading of computer viruses – and uniformly enforce their laws.

The discrepancy between the laws of the European Union that protect personal information and the lack thereof in the United States is an instance of a difference that has a significant impact on business. Should the Europeans conform to the US law or should the USA conform to the European law? If there were no interaction there might be no problem. Since there is interaction, the best way to choose is to see which is the more morally defensible position. In this instance, the best argument is in favor of the European model. The US approach of self-policing has proven ineffective, and with no sanctions for failure to protect personal information even when a site has guaranteed such protection, the approach offers consumers little or no protection. The EU's argument that they should not change because they are protecting the moral rights of consumers clearly carries more moral weight.

Computers, the Internet and the Information Age have already introduced a host of new ethical issues in business. We can expect new issues to arise as technology develops further. Some will be resolved by law. One danger is that laws will be passed as a result of lobbying by vested interests, and that these rather than moral judgments arrived at by informed popular debate will carry the day. Another is that laws will be passed that inappropriately inhibit technological development rather than simply protect human rights and well being, the general welfare, and the common good.

The Myth of Amoral Computing and Information Technology needs to be unmasked and responsibility established for the ethical issues to be seen, for our ethical intuitions to develop, and for ethics to operate as transparently and be internalized by corporations as fully as has ethics in more traditional areas of business.

References

Orwell, G. 1949: *Nineteen Eighty-Four*. New York: Oxford University Press.
Weizenbaum, J. 1976: *Computer Power and Human Reason*. New York: W. H. Freeman and Company.
Wiener, N. 1954: *The Human Use of Human Beings*. Garden City, NY: Doubleday and Co.

Further Reading

Baase, S. 1997: *A Gift of Fire*. Upper Saddle River, NJ: Prentice Hall.
DeCew, J. W. 1997: *In Pursuit of Privacy*. Ithaca: Cornell University Press.
Johnson, D. G. 1994: *Computer Ethics*. 2nd edn. Englewood Cliffs, NJ: Prentice Hall.
Johnson, D. G. and Nissenbaum, H. (eds) 1995: *Computers, Ethics and Social Values*. Englewood Cliffs, NJ: Prentice Hall.
Pennock, J. R. and Chapman, J. W. (eds) 1971: *Privacy*. New York: Atherton Press.
Rosenor, J. 1996: *Cyberlaw*. New York: Springer.
Spinello, R. A. 1995: *Ethical Aspects of Information Technology*. Englewood Cliffs, NJ: Prentice Hall.

Chapter 14

Business Ethics, Organization Ethics, and Systems Ethics for Health Care[1]

Patricia H. Werhane

John Worthy

One evening John Worthy, age forty-seven, brought home information about the new health insurance plans his employer, Factory Inc., was offering. Factory had decided to offer a choice of health plans: GoodCare, a managed care plan, or GoodCare Prime, which had a point of service option. Those who wanted to pay more for it themselves could stay with the company's old indemnity insurance.

After dinner, John and his wife Jane looked over the materials and talked about which plan they should choose. John and Jane were in pretty good health, and their younger daughter was rarely sick. Their older girl was covered by the health service at college. GoodCare's HMO had no deductible, only a small copay for office visits, and there were several doctors in their area on the plan's list of providers. They decided to sign up with GoodCare. They filled out the enrollment form and chose a primary care provider whose office would be convenient to get to; John took the papers back to work the next morning.

Two weeks later they received their member cards and handbook from GoodCare, along, with a letter encouraging them to make a "get to know you" appointment with the family doctor they'd chosen. There was no copay for the initial visit, but with one thing and another the Worthys didn't get around to scheduling appointments.

One morning, two months later, John Worthy woke up with a headache. When Mrs. Worthy called at 10:30 to say that John was experiencing a rather severe headache that came on suddenly a couple of hours previously, Fran Davis, John's new family doctor, was concerned. Unfortunately, Dr. Davis was in the middle of office hours with a very full waiting room. The physician and the Worthys were still strangers to one another, and neither the Worthys nor Dr. Davis were very familiar with the HMO's rules and procedures, since Dr. Davis's medical group was relatively new to GoodCare too.

A year ago the medical group, weary from battling payers and paperwork, sold their practice to Physician Management Services (PMS). In exchange for the practice's physical assets, a long-term contractual commitment, and a percentage of gross revenues, PMS negotiates contracts with the many HMOs and other payers for whom their physicians provide services, takes care of all the paperwork, periodically upgrades the practice's computer information system, and keeps the group within its budget. PMS receives a capitated fee from GoodCare for each enrolled patient to cover all primary care, plus outpatient laboratory and x-ray services. The HMO covers specialists and hospital care, including emergency room visits, separately. Physician Management Services pays each physician a salary, but also transfers some of its economic risk to its physicians in the form of bonuses and penalties tied to productivity and utilization. They established protocols to reduce excessive care, and set a five-patients-per-hour productivity standard. Recently, PMS has also been educating physicians about their tendency to send too many patients to the emergency room – a common response among physicians who are capitated for primary care, and whose waiting rooms have become crowded with managed care patients who pay little or nothing for office visits. Last year, high ER costs prompted GoodCare to begin assessing financial penalties on primary care providers who overused this resource.

Dr. Davis was aware that if GoodCare decided, after the fact, that John Worthy did not truly require emergency care, the patient or even she as the primary care provider could be financially at risk. Nevertheless, because she was unfamiliar with Mr. Worthy's medical history, overwhelmed at the office, and somewhat concerned by his symptoms, Dr. Davis suggested that Mrs. Worthy take John to the nearest emergency room if his headache really seemed that severe.

Edward R. Post, the emergency room physician, was concerned. When Worthy presented a little before noon, his temperature was normal, and blood pressure was 158/96. Fundoscopic examination showed no indication of elevated intracranial pressure. John said he'd had severe headaches in the past, but none for maybe the last two years. He acknowledged being a long-time heavy smoker and said he seemed to feel some pain behind one eye. During the examination he also said that his neck might feel just a little stiff, because his headache was so bothersome, it was hard for him to figure our exactly what hurt. Dr. Post could not directly feel any neck rigidity, but believed that given the severity of the headache as John reported it he should have further tests. Post explained to the Worthys that the problem was most likely just a cluster headache, a severe tension headache, or sinusitis; he did not believe that John had meningitis. But he indicated that there was a possibility, although very remote, of early bleeding in the brain, a tumor, or some other much more serious problem. And so he strongly urged John to undergo a CT scan. The Worthys asked whether the expenses would be covered by their health plan. Post replied that this hospital was not affiliated with GoodCare, and so he could not offer any assurance about reimbursement. Nonetheless, he urged the Worthys to stay for the further diagnostic evaluation.

The Worthys talked things over, but decided to leave the hospital because they were afraid the proposed tests would not be covered. Dr. Post couldn't justify insisting that John stay for tests. He suggested that since their primary care provider was busy they consider calling a neurologist in their health plan. The Worthys thought about visiting the in-plan hospital at a considerably greater distance from their home, but opted instead to return home, from where Mrs. Worthy phoned GoodCare.

Connie S. Rogers, customer service representative at GoodCare HMO, was concerned. She explained to the Worthys that if John visited the emergency department or entered the nonplan hospital near his home, and if it was not declared to be a medical emergency, the entire hospital visit could be disallowed. The Worthys recalled Post's suggestion to see a neurologist and asked if the HMO had any available. Rogers replied that GoodCare's neurologist was a Dr. Newman, and gave the Worthys his number. The Worthys phoned, but were told by Dr. Newman's receptionist that they could not have an appointment until they first received an authorization from their primary care provider. Jane Worthy, increasingly frustrated, phoned back to Dr. Davis to secure the necessary authorization. Unfortunately, Davis's phone line was busy, and calls had been temporarily transferred to an answering service. Jane left a message but, unsure when the message would reach Davis, she phoned back to the HMO.

Connie Rogers again answered. Mrs. Worthy, furious almost beyond words, insisted on talking with the president of the HMO. She was becoming panicky that her husband's worsening condition might bode something life-threatening, and was not at all sure that he could tolerate the eighteen-mile drive to the in-plan hospital. Sensing that litigation might be in the offing, Rogers indicated that although the president was not available, she would try to reach GoodCare's medical director and would talk to him on their behalf. She then phoned the medical director and explained the situation as best she could.

Michael Depp, the medical director of GoodCare, was concerned. As soon as he finished talking with Connie Rogers, he phoned Dr. Davis's office and got through promptly. Upon being updated on the Worthys' current plight, Davis indicated she would resolve the problem and phone Depp back with follow-up information. Davis first phoned the hospital emergency department and learned from Dr. Post that John had not appeared to be in an acute emergency condition, and that the Worthys had declined further evaluation for financial reasons. Dr. Davis inferred from subsequent events that John Worthy's condition seemed to be worsening, however, and that prompt referral to a neurologist was medically justified. Dr. Davis was not familiar with Dr. Newman, and did not know whether he was as experienced as other neurologists she knew in town. Nevertheless, she wanted John to be seen expeditiously by someone who could provide all the care he needed. After phoning Newman's office with the necessary referral authorization, Dr. Davis then phoned the Worthys to inform them that they were clear to visit the neurologist.

Finally, Dr. Davis phoned Michael Depp with the promised follow-up and took the opportunity to vent her own frustration. Depp listened patiently and sympathized with her difficulties. He acknowledged that the "Mickey Mouse run-around," as she'd put it, sometimes did pose real inconvenience. But he explained that GoodCare had tried other forms of cost containment for many years with little result. Thus, they installed the primary care case management model, the preferred hospital and specialist list with discounted fees, and their utilization management system. Patients were still free to visit any provider, and to receive any care they wanted. But the HMO could only assure full coverage for care it deemed necessary and appropriate. When Mrs. Worthy called Dr. Newman's office a second time to set up the authorized appointment, she told the receptionist that her husband had a "really, really bad headache," and couldn't wait until the first available slot next week. Although the receptionist did not completely appreciate the seriousness of the situation, she did juggle out a next-day appointment.

Jane Worthy was concerned. She drove John back to the ER at 11:00 PM, but even before she pulled up to the doorway, his tortured breathing had stopped. Successive attempts by the hospital staff to revive him failed. She was deeply sorry that her husband died of a massive brain hemorrhage as his cerebral aneurysm ruptured.[2]

As health care delivery, in almost all forms, moves into organizations, one can no longer focus on merely physician-patient one-on-one relationships or even on one-on-one relationships between a particular patient or professional and the provider organization such as a hospital or other care center. Health care increasingly is delivered to patient populations by healthcare professionals through complex health-care organizations run by managers and executives who themselves may or may not be professionally trained in medicine. Payers of health care delivery are no longer patients but include insurers, employers, and local, state, and national governments.

Because of these changes, much of the new work in health care ethics focuses on the ethics of healthcare provider organizations (Emanuel and Emanuel, 1996; Wong, 1998; L. Emanuel, 2000; Hall, 2000; Spencer et al., 2000; Werhane, 2000; Ozar et al., 2001). Still, an analysis of healthcare organizations may not be adequate to describe the present state of the healthcare profession and health care delivery nor deal with the complex normative issues raised by that delivery or delivery system.

In almost all its dimensions health care as it is currently delivered, rationed, or denied in the USA, is imbedded in a complex set of systems and subsystems that entail a complex set of networks of interrelationships. To deal with ethical issues in health care either from a dyadic or even an organizational perspective often belies what is really at issue and thus ignores a number of elements that are related to the issue in question. John Worthy's health care maintenance, payment, and delivery were within a complex network of managed care, employer, insurance, and delivery organizations. Worthy's employer had contracted out the health care of its employees to Physician Management Services, which, in turn, contracted with GoodCare for the healthcare delivery to these and other employees. Worthy was caught in the morass of these relationships. Yet it is difficult to pinpoint which individual or organization was at fault because of the complex structure of the system in which Worthy's health delivery was a part.

This case illustrates why one needs to address ethical issues in health care in systemic as well as in organizational terms, and why one needs to evaluate the normative content of healthcare systems as well as healthcare organizations, an evaluation that requires what the organizational and scientific literature call "systems thinking" or a systems approach. That will be the dual task of this chapter. In the next section, I shall first address the relationship of some concepts in business ethics to healthcare organizations. Then I shall expand this analysis to help us think about health care as it functions in a complex set of systems and subsystems.

I shall conclude that how a system is designed (its structure), what is included or left out – its "boundary-maintaining processes" in Laszlo and Krippner's (1998) terms – and how the value dimensions of each component of the system interact, affect decision-making. This design set has normative outcomes for the system, for those affected by, and operating within, that system, and even for some traditional ethical issues in health care such as informed consent, patient autonomy, and privacy. John Worthy could have been saved, but, given the systemic restraints, not merely by one individual professional or by his wife.

In what follows, I shall use the term "healthcare organization" to refer to any organization that manages, finances, or delivers health care. "Provider organization" refers specifically to those organizations such as medical centers, clinics, and hospitals that provide care. A Managed Care Organization (MCO) such as a Health Maintenance Organization (HMO) "integrates the financing and delivery of medical care through contracts with selected physicians and hospitals that provide comprehensive health care services to enrolled members for a predetermined monthly premium" (Inglehart, 1994, p. 1167; Wolf, 1999, p. 1634).

Business Ethics and Organization Ethics

Until recently, before managed care, business issues in the healthcare organizations that delivered care, e.g., physician offices, hospitals, clinics, and other healthcare providers, were relatively insulated from clinical issues. Today this separation of powers and of issues is less possible. In the USA, we have created a myriad of for-profit and not-for-profit healthcare organizations including managed care organizations such as HMOs that that manage, finance, and often control the delivery of health care. Payment to professionals and provider organizations is ordinarily through insurers or government agencies, not by patients, and often the extent and quality of reimbursed care is measured through capitation, rationing, DRGs set by the insurers, or, in the case of the state of Oregon, by legislators (Spencer et al., 2000).

In the contemporary healthcare setting, financial, clinical, and professional issues are all so interrelated that one cannot neatly separate out, say, the cost of an MRI from a patient's need for it, from the professional expertise that determines the desirability of that protocol, nor from the HMO guidelines that specify when and at what cost it can be administered. Thus there is a need to take into account the interrelationships between clinical, patient, professional, management, and financial aspects of those organizations as these are managed by or in HMOs.

Since much of health care is managed through HMOs, many of which are for-profit organizations, it is tempting to appeal to concepts in business ethics to sort out the complex issues that arise in these settings. More particularly, it is tempting either to take a Milton Friedman approach or a stakeholder approach to these organizational questions.

Friedmanian economics

Milton Friedman some time ago declared:

> There is one and only one social responsibility of business – to use its resources and engage in activities designed to increase its profits so long as it stays within the rules of the game, which is to say, engages in open and free competition without deception or fraud (Friedman, 1970, p. 126).

This often-misquoted statement does not advocate that "anything goes" in commerce. Law and common morality should guide our action in the marketplace just as they guide our actions elsewhere. Nevertheless, given that qualification, which is an important one, managers' first duties and fiduciary duties are to owners or shareholders. Ordinarily these duties are to maximize return on investment, although in some companies the mission statement directs managers to other ends as well.

Friedman's depiction of the relationship between ethics and business has been influential in changing the model of contemporary healthcare delivery. The promise of managed care has been that self-interested commercial competition between providers and insurers will be a sufficient mechanism to improve the efficiency and reduce the cost of health care, without imperiling quality. Yet there are a number of difficulties with this argument even as it applies to the practice of commerce or business, and even greater difficulties when applied without qualification to healthcare management and delivery.

One difficulty is that, in fact, many of the best for-profit corporations do not operate under Friedman's philosophy. In a six-year project, James Collins and Jerry Porras, set out to identify and systematically research the historical development of a set of what they called "visionary companies," to examine how these companies differed from a carefully selected control set of comparison companies (Collins and Porras, 1994, p. 2). Collins and Porras defined the visionary company as the premier organization in their industries, as being widely admired by their peers, and as having a long track record of making a significant impact on the world around them (p. 3).[3] What was different about visionary companies and comparison companies? Each operates in the same market and each has relatively the same opportunities. Still, Collins and Porras (1994, p. 8) state:

> Contrary to business school doctrine, "maximizing shareholder wealth" or profit maximization" has not been the dominant driving force or primary objective through the history of the visionary companies. Visionary companies pursue a cluster of objectives, of which making money is only one – and not necessarily the primary one. Yes, they seek profits, but they are equally guided by a core ideology – core values and a sense of purpose beyond just making money. Yet, paradoxically, the visionary companies make more money than the more purely profit-driven comparison companies.

Having dispelled Friedman's edict as the only acceptable normative framework for business organizations, there *is* one sense in which Milton Friedman's version might be useful in thinking about healthcare organizations. Healthcare organizations are, at least in theory, created for one purpose: to manage, evaluate, finance, and/or deliver health care to patients and patient populations. If their mission is patient or population health, then as rational agents they should act so as to maximize the treatment and well being of their designated populations. Rewording Friedman,

> There is one and only one social responsibility of any healthcare organization: to use its professional and economic resources and engage in activities designed to treat and improve the health of its patient populations so long as it stays within the rules of the game . . . (Werhane, 2000, p. 173).

This formulation puts in perspective the unique feature of healthcare organizations that distinguishes them from other types or organizations including for-profit non-health related corporations. Actions of a provider organization that do not maximize patient or population treatment, or actions of an HMO that do not manage the delivery of that treatment effectively and successfully over a defined population, would, on this account, be irrational and indeed, morally wrong, given the mission of these healthcare organizations (Werhane, 2000).

Still, one of the "rules of the game" in the present economic climate might be the proviso that these organizations must be economically viable, that is, minimally, they must break even or create the ability to pay their debts. Even charity hospitals are under such economic constraints. Thus, even given a reformulated edict of Milton Friedman, can we simply subsume all healthcare organizations including provider organizations and HMOs, under the philosophical umbrella of commerce? Several characteristics of *healthcare* organizations complicate or even preclude such a move. Stakeholder theory helps us to sort out these complications, and an analysis of healthcare markets helps to distinguish health care from other types of market-driven organizations.

Stakeholder theory and stakeholder priorities[4]

A stakeholder is any individual or group whose role-relationships with an organization

- helps to define the organization, its mission, purpose, or its goals, and/or
- "is vital to the survival, and success [or well-being] of the corporation" (Freeman, 1999, p. 250), or
- is most affected by the organization and its activities.

Let us assume for our purposes that all stakeholders in question are individuals or groups (including institutions) made up of individuals. If stakeholder interests have intrinsic value, then, according to R. E. Freeman, the "father" of stakeholder theory, in every stakeholder relationship, the "stakes [that is, what is expected and due to each party] of each are reciprocal, [although not identical], since each can affect the other in terms of harms and benefits as well as rights and duties" (Freeman, 1999, p. 250). Therefore stakeholder relationships are normative reciprocal relationships for which each party is accountable. Figure 14.1 illustrates some of those kinds of relationships in a typical healthcare organization.

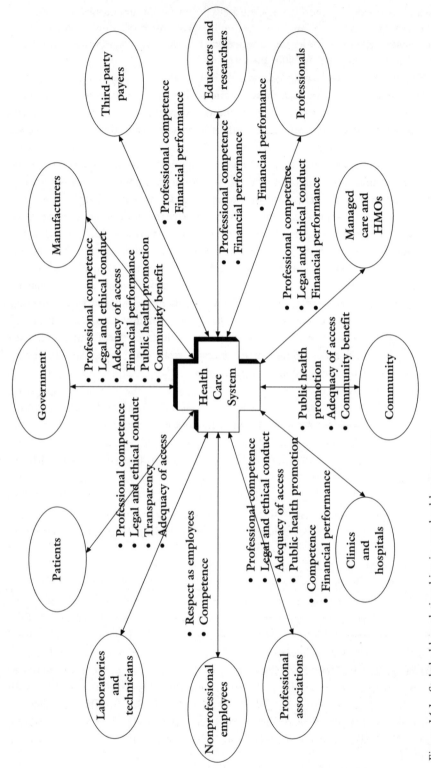

Figure 14.1 Stakeholder relationships in our health care system
Source: Emanuel and Emanuel (1996)

One of the challenges of stakeholder theory is to evaluate and prioritize various stakeholder claims with each other and with the profitability (or economic survivability) criterion Friedman and other economists advocate. In healthcare organizations, however, because of their unique features, the prioritization of stakeholder and claims is relatively more clear-cut.

By the fact of being a *healthcare* organization, the primary stakeholders in any healthcare organization are, or should be, its patients or patient population it serves. The difference between garden-variety corporations and any health care organization, even HMOs, (whether a for-profit organization or not) is the primary mission is always the financing, management and/or delivery of health services to individuals and populations. Moreover, since health care deals with individual persons, patient autonomy and informed consent are part of this equation. Indeed, Dr. Post, the ER physician in the Worthy case, in his comments on the aftermath of the case, stated, "I acceded in Mr. Worthy's decision to decline my recommendation to have a CT scan. . . . I believe strongly in patient autonomy and the right to choose" (S4–5) (Ozar et al., 2001).

The basic value-creating activities of healthcare organizations are the management, payment, and delivery of patient care. Such delivery requires professional expertise, without which the organization will fail, whatever its goals. Therefore, healthcare professionals are the second most important stakeholders both for HMOs and provider organizations. Typically, healthcare professionals belong to, and are accredited by, independent professional associations. Many if not all professionals consider themselves primarily bound by the ethical prescriptions of their profession, preeminent among which are their duties to their patients. One of Dr. Davis's dilemmas in the Worthy case was the conflict between her professional duty to patient health and the capitation requirements of GoodCare, which affected her compensation and the compensation of her medical group. As she stated, in commenting on the case, ". . . [I]t's increasingly important (for my financial well-being and the plans') that I authorize only 'appropriate' referrals" (S3).

Financial stability is the third priority in healthcare organizations, which, in for-profit organizations, is translated into shareholder value, as the third most important stakeholders. Long-term organizational viability that includes financial stability is necessary for the continuation of any of these organizations and part of the guarantee of the quality of its services, even charity organizations. Indeed, it is not odd that healthcare organizations are concerned with efficiency, profitability or at least, economic survival. But the trouble begins when a healthcare organization realigns its mission or creates an organizational culture in which efficiency, productivity, and/or profitability become the overriding priorities, as may have been so in the Worthy situation. Dr. Depp's statement after the death of Worthy, "The HMO has also adhered to a firm policy of requiring primary care provider approval for all specialty referrals . . . to protect our members from getting unneeded specialty services" (S8) illustrates this preoccupation for rules and efficiency.

Part of professional responsibility as defined by every healthcare professional's code of ethics (and spelled in the Code of the Association of Health Care Executives as well! [www.ache.org]) is commitment to community and public health. Despite the ability of HMOs to define and restrict the patient population they will serve, community access and public health are always part of the accountability equation, because of the simple societal expectation that healthcare organizations and professionals *should* serve public health needs. One of Dr. Post's problems as an ER physician was that his hospital was in a poor community. The commitment to that community forced him to consider whether to encourage Worthy to have a CT scan if it would not be reimbursed.

Stakeholder prioritization creates values prioritization as well, in health care organizations. If the primary stakeholder is the patient and patient populations, then the first goal of any healthcare organization should be the autonomy and care of its patients. The second goal is the encouragement, respect, and well being of its professional staff and their decisions, the third is financial viability, and the fourth, but not least, community health.[5]

Given these priorities as provisos, can we nevertheless treat healthcare organizations like other businesses? There is a further complication, the nature of healthcare markets.

Healthcare markets

There are a number of factors that complicate healthcare markets, adding to the questionability of treating healthcare organizations univocally like other business corporations. These factors include the distinction between customers/payers and consumers/patients, information asymmetries, and the distortion of supply-and-demand models.

The correlation between consumers and payers is very different in this organization than in the usual business. In provider organizations, recipients of healthcare services are usually not the payers. Various forms of insurance, employer sponsored health plans or government agencies (the "customers") purchase health coverage for the individuals and patient groups who are the actual and potential patients (the "consumers"). This three-way relationship complicates accountability between the parties affected in healthcare delivery. Moreover, unlike the typical consumer, the patient, like John Worthy, may have limited choices in delivery options. "Buyer Beware" is not an appropriate slogan for healthcare consumers. Even in those cases where the patient is also the payer, the consumer/patient is often ill and vulnerable. So, unlike ordinary consumers, patients are not always able to exercise their choices coherently.

Coupled with patient vulnerability, healthcare patients are seldom "fully informed." There is an obvious information asymmetry between HMOs and provider organizations, between managers and healthcare professionals, and between professionals and customers or patients regarding knowledge about health. There is also an information asymmetry between healthcare organizations. Competitive HMOs do not have access to consumer (i.e., patient) information in ways in which they have access to market information in other business enterprises. So, ordinary competitive relationships are not possible in the healthcare market. So, ordinary competitive information is not always available in the healthcare "market."

Finally, supply-and-demand curves are skewed in the healthcare industry. Healthcare organizations cannot respond to all market demands, in particular, to the demands of the uninsured. Some patients or patient-groups cannot pay for what they consume while others pay for more than they consume.

These factors, and there are others, give ample evidence that the distinguishing features of healthcare organizations warrant their separate study. Business ethics provides some tools for that study, but this does not merit merely conflating HCOs with other commercial organizations.

Returning to the John Worthy case, does an organizational analysis of this situation help in sorting out this situation? Focusing on Worthy, his autonomy, his implicit consent to the healthcare plan, and his refusal to heed the recommendation of Dr. Post, the ER physician, because that hospital was not affiliated with GoodCare contributed to his death. The prioritization of patient health by Dr. Davis, GoodCare, and the emergency room, would have helped to alleviate this problem. But each of these people, and GoodCare itself, was functioning in a complex network or system of interrelationships all of which complicated the situation. Each individual was caught in the maelstrom of this system and no one could or did sort through and prioritize these relationships in ways that might have saved Worthy. GoodCare itself was mired in rules that helped most of its patients, but was ill suited to emergency situations. Thus the case calls for a more complex analysis.

Systems and Systems Ethics

A truly systemic view [of current health care] . . . considers how [this set of individuals, institutions, and processes] operates in a system with certain characteristics. The system involves interactions extending over time, a complex set of interrelated decision points, an array of [individual, institutional, and governmental] actors with conflicting interests . . . and a number of feedback loops (Wolf, 1999, p. 1675).

What do we mean by a *healthcare system*? There are at least two ways to think about systems that are helpful for our purposes. First, a healthcare system can be defined as "assemblages of interactions within an organization or between organizations" (Emanuel, 2000, p. 152). These "assemblages" are governed by

1   organization arrangements or structure
2   attributes that organize and shape an institution
3   the interrelationships between organizations, and/or
4   procedures and processes that are adapted by an organization or a set of
    organizations.

Under this rubric health care systems are networks of relationships between individuals, between individuals and organizations, between organizations, and between individuals, organizations, institutions, and government. On a macro level a healthcare system, in the case of the USA, includes government agencies that regulate the health care industry and create public policy, government payers including Medicare and Medicaid, public policy (and public policy think tanks), insurers, employers and employer health plans, HMOs, MCOs, health care centers (including academic medical centers), hospitals, nursing homes, laboratories, pharmaceuticals and pharmacists, healthcare networks, professionals and other care givers, (both employed and independent professionals), researchers, writers, lawyers, healthcare executives, managers and other employees, professional and academic associations, patients and patient populations, social workers. The system is defined by the myriad of networks and interrelationships between these institutions, organizations, employers, managers, professionals, care givers, payers, patients, and managers. Thus systems under this rubric are social networks of interactions between individuals and groups of individuals within and across institutions.

A second approach to thinking about healthcare systems is best described by Laszlo and Krippner's definition of a system as "a complex of interacting components together with the relationships among them that permit the identification of a boundary-maintaining entity or process" (Laszlo and Krippner, 1998, p. 51). A "system" under this definition refers to a model or framework, a structured set of methodologies, rules or processes that frame a certain approach, protocol or decision process. On this account, a systems approach embeds a model that includes a set of techniques or procedures to deal with a bounded class of phenomena. For example, processes to reduce house office fatigue, to test blood, to diagnose certain diseases, or to catch medication errors are systems protocols that function similarly within and/or across organizations. In framing the process or prescribing the set of rules for procedure this approach also limits or proscribes as well so that the set of rules are boundary-maintaining in Laszlo and Krippner's sense of the term. These processes or rules are protocols that are adapted by many individuals and organizations engaged in the procedures in question, and which protocols are adapted will obviously affect the network of individuals and institutions where they are adapted.

These two approaches to thinking about systems are interconnected. A systems protocol to catch medication errors might be adapted by a number of organizations and within each organization that adaptation helps to define and frame the way in which that institution operates and how its operations affect its professionals and patients. Rules, procedures, and other arrangements within a particular organization shape, which protocols are adapted for medical procedures and how those are interpreted, and also affect or are affected by HMOs, MCOs, and other insurers or payers of health care. An HCO that has a reputation for repeated medication errors, for example, will likely attract attention to insurers and other payers of patient care at that organization and eventually affect that organization and its structure. Conversely, the structure and mission of a particular organization of a healthcare system may preclude the adoption of certain protocols. For example, capitation or coverage limitations by insurers or the government on treatment may preclude the practice of certain experimental protocols, or, in the case of Worthy, the use of an unspecified emergency room.

What is characteristic of both types of systems is that any phenomenon or set of phenomena that are defined as a system has properties or characteristics that are lost or at best, obscured, when the system is broken up into components. For example, in studying Worthy's healthcare system, merely analyzing GoodCare will obscure many of the issues in the case. Similarly, in viewing organizations such as GoodCare, if one focuses simply on its organizational structure, or merely on its mission statement, or only on its employees or participants, one loses the interconnections and interrelationships that characterize that system or subsystem. Similarly, if one isolates one component of a protocol for study, one is no longer studying the protocol (Laszlo and Krippner, 1998, p. 53). The kinds of systems we are concentrating on in this paper, healthcare systems, have another characteristic. Each type of system or subsystem is purposive or goal-oriented. Protocols and procedures are developed with outcomes in mind, and a good procedure is one that produces clear and consistent outcomes as defined by the structure and methodology of the procedure. Indeed, the prescribed outcomes of any protocol create the boundaries for that protocol. Organizations and institutions also have goals that are usually reflected in their mission statements or other statements of purpose. When one looks at the macro system of health care in this country, the goals are confusing and less clear. Nevertheless, one usually ascribes goals to healthcare systems, e.g., patient, patient populations and/or public health, although this ascription is sometimes a normative prescription rather than a description of the purposes and goals presently in place.

The goal-orientation of healthcare systems accounts for their normative dimensions. As has been argued extensively elsewhere, organizations as well as individuals have purposes and goals that carry with them moral obligations, and we hold organizations and institutions, as well as individuals, morally accountable (French, 1979; Werhane, 1985; Spencer et al., 2000; Ozar et al., 2001). While it is less transparent that systems are moral agents of some sort, it is true that the structure, interrelationships, and goals of a particular system produce outcomes that have normative consequences. An alteration of a particular system or parts of that system will often produce different kinds of outcomes. Systems that consist of networks of relationships between individuals, groups, and institutions are relationships between people. Thus, how the system is construed, how it operates, affects and is affected by individuals. The character and operations of a particular system or set of systems affect those of us who come in contact with the system, whether we are patients, the community, professionals, managers, or insurers. That we do not have universal healthcare coverage in the USA, for example, not only affects the uninsured, but also has economic and social consequences for communities, healthcare providers, and professionals. Finally, systems as well as organizations and individuals are often causally responsible for healthcare delivery and clinical performance. The systems of payment for healthcare delivery, for instance, affect the quality and kind of delivery available to many patients, as Worthy discovers. Thus moral responsibility is incurred by the nature and characteristics of the system in question (Emanuel, 2000).

Systemic arrangements and organization networks create roles and role responsibilities, rights, and opportunities that affect individuals and individual activities and performance. What is less obvious is that one can take a single organization or a single individual functioning within that organization or system and apply different systems matrices to that organization with differing outcomes. The preoccupations of subsystems and individuals functioning within these systems and the ways values and stakeholders are prioritized affects the goals, procedures, and outcomes of the system or subsystem in question. On every level, the ways we frame the goals, the procedures and what networks we take into account makes a difference in what we discover and what we neglect. These framing mechanisms will turn out to be important normative influences of systems and systems thinking.

For example, a salaried healthcare professional operating within a strict capitation HMO such as Dr. Davis, may see her role as a professional differently than, say, an individual physician in a small independent practice. Indeed, different mindsets operative in the Worthy case prioritize events and their importance differently, thus creating part of Worthy's problem. Sometimes, as in this instance, the professional model outlined by the Hippocratic Oath is replaced by or blurred with economic interests. Then individual patient need as determined by healthcare professionals is evaluated according to the criteria of efficiency and cost, and attention to individual patients is replaced by a group identification to a defined patient population and carefully prescribed rationing. The Worthys were concentrating on themselves and what they took to be an individual patient-physician relationship with Dr. Davis. Dr. Davis, with a bloated caseload and pressures to see as many patients as possible, focused on current patients, the exigencies of that day, and GoodCare's capitation requirements. Dr. Newman's office was preoccupied with the HMO rules, while the emergency room was concerned with Worthy's coverage as well as his autonomy. Depp and GoodCare were interested in patient populations, costs and benefits of healthcare financing and delivery, and what they could deliver productively and with efficiency to their defined population. These mind sets and their priorities set differing boundary conditions that scarcely overlapped in ways that could have benefited Worthy. Different perspectives frame the goals and expectations of the HCO differently with obviously differing outcomes.

Systems thinking

What do we mean by "systems thinking" or a "systems approach?" For our purposes systems thinking presupposes that most of our reasoning, experiencing, practices and institutions are interrelated and interconnected. Almost everything we can experience or think about is in a network of interrelationships such that each element of a particular set of interrelationships affects the other components of that set and the system itself, and almost no phenomenon can be studied in isolation from all relationships with at least some other phenomenon. Systems thinking, then, involves two kinds of analysis. In a systems approach, "concentration is on the analysis and design of the whole, as distinct from . . . the components or parts . . ." (Ramo, 1969, pp. 11–12). Systems thinking requires conceiving of the system as a whole with interdependent elements, subsystems, and networks of relationships and patterns of interaction. Studying a particular component of a system or a particular relationship is valuable under this rubric only if one recognizes that that study is, at least in part, an abstraction from a more systemic consideration.

Second, few systems are merely linear and few, including healthcare systems, are closed systems that are not constantly in dynamic processes of changing and reinventing themselves. Because "the fundamental notion of interconnectedness or nonseparability, forms the basis of what has come to be known as the Systems Approach, . . . every problem humans face is complicated[and] must be perceived as such" (Mitroff and Linstone, 1993, p. 95). So each system or subsystem, because it is complex and entails a multitude of various individual, empirical, social, and political relationships, needs to be analyzed, and analyzed from multiple perspectives. The downside of not taking this sort of approach is obvious in the Worthy case. Looking at Worthy's situation merely from his perspective and that of his wife was disabling, just as disabling as examining this problem merely from the perspective of Dr. Davis or Dr. Post.

A Multiple Perspective method postulates that any phenomenon, organization, or system (or problems arising for or within that phenomenon or system) should be dealt with from a number of perspectives, each of which involves different world views where each challenges the others in dynamic exchanges of questions and ideas. Mitroff and Linstone suggest that in business, economic, and public policy contexts one needs to look at problems from a technical, or fact-finding point of view, from an organizational or social relationships perspective, and from an individual perspective, ranking problems, perspectives and alternate solutions, and evaluating the problem and its possible resolution from these multiple perspectives (Mitroff and Linstone, 1993, ch. 6). While it is never possible to take account all the networks of relationships involved in a particular system, and surely never so given these systems interact over time, a multiple perspectives approach forces us to think more broadly, and to look at particular systems or problems from different points of view. This is crucial in trying to avoid problems such as Worthy's, because each perspective usually "reveals insights . . . that are not obtainable in principle from others" (Mitroff and Linstone, 1993, p. 98). It is also invaluable in trying to understand other points of view. A Multiple Perspectives approach is essential if, for example, for-profit healthcare systems are to understand what is at stake for the uninsured, or what is at risk if professional staff is overburdened with efficiency requirements or is reduced. This kind of approach is critical for not-for-profit healthcare organizations to help them understand the economic dynamics of healthcare delivery, and such an approach is important for healthcare consumers so that people like John Worthy can comprehend what sort of system they have enrolled in.

A multiple perspectives approach to healthcare systems

In examining ethical issues in healthcare systems, subsystems, and organizations, a Multiple Perspectives approach might involve describing the system and subsystems in question, and an examination and evaluation of the network of organizational, relational, and individual perspectives. One investigates how a particular configuration of a system or subsystem affects individuals, in this instance, healthcare delivery, community and public health, and micro issues such as patient autonomy, access, informed consent, privacy, and other important matters of concern to those delivering and receiving care. One evaluates the boundary creating processes, to be clear about what is left out, as well as accountability relationships, as we illustrated earlier. Then one evaluates both by prioritizing the goals of the system and indeed, by evaluating those goals (including the professional, organizational, economic and sometimes, political norms) implicit in the system.[6] The aim is three-fold: to understand the system and its complex interrelationships; to evaluate that system, its relationships, and the moral responsibilities embedded therein; and to think through possible solutions or resolutions of the issues in question that take into account these multiple perspectives, and individual as well as organizational and systems responsibility.

The first, a descriptive or "technical" perspective, includes the following. First one describes the system in question, as we tried to outline the US healthcare system in the beginning of the paper, and the health care system in which Worthy was involved. Included in the description are networks of interrelationships between individuals, groups, organizations, and systems, and the number, nature, and scope of subsystems in the system in question. Stakeholder analysis is useful in this context. By enumerating the various stakeholders involved in or affected by this system, and their interrelationships and accountabilities, one can get clearer on the complex nature of the system and its outcomes. Worthy's employer presented him three healthcare alternatives. He accepted one alternative, mainly for cost reasons without considering the positive aspects of other choices. His primary physician, Dr. Davis, was part of that GoodCare system, about which she knew very little. She was measured by GoodCare on volume of patients seen and on capitation criteria that restricted her decision making. GoodCare itself had developed a series of rules and regulations that prevented it from being clear on its alleged mission to health. Dr. Post, the ER physician, made choices on the basis of patient autonomy but his choices were also affected by the fact that his hospital took in many indigent and working poor patients and needed to be careful to seek out paying patients as well. So, the economic pressures on these stakeholders affected their decisions, even Worthy's.

In this process, it is also helpful to outline the boundaries and boundary-creating activities so that it is clear what is not included in the system. But different stakeholders will outline the boundary conditions differently because of the way they prioritize the value creating activities of the system. For example, Fran Davis, the Worthy family doctor, said,

> I made the decision not to see Mr. Worthy in the office and recommended instead that he go to the emergency room if the pain "seemed that severe . . ." . . . It's increasingly important (for my financial well-being and the plans') that I authorize only "appropriate" referrals (S3).

In other words, she prioritized the patients on her schedule and her financial well-being ahead of what turned out to be a critical situation. Similarly, Dr. Post claimed, "I believe strongly in patient autonomy and the right to choose . . ." and argues further, "the chance that those tests [Worthy's] would not be reimbursed poses a dilemma . . ." (S5). So Dr. Post prioritized patient autonomy and community health provision ahead of Worthy's particular condition. Connie Rogers, the customer service representative at GoodCare, who would not refer Mrs. Worthy to the President of GoodCare had other priorities. One was the GoodCare rules for referrals. The second was the company president's edict that "he wants us to offer him solutions, not problems." (S6) Note that both physicians and Ms. Rogers, were each trying to do his or her best in the situation. But this illustrates how prioritization of stakeholders and values (including economic values) changes the perception of boundary conditions and affects decision making.

Linked to the boundary conditions and stakeholder prioritization are the accountability relationships between each stakeholder and element of the system in question. It is tempting to conceive those dyadically as Figure 14.1 illustrated and, from an organizational approach, a dyadic description of accountability may be adequate. But healthcare organizations are parts of more complex systems, and these relationships are much more overlapping and interlocking. See Figure 14.2 for a partial diagramic depiction of some of these. Being clear about these relationships, and how each individual and each element of the system are or should be accountable to each other helps to clarify where decisions go wrong.

Imbedded in this process are the goals or purposes of the system, or in the case of health care or a healthcare subsystem, what goals it *should* have, and how these are prioritized, since the goals a system has will affect its structure, interrelationships, and outcomes. These prioritized goals then become the evaluative elements overlaid on the descriptive grid. In the Worthy case, the goal of any part of this

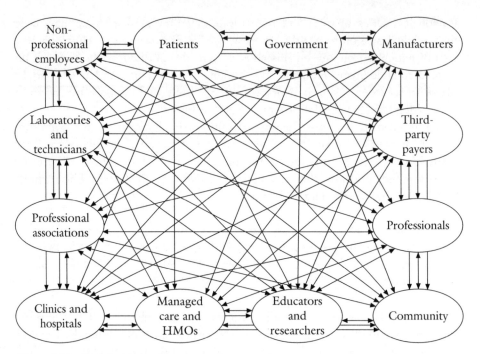

Figure 14.2 Stakeholder systems networks

system should be first, and primarily, patient well-being. Yet these were sometimes confused with rule-following and efficiency at GoodCare. The reward system for its physicians was based on a capitation system that seemed to allow no loopholes for emergencies. Dr. Post's hospital was in financial trouble, so his worries included those economic issues as well. GoodCare is not an evil organization bent on eliminating its consumer-patients. Dr. Davis and Dr. Post are caring, well-trained, physicians. Economic viability and financial survival are not wrong-headed aims. Following rules is ordinarily a good way to operate. However, it is the ways these elements are prioritized that gets GoodCare and its physicians in trouble. Yet, if this system had an agreed upon overlapping set of goals, if each was clear on what these were and how they were to be prioritized, then patient well-being and professional judgment might have been placed ahead of rules and economic and efficiency concerns.

There is one more perspective to consider in the Worthy case, that of individual responsibility, the responsibilities of the professionals, managers, and of John Worthy himself. A systems approach should not be confused with some form of abdication of individual responsibility. As individuals we are not merely the sum of, or identified with, these relationships and roles, we can evaluate and change our relationships, roles, and role obligations, and we are thus responsible for them. That is, each of us is at once byproducts of, characters in, and authors of, our own experiences. The physicians and other healthcare professionals in the Worthy scenario each had responsibilities as defined by their profession, the responsibility to patient care and well-being. While employment demands may have conflicted with that responsibility, as professionals, that Hippocratic Oath is supposed to take precedence. Interestingly too, many healthcare executives now are members of a professional association as well, the American College of Healthcare Executives. Part of that professional code states, "[t]he fundamental objectives of the healthcare management profession are to enhance overall quality of life, dignity, and well being of every individual needing healthcare services" (visit www.ache.org). The GoodCare organization, at least as evidenced in this case, created barriers to these professional responsibilities; still the professional "actors" in this case, by accepting their roles as professionals, had responsibilities that should have taken precedence.

John Worthy, too, had responsibilities – responsibilities to be familiar with his health coverage and its limits, and to make an appointment to see Dr. Davis before he became ill. He, too, was responsible, and we cannot mitigate all of that responsibility through blaming the health system in which he found himself.

We can now evaluate John Worthy's particular dilemma and the problems at GoodCare. Earlier we argued that part of the issue was a misprioritization of stakeholders and stakeholder concerns in creating organizational goals at GoodCare, with the capitation pressures on Dr. Davis, the hospital economic pressures on Dr. Post, and cost constraints of Worthy's employer, who simply "farmed out" its employees' health care, because "we . . . need to control our operating costs, of which health care premiums are a large part" (S10). But simply placing patient and patient population health as the first priority does not, in itself solve the problem. Everyone in the Worthy scenario thought they *were* putting patients first, even though some confused rule-following and financial survival with that priority. Dr. Post gave Worthy a choice, but given his condition, it was not an informed one. Given this healthcare system, the first priority of patient health has to be operationalized in a manner that makes sense to all parties under the pressures the ordinary patient, healthcare professional, or executive faces every day. One approach is the "reasonable person" or "prudent layperson" standard. This standard, in brief, argues that even under managed care, one of the "rules" should be that payment is authorized "for emergency and other services when a reasonable person believes his or her condition requires emergency evaluation or treatment" (S6). While this standard appears to be fuzzy, it turns out that reasonable people will usually agree about such conditions. We all agree that Worthy should have received emergency care even in a unit not ordinarily covered by GoodCare. But neither Worthy nor Dr. Post nor even Michael Depp, the Medical Director at GoodCare thought this was possible. Indeed, Dr. Depp argued, "Looking back on what happened, I don't really think our system failed Mr. Worthy" (S9).

Another related approach is to consider which core values are at stake in healthcare management and delivery, prioritize those, and use those as the basis for one's decision in crisis situations such as Worthy's. Prioritizing, the well being of the patient (as well as his autonomy) are and must be, the first considerations.

Otherwise the organization will fail as a *healthcare* organization. Moreover, if the Collins and Porras study has validity, such prioritization of patient well being and professional expertise will allow healthcare organizations to succeed, even become profitable.

But let us assume that GoodCare and its professional and managerial staff know all of this and in fact try to prioritize patient care and respect for professionals, even though some of their systems procedures belie this assumption. There is a third challenge. Dr. Davis, Dr. Post, Michael Depp, Connie Rogers are all in the middle of large organizations – they are employees. How do they lead "from the middle" and make what we, after the fact, declare as the "right" decisions? If, as professionals they have duties specified by their professions, and if these are to override other claims, then, first, they have to be operationally committed to that prioritization. Secondly, as professionals, they have to look for allies within GoodCare, challenge the rule-bound status quo, and make a space for the value of patient care. While this appears to be asking a great deal of these individuals, in fact there is evidence that such forms of leadership are very effective in challenging organizational authority and systems constraints (Bruner et al., 1998, pp. 251–75; Nielsen, 2000). Such leadership was patently absent in John Worthy's situation. If only one of these professionals had spoken out, raised the issue of patient priority, and taken professional responsibility, John Worthy might be with us today.

To summarize, what I am suggesting is that what was lacking in the Worthy case was self-awareness of the systems in which these actors were operating, evaluation of the system, organizations, and sub-systems in question, and then, finally, courage to make changes both in decision-making and later, to organizations in question and to the system itself. What is missing in this scenario is what I have called in another place, "moral imagination," "the ability in particular circumstances to discover and evaluate possibilities not merely determined by that circumstance, or limited by its operative mental models, or merely framed by a set of rules or rule-governed concerns" (Werhane, 1999, p. 93). In systems thinking what is required is moral imagination, now operating on organizational and systemic levels as well as within individual decision-making.

Systems thinking and traditional health care issues

Let us step back from the Worthy case and consider another application of systems thinking. Given the present state of healthcare payment and delivery in the USA, a systems approach is essential in dealing adequately with more traditional ethical issues in medicine. In a recent article on informed consent Susan Wolf uses that example to argue that merely considering patient informed consent by the physician at the point of treatment (a dyadic approach) is an oversimplification of the complex arrangements in health care systems and bypasses many elements that affect patient consent. Systemic arrangements demand informed consent concerning subscription to a plan, insurance and healthcare coverage, patient information sharing and transfer, rationing, and other points of care. It is precisely in this network or web of relationships that patients become ill-informed about their coverage, options, insurance, etc. Merely to think of informed consent in the patient-healthcare professional one-on-one encounters will not take into account how that patient is insured, how the professional and the healthcare center are reimbursed, capitation and rationing limitations (which may be proscribed by the employer of the patient, the insurer, the state, Medicare or Medicaid, or by other criteria), patient options in treatment or choices to go to another healthcare center. Obligations to inform patients run all the way through the healthcare system and not merely at entry or before treatment. It is not merely the *physician's* duty to inform her patients since that is placing an undue burden of knowledge on healthcare professionals. These duties run throughout all parts of the system as well. Disclosure and full information needs to be disseminated at every stage, not merely at the point of treatment (Wolf, 1999).

A similar analysis reveals the complexity of protecting the privacy of medical records. In analyzing privacy issues, traditionally the focus was often on the protection of patient records by the physician or the hospital. Under the present health care delivery system, this, in fact, has little affect on protecting these records. Indeed, even in the "olden days," one's records were subject to pervue by those working in the physician's office, by nurses, interns, residents and other attendants at the hospital, one's pharmacy, laboratory, and by any other medical facility with which one had contact.[7] Today, one's insurance company, employer, laboratory, hospital or other healthcare center usually has access to these records. Insurance databases often have access to information. Records of those on Medicaid and Medicare or claiming disability or workers compensation are available to state and federal government agencies. Anyone using the internet for health advice or for ordering prescriptions exposes herself to information sharing. While federal medical records safeguards are being proposed, these would require patient written consent before disclosure in even the most routine cases such as claims payment. Such legislation might protect patient privacy to some extent, but operationalizing written consent in practice might create overwhelming complications. And since every patient would have to give consent for her treatment and insurance, the result would not be to protect the privacy of medical records except in some instances from managed care organizations other than one's own, or perhaps from online advertisers and marketers who often share consumer/patient lists. What appears to be simple protection of a patient's records in fact must be approached systemically in order to comprehend what is at stake and to achieve any results (Murray, 1999, p. A12; Pear, 2000, p. A1; Hodge et al. 1999).

To conclude, systems thinking is essential if we are to understand, evaluate, and change health care payment and delivery in this country. Nevertheless, despite the importance of systems thinking and systems analysis in health care, and this is the final point of the paper, no healthcare system or subsystem is or need be thought of, as a closed static system. Healthcare systems are dynamic, and revisable phenomena, created and changed by individuals. But until we comprehend the complexity of the systemic interrelationships within and across systems we cannot successfully evaluate the system or subsystem in question and begin to make changes that are critical if we are to avoid unnecessary deaths such as John Worthy's. Nor, if Susan Wolf is right, can we deal adequately with traditional ethical issues in health care. This paper is an initiation of that set of thinking processes.

Notes

1 This paper has benefited greatly from the work of Linda Emanuel and Susan Wolf, and from collaborative work with Ann Mills, Mary Rorty, and Edward Spencer and the comments of Norman Bowie and Andy Wicks.

2 Reprinted by permission from the *Hasting Center Report, Special Supplement*, 1998: What Could Have Saved John Worthy? July–August. S1–S12.

3 The long-term financial performance of each has been remarkable. A dollar invested in a visionary company stock fund on 1 January 1926, with dividends reinvested, and making appropriate adjustments for when the companies became available on the stock market would have grown by 31 December 1990 to $6356. A dollar invested in a comparison stock fund composed of these companies would have returned $955 – more than twice the general market, but less then one sixth of the return provided by the visionary companies. That dollar invested in a general market fund would have grown to $415 (Collins and Porras, 1994, pp. 4–5).

4 See Jones et al., chapter 1 in this volume, for a complete and updated version of this theory.

5 Ozar et al. (2001) postulate other priorities including unmet healthcare needs, advocacy for social policy reform and community benefit. I have gathered those together in the "community and public health" category. Ozar et al. also place organizational solvency and survival in the list of secondary priorities. I disagree with this prioritization.

6 In analyzing the ethics of systems, Linda Emanuel proposes an evaluative grid that sets out the purpose, structure, processes and outcomes of a particular system against professional, political, and economic models (Emanuel, 2000, Table 1, p. 161). While the details of that grid are certainly subject to more debate, this approach pushes us into the direction of more broad-based systems thinking and into more creative and imaginative ways to analyze and evaluate healthcare systems. In the case of Worthy, we are working on a more micro level, dealing with issues within the US healthcare system and the system of GoodCare. Moreover, using Emanuel's grid, one has to sort out and evaluate professional, political, and economic models as they apply to health care. Our prioritization in the previous section of patient health and autonomy, professional competence and excellence, economic viability, and public health, is one example of such a evaluative scheme. While many will argue as to the sequencing of these priorities, some sort of prioritization is implicit in any list of professional, political and economic norms, and making those explicit helps to clarify where there is congruence.

7 A physician writing about confidentiality of patient information did an informal survey and found that 75 clinicians or employees had legitimate access to his patient's record, which meant that they were in some measure engaged in his patient's care (Mark Siegler, 1982).

References

Bruner, R., Eaker, M., Freeman, R. E., Spekman, R. and Teisberg, E. O. 1998: Leading from the middle. *The Portable MBA*. New York: Wiley, 251–75.

Collins, J. and Porras, J. 1994: *Built to Last*. New York: Harper Business.

Emanuel, L. 2000: Ethics and the structures of health Care. *Cambridge Quarterly*. 9, 151–68.

Emanuel, E. and Emanuel, L. 1996: What is accountability in health care? *Annals of Internal Medicine*. 124, 229–39.

Freeman, R. E. 1999: Stakeholder theory and the modern corporation. In T. J. Donaldson and P. H. Werhane (eds.), *Ethical Issues in Business* (6th edn) Upper Saddle River, NJ: Prentice-Hall, Inc., 247–57.

French, P. 1979: The corporation as a moral person. *American Philosophical Quarterly*. 16, 207–15.

Friedman, M. 1970: The social responsibility of business is to increase its profits. *New York Times Magazine*. 13 September. 122–6.

Hall, R. T. 2000: *An Introduction to Healthcare Organizational Ethics*. New York: Oxford University Press.

Hodge, J. G. Jr., Gostin, L. O. and Jacobson, P. D. 1999: Legal issues concerning electronic health information: Privacy, quality and liability. *Journal of the American Medical Association*. 282, 1466–71.

Inglehart, J. K. 1994: Physicians and the growth of managed care. *New England Journal of Medicine*. 33, 1167.

Laszlo, A. and Krippner, S. 1998: Systems theories: Their origins, foundations and development. In J. Scott Jordan (ed.) *Systems Theories and a Priori Aspects of Perception*. Amsterdam: Elsevier.

Mitroff, I. I. and Linstone, H. 1993: *The Unbounded Mind*. New York: Oxford University Press.

Murray, S. 1999: On medical-privacy issue, the doctor finally may be in. *Wall Street Journal*. 20 August A12.

Nielsen, R. P. 2000: The politics of long-term corruption reform. *Business Ethics Quarterly*. 10, 305–17.

Ozar, D., Emanuel, L., Berg, J. and Werhane, P. H. 2001: Organization ethics in health care: A framework for ethical decision-making by provider organizations. AMA Working Group on the Ethics of Healthcare Organizations. Report 2000. *Annals of Internal Medicine*. Forthcoming.

Pear, R. 2000: Clinton will issue new privacy rules to shield patients. *New York Times*. 20 December.

Ramo, S. 1969: *Cure for Chaos*. New York: D. Mackay Co.

Siegler, M. 1982: Confidentiality: A decrepit concept. *New England Journal of Medicine*. 307 (24), 1518–21.

Spencer, E., Mills, A., Rorty, M. and Werhane, P. 2000: *The Ethics of Healthcare Organizations*. New York: Oxford University Press.

Werhane, P. H. 1985: *Persons, Rights, and Corporations*. Englewood Cliffs, NJ: Prentice-Hall Inc.

Werhane, P. H. 1999: *Moral Imagination and Management Decision Making*. New York: Oxford University Press.

Werhane, P. H. 2000: Stakeholder theory and the ethics of healthcare organizations. *Cambridge Quarterly.* 9, 169–81.

Wolf, S. 1999: Toward a systemic theory of informed consent in managed care. *Houston Law Review.* 35, 1631–81.

Wong, K. L. 1998: *Medicine and the Marketplace.* Notre Dame IN: Notre Dame University Press.

Further Reading

Berwick, D. M. and Nolan, T. W. 1998: Physicians as leaders in improving health care. *Annals of Internal Medicine.* 128, 289–92.

Chapter 15

The Ethical Dilemmas of the Biotechnology Industry

Lisa H. Newton

Introduction: The Owl Attempts to Fly at Dawn

The Owl of Minerva is supposed to fly at twilight, when all the data are in, the mistakes made and chewed over, everything said that can be said, and the philosopher may reflect on the subject in peace. For this topic, the ethical dimensions of the business of biotechnology, twilight is unimaginably far away. As I set pen to paper (or mouse to CPU) in the summer of the year 2000, two projects – one private, one public – have jointly, within the month, assembled a working model of the human genome; the uses of this knowledge are the subject of vigorous dispute. And who should own it, or profit from it, either by selling information or by selling the pharmaceuticals derived from it? Meanwhile, a firestorm rages around the development and sale of genetically modified organisms for agricultural purposes, a storm that ultimately involves all global trade arrangements. What follows in this article is an attempt to bring a philosophical perspective on an enterprise still in its tormented beginnings, rather like an essay on the applications of Just War Theory to the conduct of a particular conflict, written in a foxhole with the first shells of that conflict bursting around. This is a very preliminary study, but absolutely necessary if the mistakes are not to be made before anyone has a chance to think about them. If we are to achieve any insight at all into the dilemmas of biotechnology, the Owl is going to have to become used to some very bright early morning sunlight.

Untimely Born

The industry, or industries, dependent on biotechnology bear an unwanted distinction: they have been the targets of moral attack since well before they came into being. Only slavery, in the history of free market capitalism, aroused a more intense conviction that the entire motive of an industry is morally flawed. From the first, we have had doubts about the manipulation of the basic materials of life itself for the purpose of making a profit. But those doubts take at least three forms, and only one can concern us here. Before we can talk about the ethical dilemmas that confront these industries, we will have to distinguish among the kinds of moral criticism that confront them, since they bear with very different moral force on the businesses involved.

Objections to the knowledge itself

First, there are the *theological* (or quasi-theological) objections to biotechnology. These objections call attention to the sacred nature of life itself, and express serious (if nameless) fears about tinkering with it. In a revealing article in *The New York Times* international section in July of 1998, Michael Specter quotes a traditional farmer in Germany, denouncing the US attempts to "change the basic rules of life" by the genetic engineering of common agricultural crops – producing "genetically modified organisms," or GMOs. Such changes were not for him, he insisted. "Here we are going to live like God intended" (Specter, 1998). Why does God hate GMOs so much in Europe? It's a good question, but not one we can take on in this paper, which deals with the for-profit operations of the corporations and individuals of the free-market economy. Theology will take us beyond our boundaries (or turn this article into a book). We must, however, take seriously the effects of public perception on market behavior, and the complex shaping of public perceptions by market-related communications.

Concern for the biosphere

Second, there are the *environmental* objections to biotechnology. These objections focus not on the consequences of the problematic technology, whatever it may be, for human rights and interests (the ordinary focus of business ethics) – at least not in the foreseeable future. They focus instead on the values that Aldo Leopold associated with the ethic of the Land itself (Leopold, 1949). These values include biodiversity (the preservation of all existing natural species in the environment), integrity of the ecosystem (freedom from invasion by human activity or exotic species), and resilience (the ability of the ecosystem, or the biosphere, to recover from natural shocks). Such objections, for instance, are raised against many GMOs, including genetically engineered salmon, which gain weight much faster than wild salmon and are therefore profitable to raise and sell. If they get loose from their pens, however, they might mate with the wild salmon. As the engineered salmon are bigger, they would have an evolutionary advantage, and might eventually replace the wild salmon. From the human point of view, so much the better. From the point of view of biodiversity and the integrity of the ecosystem, so much the worse, for a natural species will have been forever altered by human meddling. The rule for this paper is simple: To the extent that environmental impact has human consequences, we shall consider it; to the extent that the ecosystem apart from humans is in question, we cannot.

We will also consider objections that seem to take into account only species other than human, when they raise symbolic or other issues that directly affect public welfare or perceptions. For instance, one apparently environmental objection is raised with respect to crops engineered to carry new traits, whose pollen, flying freely among the wild plants, may carry those to plants in the wild. A cardinal example of such a problem is the danger that may be posed to the larvae of monarch butterflies, that feed on the milkweed plant, when pollen from corn engineered to contain insecticide blows upon the milkweed (Yoon, 1999; *New York Times* 1999: Editorial, "A Warning From the Butterflies," 21 May; Carey, 1999). To the extent that we are talking only about butterflies and milkweed, the objections might seem to be solely environmental (and not well taken at that: the results of the single study are disputed, and even if valid, the pollen transfer threatens neither milkweed nor monarchs). But the monarch butterfly is more than an insect. Like the bald eagle, it is a powerful symbol of the beauty of the wild environment, and is closely linked with our perception, often felt more than articulated, that that beautiful environment is fragile and threatened. For this reason, any perceived threat to the monarch arouses reactions that go well beyond the self-interested calculations of the relative advantages and disadvantages of engineered corn, and for this reason we will have to take it seriously as impacting the market.

Attempts to do business ethically

The ethical focus of this paper is very narrow, and has to be. We are dealing only with the ethical dimensions of the new biotechnology industry, the problems raised by its operations for human rights and interests. At best, even this analysis is only a preliminary sketch: the industry is very young, its products are very problematic, the possibility of abuse of its knowledge base is very real, and even its claim to operate within the system of private property is disputed. Let us say a few words on these aspects of the ethical environment surrounding biotechnology and the market, and then take on three representative disputes as an introduction to ethical reflection in this field.

First, the "products" of biotechnology are difficult to define, let alone evaluate for safety and effectiveness. Genetically modified corn is not like the Pinto car, one of a huge and known species, whose variations can be investigated against a background of known characteristics and government standards. The magnitude of the distance between an established line of automobiles and a new one is usually calculable (and usually small). The distance between regular corn and a GMO just is not calculable: it is either infinitesimal (amounting to no more than a normal variation that might occur in nature) or immense (amounting to the distance between Nature and the untested assumptions of ignorant humans). If the former is correct, there is no need for distinguishing the new from the old, and the GMO is hardly a "product" at all. If the latter is correct, what kind of testing would ever be reassuring? Unfortunately, the decision to regard the GMO as one or the other, at present, is in the hands of the media and the political process. How should a company that markets such products ensure their safety for the ultimate consumer, meet the objections of competitors and non-governmental organizations (NGOs) in their proposed markets, and define the directions and limits of future products of this sort? These questions are not separable from other, larger questions, involving world trade in agricultural goods and the World Trade Organization (WTO) that regulates it, the economic situation of the small farmer and the future of agriculture in every country in the world.

Second, the Free Market system depends upon the legal and moral protection of the institution of private property; we cannot buy or sell unless we own, unquestionably, what we sell prior to the sale, and will own, safely, what we buy after it. Intellectual property is like any other property: if an idea or process is my idea, my discovery, my product, I can take out a patent on it. I have free and exclusive right to the use and licensing of that process or discovery during the life of that patent, and any party who would use it must pay me for a license. Does that include the genes discovered during the process of sorting out the human genome? How about the proteins that the genes turn out to be responsible for synthesizing? Above all, does that include drugs and other modes of therapy developed from all this new knowledge? Does it matter that much of the information assembled by the private parties taking out the patent was actually uncovered by a taxpayer-financed project? Who ultimately has the "right" to all of this new information? The question of the legitimacy of patenting genetic discoveries cannot be separated from larger political and economic questions about the pharmaceutical industry in general. Are its profits too high? Does the burden of drug costs lie unfairly on the backs of senior citizens, who concededly consume a disproportionate share of pharmaceuticals in the USA? (Should such costs be borne by the taxpayer?) What are the obligations of pharmaceutical companies (as opposed, say, to toy companies) to subsidize the purchase of their products for the poor in this country and across the world? In any survey of the moral implications of new uses of genetic knowledge in pharmaceuticals, there is very little solid moral ground in the pharmaceuticals industry on which to plant the transit.

Third, now that we have amazed ourselves by sorting out the human genome, what is the potential for the use of that knowledge? How will that knowledge in fact be used? Who will decide how that knowledge will be used? In the literature of this project looms a shadowy but overwhelming fear, occasionally tinged with theology, but also very practical and political, about the threat of loss of privacy in the penetrating glare of the new knowledge, genetic and otherwise. The fear stems from the enormous power that can be wielded by one who holds this knowledge. My entire genome, it may be, can be traced from one drop of my blood, possibly from a snippet of my hair or a flake from my skin left on my bed sheet. Once known, the holder of that knowledge could tell (it may be) how long I will live, of what diseases I will suffer and die, how well I will get along with others, and whether or not I will commit a crime. On the basis of that knowledge, its holder could decide what kinds of health or life insurance I will be sold and at what cost, what employment I will be chosen for, and possibly, that it would be a good idea to put me in jail now and save the trouble of doing it later. Of particular concern to the US consumer, in this era of "managed care" in which the distribution of health care is largely controlled by for-profit health maintenance organizations (HMOs), is the possibility that such information would become available to the insurance companies that administer the HMOs. Insurance companies have the right to tailor access and cost of every other kind of insurance to the risk posed by the insured; why not in health care also? Again, questions regarding genetic information so used are not separable from very serious questions concerning the entire health care regime in the USA at this time. The moral position of the HMO vis-à-vis the patient is in violent flux in the popular press and in the philosophical literature, and it may be some time before it is settled in any area.

Evident in the questions above is one of the leitmotifs of this paper: novel and troubling as they may be in and of themselves, the dilemmas of biotechnology are also inseparable from the most intractable and polarizing political and economic disputes of this nation and the world at this time. We *do not know* what to do about overwhelming march of world free trade and the plight of the small farmer (or any small producer) worldwide. We are *afraid* of our loss of privacy and the power wielded by governments and private companies in determining the conditions of our lives. We *have no formula* for the just and responsible provision of health care in this country, including regulation of the industries that profit from it. Of all times for an industry to be born, the "life sciences" industry, biotechnology, has picked the worst. These larger contexts and these difficult times must be kept in mind in consideration of the industry-specific problems that follow. The first problem concerns the warrant of merchantability of genetically modified foods: what responsibilities do Monsanto and its competitors have for assuring their safety? The second concerns the place in the private property system for knowledge of the genome: should Incyte and its competitors be allowed to patent genes, proteins, and other basic elements of life? The third concerns our privacy and the operations of our health care industry: should information about our genetic makeup be available to insurance companies on the same basis as information about our driving?

Genetically Modified Crops:
The Controversy over the "Frankenfoods"

A success story suddenly goes sour

The problem and the possibilities that led to the genetic engineering of market crops are not new. For almost fifteen years, we have known that crops could be engineered by the techniques of recombinant DNA to have characteristics that would be desirable – even that it was possible to take a beneficial gene (that repels insects, for instance) out of one species and put it into another, which thereafter, with all its children, would have that trait (Specter, 1998). Crops, for instance, could be granted resistance to weed killers – saving farmers, in the case of genetically engineered tomatoes, potentially $30 per acre each season by reducing the need for hand or mechanical tilling. Obvious business opportunities awaited the chemical companies who engineered seeds resistant to their own herbicides. We have also known for a long time that we would have to do something to improve the productivity of agriculture worldwide. In 1999, it took one hectare, two and a half acres, to feed four people, according to Maria Zimmerman, who is in charge of agricultural research for the sustainable development department of the UN Food and Agricultural Organization. A projected increase in demand, stemming from a higher population living at a higher standard of living, will require that hectare to support six people in about 20 years. The obvious question was, can we put our intriguing technology to work to solve the world's food problems? Robert B. Shapiro, CEO of Monsanto, set out to do just that.

Robert Shapiro took control of the Monsanto Company in 1995 with a clear mandate and intention to reshape the conglomerate away from its beginnings in chemicals (including PCBs, dioxin and Agent Orange!) toward a new birth as a Life Sciences enterprise. Foods, seeds and pharmaceuticals can all be enhanced with the new biotechnology, as he knew, and he intended to capitalize on the new science to reshape those industries.

> A lawyer and a former urban-affairs professor, Shapiro had become the unlikely Johnny Appleseed of genetic modification, promoting his vision of a world where there are not simply foods and drugs but foods that take the place of drugs. . . . "[T]he application of contemporary biological knowledge to issues like food and nutrition and human health has to occur [Shapiro argues];. . . . People want to live better, and they will use the tools they have to do it. Biology is the best tool we have" (Specter, 2000, p. 60).

The last decade of the twentieth century had seen some amazing advances in biotechnology. Monsanto had developed glyphosate, a powerful and safe herbicide marketed as Roundup, and was beginning to engineer "Roundup Ready" plants that would resist it (Benbrook and Moses, 1986). Altering hormones by genetic engineering, and injecting them into cattle, was creating cows with more beef and less fat (Brody, 1988). Then Monsanto and others produced a line of plants (primarily potatoes and corn) that contained their own insecticide, by inserting *Bacillus thuringiensis* (Bt), a natural insect-killer, into their genes. The developments were widely welcomed and adopted by farmers. There had been no transgenic crops available for planting in 1990; by 1995, four million acres of transgenic crops were under cultivation; by the end of the century, more than 100 million. "In the United States, half of the enormous soybean crop and more than a third of the corn are the products of biotechnology" (Specter, 2000, p. 61).

Controversy over the desirability of GMOs – begun with Jeremy Rifkin's attacks on the Flavr Savr Tomato in 1993 (Seabrook, 1993) – acquired new momentum with this development. Environmentalists fought the use of bioengineered Bt. The protest came primarily from organic farmers, who used Bt exclusively for their crops just because it was a naturally occurring organism; they were worried about "acquired resistance," the danger that bugs might become immune to Bt (Naj, 1989). (In any species of insect, some individuals will naturally be resistant to any insecticide. The extensive use of a pesticide selects for those individuals, who, without competition from others, will thrive and multiply, eventually making the insecticide useless against that species.) The best answer to the charge was that the Bt plants at least got rid of large amounts of toxic spray. Consider Monsanto's Bt-bioengineered cotton plant. Before this plant was available, cotton planters put 100 million pounds of agricultural chemicals on their crop each year, most of it insecticide. Now they did not have to do that. Even environmentalists conceded the improvement (Slutsker, 1990).

By 1998, activist objections had flowered into a powerful popular, even populist, movement, that had succeeded in getting GMOs banned in much of Europe (Specter, 1998). The appeals that drove the movement have a puzzling disconnect with reality: as above, they include the horror of the Holocaust, also the fear of a repeat of "Mad Cow Disease," referring to an episode of bovine spongiform encephalopathy (BSE) in the UK some years ago. What does that episode of bovine infection have to do with bioengineering of corn? The comparisons are instructive: First, profit-oriented innovations had led farmers to include the offal of slaughtered animals in feed for their herds of beef cattle, and that is how the cows became infected in the first place. Second, even as infected cattle staggered and fell before the television cameras of three continents, scientists plausibly argued that such disease could not possibly affect humans, so British beef was quite safe. Third, after all the scientists promised it wouldn't happen, and all government agencies pooh-poohed the danger, some people who ate that beef became very sick. Proving? That businessmen are greedy, that science, in the pay of industry, is not always honest or right, and that the regulators, also funded by industry, cannot always be relied upon. BSE has no other role in this controversy, but it is a very strong supporting role: The BSE controversy served to undermine the authority of regulatory authority and scientific pronouncements, and that undermining turned out to be very important in the outcome of the GMO debate. We'll see those cows again.

Terminators and monarchs

In the middle of 1999, the volume of the war increased noticeably as a new controversy erupted. Monsanto had acquired Delta, a seed firm that had engineered a new kind of gene, instantly dubbed the "terminator gene," that would make sure that its bioengineered plants had no progeny. Why do this? An unsigned editorial on 9 October 1999 in *The Economist* entitled 'Fertility Rights' explained:

> Terminator is a set of genes that act as a series of molecular switches. These switches are set off by a chemical signal sprayed on genetically tinkered seed. Although the plant springing forth from that seed is healthy and can go about its business of producing grain, say, quite normally, the grain that it produced will not grow if planted, because the activated terminator gene has killed off the seed's reproductive bits. This means that farmers who want to grow a plant with the same genetically engineered traits next season have to go back to the company for more seeds.

A new uproar greeted the news. Monsanto was seen as depriving poor farmers of the developing world the possibility of saving their seeds. More ominously, those genes might spread, by pollen, to the fields of neighboring farms, injecting themselves into the seeds of traditional crops, and making it impossible for farmers planting traditional crops to save their seeds from year to year. Underlining the horror was the fact that farmers could not know that their seeds were contaminated until a new crop planted simply failed to germinate, and their family starved (Feder, 1999). Eventually Shapiro had to bow to pressure from the Rockefeller Foundation, and formally promised not to commercialize the genetic engineering of seed sterility.

> Given its parlous public image, Monsanto must be hoping that its move will buy it a little goodwill. The terminator technology has raised such interest in the industry, and caused such an outcry in society, because it is a neat and potentially powerful way for biotechnology firms such as Monsanto to protect the intellectual property locked in genetically modified seeds . . . (*Economist*, 'Fertility Rights', 9 October 1999).

On the other hand,

> the battle highlights the difficulty of protecting intellectual property when the products are sophisticated genetic technologies. Monsanto and other firms have said the terminator is a legitimate way to recoup the billions of dollars they have poured into developing bioengineered crops with traits such as insect resistance (*U.S. News and World Report*, 1999: Editorial, October 18, 1999, p. 83).

The tide turned even more decisively against Monsanto in the spring of 1999, as engineered corn was accused of being dangerous to Monarch butterflies (Yoon, 1999). Suddenly, wrote John Carey, covering science from Washington for *Business Week*, foes of bioengineering in the food supply have their own potent symbol: the beloved monarch butterfly. In mid-May, Cornell University researchers reported that pollen from corn altered to slay corn-borer pests can land on neighboring milkweed plants, where it can kill monarch butterfly caterpillars. The finding has biotech foes exulting. "The monarch butterfly experiment is the smoking gun that will be the beginning of the unraveling of the industry," says Jeremy Rifkin . . . The findings cast genetically altered food plants in a new light. They may benefit farmers and consumers, but now opponents have evidence that there could be worrisome ecological effects on other species.

Both Greenpeace and the Union of Concerned Scientists are now asking the EPA to pull the seeds off the market (Carey, 1999). "The industry is in big trouble," according to agriculture consultant Charles Benbrook. "It misplayed its hand by overstating its command of the science and its knowledge of the consequences." If biotech companies had considered unintended side effects years ago, they would not, he argued, be on the defensive now. "The industry 'asked for trouble, and they got it,' says monarch expert Lincoln Brower of Sweet Briar College" (Carey, 1999). The judgment seems harsh; who could have suspected damage to monarchs? But that is just the point, of course.

None of this furor was of any environmental relevance. Monarchs are not endangered or even plausibly threatened in their northern range (their southern hibernation range in Mexico, woodlands periodically raided by very poor farmers, are a different story). Milkweed is certainly not endangered, and grows in plenty of locations nowhere near cornfields. When it does show up near a cornfield, the farmers tend to get rid of it, not for worry about the monarchs, but because it is a pesky invasive weed. Pollen does not blow very far. The danger to monarchs from Bt-engineered corn is somewhere between negligible and nonexistent, although trying to conduct field tests to establish this point would be prohibitively expensive (Yoon, 2000). None of this slowed down the campaign to uproot the corn.

"If the current British furore over genetically modified foods were a crop not a crisis," chortled *The Economist* in June of 1999,

you can bet Monsanto or its competitors would have patented it. It has many of the traits that genetic engineers prize: it is incredibly fertile, thrives in inhospitable conditions, has tremendous consumer appeal and is easy to cross with other interests to create a hardy new hybrid. Moreover, it seems to resist anything that might kill it, from scientific evidence to official reassurance. Now it seems to be spreading to other parts of Europe, Australia and even America. There, regulators will face the same questions that confront the British government: how should the public be reassured, and how can the benefits of GM foods be reaped without harm, either to human beings or to the environment?

At least, *The Economist* ('Who's afraid? 19 June 1999) consoled us, the USA doesn't have to deal with the Prince of Wales, who had for religious reasons taken a very public position against GMOs. The editorial went on to point out that this unforeseen consumer backlash "threatens to undermine both this new technology and the credibility of the agencies that regulate it." That, they would have us recall, was the major effect of the fallout from Mad Cow disease. (There go those cows again). By repeated infections of scandal, and general suspicion (fanned by NGOs) that government is in league with the biotech industry, food fears seem to have developed a resistance to official reassurance, much as insect species develop resistance to pesticides.

The public relations battle

Monsanto was doing something wrong, and nothing in the management manuals could tell them just what. They seemed to have science on their side, government regulatory agencies had been supportive, and they thought they could really improve the nutritional status of the world (while making money for their shareholders). Where did all this hostility come from? The major factor, as anyone could see by the fall of 1999, was that in none of their calculations had they anticipated the reaction to GMOs from the NGOs like Greenpeace and Environmental Defense (formerly the Environmental Defense Fund). After all, to whom is a business, a for-profit publicly held corporation, accountable? Two accounts dominate the literature. One holds that the corporation is accountable only to its owners, the shareholders. This view is generally propounded by the Wall Street-oriented business commentary, upheld by a significant stream of our legal tradition, and will constitute the assumption of the next section. The other, associated with the liberal reform movement that infused the corporate world in the 1970s and into the 1980s, holds that good management must weigh the claims of all the "stakeholders," all who will be affected by the decisions of the corporation (Freeman, 1984). Both views are logically consistent, and both are widely espoused. But neither one of them include the NGOs as parties who will demand an accounting, and the NGOs, from case to case, continue to take corporations completely by surprise. Monsanto, Novartis, and the other players in the biotech farming industry were no exception.

Even as the battle goes on, with everyone swearing the GM foods are safe, all food processors are going back to buying conventional foods (Magnusson et al., 1999). This retreat from the new crops hurts farmers, and incidentally undermines the battle against protectionism in world trade. The stakes are high. Overseas shipments of US crops came to $46 billion last year, giving us a $5 billion trade surplus in farm products. Half of US soybeans and one third of US corn are genetically modified. About 60 percent of processed food, and virtually all candy, syrup, salad dressing, chocolate, have GM material in them. Monsanto had hoped to reap $881 million by 2003 in licensing fees for its high-tech seeds. It appears that they will fall far short of that target (Magnusson et al., 1999).

Now, the bio-food phobia is catching on in Japan. Brewers have sworn off GM corn, and the government is mandating labeling for 28 different products containing GM food. Japanese tofu makers, responding to public sentiment, are switching to non-GM soybeans, jeopardizing some 500,000 tons of imports, most of them from the U.S.

A measured defense of GMOs has been offered. John Carey and others presented a solid examination of the whole topic ("Are Bio-Foods Safe?") in *Business Week* toward the end of 1999 (Carey et al., 1999); Margaret Kriz did the same in "Global Food Fights" in *The National Journal* (Kriz, 2000). Both pieces pointed out that genetically engineered foods had indeed been tested, certainly much more than conventional foods were ever tested, and that time and again, the proof of the pudding had been in the safe eating. But defenders were badly out numbered, or at least outshouted.

Eventually Monsanto and other firms hired a Perception Management firm to help. Full-page ads bloomed in the press in the spring of 2000 ("Biotechnology gives her a better way to protect her crop – and her grandchildren's planet"; "When leukemia laid him low, biotechnology helped get him up and running again"), and a widely distributed colorful brochure, "Good Ideas Are Growing," sponsored by the industry association, the Council for Biotechnology Information. Will this campaign work? Ross S. Irvine, in a special article in *O'Dwyer's* PR Services Report, thinks the whole campaign is ridiculous. "The Council for Biotechnology Information is spending more than $50 million for an advertising campaign to convince consumers that biotech food is safe to eat and not a threat to the environment," in an effort, probably useless, to keep Frankenfood fear out of the USA. "They are basically throwing the money away because feel-good image ads just don't make it in the era of the Internet." Irvine recommends that Monsanto become a "netwarrior," using the internet to reach new audiences and undermine the Internet attacks against it (Irvine, 2000). Someone must have been listening. The Council for Biotechnology Information ("Good Ideas Are Growing") now has a website, www.whybiotech.com, in addition to its full-page ads, booklets, and an 800 number (1-800-980-8660). Maybe it will do the industry some good. But it will be catch-up ball all the way, and that may not be the best way to go.

Meanwhile, policy and action on GMOs, are very inconsistent. There is still no satisfactory explanation for the fact that GMOs have been a non-issue in the USA and anathema in Europe. Worries about food safety and worries about public relations seem to be inseparable. Cries for "labeling" of all GMO food seem to go unheard. Genetically modified crops continually to be widely grown even as the conflicts multiply. Novartis, a Swiss pharmaceutical giant, makes and sells genetically modified corn and soybean seeds, while Gerber Products, one of its subsidiaries, has virtuously banned all genetically modified ingredients from its baby-food formulas. Heinz has banned GMOs from its baby foods but not its other products. McDonald's will not accept genetically modified potatoes for its fries, but it cooks them in vegetable oil made from modified corn and soybeans. Pepsi Cola uses corn syrup made from genetically modified corn, but Pepsico's Frito-Lay division won't use that corn in its chips. But for a company to maintain even a limited ban successfully, it must have extraordinary knowledge of its sources. Most companies buy products on the open market, and most food suppliers have no idea whether or not there are GMOs in the mix. The "labeling" agenda would be very hard to carry out even if everyone thought it was a good idea. (Barboza, 2000) Where do we go from here? Shapiro goes home; Pharmacia, which bought out Monsanto, wants to concentrate on its pharmaceutical divisions.

Patenting Life: The Uses of the Genome

Another firestorm is brewing over the patenting of genetic material, and the threats to privacy if genetic knowledge becomes publicly available. How is intellectual property to be protected in this new field? Or is the whole effort to make "property" out of genetic knowledge misguided?

The history of the mapping of the human genome is instructive. The Human Genome Project (HGP) started up in 1990 as a public project, an international consortium of teams of scientists. Its objective was to map the entire human genome. It planned to do this by the year 2005 for $3 billion, supplied by the Wellcome Trust in the UK and the US National Institutes of Health (NIH). The leaders are James D. Watson and his immediate successor, Francis Collins, of the NIH, and John Sulston of the Sanger Center in Cambridge, England. They have consistently sought, and received, contributions from all nations, and have made their project readily available, posting all results on the World-Wide Web as they went along. Suddenly, in 1998, the public project found itself joined, as an unexpected companion in exploration, by a private, for-profit, project, Celera Genomics, led by Craig Venter, formerly of the NIH. Celera is backed by investors, who intend to profit from subscriptions to the Celera database, which should be of enormous interest to manufacturers of drugs. With genetic knowledge, future companies should be able to patent discoveries for their use in engineering profitable organisms, as above, or creating drugs that would be tailored to an individual's genetic capacity. Venter proposed a 2003 deadline for completing Celera's work in sequencing; he was immediately joined in this objective by the public consortium. The spring of the year 2000 found itself entertained by their competition, inspired by their progress, and ultimately rewarded, in June 2000, by their joint announcement that 90 per cent of the project was now complete.

But the enterprise does raise some questions, does it not? Since the private venture, while adopting some novel approaches to mapping, was able to succeed only by regularly scarfing up the publicly available results of the public venture, why should the private corporation have the rights to exploit those results for private profit? Further, does the notion of "patenting life," life that we did not really create, raise philosophical questions on its own?

Let us review. What can be patented? To patent something in the US Office of Patents and Trademarks (PTO), it must be "useful" (most Rube Goldberg machines are ruled out here), "novel" (don't try to patent the wheel again), "nonobvious" (warming the pie by putting it out in the sun can't be patented), and must be sufficiently described so that someone skilled in the field could use it. The "patented" discovery is very different from the "trade secret": You want to keep your trade secrets secret, even to the point of concealing the fact that there *is* a secret. But if a competitor should figure out on his own how to duplicate that discovery you've been keeping secret, you're out of luck; it's his discovery now, and he can go ahead and market it. The patent, by contrast, is public from the day it is registered. You *want* your competitors to know about it. You even want them to use it. But first they've got to get your permission and pay you royalties or some other fee for using it. And if one of your clever competitors should discover the patented innovation on his own, even totally oblivious to your discovering it first, *he's* out of luck; you still get royalties. Why did we ever permit patents? Because we want to encourage creative enterprise and invention, and the best way we know how to do that is to allow the inventor to profit from his discovery. So we allow an extended period of time during which the inventor controls all uses of his invention, and can profit from them. Under the protection of these laws, it should be noted, technological business has flourished in the USA. For there is a secondary benefit: in a field undergoing rapid growth, where a number of competitors may be supposed to be reaching for the same advances, publishing each patent saves everyone else the time it would take to discover it (while making it not worth discovering). The field can grow by leapfrogs instead of one step at a time. From the point of view of the public interest, there is ample justification for protecting the patent.

But how can discoveries of sequences of genetic material satisfy the criteria for patenting? It certainly is "useful" to map the genome, and to know how it operates, as it is useful to know how the Missouri flows home to the Mississippi. That makes it worthwhile to map the Missouri, but not legal to patent it. (To drive home the comparison, when President William Clinton announced the mapping of the genome, he compared the occasion it to Thomas Jefferson's receipt of the map of the Missouri River from Merriwether Lewis.) The human genome is certainly not "novel"; it's been around for millennia, most of it. It is just as certainly not obvious, so that should help, but the problem is that it is not really clear to anyone, even those most versed in its mysteries, which means that we cannot be quite sure what they are patenting. So what the genomic explorers have patented, for the most part, are the methods used to break down the genome and describe its peculiarities. Should they be allowed to do even this? If Merriwether Lewis could not sell the Missouri or the right to look at it, could he at least sell his maps, protected against other travelers who might make such maps, for awhile? I tend to think not. Yet the substances developed from knowledge of the genome are private property, and very profitable property at that.

> Human growth hormone, insulin, and erythropoietin – protein drugs with billions of dollars in combined annual sales – are all manufactured using patented DNA sequences. Given the incentive of 20-year patent protection, several dozen new drugs have been brought to market (with hundreds more in the pipeline) by a U.S. biotech industry that now numbers 1,200 companies and counts $13 billion in sales, . . . (Regalado, 2000, p. 50).

Does the policy justification that underlies the Patent and Trademark Office extend to this application? It depends on how you see the genome. On the one hand, it may be one more privately exploitable bit of raw material for commercial enterprise. Only God Can Make a Tree, the poet reminds us, but that does not prevent us from owning trees, cutting trees, sawing, slicing and pulping trees for our own uses, without public outcry so far (except in environmentally sensitive areas). The fact that the genome, and information about the genome, are part of God's creation does not on the face of it rule out profitable use. But it should rule out patentability: no "natural object," or "product of nature," can pass the test of "novelty."

> However, when it comes to human genes . . . legal precedent offers a way around that prohibition, namely that genes captured and identified in the lab aren't in their natural form. In order to be studied, genes are copied, abbreviated, spliced into bacteria or otherwise altered. From the point of view of patent law, a gene is just another man-made chemical (Regalado, 2000).

But wait: if it is the intervention, the splicing process, that is being patented, well and good. But if it is the information about the gene, discovered by that process, that is in question, how can such information about the natural world be patented?

The justification of the patent, as above, is that it encourages research. But in the maze of patents in the genomic industry – patents covering genes, the proteins that they encode, and any use at all that may be made of that knowledge – the net result may be the reverse. Take, for example, the case of G. D. Searle's Celebrex, a powerful painkiller of great use in the treatment of arthritis. The University of Rochester, as it happens, had obtained what is known as a "submarine patent" on a gene called Cox-2. The patent specifies no drugs or treatments in particular, it just claims the right to all drugs anywhere that might act on that site in the genome. Celebrex, developed without any knowledge of Rochester's patent, is highly effective against the pain of arthritis because it blocks the enzyme encoded by Cox-2. Many people suffer from arthritis, and Celebrex was very profitable indeed, bringing the company $1.5 billion in sales in its first year. So Rochester's submarine surfaced and demanded royalties. Searle protested that it had developed the drug all by itself with private money, and did not see why it should pay royalties to a University whose discovery of the basic science under-lying its drug had been paid for by federal grants (Regalado, 2000, pp. 51–2). Who's right?

The private business perspective – that companies should patent and exploit the genome in all ways possible for profit, for the greater good of the public in the long run – has vigorous defenders. Lee Silver, for instance, in a summer Op-Ed, criticized President Clinton and Prime Minister Tony Blair for their joint sugges-tion, on announcing the effective decoding of the genome, that all scientific data on the human genome "should be made freely available to scientists everywhere." There's nothing wrong with science for profit, he argues, and in the long run the public will benefit from having the information.

> In no other arena of business would there be a debate over the right of a com-pany to control and profit from the packaging of information that it discovered and made publicly available. Unfortunately, biotechnology isn't like any other business. The public is understandably nervous about the idea of companies profiting from our genetic code. But if the goal is to make this genetic information useful as soon as possible, the debate should be focused on fair business practices and regulatory issues, not on ethics (Silver, 2000).

Another perspective is suggested by Seth Shulman, author of *Owning Our Future*, a 1999 study of the future of the genome project. After tracking some of the insane difficulties of trying to do research while navigating through a half-patented genome, he proposes some general principles to govern the allocation of "rights" to its use:

> The key is to treat this as a vital public policy issue rather than a strictly legal or scientific one. The first thing to remember is that the human genome is a precious inheritance of the human species. For this reason alone, it deserves special treatment. Second, the project to decode the human genome has, for more than a decade, been the mission of a publicly funded project that will ultimately cost some $3 billion. Given this outlay of funds by taxpayers, the public has every right to demand that the genome is used wisely and not simply handed over for private gain. And finally, we must recognize that – with the recent, momentous milestone of a completed working draft of the human genome – the time to act is now (Shulman, 2000).

Shulman suggests five policy "steps" – steps that will require federal law and international treaty – to keep the genome for all purposes of the common good and avoid the legal deathtraps that currently threaten the paths of research.

The first is to create "the world's first IP-Free Zone," by declaration that the genome's raw sequence data cannot be privately owned. "[T]things work best when seminal information assets . . . are pooled and shared. . . . Like public lands or public libraries, pooled knowledge assets must be made freely available and protected within a framework that preserves their integrity" (Shulman, 2000).

The second is to declare a moratorium on gene patenting "until we can all agree on sensible rules." Right now these broad grants of proprietary rights "may confer power to block off whole areas of scientific development, without compensating benefit to the public." The PTO is considering adding the words "substantial, specific, and credible" to "use," so as to make companies specify exactly how the portion of the genome that they intend to own might be used. (At present, they can wait, as above, until G. D. Searle or someone else discovers a profitable use and then sue for royalties. That doesn't seem fair.)

Third, we should institute a compulsory licensing system. Right now, the owner of the patent may simply exclude others from any use of the product. Where public health is at stake, excluding researchers from access to needed information is too high a price to pay for capitalistic privilege.

Fourth, we should establish a "zoning commission," with a membership composed of all major stakeholders, to set standards and shape policy in this area. The zoning of land has taught us that the value of all properties can be supported by good rules properly adhered to.

And fifth, we should remember to put public health first. The question of long term impact on public health – amount of research enabled, number of pharmaceutical products brought out, general access to helpful developments – should be the touchstone of all genome policy (Shulman, 2000).

Shulman notes that in his appeal to the public good and public access, Clinton had done little to ease uncertainty in the field – indeed, the value of high-tech stocks plummeted at the very words, "public access." But he "got it right when he called upon us to 'ensure the profits of human genome research are measured not in dollars but in the betterment of human life'" (Shulman, 2000).

The Uses of the Genome: Profits vs. Privacy

The discovery and its reception

When it's not being used to patent profitable chemicals, what else might the decoding of the human genome have in store for us citizens? The best commentaries on the decoding of the Genome were unintentional. The *Connecticut Post*, for instance, on Tuesday, 27 June 2000, published the Associated Press account of the successful cracking of the genetic code, under the headline "ABCs of DNA." After the first paragraph or so, readers were invited to follow the story to the interior pages: "Please see NEW on A8." Just below it, a staff writer, Peter Urban (2000), had a companion article, "Democrats offer bill to block genetic bias," also continued on the inside: "Please see FEARS on A8." The decoding of the genome is an absolutely fantastic scientific accomplishment, rivaling any exploration yet attempted, holding out hopes of true cures to some of our worst diseases, giving us glimpses of hitherto unsuspected horizons, all gloriously NEW.

But how will it in fact be used? To help us? Or to tell everybody that has any interest at all in discriminating against us – the government, the employer, the insurance company – about all our weaknesses, to make us terribly vulnerable before those with power, prospects that fill us with FEARS?

What kind of threat to privacy?

We have always known that the boundaries of the self were variable, socially defined, and insecure. What counts as the inviolable perimeter of the self, the symbolic skin that supplements the physical as a barrier between what is safely inside and what is not, is subject to change. The self was easier to define and protect, perhaps, before we knew there was such a substance as deoxyribonucleic acid (DNA), let alone that each one of us has a unique combination of the proteins and bases that make it up. Is my DNA at least protected by even the narrowest definition of the right of privacy? Could there be anything more personal?

Suppose my DNA were known to my enemy. Instantly there is the threat of new and sci-fi spectacular forms of abuse. Right now, we know that an "identity" can be stolen if a social security number, driver's license or credit card number falls into the wrong hands. Criminals can use an identity stolen from me to buy a car, use it in a crime, run up a tab at Circuit City, and have me blamed for the whole thing. If they're clever, they can clean out my bank accounts, sell my house, and leave me penniless. The only hope I have to prove that these criminals are not me is that they will leave fingerprints somewhere. Fingerprints are uniquely, physically, permanently, ours, and fingerprints will identify the real criminals. The FBI is now saying it would rather use DNA for such unmistakable identification of criminals. They could take DNA from everyone in the country, put together a huge database, and catch every criminal who left a fingernail scraping or a drop of blood behind at the crime scene. But what if that identity could be stolen, too? All a thief would need would be a scraping from my beach chair. Could my identity be stolen if my DNA were available for use? Possibly such information could be used to violate the new security systems that use physical signatures instead of ID cards?

Where science fiction leaves off and the health care system begins, there is the health management organization (HMO), or similar organization designed to ration health care for the purposes of cutting costs. Many of us now have health insurance. Health insurance is a straightforward business arrangement. Individuals or families can buy health insurance on their own, from some private insurer who offers such coverage, on an analogy with fire or homeowners' insurance. Companies can arrange to have their employees covered collectively by some insurance plan through deductions from their pay, on an analogy with a pension plan. The benefits of the health insurance plan, in either case, may vary widely: as with any insurance, the insured (or the company) can opt for a more expensive plan that covers more contingencies, or a less expensive plan that covers fewer contingencies.

In any plan, the insured is issued a contract by the insurance company that is supposed to spell out what is covered, for how much, and what is not, and the insured is supposed to agree to it. It sounds very simple, and entirely in accord with our market tradition, certainly with the tradition of buying insurance: a willing buyer purchases known benefits from a willing seller, and both are better off for the exchange.

How does knowledge of our DNA fit into the health insurance business? It all comes down to "risk." If knowledge of our DNA affects the company's assessment of risk, then it will figure in our fate at the hands of the companies. Insurance is a device to spread risk so that the whole damage of an ordinary calamity will not fall on the sufferer. Since the rates collectively must cover the claims collectively, it is in everyone's interest to limit the claims. It is in the company's interest not to have, as subscribers, people who are likely to experience the catastrophe contemplated, for these people will file claims. And it is in my interest, as subscriber, not to share my pool with high-risk persons, for the payment of their frequent claims will drive up the cost of the premiums.

No insurance company could survive a requirement that it offer equal access and equal premiums to all. Every insurance company will try to insure all and only those who will never make claims. In automobile insurance, that means a preference for mature drivers; in fire insurance, that means a preference for residences with smoke alarms and commercial buildings with sprinklers; and in health insurance, that means a preference for non-smokers and people who at least are not sick already, and are less likely than others to get sick – the young, the suburban, the educated. The practice of discovering and insuring only those who will be unlikely to make claims – "skimming" (the cream), or "creaming" – is entirely acceptable. Insurance companies are even legally permitted to discriminate by age and sex – note the bias in automobile insurance against young males. We may not expect that they will treat a health care subscribership any differently (Bodenheimer, 1999).

If – and this is a set of ifs deemed generally probable, if not inevitable – we manage through our superb science to link much debilitating disease in later life to genetic traits discernible at birth, and if we are permitted to classify such traits as "pre-existing conditions" that insurance companies are not bound to cover, and if DNA screening becomes universal (the FBI model) or at least required in order to obtain health insurance, and if no legislation arises as barriers between insurance company policies and insurance company shareholder interests – we may expect that the HMOs will candidly screen applicants by DNA profile. Nor is this merely an empirical prediction (although it is that). As long as shareholders have a right to have their companies optimize the profit picture, the companies will be morally obligated to use DNA profiling to reduce the claims probabilities.

Why do these conclusions grate on our nerves? Almost half of the American people are now invested in the stock market, from the day traders who do it full time to the teachers whose pension funds depend on the profitability of the private sector. Any of us who are interested in our retirement ought to be grateful for the care that these corporations are taking not to waste the money we have put into them, money that we can spend on our own needs when the pension fund pays out. Yet somehow, the notion that circumstances over which we have absolutely no control – the chromosomes assembled when we were but zygotes – will determine our access to health care, rings a very sour note in our belfry. We are left in the kind of conflict that is typical of this field. On the one hand, we have an interest in the continuing profitable workings of the free market. On the other hand, we have no national consensus on how, and whether, health insurance companies may make their money. There is a powerful feeling in the nation that health care ought to be available to everyone, free or almost so, and that the sicker and frailer you are, the greater your access should be. That's not the way insurance works now, and if the managers of the genome make contact with the managers in Hartford, it will work even less that way in the future.

The Challenge to Management: An Uncertain Future

In sum, and, in view of the limitations appropriate for this paper, in very brief, what characteristics, and characteristic action, should we look for in the biotechnology manager who is genuinely trying to do a good job? In this industry, perhaps uniquely, it is the wrong time to conclude with a call for visionary leadership, mind that grasps the intellectual puzzles of the field, heart that reaches out in compassion to a world afflicted with poverty and want, and will that strives always for the common good. That litany perfectly describes Monsanto's Robert Shapiro, and look what happened to him. It may seem unfashionable in the field, but I think right now we need fewer visionaries and more managers – fewer people with schemes to revolutionize business and science, and more people with the patience to listen, to negotiate, to make concessions, and to try experiments in partnership with groups they don't like. Yeats' "Second Coming" comes to mind, although not as the poet intended. The best in this field lack all conviction, and appropriately so, since the field is very new, the consequences of its work highly speculative, and the moral dilemmas unprecedented. The worst, if so you would characterize the NGOs who proclaim rumors as scientific fact and monger fear as a route to power, are full of passionate intensity all over the Internet. But the worst represent us in some forum that we cannot yet name; they are guarding for us something that we are sure is valuable, although we cannot always describe it or say why. What fascinates us, about the three cases taken as exemplars of the biotechnology dilemma, is that at the heart of each is something precious that we did not create, that we could not replace, and that seems to be threatened by business. The routine growth of the crop in the field, on which we have depended for 10,000 years and depend to this day, our health, the stuff of life itself, the code of our inmost being, and the guarantee of privacy for the self – the promise that we can be whom we like and tell what we like about ourselves to an unsympathetic world – all seem to be in the path of the bulldozer of globalized free enterprise. Now we need managers who can listen to the fears, feel them, let us help work them out, cooperate with governments in legislation halting the progress of biotechnology for a time if that is what is needed, and form partnerships with Greenpeace and the other NGOs to chart the future of biotechnology. It is time for non-threatening managers, and visionaries are rarely non-threatening. Let us seek cooperators.

Then where is the future of biotechnology? The answer to that question demands a crystal ball, not a strategic plan. We can say this, as a logical possibility: Right now one of the fields that is moving too fast for the human eye to follow is silicon chip technology, outstripping even "Moore's Law" that predicted in 1965 that the power of the computer chip would double every year. ("In 1965, when Moore wrote his article, the world's most complex chip was right in his lab at Fairchild: It had 64 transistors. Intel's new-model Pentium III, introduced last October, contains 28 *million* transistors" (Mann, 2000, emphasis in original).) The other field that is moving too fast to comprehend is biotechnology. What happens when they intersect? Carbon and silicon have many of the same chemical properties. Could we use molecules, little bits of life, as components of our computers? Yes, we could, and that will be the next thundering explosion in the biotechnology eruption (Rotman, 2000; Sivitz, 2000; Kagan, 2001). First applications of miniature molecular computers might be injectable cells that monitor for toxins in the bloodstream or manufacture drugs in the body (Garfinkel, 2000; Wortman, 2001). After that, the possibilities are endless. Let us hope that, by the time they materialize, we will have mastered the art of negotiating the future with the guardians of the human legacy.

References

Barboza, D. 2000: Modified foods put companies in a quandary: Science is called sound but public is not sure. *The New York Times*, 4 June, 1, 34.

Benbrook, C. M. and Moses, P. B. 1986: Engineering crops to resist herbicides. *Technology Review*. November/December, 55ff.

Bodenheimer, T. 1999: Physicians and the changing medical marketplace. *The New England Journal of Medicine*. 340 (7), 584–8.

Brody, J. E. 1988: Quest for lean meat prompts new approach. *The New York Times*, Tuesday, 12 April, C1, C4 (Science section).

Carey, J. 1999: Imperiled monarchs alter the biotech landscape. *Business Week* 7 June, 36.

Carey, J. Licking, E. and Barrett, A. 1999: Are bio-foods safe? *Business Week* 20 December, 70.

Feder, B. J. 1999: Plant sterility research inflames debate on biotechnology's role in farming. *The New York Times*, Monday, 19 April, 19.

Freeman, R. E. 1984: *Strategic Management: A Stakeholder Approach*. Boston, MA: Pitman.

Garfinkel, S. 2000: Biological computing. *Technology Review*. May/June, 70–7.

Irvine, R. S. 2000: 'Netwarriors' fight way to top in corporate PR. *O'Dwyer's* PR Services Report, May, 1.

Kagan, C. 2001: Flexible transistors. *Technology Today.* January February, 100.

Kriz, M. 2000: Global food fights. *The National Journal* 32 (10) 688 4 March.

Leopold, A. 1949: The land ethic. In *A Sand County Almanac,* New York: Oxford University Press, 201ff.

Magnusson, P. Palmer, A. T. and Capell, K. 1999: Furor over 'Frankenfood.' *Business Week,* 18 October, 50.

Mann, C. C. 2000: The end of Moore's Law? *Technology Review.* May–June, 42–8.

Naj, A. K. 1989: Can biotechnology control farm pests? Specialty plants may cut need for chemicals. *The Wall Street Journal,* Thursday, 11 May.

Regalado, A. 2000: The great gene grab. *Technology Review.* September/October, 48–55.

Rotman, D. 2000: Molecular computing. *Technology Review.* May/June, 52–8.

Seabrook, J. 1993: Tremors in the hothouse: The battle lines are being drawn . . . the first genetically altered supermarket tomato. *The New Yorker* Brave New World Department, 19 July, 32–41.

Shulman, S. 2000: Toward sharing the genome. *Technology Review.* September/October, 60–7.

Silver, L. 2000: Who owns the human genome? *The New York Times,* Thursday, 16 March, Op Ed.

Sivitz, L. 2000: When the chips are down: scientiest seek alternatives to a computer technology nearing its limits. *Science News.* 158, 350–1, 25 November.

Slutsker, G. 1990: The lesser of two weevils. *Forbes* 15 October, 202–3.

Specter, M. 1998: Europe, bucking trend in U.S., blocks genetically altered food. *The New York Times,* A1, A8.

Specter, M. 2000: The Pharmageddon riddle. *The New Yorker,* 10 April, 58–71.

Urban, P. 2000: Democrats offer bill to block genetic bias. *Connecticut Post* 27 June, A1, A8.

Wortman, M. 2001: Medicine gets personal. *Technology Review.* January February, 72–8.

Yoon, C. K. 1999: Altered corn may imperil butterfly, researchers say. *The New York Times,* Thursday, 20 May, A1, A25.

Yoon, C. K. 2000: What's next for biotech crops? Questions. *The New York Times,* Tuesday, 19 December, F1, F5 (Science Times).

Further Reading

Goldburg, R. 1990: Biotechnology's bitter harvest: Herbicide-tolerant crops and the threat to sustainable agriculture. *Report: Biotechnology Working group,* Environmental Defense Fund 1990 (now Environmental Defense).

Sun, M. 1986: Engineering crops to resist weed killers. *Science* 231, 1360–1, 21 March.

Yoon, C. K. 2000: Altered salmon leading way to dinner plates, but rules lag. *The New York Times,* Monday, 1 May, A1, A20.

Chapter 16

Trust and the Future of Leadership

Joanne B. Ciulla

Business ethics scholars have always tipped their hats to business leaders – "the ethics of the organization come from the top" – and leadership studies scholars have always tipped their hats to ethics – "leaders should have high ethical standards." Yet until recently, these polite acknowledgments have not led them into deeper investigations. Yes, the ethics of a business leader has an influence on the ethics of a business. What is less obvious is the role ethics is playing in the rapidly changing role of leaders and the very concept of leadership in both business and politics. This paper examines the changes in the world and workplace that have led to a greater emphasis on the role of trust in leadership. I begin by examining how some philosophers, writers, and social scientists have thought about leadership. This will not be comprehensive history, but rather a selective one that provides the terms for understanding the changing face of leadership today. I'll then discuss the social factors that have changed the nature of leadership. Lastly, I will talk about future research that may offer insight into how leadership, values, and moral decision making are shaped by access to other cultures.

Leadership Yesterday

Ancient writers

Ancient writers have talked more about the ethics of leaders than leadership scholars of the twentieth century. We begin by looking closely at Plato's work on the subject because he had some very useful things to say about the ethics of leaders. In his early works, he firmly believed that the wisest and most virtuous people would make the best leaders, but he later realized that virtue and wisdom was not enough to get things done. In *Epistle VII* Plato gives a personal account of how he gained insight into leadership during his visits to Syracuse. The first time he was invited there by the tyrant Dionysius I. Plato tells us that he was disgusted by the decadent and luxurious lifestyle of Dionysius' court. When Plato returned to Athens he set up his Academy, and went on to write *Republic*. In *Republic*, he argued that the perfect state would only come about by rationally exploiting the highest qualities in people through education. A philosopher king who was wise and moral would lead such a state.

About 24 years after his first visit to Syracuse, Plato was invited back by Dion, who was Dionysius' brother-in-law. By this time Dionysius I was dead. Dion had read *Republic* and wanted Plato to test his theory of leadership education on Dionysius' son Dionysius II. This was an offer that Plato couldn't refuse, although he had serious reservations about accepting it. The trip was a disaster. Plato's friend Dion was exiled because of court intrigues. Plato left Syracuse in a hurry, despite young Dionysius' pleas for him to stay. On returning to Athens, Plato wrote,

> the older I grew, the more I realized how difficult it is to manage a city's affairs rightly. For I saw that it was impossible to do anything without friends and loyal followers . . . The corruption of written laws and our customs was proceeding at such amazing speed that whereas when I noted these changes and saw how unstable everything was, I became in the end quite dizzy (Epistle VII, 325c–26).

After his visits to Syracuse, Plato altered his view of leadership. He realized that wisdom and virtue of a philosopher king would not take him far without friends. In *Republic*, Plato entertained a pastoral image of the leader as a shepherd to his flock, an image also found in the *Bible*. But after his experiences in Sicily, Plato wrote *Statesman* in which he says leaders are not like shepherds and followers are not like sheep. Shepherds are very different from their sheep, whereas human leaders are not much different from their followers. Furthermore, people are not sheep; some are meek and cooperative, whereas others are contentious and stubborn. Hence, Plato's revised view in *Statesman* is that leaders are really like weavers. Their main task is to weave together into a society different kinds of people such as the meek and self-controlled and the brave and impetuous. Near the end of *Statesman*, Plato explains that since we can't always depend on leaders to be good, we need the rule of law. In other words, good laws help us to survive bad leaders. If we follow the progression of Plato's work on leadership, he goes from a profound belief that it is possible for some people to be wise and benevolent philosopher kings, to a more modest belief that the real challenge of leadership is making loyal friends and getting people who don't like each other, don't like the leader, and don't want to work together, to work towards a common goal.

Plato also provides some gems of insight into leadership in Books I and II of *Republic*. In Book I Plato tells us that just people will not want to rule because they realize that justice requires them to act in ways that are not in their self-interest. This explains why we are sometimes nervous about people who seem *too* eager to take on leadership positions. We worry that they want the job to serve their self-interest or that they fail to understand the moral responsibilities of the position. In Book II, Plato provides a thought experiment for understanding the ethical temptations specific to leaders. In "The Ring of Gyges," he tells the story a young shepherd who finds a ring that can make him invisible. He uses the ring to gain power and wealth. Glaucon, the protagonist in the dialogue, argues that the only reason people are just is because they are held accountable and have no choice. Yet, if they had a choice, as Gyges of Lydia did, most people would be unjust. Leaders at the top of organizations either have this freedom or sometimes think they do. One of our concerns about leaders is that they will abuse their power because they have less people to whom they are accountable.

Many writers throughout history have focused on the temptations of power. The biblical story of "David and Bathsheba" is one such example. It is all the more interesting because King David is God's chosen ruler. Yet, in the story of "David and Bathsheba," David falls off the moral path by seducing Bathsheba, the wife of Uriah, his best officer on the front. When Bathsheba becomes pregnant, David tries to cover it up. When the cover-up fails, he arranges to have Uriah killed. Like President Clinton's sex scandal and numerous leadership scandals throughout history, David's cover-up is worse than the crime. Cover-ups are often worse because that is when leaders tend to most abuse their power, and the trust and loyalty of their followers.

Numerous other philosophers of the ancient Western world such as Aristotle, Plutarch, and Cicero wrote about leadership. In the Eastern world, some of the most famous scholars such as Lao-tzu and Confucius focused on the character and moral obligations of a leader. For Lao-tzu, the best leaders are not conspicuous. In *Tao-Te Ching*, he says that the best rulers are those whose existence is merely known by people, after that are those who are loved, then feared, and last are leaders who are despised. In his *Analects* Confucius writes about the "chün-tzu," which literally means "son of the ruler" but is translated as the "superior man." Like Plato, his superior man is well educated. Confucius says the good leader leads on the basis of moral principles not his own profit. Ancients from the East and West knew that power was a key moral challenge for leaders and that the very role of leader required self-discipline and the ability to put the interests of others first. Both Lao-tzu and Confucius portray the leader as someone who serves followers. Contemporary writers such as Robert Greenleaf draw their ideas of servant leadership indirectly from these traditions.

Great men and charismatics

Niccolo Machiavelli was more interested in strategy and power than the ethics of leadership. The Prince was someone who developed the instinct, cunning, and tactics to be effective at getting and holding power. He was clever and amoral, but not always moral. Machiavelli's Prince was closer to the way some modern theorists, especially in business, have thought about leadership. For them, leadership is a series of techniques and skills that help make leaders get the job done.

Machiavelli seemed to think that anyone could learn to be a leader, whereas Plato thought you needed to be born with the right stuff and then educated. Many people today still carry with them the "Great Man" theory – that leaders are born and not made. They believe that inborn personality traits, not values catapult leaders to greatness. This theory has been articulated in many different ways. In his book, *On Heroes, Hero Worship, and the Historic in History*, Thomas Carlyle (1902) wrote about how great men like Napoleon changed the face of human history. Carlyle said that we had to search for the "ablest" man to be our leader and then submit to him for our own good. Leadership then was based on the traits that a person had at birth. The author Leo Tolstoy disagreed with Carlyle. In his novel *War and Peace* (Tolstoy, 1983), he writes, "it is incomprehensible that millions of Christian men killed and tortured each other because Napolean was ambitious . . ." Tolstoy said great men are nothing more than labels that give names to events. People become leaders not simply because of their innate qualities, but because they are the right people, in the right place, at the right time. In other words, leaders don't make history; history makes leaders.

Charismatic leadership is a close relative to the Great Man Theory and a more generalized species of a trait theory. It too attributes leadership to the personal qualities of an individual. Charismatic leaders have powerful personalities. The distinguishing feature of charismatic leadership is the emotional relationship that leaders establish with their followers. Max Weber describes charisma as "a certain quality of an individual personality by virtue of which he is set apart from ordinary men . . ." According to Weber, the authority of charismatic leaders over their followers is not rational and the institutions they run do not operate by rational routine rules. Weber tells us that the legitimacy of charismatic leaders comes only from recognition of and belief in charismatic inspiration by followers. Charismatic leaders range from John F. Kennedy, who inspired a generation to try and make the world better, to the cult leader Jim Jones, the Evangelical religious leader who lead 913 of his followers into a mass suicide. Charismatic leaders can be the most effective leaders, but they can also be the most dangerous.

From character to personality

It is interesting to note that early in American history, thinkers such as Benjamin Franklin believed that good character was the key to becoming a success in life. A product of the Enlightenment, Franklin thought people should strive for wealth so that they could use it in a humane way to help society. So for Franklin, leadership would come more from one's moral virtues, than personality traits. In the eighteenth and nineteenth centuries business leaders were lauded for their good character. America is somewhat distinct in its history of celebrating the values and character of business leaders. For example, in the nineteenth century, William Makepeace Thayer specialized in biographies of chief executive officers. His books focused on how the virtues leaders formed early in life contributed to their success. As the number of business journalists grew in America, some dedicated themselves to lionizing business leaders. The Scottish immigrant Bertie Charles (B.C.) Forbes elevated the moral adulation of business leaders into an enduring art form that is still imitated by business publications throughout the world today. When he started *Forbes Magazine* in 1916, Forbes described it as "a publication that would strive to inject more humanity, more joy, and more satisfaction into business and into life in general." His goal was to convey Franklin's message that work, virtue, and wealth lead to happiness and social benefit. But there were other forces at work in business journalism that have had a far greater influence on the ethics of leaders and business today. The end of the nineteenth century saw the advent of the "muckraker" journalists, such as Ida Tarbell, who wrote scathing accounts of John D. Rockefeller's monopolistic business practices at Standard Oil. These journalists were more interested in exposing unethical business leaders than they were praising them. The role of the press in business and other areas, would become a key influence in shaping the ethics of business and political leaders.

The eighteenth and nineteenth century advocates of the work ethic preached that strong moral character was the key to wealth. By the early twentieth century, the emphasis on moral character shifted to an emphasis on personality. This change was epitomized in Dale Carnegie's 1936 classic *How to Win Friends and Influence People*, where psychology, not morality, was the key to success in business. This was true in leadership studies as well. Twentieth century scholars were more interested in studying the personality traits of leaders than their values. In part this is because most of the leadership research was done by social scientists (usually psychologists), who were often captives of positivism, working under the mantra of value free social science.

From traits, to behaviors, to contingencies, and transformations

In 1948, after reviewing more than 120 studies concerning the traits of leaders, noted leadership scholar Ralph Stogdill concluded that after almost a century of social science research, he was unable to discern a reliable and coherent pattern of traits found in leaders. Other researchers of the time had been looking at the behaviors, instead of the traits of leaders. They wanted to discover the best leadership "style." Kurk Lewin and his associates conducted one of the classic studies to see what leadership style was most effective in terms of group productivity and follower satisfaction. The styles measured were autocratic, democratic, and laissez-faire. This study found that the democratic style was slightly more effective. Lewin's research shifted the focus of research from what the leader was like to how he or she led. Researchers then began to measure leadership effectiveness in terms of leaders' orientation toward people and their orientation towards tasks. They found that some leaders were effective because they focused on building strong relationships with employees, whereas others were effective because they focused on the tasks at hand. Researchers soon realized that their study of leader behaviors needed to include more variables. The context of leadership and the kind of work people had to do were also important. So at the end of the twentieth century, many scholars used a contingency approach that looked at the context of leadership as well as the leader behaviors.

Twentieth-century social science research into leadership offered fragmented insights into leadership, but not a picture of it. Their question was: "What is it that makes leaders effective?" But the deeper question (especially in a democratic society) was: "What is it that makes people want to follow leaders of their own free will?" James MacGregor Burns' theory of transforming leadership offered an answer to this question. In his 1978 classic, *Leadership*, he tells us that people follow leaders who are able to make them care about shared moral values. Burns says leaders have to operate at higher need and value levels than those of followers. He contrasts transforming leadership with transactional leadership. Transactional leadership is based on incentives and leaders and followers often have different goals. Whereas in transformational leaders look for potential motives in followers and they seek to satisfy followers' higher needs and engage them in thinking about values and larger issues. According to Burns, transforming leaders have strong values, but they do not force them on others. The transforming leader engages followers in a dialogue about the tension and conflict within their own value systems. Ultimately, the goal of a transforming leader is to develop and empower followers so that they can lead themselves.

Burns' theory was distinctive at the time in its emphasis on the role and influence of followers. He believed that the dialectic that took place between leaders and followers could potentially improve the values of leaders. Other theorists such as Bernard Bass and Jay Conger argued that transformational leaders were also charismatic. However, unlike the emotional charismatic leader, the transformational leader engages followers on an intellectual level as well. Transformational leadership is not without critics. For example, Michael Keeley has argued that those transformational leaders still face some of the same pitfalls of charismatic leaders. A transforming leader might well engage people in a higher cause, but what if it is a bad one? Evoking James Madison's fears about the conflict of factions in a democracy, Keeley argues that it is just as dangerous to try to persuade everyone to hold the same interests, as it is to restrict the freedom of groups to pursue their own interests. Keeley does a nice job of illustrating how repressive transformational leadership might be in the workplace.

The last 100 years of social science research in leadership does not offer a conclusive description of what makes someone a leader. However, the real value of this research is that it isolated some of the variables that we need to understand leadership. Those variables are traits, charisma, task orientation, relationship orientation (which would also include democratic and autocratic leadership styles), and last but not least, contextual influences. Transformational leadership is a normative theory that prescribes what the leader/follower relationship should be like. The one thing all researchers implicitly or explicitly imply is that leadership is a specific kind of relationship between leaders and followers. Perhaps the greatest contribution of Burns' book was that it demonstrated that an interdisciplinary approach could provide a more satisfying picture of leadership. The history of leadership studies also shows that the study of individual leaders only makes sense as part of a broader study of where they stand in history and in a cultural context.

This short, but by no means complete, history of leadership was designed to bring out the ideas about leaders and the ethics of leadership that are still part of the discussion today. We are often concerned about the ability of leaders to exercise power in just and unself-interested ways. People still raise the question, "Are leaders born or made?" Can leaders be taught? Is leadership mainly about techniques and strategies? To what extent is leadership largely dependent on social or historical conditions? Does one have to have charisma to be a leader? Is leadership a quality of personality or character? And finally, is the job of a leader to transform followers by moving them to a higher moral plane?

Leadership Today

Ethics and effectiveness

One thing that has come out of the study of leadership is that legitimate leadership is about more than a title, a position, money, or power. Not all Presidents and CEOs are leaders, whereas some secretaries and janitors are. Immoral or amoral business leaders, gangsters, black marketers, and monopolists may have power over others and the market, but in today's world, coercive power does not give them legitimacy as leaders. So if leadership is more than position, money, and power, what is it?

Some contemporary scholars believe that if they could agree on a common definition of leadership, they would be better able to understand it. One such scholar is Joseph Rost who gathered together 221 definitions of leadership in his quest for *the* definition. After reviewing all of his definitions, we discover that the definition problem was not really about definitions per se. All 221 definitions say basically the same thing – leadership is about one person getting other people to do something. Where the definitions differ is in *how* leaders motivate their followers and *who* has a say in the goals of the group or organization. For example, one definition from the 1920s said, "Leadership is the ability to impress the will of the leader on those led and induce obedience, respect, loyalty, and cooperation." Another definition from the 1990s said, "Leadership is an influence relationship between leaders and followers who intend real changes that reflect their mutual purposes." We all can think of leaders who fit both of these descriptions. Some leaders use their power to force people to do what they want, others work with their followers to do what everyone agrees is best for them. The 1920's definition is transactional and based on a strong task orientation. Rost's 1990's definition is transformational and based on a relationship orientation (Rost, 1991). The real difference between the definitions rests on their normative assumptions. The underlying question is "How should leaders treat followers and how should followers treat leaders?"

The scholars who worry about constructing the ultimate definition of leadership are asking the wrong question, but inadvertently trying to answer the right one. The ultimate question about leadership is not "What is the definition of leadership?" The whole point of studying leadership is, "What is good leadership?" The use of word *good* here has two senses, morally good and technically good or effective. In the past leadership scholars were more interested in the question of what made leaders successful or effective. (Plato went the opposite route. He started out focusing on the morality of leaders and then had to think about what it took to make leaders effective.) Today we are interested in both aspects. When we say, "She is a good leader" we mean she is effective *and* she is ethical.

The question, "What constitutes a good leader?" is central to public debates about leadership. We want our leaders to be effective and morally good. Nonetheless, we are often more likely to say leaders are good if they are effective, but not moral, than if they are moral, but not effective. Leaders face a paradox. They have to stay in business or get reelected to be leaders. If they are not minimally effective at doing these things, their morality as leaders is usually irrelevant, because they are no longer in charge. What we hope for are leaders who know when ethics should take priority over effectiveness. For example, in business this may mean knowing when employee safety or protection of the environment are more important than profits. History tends to dismiss as irrelevant the morally good leaders who are unsuccessful. President Jimmy Carter was a man of great personal integrity, but during his presidency, he was ineffective and generally considered a poor leader.

The conflict between ethics and effectiveness and the definition problem are apparent in what I have called, "the Hitler problem." The answer to the question "Was Hitler a good leader?" is yes, if a leader is defined as someone who is effective at getting people together to perform some task. The answer is no, if the leader gets the job done, but the job itself is immoral and/or is done using immoral means. In other words leadership is about more than being effective at getting followers to do things. The quality of leadership also depends on the ethics of the means (which also includes the leader/follower relationship) and the ethics of the ends of a leader's actions. For example, the folk hero Robin Hood uses unethical means to achieve morally worthy ends – he steals from the rich to give to the poor. Most of us would prefer to have leaders who do the right thing, the right way, and for the right reasons.

The changing work context

Today most leadership scholars agree that morally good and effective leadership depends on the situation, cultural norms and values, and the historical context. Leadership is a moral and psychological relationship but it is also a social construction. In the twenty-first century a number of forces have not only altered the context of leadership, but have altered the way leaders exercise their power and influence.

To understand how social context affects the idea of business leadership, let us go back to the autocratic definition from the 1920s. This model of leadership was for industrial mass production done mostly by workers with a low level of education and skill. The leader/follower relationship was simple. Managers decided what was to be done and how to do it. Employees did what they were told. They weren't asked to do more. Workers did not question the authority of the leader because they did not have the knowledge or the courage to do so. Under scientific management and industrialization workers were deskilled. The ethical relationship between leader and follower was purely transactional. "If you do as you are told, I will pay you what I promised." A leader's source of power and authority came from his or her position, superior knowledge, control of resources, and ability to reward or punish.

The model of leadership from the 1990s is quite different. It states that leadership is an "influence relationship between leaders and followers" as they pursue shared goals. It implies that followers have a say in the work process and exert some influence over their leaders. This change in definition does not necessarily mean that business leaders had become more enlightened, but that the nature of businesses and the norms of society had changed. As sociologist Daniel Bell observed, a post-industrial society is one in which most people are employed in jobs that are unrelated to making or growing things. He wrote: "In the daily round of work, men no longer confront nature, as either alien or beneficent, and fewer now handle artifacts and things." More people work in cooperative settings with their minds and not their hands. The value of employees' intelligence, skill, and creativity or what is now called "human capital" has grown. Leadership changed because the tasks and the followers changed.

One way that leadership began to change at the end of the twentieth century was in the way that leaders could effectively influence employees. Leaders' traditional sources of power are the power of their position, their ability to reward or punish, their ability to control information, their expertise, and their personal qualities (also called referent power). By the turn of the twenty-first century, leaders in business and other areas began to realize that they could not exercise many of these traditional sources of power as they had in the past. In industries that required human capital, leaders had to court the good will of employees so that they would use their talents to achieve the company's goals. This cannot be done by exerting positional power, or simply giving out rewards and punishments. Businesses hire an army of organizational psychologists, pop psychologists, trainers, consultants and motivational speakers to get at the good will of employees. By the end of the twentieth century, these approaches produced diminishing returns (and perhaps they never really worked). Good will, commitment, loyalty and trust are about the moral not psychological relationships. Workers today are not only better educated than workers of the 1920s, they are better informed. They can go to the business section of any bookstore and discover what the latest management fad is trying to do to them.

Given the growing complexity of the technology, employees in organizations often have greater expert power than business leaders. Leadership in industries where employees hold an enormous amount of expert power is among the most challenging. Here leaders cannot use coercive power (because employees will leave), they do not have expert power, and they do not have as much control over information as they did in the past. They can and do use rewards, such as stock options, to keep employees, but this is sometimes not enough to gain their good will and loyalty. Even less skilled employees have the power to make life miserable for business leaders. Technologies that give employees greater access to information have altered the relationship of employers to employees. Access to information, goods, and services in the global economy redistributes power in the workplace and in society. For better or worse, the media also plays an empowering role. Unhappy workers can go to the newspaper with unflattering stories. Corrupt and angry employees can pass on sensitive information to a competitor or sabotage the computer system. Individual workers are now able to do greater harm and greater good than ever before.

A large part of the world is still at the industrial or pre-industrial stage of development, where the command and control leadership methods of the 1920s may seem appropriate. Businesses in the post-industrial world seek cheap labor and suppliers for their products in the developing world. A factory owner in a developing country may overwork his or her workers, hire child labor, or even buy children as laborers. Some might argue that this is appropriate behavior for that country's stage of economic development. After all, countries in the West did the same things during their industrial revolutions. However the buyers of these products are often companies or people from Western countries. Today with the help of consumer groups and the media, businesses and business leaders' reputations can rise or fall on the behavior of people in far off lands. For example, if a major toy company stops doing business with a factory that has inhuman labor practices or pollutes the environment, other factories in that country may clean up their acts to get or keep the toy company's business. While many people like to complain about the press, it has played an invaluable role in improving the ethics of businesses and leaders. Revelations of unethical business practices not only create bad publicity, but elicit consumer boycotts, condemnation by stockholders, civic, and religious leaders. These can harm businesses and the ability of a business to either operate or continue to operate in some countries. The unethical behavior of a supplier may harm credibility of the business leader, which will certainly make him or her less effective. Hence, when businesses are held morally responsible for businesses that they do not control they resort to rewards and punishments to influence the behavior or suppliers.

Throughout the world the positional power of leaders in business and politics is eroding. Like Plato, we have come to realize that leaders are not much different than the rest of us. Leaders' job titles don't make them any better unless they do their jobs well. The reason why attitudes towards leaders is changing is because people throughout the world, increasingly know more about their leaders than ever before. When we read news reports about the private affairs of leaders or their unsavory business deals, it becomes difficult to hold them in awe. Those who believe that all the truly great leaders are gone, might think differently if they knew as much about the heroes of the past as we do about our leaders today. While some of the offices and institutions such as the US Presidency or the British royal family still garner respect, this respect is not automatically transferred to the people who hold these offices.

One cannot underestimate the impact of a better-educated work force and consumers, information technologies, and the media on how people think about leadership and how leadership is exercised. The number of countries that are able to totally control information is slowing diminishing. With the advent of wireless technologies, the leaders in these countries will find the task of keeping information out formidable. Political tyrants and their corrupt business cronies are protected by the abject poverty of their people that creates the information divide. As long as leaders control either the flow or the content of information, the ring of Gyges protects them. However, if leaders of countries or businesses want access to money from the international capital market, they will have to remove the ring to meet the growing demands of transparency. Ethical leaders have little to hide. In the long run it will be more difficult for leaders of all stripes to hide what they don't want the public to see. But does this mean that leaders will be more ethical in the future?

Ethics and the concept of leadership

I have tried to show how, in the workplace of the twenty-first century, business leaders' use of rewards, punishments, expert power, and control of information are increasingly less effective than they used to be. Furthermore, leaders themselves have less control over the fortunes of their business. If they are not at the mercy of stockholders, boards and the stock market, they still face the press, consumer groups, and government regulations. In an increasingly interdependent global economy, business leaders contend with currency fluctuations, and the natural disasters and economic and political misfortunes of people in far away places.

I have also discussed how better educated followers and increased access to information about leaders from the press and via various information technologies have made followers more powerful and leaders more watched and less revered. One might conclude that these factors will make for more ethical leaders. However, there are a number of objections to this line of thought. Not all information is good information – the Internet is also filled with false, unfounded, and slanted information. Leaders can and do use these same technologies to punish opponents, mislead and exploit followers, cover their misdeeds and the misdeeds of their businesses. They might also use information to spy on employees or citizens. Furthermore the media is sometimes biased and sensational. There is currently enormous concern that a few powerful media moguls and conglomerates will eat up outlets and present their own views of the truth. Leaders who know the press can make or break them, hire media consultants to manipulate the press. We even blame the media for lowering public morality and encouraging cynicism. This is why I am not saying that education, information technologies, and the media will make leaders more ethical; however, I am arguing that these factors have put ethics into the center of public discussions about leadership. The quality of this discussion ranges from that of a sensationalist TV talk show to a reasoned debate. Nonetheless, both are still discussions about morality.

It is easy to underestimate how interesting the subject of ethics is to most human beings. We are particularly fascinated by immorality, and this fascination is heightened by the fact that people attempt to keep their immoral behavior secret. Throughout history the morality and immorality of people has long been the theme of entertainment. Immorality is often the subject matter of gossip, soap operas, comedies, tragedies and dramas. This is why the media like to uncover scandals and unethical practices; immorality sells newspapers and draws an audience. Combine the public's fascination with immorality with their interest in power and money, and it is easy to see why the ethics of leaders are in the public eye today.

All of these factors might lead one to the conclusion that since leaders are watched closely, they are forced to behave ethically. However, we know that is not always true. First, because sometimes the public notion of morality is misguided and sometimes leaders have no sense of shame. Second, because, some leaders suffer from the same human frailty found in King David. They believe that they can use their power to outsmart everyone else. (King David believed this even when he knew God was watching!) Third, in some cultures the media attention given to leaders and the attention leaders give to the media have blurred the line between leadership and celebrity. When leaders are regarded as celebrities, people tend to look for the traits of charisma in their leaders. For the most part, business leaders escape this celebrity, but they are affected by the outcome of this perception of leaders.

Charisma and trust

Robert C. Solomon has argued that the focus on charisma distracts us from the emotional complexity of leadership. He believes that charisma is not a quality or set of emotions, but rather a generalized way of explaining an emotional relationship that really should be analyzed in terms of trust. Solomon says that trust is an emotional as well as a moral relationship. Often in public discourse about leaders, people focus on whether leaders are likeable, exciting, or if they make them feel good, rather than whether leaders can be trusted. As Solomon points out, we often spend more time talking about how leaders earn trust than we do about followers giving trust. Giving trust is a difficult and dynamic set of emotions. It is the burden of followers to decide whether to trust or not to trust their leaders. This is the decision that makes or breaks a leader in today's world.

Earlier we looked at the sources of power available to leaders. The last one was called "referent power." This includes the personal qualities of leaders, including their virtues and personality traits. A leader who is deemed by followers as morally worthy of trust and respect, has "referent power." People voluntarily follow leaders whom they trust and respect as persons. Leaders have to earn trust and respect through their actions in business and their treatment of all stakeholders, but the real burden is on the followers who must give trust.

Trust and respect are the most difficult things for business leaders to establish in organizations, in part because there are so many externalities that business leaders cannot control. Try as they may, there are no short cuts to trust, and being trustworthy is not something leaders can fake for long. The rewards of trust are astounding. In businesses that operate with a high level of trust, there is more good will and less need for costly oversight. Trusted leaders get what Edwin Hollander calls "idiosyncrasy credits" from their followers. Leaders get idiosyncrasy credits when followers trust them and are willing to let them deviate from the norm. These so-called "credits" give leaders more latitude for making changes. Organizations that have high levels of trust are potentially more innovative because employees aren't afraid to take risks. Francis Fukuyama has made similar observations about the benefits of trust within cultures. He argues that a nation's well-being and ability to compete is conditioned by the level of trust in society. Fukuyama found that societies in which people have a high level of trust are socially and economically better off than low trust societies. People also have an easier time adapting to change when they feel secure with their leaders. In a fast changing world people seem to have a greater need for leaders they can trust. As Ronald Heifetz has demonstrated, part of the task of leaders today is to help people adapt to the changes and resolve conflict between their values and the new realities that they face.

Leadership Tomorrow

Connective leadership

The conflict that I set up earlier between ethics and effectiveness may be a false dilemma that hinges on what we mean by the word "effective" and "effective" at what. I have been arguing that trust and ethics are increasingly necessary, but not sufficient conditions for effective leadership. People everywhere long for leaders that they can trust and respect. They will follow such leaders without coercion and without promise of reward. This is not necessarily because, as transformational theorists argue, these leaders have elevated them to a higher moral plane, but because they trust their leaders and recognize the value of what they want to do. Leadership has gotten more personal, while at the same time leadership has been dispersed among more people. The line between leaders and followers is more fluid. We know more about our leaders. It is increasingly difficult to lead alone; leaders need other leaders to help them.

Leadership today is primarily concerned with a variety of relationships. Jean Lipman-Blumen describes the new context of leadership as the connective era. Old geopolitical alliances are dissolving and the connections between people, ideas and the environment are tightening. Technology crosses political boundaries, which no longer prevent people from moving into other people's space. She says leaders now operate in a world torn by interdependence and diversity. The fact that our economy, politics, and environment are intertwined with the rest of the world's, causes many groups to retreat to the ancient certainties of the tribe. As Lipman-Blumen and others such as Benjamin Barber and Samuel Huntington have pointed out, this leads to clashes between the commercial world and racial, ethnic, religious, and cultural values. This clash occurs not only on a global level, but on local levels in organizations and societies of increasing diversity.

This is an unsettling era for many people, but it is also is one where success in business and politics is more likely to come from creatively building networks and partnerships than from going it alone. These partnerships may be long-term or short-term, depending on the task at hand. In business Lipman-Blumen says organizations will have to be flexible to compete. One way to gain this flexibility is to build up a network of connections with other organizations and in other parts of the world. This entails a different set of leader behaviors and traits. The first important skill will be the ability to not only make friends, but create a network of people and organizations. Again it is interesting to note that as these networks expand, so will the knowledge of who is a good partner and who isn't. Trustworthiness, will be a key trait in this kind of leader. Lipman-Blumen believes that competition in this environment may be less productive than cooperation. So leaders will also need to be skilled in negotiation and conflict resolution. Successful negotiators and mediators are often those who all parties trust. Lastly, Lipman-Blumen describes connective leaders as those who support democracy and act as servant leaders who serve the interests of society, not themselves.

While Lipman-Blumen's analysis of the connective era is compelling, it also contains the seeds of what would make her image of a connective leader a failure. As she points out in her book, *Connective Leadership*, the response to globalization has broken people up into tribal groups. The dark side of this picture is that leaders, under pressure to meet short-term goals in a very competitive world will become even more ruthless in business. We already see businesses forming mega banks, oil companies, and telecommunications companies in an attempt to crush smaller businesses. In politics the call of every religious or ethnic group that feels threatened could be met by leaders who rule by cultivating their fears instead of their trust. Rather than a world symbolized by people holding hands, we could have a post-apocalypse world of ruthless road warriors. Yet, even if the latter were the future, the leaders who were able to form alliances and gain the trust of others, might still have the competitive advantage. As we look at the world today, we realize how right Plato was. The world is increasingly a place where leaders can't go it alone without friends for long. When they try to do so, they often inflict enormous suffering on their followers and other stakeholders. The diversity and disappearing borders of the world make weaving together the different threads of followers a formidable challenge. Leaders need to earn trust before they can weave together diverse people.

Bridge leaders

One of the biggest problems with the leadership research is that it is largely from the USA. Yet, throughout the world there are many kinds of leaders and ways of leading. The ultimate research question about leadership is "What can we learn about good leadership that is applicable everywhere?" I think this is a normative question, closely related to the ultimate question in ethics: "Are there universal moral principles?" The cultural relativists have told us that every culture has its own norms and values; however, people often think their culture's values are best because they are the only one's they know. In a world where national and cultural boundaries are easily crossed, we have access to a variety of moral systems and values.

Consider the case of the Oba of Benin. The Obas have been the tribal rulers of Benin for 800 years. The current Oba has a Cambridge law degree, yet he leads with the aid of a soothe-sayer who helps him make decisions by reading chicken entrails. How does this man think when he makes important moral decisions? He has been exposed to at least two cultural models of leadership and morality. Like anyone visiting a foreign culture, there must have been values that he liked and/or hated about English culture. He can pick and choose from the values and practices of both cultures. For me the interesting question is, "If he has such a choice, how does he choose?" "What does he choose? and "Does having this choice make a difference to how he leads?"

Almost every culture has tales about young people who leave home to seek their fortune, experience different cultures and adventures, and then return home different and often wiser. There are even cultures where leaving home and return- ing is a formal rite of passage. We call these "Prodigal Son" stories.

The message of such stories varies. Sometimes, the prodigal sons return with a greater appreciation of what they have at home. Sometimes, prodigal sons and daughters bring back new ideas that make home better; in other cases their new perspective on the world makes them unhappy and/or outcasts in their home. One way to learn about what values and ideas leaders would choose, if given a choice, is to study the ones who are prodigal sons and daughters. Businesses are filled with such people, who grew up in one country and have spent their business lives in different cultures. What do they bring to leadership? What ethical conflicts do they face being between different cultures? How do they choose between value systems? How will these people alter the face of leadership in business?

My hypothesis is that the expanded moral repertoire of prodigal sons and daughters enhances their moral imagination and ability to build bridges between cultures. They may use their expanded moral repertoires to come up with novel solutions to problems of leadership and perhaps leadership itself. Clearly not all prodigal sons and daughters exercise this skill; however, the ones that do I call "bridge leaders." By exposure to the values of another culture, a leader gains an expanded moral repertoire because he or she has access to different norms of social responsibility and obligation (including ideas about liberty, equality, rights, community, etc.), personal accountability, respect for persons, and most importantly different approaches to moral reasoning. These expanded moral repertoires allow them to be a bridge between conflicting value systems within their own culture or between their culture and other cultures. As bridges, their moral repertoires are not necessarily a synthesis of cultures or a conjunction of cultures, but a new way. Bridge leaders would have some of the talents of connective leaders, but their real strength would be in their ability to understand other values systems and to build trust with a wide variety of people, across large cultural divides.

Conclusion

In this paper, I have been trying to show how fundamental ethics is to the idea and practice of leadership today and in the future. We do not know the impact of globalization in the future. What we do know is that the neatly carved political world of the nation state seems to be falling away to a borderless world where business people and markets seem to call the shots. Business leaders of large corporations have responsibilities that look more like those of national leaders. The moral responsibilities of business leaders are wider and affect larger constituencies. As always, business leaders will have to be knowledgeable, but they will also have to have self-discipline, moral imagination, and a track record of honesty and integrity. I have argued that trust is a necessary condition for long-term effective leadership. In a fast changing diverse world, trust is difficult to find and sometimes quite frail, but as such, it is also the most valuable commodity any leader can get and any follower can give.

References

Burns, J. M. 1978: *Leadership*. New York: Harper and Row.

Carlyle, T. 1902: *On Heroes, Hero Worship, and the Heroic in History*. New York: Ginn and Co.

Carnegie, D. 1998: *How to Win Friends and Influence People*. New York: Pocket Books. First published 1936.

Lao, T. 1963: The Lao Tzu (Tao-te-ching) In W.-T. Chan (ed.) *A Source Book in Chinese Philosophy*. Princeton: Princeton University Press, 139–76.

Lipman-Blumen, J. 1996: *Connective Leadership*. New York: Oxford University Press.

Plato 1992: *Republic* (Grube, G. M. A, Trans.) Indianapolis: Hackett Publishing Co.

Plato 1992: *Statesman*. (Skemp, J. B. trans). Indianapolis: Hackett Publishing Co.

Plato 1962: *Epistles: A Translation with Critical Essays and Notes*. Morrow, G. R. (ed.). New York: Bobbes-Merrill.

Rost, J. 1991: *Leadership for the Twenty-first Century*. Westport, CT: Praeger.

Tolstoy, L. 1983: *War and Peace*. (Maude, L. and Maude, A. Trans.). New York: Oxford University Press.

Further Reading

Barber, B. 1996: *Jihad vs. McWorld*. New York: Random House.

Bass, B. 1989: *Leadership and Performance Beyond Expectations*. New York: Free Press.

Bass, B. (ed.) 1990: *Bass and Stogdill's Handbook of Leadership*. New York: Free Press.

Bell, D. 1999: *Coming of Post-Industrial Society*. New York: Basic Books.

Bennis, W. G. 1989: *On Becoming a Leader*. Reading, MA: Addison-Wesley.

Bennis, W. and Nanus, B. 1985: *Leaders: Strategies for Taking Charge*. New York: Harper Collins.

Ciulla, J. B. (ed.). 1998: *Ethics the Heart of Leadership*. Westport, CT: Praeger.

Ciulla, J. B. 2000: Bridge leaders. In B. Kellerman and L. R. Matusak, (eds) *The Cutting Edge: Leadership 2000*. College Park, MD: The James McGregor Burns Academy of Leadership.

Ciulla, J. B. 2000: *The Working Life: The Promise and Betrayal of Modern Work*. New York: Times Books.

Confucius. 1963: *Analects*. In W.-T. Chan, (ed.) *A Source Book in Chinese Philosophy*. Princeton: Princeton University Press, 19–46.

Conger, J. and Kanungo, R. N. 1988: *Charismatic Leadership: The Elusive Factor in Organizational Effectiveness*. San Francisco: Jossey-Bass.

DuPree, M. 1989: *Leadership as an Art*. New York: Dell Publishing.

Forbes, B. C. 1947: Fact and comment. *Forbes*. 60, 1 October.

French, J. and Raven, B. 1959: The bases of social power. In D. Cartwright (ed.) *Studies in Social Power*. Ann Arbor, MI: Research Center for Group Dynamics Institute for Social Research, University of Michigan, 150–67.

Fukuyama, F. 1995: *Trust*. New York: Free Press.

Fuller, T. (ed.). 2000: *Leading and Leadership*. Notre Dame: University of Notre Dame Press.

Gardner, H. 1995: *Leading Minds*. New York: Basic Books.

Gardner, J. W. 1990: *On Leadership*. New York: The Free Press.

Greenleaf, R. K. 1977: *Servant Leadership*. New York: Paulist Press.

Heifetz, R. A. 1994: *Leadership Without Easy Answers*. Cambridge: Harvard University Press.

Hollander, E. 1958: Conformity, status and idiosyncrasy credit. *Psychological Review*. 65, 117–27.

Huntington, S. P. 1993: The clash of civilizations. *Foreign Affairs*. 72 (3), 22–49.

Keeley, M. 1998: The trouble with transformational leadership. In J. B. Ciulla (ed.) *Ethics the Heart of Leadership*. Westport, CT: Praeger.

Lewin, K., Lippitt, R., and White, R. 1939: Patterns of aggressive behavior in experimentally created social climates. *Journal of Social Psychology*. 10, 271–99.

Machiavelli, N. 1954: *The Prince*. (Thompson, H. Trans.) New York: The Limited Editions Club.

Moore, B. V. 1927: The may conference on leadership. *Personnel Journal*. 6, 124.

Solomon, R. C. 1998: Ethical leadership. Emotions and trust beyond charisma. In J. B. Ciulla (ed.) *Ethics the Heart of Leadership*. Westport, CT: Praeger, 94–105.

Stogdill, R. M. 19xx: Personal factors associated with leadership: A survey of the literature. *Journal of Psychology*. 25 (194), 35–71.

Weber, M. 1968: Pure types of legitimate authority and the nature of charismatic authority and its routinization. (Eisenstadt, S. N. Trans.). *Max Weber on Charisma and Institution Building*. Chicago: University of Chicago Press, 46–52.

Wren, J. T. (ed.). 1995: *Leader's Companion*. New York: Free Press.

Yukl, G. 1998: *Leadership in Organizations*. Upper Saddle River, NJ: Prentice Hall.

Index